# Integration of Ecosystem Theories: A Pattern

by

**Sven Erik Jørgensen**

Royal Danish School of Pharmacy,
Department of Environmental Chemistry,
Copenhagen, Denmark

KLUWER ACADEMIC PUBLISHERS

DORDRECHT / BOSTON / LONDON

ISBN 0-7923-1985-0

Published by Kluwer Academic Publishers,
P.O. Box 17, 3300 AA Dordrecht, The Netherlands.

Kluwer Academic Publishers incorporates
the publishing programmes of
D. Reidel, Martinus Nijhoff, Dr W. Junk and MTP Press.

Sold and distributed in the U.S.A. and Canada
by Kluwer Academic Publishers,
101 Philip Drive, Norwell, MA 02061, U.S.A.

In all other countries, sold and distributed
by Kluwer Academic Publishers Group,
P.O. Box 322, 3300 AH Dordrecht, The Netherlands.

*Printed on acid-free paper*

# CONTENTS

7

# Preface

Ecosystems are still a puzzle for mankind. We would like to be able to know their reactions and control them, but repeatedly we have been surprised by their unexpected reactions to our somewhat hasty actions. We unfortunately have to admit that our present knowledge about ecosystems and their true nature is rather limited.

Many excellent contributions to a more profound understanding of ecosystems have been launched during the last two decades, but if you do not know the field, it looks as if all the presented ecosystem theories are in complete discord with each other. However, ecosystems are extremely complex and only a pluralistic view will be able to reveal their basic properties. The different approaches therefore have much more in common, when you go deeper into the core material, than the first superficial glance will be able to tell and there is therefore a natural need for a unification of the various approaches to ecosystem theories.

It has for many years been my desire to attempt to make a unification of the many excellent thoughts, ideas and observations about ecosystems, that scientists have contributed. These thoughts, ideas and hypotheses have not been made in vain. They all contain a part of the truth about ecosystems and I have felt that it was almost my duty to attempt to find the "red thread" in all these important contributions to science. It is the aim of this volume to attempt to integrate all these contributions into a beautiful pattern, which will form a tentative comprehensive ecosystem theory. It may contain artifacts, it may in some hopefully minor, parts be completely wrong, but it will have the strength of being one unifying, comprehensive theory, based upon the many fruitful results already attained, and it can therefore serve as a reference framework for further contributions and ideas in ecosystem theory. It is my ambition that this volume will synthesize the already existing theories in one unifying theory, which can serve as a platform for discussion and further progress of ecosystem theory. I hope that I am thereby contributing to the development in our understanding of ecosystems, because that is urgently needed here and now due to the many immense, apparently incalculable global problems, which mankind is facing and which call for a solution in very few years.

I am grateful to all the contributors to ecosystem theory, i.e., all the authors, to whom I refer in the text - see the full list of references . They have all made a smaller or larger piece of the pattern, which I attempt to present as an entity...a completed pattern. Without their contributions there would be no pattern, and let me emphasize that the pattern *is tentative* and only a first attempt to construct a common framework for further development of ecosystem theory. Furthermore, it may be too ambitious a task, but if the "union of theories" I am presenting would create discussions, be criticized (heavily), give inspirations to new ideas and thereby changes of the pattern, the aim of this volume has been fulfilled. It must only be considered a first attempt to make a synthesis of already existing material and ideas to contribute to further development by unifying existing ideas in stead of presenting a new set of ideas, which would only have added to the confusion.

The volume draws heavily of course, on the existing literature about the different presented theories. However, it is attempted to limit the presentation of the theories to the basic ideas, concepts and their ecological implications. It would require several thousand pages to present all details about the various theories. For those who are interested in more knowledge - more details - about a specific viewpoint or theory, it is recommended to go to the basic books or the original references. This volume will only present the core material needed to construct a first tentative pattern of an ecological theory.

The book was not written for mathematicians and the mathematics has deliberately been presented not in the most rigorous, but rather in the most accessible form. The aim of the book is to initiate as broad a discussion as possible on ecosystem theory.

Many of presented contributions are based upon the application of models. Although models are a powerful tool, they are imperfect. We attempt to capture the characteristic features of natural ecosystems by the use of models, but real ecosystems are far more complex than the models and it is still an open question, as to what this immense complexity implies for the properties of ecosystems. Most ecosystem theorists, however, use models to find model independent properties, i.e., properties that the model possesses independently of the ecosystem being modelled and independently of the complexity of the model, provided it is sufficiently complex to contain the essential features of the modelled ecosystem. I am fully aware of these limitations of models, but we have no other choice to day.

The excuse for the book should maybe more honestly be formulated and summarized as follows: I have felt deeply in the roots of my soul for at least the last ten years that there is an urgent need for a synthesis, a unification, of existing excellent contributions to ecosystem theories to meet the pluralistic challenges of ecological sciences. So, I had to try to meet this challenge and the result is this book.

During the development of this volume I have had opportunity to discuss the content, get fruitful criticism as feedback and be inspired with new thoughts by several of my scientific colleagues and I would like to thank them all for their very valuable support. Listed in alphabetic order, they are: Leif Albert Jørgensen, James Kay, Boris Kompare, Dmitjri Logofet, Henning Mejer, William Mitsch, Søren Nors Nielsen, Peter Skat Nielsen, Bernard Patten, Jørgen Salomonsen, Erik Schneider, Milan Straskraba, Yuri Svirezhev, Peter Symes, Robert Ulanowicz and Richard Vollenweider.

Columbus, Ohio, U.S.A. 4. of July 1991 (first draft).
Copenhagen, Denmark 21. April 1992  (final text).

# 1. INTRODUCTION: RECENT TRENDS IN SCIENCE

## 1.1. How Did It start?

This book is about the emergence of a new ecology - ecosystem ecology, which was initiated in the scientific community in the fifties; see for instance von Bertalanffy (1952) and E.P. Odum (1953). The real "take off" with tail wind coming from society started, however, round the mid sixties as a result of the environmental discussion, triggered by - among many outstanding environmental books - Rachel Carson's book "Silent Spring" (1962), while Koestler's book "The Ghost in the Machine" (1967) contributed to the initial development of system theory. "Limits to Growth" Meadows et al 1972) should also be mentioned in this context as an initiator of environmental discussion, which provoked a further need for a new and more holistic ecology.

Ecology was a scientific discipline without any roots in the society before these books. If 30 years ago you had asked the man on the street: "What is ecology?" he would not have been able to answer the question, while every schoolchild today will know the meaning of the word "ecology."

The environmental crisis has however, not only made ecology a useful scientific discipline for society, but it has radically changed what ecology is and stands for. The ecologists were taken down from their ivory tower and confronted with the environmental problems. The need for a more quantitative ecology as a tool in environmental management has provoked further development within ecology, which has initiated a recognition of the importance of complexity. Science was confronted with a new challenge: how to deal with complex systems? What properties do they have? Can we at all describe them quantitatively? Should we learn from the more exact sciences such as physics, nuclear physics, astronomy and chemistry? Or do we need to find new ways, because ecology is different from physics and chemistry?

Physics, astronomy and chemistry have, however, been changed parallel to these developments. The trends in these scientific disciplines have also been towards the solution of ever more complex problems. The number of "known" nuclear particles has increased rapidly during the last three decades. Nuclear physics uses very complex models to describe the nuclear properties of protons, neutrons and electrons. The focus on the chemistry of biological systems has revealed that there is a long way to go before we can give a complete description of the chemistry of nature. Astronomy has added similarly to the complexity by the interpretation of astrophysical observations such as black holes, birth of stars, the evolution of stars etc. New theories about the creation of the Universe by a "big bang" and about the expanding Universe have only added to this complexity.

In the fifties science still discussed a possible "World Equation" and expected the discovery of such an equation, which could explain "everything," to be round the corner. This idea has been left now in the recognition of the enormous complexity of nature.

All these trends would, however, never have been able to cause any new developments in science, if we had not obtained the tools to deal with complex systems. Without the development in computer science, these processes in science would have stopped through lack of internal inertia. Without a new far from equilibrium thermodynamics and without new mathematical tools such as catastrophe theory, fractal theory, cybernetics and network theory, the development of ecosystem science would never have reached the point of today.

It is the aim of this book to present what may be called "A holistic Ecology" or even more informatively "A holistic Ecosystem-Ecology," resulting from complex interactions between environmental problems, the development in other sciences, computer science, new mathematical tools and the development in ecology towards systems ecology. The presentation will concentrate on the developments in ecology, but to understand these processes of developments, it is also necessary to understand all the components, that have contributed to them. Therefore the book will touch on quantum mechanics, non-equilibrium thermodynamics, catastrophe theory, fractal theory and network theory and illustrate these theories by their applications on ecological examples.

A comprehensive ecological theory is not available, yet, but many elements of such a theory have already been presented. At first glance they are very different and a unification seems impossible. However, such complex systems as ecosystems can *not* be described by the use of only one viewpoint. Many viewpoints are needed simultaneously to give a full coverage of all the many and different aspects of ecosystems and their system properties. Therefore a pluralistic view is the only possible foundation for a comprehensive ecosystem theory and the scientific problem seems more to be able to unite the presented elements of an ecosystem theory into one comprehensive theory than to demonstrate which of the different views give the most correct description of nature. It is the aim of this book to attempt to draw parallels between two or more ecological theories and thereby show that the various

14

ecological theories are to a certain extent different entrances to the same matter. This book attempts to make a synthesis of several presented ecological theories, based on a pluralistic view. Many parallels can be drawn between the theories. It is my hope that this volume will contribute significantly to development of the comprehensive ecological theory, that we are missing and so much looking forward to.

## 1.2 Physics versus Ecology

When science reawakened after the Middle Ages, a scientific revolution took place from Galileo to Newton and Lavoisier, but it was only the physical sciences that experienced this first scientific flowering.

Since the seventeenth century, when Newton first described the law of motion, science has indeed been dominated by the view that the Universe is a mechanism ultimately reducible to behaviors of individual particles that are under control of determinate forces. In a Newtonian world no real changes or evolutions occur only endless rearrangement of particles. Perhaps the most characteristic feature of classical physics was its strict determinism, which is well expressed by Galileo's famous statement: measure everything that is measurable and make measurable everything that is not (yet) measurable.

The classical thermodynamics developed during the nineteenth century introduced notions of flux and changes, but the interpretation of the second law insisted that all changes are part of a cosmic degeneration toward the death of heat.

The biological sciences did not really come to life before the beginning of the nineteenth century. The British physicist Rutherford mentioned as late as the beginning of this century that biology was nothing more than "postage stamp collecting" due to its overwhelming interest for systematic details. Biology was still not able or even interested to explain, why life was different from inert matter; Darwin (1859) was one of the few exceptions, but his view did not change the predominant picture of biology in the nineteenth century.

The difference between physics and biology may best be described by a few statements by the well-known physicist Weinberg (1975): "One of man's enduring hopes has been to find a few simple laws that would explain why nature with all its seemingly complexity and variety is the way it is." Surely no biologist would ever express such a (ridiculous) hope. And to quote Weinberg further: "Today the closest we can come to a unified view of nature is a description in terms of elementary particles and their mutual interactions."

15

The basic ideas that physicists and many scientific philosophers in the beginning of this century had were that life obeys the laws, that are valid for inert matter and there are no other laws.

The reactions of biologists to this statement may be classified in two groups: The majority and in particular those working with physiology adopted the physicalist interpretation. Everything was mechanistic, everything was deterministic and there were no unexplained residues. The other class of biologists opposed this view and felt that physics was insufficient to explaining life, and that living matter contained some extra force or constituent, that was outside the realms of physical and chemical sciences. Those who made these claims were called vitalists. For the extreme vitalists physics and biology were two separate sciences.

The controversy between physicalists and vitalists continued for well over 100 years, but about 50 years ago it became clear that neither the physicalists nor the vitalists had found the right answer. There were phenomena in living nature that could *not* be explained by the reductionist physicalist approach, and there were no vital forces or constituents, that were inconsistent with physics and chemistry. It is also interesting that some of the leaders of quantum mechanics, Niels Bohr, Schroedinger and Pauli postulated, that someday science would discover unknown physical laws operating in living, but *not* in inert matter.

Physical sciences were dominated until well into this century by a quest for laws and the most impressed biologists also tried to explain all biological processes and phenomena by application of laws, for instance in genetics. A belief in universal laws implies a belief in the possibilities of absolute predictions. The best test for the validity of an explanation was therefore for physicists the correctness of predictions.

In the classical literature of physics it has been stated repeatedly that experiments, or rather repeatable experiments are the only valid method of science. Biology also uses experiments, but not to the same extent and not as the only method.

As late as the fifties science had a different spirit than today. It was expected that a full explanation of nature was round the corner. The optimism regarding what science was able to achieve during the next fifty years was much higher than today. The concepts of energy and mass were well defined and atomic compositions well known. Man mastered nuclear power. Only the uncertainties introduced by quantum mechanics somehow disturbed the picture and were not yet fully accepted. Einstein and Bohr discussed their validity and Einstein never fully accepted them: "God is not playing dice," Einstein said. A world equation, which could explain all forces in one equation, was expected to be at hand, as already mentioned in Section 1.1; an equation that could explain the entire physical world at least.

It can be concluded from this very short review of the incongruity and incompatibility of physical and biological sciences in the past centuries and up to 40 years ago that these two sciences have been observing nature from two completely different angles and in the next section we shall look into what has happened the last 40 years. Has the contrast between the two sciences increased or decreased since the mid-fifties?

## 1.3. Ecology and Physics

Today we acknowledge that we do not know the origin of the world and admitting this ignorance makes it much easier for physicists and ecologists to come together. The world is much more complex than previously thought. Many more nuclear particles were discovered during the last three decades in nuclear physics and the rise of ecology has brought out the difficulties of learning all details of the complex phenomena of nature.

It was demonstrated that predictions are not a necessary part of causality, because in complex systems one can give posterior explanations of events, which one can not predict with complete certainty. Predictions in meteorology, cosmology and other physical sciences have exactly the same properties as those of biological sciences, because they all deal with complex systems.

The modern development in biology does not consent to either of the two classical views, presented in Section 1.2, but transcends both in a new and third one. It appeared to be the goal of ecological research to resolve the complex entities and processes that confront us in living nature into elementary units in order to explain them by means of summation of these elementary units and processes. Biochemistry and classical cell biology can present many good examples of these ideas. However, the actual whole shows properties that are absent from its isolated parts. The problem of life is that of organization of the components and the emerging properties of the entire living system due to this organization and in addition to the sum of properties of the individual components - synergism in contrast to simple algebraic addition.

Sciences oscillate to a certain extent between periods of new observations and analysis - a reductionistic period - and periods of synthesis and new holistic theories. The best illustration of these changes is the period of physics from 1870 till 1935. In the first part of this period many new discoveries were made: photoelectrical effect, radioactive radiation, new chemical elements and so on, but it was not possible

17

to unify these observations into one more holistic theory. This happened in the second part of the period with the emergence of the relativity theories and the quantum theory. First observations and analysis, which bring new elements to a theory and then the elements are brought together in a synthesis.

Science including physics has known a similar period between 1960 and 199.... Or maybe the period will last 10-20 years more to the year 2010 or 2020? The first part of the period has been used to find new nuclear particles and today nuclear physics is working on a new theory on the forces inside atoms.

Ecology illustrates in the same period the same shift from analysis towards synthesis. Due to the increasing interest in environmental problems, resources were applied in the field of ecology during the sixties and seventies to reveal the properties of biological components to pollution and get quantitative knowledge about ecological processes. The time seems now right to attempt to synthesize this knowledge into a more basic theory for ecosystems and this book presents such an attempt. What is needed is a unification of the existing elements of an ecological theory into one comprehensive, pluralistic theory. This book will hopefully contribute to this development.

This description of the development in sciences must not be interpreted as if all scientists in one period work analytically, while in the next they all try to synthesize. In both periods there are scientists, who develop analytical approaches, while other scientists focus on synthesizing, but it is more the general tendencies of development in the scientific disciplines, which are changing. Although the general tendency in ecology is still dominated by analytical work, there are more and more papers being published that contribute to a holistic ecosystem theory. However, an even stronger development in the direction of a more holistic ecosystem theory is needed. This will be touched upon in Section 2.1, where the two types of ecology are compared and found to be controversial. A unification of the two ecologies would also be an advantage for further development of the ecological science, as will be discussed further in Section 2.1.

The acknowledgments of the complexity of nature and the need for new synthesis have brought physics and ecology closer. The same goes for quantum mechanics, which is based upon the need for pluralistic viewpoints to cover a full description of nature. The complexity of ecosystems cannot be dealt with unless descriptions from many different viewpoints are put together in a total, i.e., a holistic picture. Section 2.3 covers in more detail the application of quantum mechanics to ecology including the presentation of an ecological uncertainty relation to account for the limitations of our observations set by the immense complexity.

Many of the new and synthesizing approaches in ecology, which are here presented as a new and more holistic ecology, are based upon thermodynamics, which may be considered a holistically oriented scientific discipline in chemistry and physics. A simple example can easily illustrate the holistic thinking behind thermodynamics. A reductionistic description of the molecules in a room will require that the velocity and direction of the movement of every molecule are known. The thermodynamic approach uses only the temperature for such a description, as it is known that the kinetic energy of a molecule is proportional to the absolute temperature. The contributions from thermodynamics to ecology are covered in Chapters 4, 5 and 6.

## 1.4. Recent Trends in Science

Biology (ecology) and physics developed in different directions until 30-50 years ago. There have since been several indications of a more parallel development as mentioned in Section 1.3. The parallel development has its roots in the more general trends in science, which have been observed during the last decades.

The basic philosophy or thinking of sciences is currently changing along with other facets of our culture such as arts and fashions. During the last two to three decades, we have observed such a shift.

The driving forces behind such developments are often very complex and are very difficult to explain in detail, but it will be attempted to indicate at least some of tendencies in the development (which are also consistent with the discussion of the controversy and parallelism between ecology and physics mentioned above and which can be considered as a summary of the author's message in Chapter 1) :

1. The sciences have realized that the world is more complex than we thought some decades ago. In nuclear physics we have found several new particles and faced with environmental problems we have realized how complex nature is and how much more difficult it is to cope with problems in nature than in laboratories. Computations in sciences were often based on the assumption of so many simplifications, that they became unrealistic.

2. Ecosystem-ecology - we may call it the science of (the very complex) ecosystems - has developed very rapidly during the last decades and has evidently shown the need for systems sciences - also for interpretations, understandings and implications of the results obtained in other sciences, including physics.

3. It has been realized in sciences that many systems are so complex that it will not be possible to know all the details. In nuclear physics there is always an uncertainty in our observations, expressed by Heisenberg's uncertainty relations. The uncertainty is caused by the influence of our observations on the nuclear particles. We have a similar uncertainty relation in ecology and environmental sciences caused by the complexity of the systems. A further presentation of these ideas is given in Chapter 2, where the complexity of ecosystems is discussed in more detail. In addition, many relatively simple physical systems such as the atmosphere, show chaotic behavior, which makes long term predictions impossible, see Chapter 10. The conclusion is unambiguous: we can not and will never be able to, know the world with complete accuracy. We have to acknowledge that these are the conditions for modern sciences.

4. It has been realized, that many systems in nature are irreducible systems (Wolfram 1984 a and b), i.e., it is not possible to reduce observations on system behavior to a law of nature, because the system has so many interacting elements that the reaction of the system cannot be surveyed without use of models. For such systems other experimental methods must be applied. It is necessary to construct a model and compare the reactions of the model with our observations to test the reliability of the model and get ideas for model improvements, construct an improved model, compare *its* reactions with the observations again to get new ideas for further improvements and soforth. By such an iterative method we may be able to develop a satisfactory model that is able to describe our observation properly. The observations have thereby not resulted in a new law of nature but in a new model of a piece of nature; but as seen by description of the details in the model development, the model should be constructed on the basis of causalities, which inherit basic laws. This broader use of models as an instrument in science will be discussed in more detail in Chapter 3, Section 7.

5. As a result of the tendencies 1-4, modelling as a tool in science and research has developed. Ecological or environmental modelling has become a scientific discipline of its own - a discipline which has experienced rapid growth during the last decade. Developments in computer science and ecology have of course favored this rapid growth in modelling as they are the components on which modelling is founded. This development is touched upon in Chapter 3, Section 7.

6. The scientific analytical method has always been a very powerful tool in

research. However, there has been an increasing need for scientific synthesis, i.e., for putting the analytical results together to form a holistic picture of natural systems. Due to the extremely high complexity of natural systems it is not possible to obtain a complete and comprehensive picture of natural systems by analysis alone, but it is necessary to synthesize important analytical results to get system-properties. The synthesis and the analysis must work hand in hand. The synthesis (for instance in the form of a model) will indicate which analytical results are needed to improve the synthesis and new analytical results will then be used as components in the synthesis. There has been a clear tendency in sciences to give the synthesis a higher priority than previously. This does not imply that the analysis should be given a lower priority. Analytical results are needed to provide components for the synthesis, and the synthesis must be used to give priorities for the needed analytical results. No science exists without observations, but no science can be developed without the digestions of the observations to form a "picture" or "pattern" of nature either. Analysis and synthesis should be considered as two sides of the same coin. Vollenweider (1990) exemplifies these underlying ideas in limnological research by use of a matrix approach which combines in a realistic way reductionism and holism, and single case and cross-sectional methodologies. The matrix is reproduced in Table 1.1. (reproduced from Vollenweider 1990) and it is demonstrated here, that all four classes of research and integrations of them are needed to gain a wider understanding of, in this case, lakes as ecosystems.

**Table 1.1.**

|  | **Matrix approach and pathways to integration.** | |
|  | **Reductionistic / analytical:** | **Holistic / integrative:** |
| --- | --- | --- |
| **In-depth single case** | Parts and processes, Linear causalities, etc. | Dynamic modelling, etc. |
| **Comparative cross-sectional** | Loading-trophic state; General plankton model, etc. | Trophic topology and metabolic types, homeostatis, ecosystem behavior. |

7. A few decades ago the sciences were more optimistic than today in the sense that it was expected that a complete description of nature would soon be a reality. Einstein even talked about a "world equation," (see Sections 1.1. and 1.3), which should be the basis for all physics of nature. Today it is realized that it is not that easy and that nature is far more complex. Sciences have a long way to go and it is not expected that the secret of nature can be revealed by a few equations, but that it will be necessary to apply many and complex models to describe nature.

## 1.5. The Ecosystem as Object of Research

Ecologists generally recognize ecosystems as a specific level of organization, but the open question is the appropriate selection of time and space scales. Colinvaux (1973) argues that any size area could be selected, but in the context of this volume, the following definition presented by Morowitz (1968) will be used: "An ecosystem sustains life under present-day conditions, which is considered a property of ecosystems rather than a single organism or species." This means that a few square meters may seem adequate for microbiologists, while 100 square kilometers may be insufficient if large carnivores are considered (Hutchinson, 1978).

Population-community ecologists tend to view ecosystems as networks of interacting organisms and populations. Tansley (1935) found that an ecosystem includes both organisms and chemical-physical components and it inspired Lindeman (1942) to use the following definition: "An ecosystem composes of physical-chemical-biological processes active within a space-time unit." E.P. Odum (1953) followed these lines and is largely responsible for developing the process-functional approach, which has dominated the last few decades.

This does not mean that different views can not be a point of entry. Hutchinson (1948) used a cyclic causal approach, which is often invisible in population - community problems. Measurement of inputs and outputs of total landscape units has been the emphasis in Bormann and Likens (1967) functional approaches. O' Neill (1976) has emphasized energy capture, nutrient retention and rate regulations. H.T. Odum (1957) has underlined the importance of energy transfer rates. Quilin (1975) has argued that cybernetic views of ecosystems are appropriate and Prigogine (1947), Mauersberger (1983) and Jørgensen (1981) have all emphasized the need for a thermodynamic approach for the proper description of ecosystems.

For some ecologists ecosystems are either biotic assemblages or functional systems. The two views are separated. It is, however, important in the context of ecosystem theory to adopt both views and to integrate them. Because an ecosystem cannot be described in detail, it cannot be defined according to Morowitz's definition, *before* the objectives of our study are presented. With this in mind the definition of an ecosystem used in the context of ecosystem theory as presented in this volume, becomes:

**An ecosystem is a biotic and functional system or unit, which is able to sustain life and includes all biological and non-biological variables in that unit. Spatial and temporal scales are not specified a priori, but are entirely based upon the objectives of the ecosystem study.**

Currently there are several approaches (Likens 1985) to the study of ecosystems:

1) Empirical studies where bits of information are collected, and an attempt is made to integrate and assemble these into a complete picture.

2) Comparative studies where a few structural and a few functional components are compared for a range of ecosystem types.

3) Experimental studies where manipulation of a whole ecosystem is used to identify and elucidate mechanisms.

4) Modelling or computer simulation studies.

The motivation (Likens 1983 and 1985) in all of these approaches is to achieve an understanding of the entire ecosystem, giving more insight than the sum of knowledge about its parts relative to the structure, metabolism and biogeochemistry of the landscape.

Likens (1985) has presented an excellent ecosystem approach to Mirror Lake and its environment. The study contains all the above mentioned studies, although the modelling part is rather weak. The study demonstrates clearly, that it is necessary to use *all* four approaches to achieve a good picture of the system properties of an ecosystem. An ecosystem is so complex that you cannot capture all the system properties by one approach!

Ecosystem studies are widely using the notions of order, complexity, randomness and organization. They are used interchangeably in the literature, which causes much confusion. As the terms are used in relation to ecosystems throughout the volume, it is necessary to give a clear definition of these concepts in this introductory chapter.

According to Wicken (1979 p. 357) randomness and order are each other's antithesis and may be considered as relative terms. Randomness measures the amount of information required to describe a system. The more information is required to describe the system, the more random it is.

Organized systems are to be carefully distinguished from ordered systems. Neither kind of systems is random, but whereas ordered systems are generated according to simple algorithms and may therefore lack complexity, organized system must be assembled element by element according to an external wiring diagram with a high level of information. Organization is functional complexity and carries functional information. It is non-random by design or by selection, rather than by a priori necessity.

Saunder and Ho (1981) claim that complexity is a relative concept dependent on the observer. We will adopt Kay's definition (Kay, 1984, p.57), which distinguishes between *structural complexity* , defined as the number of interconnections between components in the system and *functional complexity*, defined as the number of distinct functions carried out by the system.

Appendix 1 gives a list of definitions of concepts applied in the text. The definitions are partly taken from Kay (1984).

# 2. DO WE NEED A NEW, HOLISTIC ECOLOGY?

## 2.1. Two Ecologies

Ecology is the scientific study of the relationship between organisms and their environment. In this definition it is embedded that ecology may be approached from two sides: a reductionistic, where the relationships are found one by one and put together afterwards and a holistic one, where the entire system is considered and it is attempted to reveal properties on the system level.

Essentially reductionism is a watchmaker's view of nature. A watch can be disassembled into its components and it can be assembled again from these parts. Reductionists think of the most complex systems as made up of components, which have been combined by nature in countless ingenious ways and which can be assembled and disassembled. Reductionistic thinking in science is based on Newtonian physics, which has been so successful in all branches of science and been the initiator of the successful industrial period, that began in the eighteenth century.

In the 1870s the famous physicist Ludwig Boltzmann attempted to neutralize the challenge of entropic holism by proving that Newtonian mechanics was still universally true on the reductionistic level of atoms and molecules. Boltzmann argued, that in complicated systems consisting of for instance trillions of atoms or molecules, it becomes less and less likely that they will all stay in an ordered relationship, so that when ordered relationships do occur, they will break down relatively quickly. Reductionists now imagined that the end of the Universe would be a state of general homogeneity: the heat death, where a meaningless and formless cosmos would govern. By introducing probability Boltzmann saved reductionism from being corrupted by holism, proving that entropy was simply an expression of Newtonian order, or rather, disorder.

For science a phenomenon is orderly if its movement can be explained in the kind of cause-and-effect scheme represented by a differential equation. Quickly scientists came to rely on linear differential equations, in which small changes produce small effects and large effects are obtained by summing up small changes.

Reductionistic ecology examines the relationships between organisms and their environment one by one. The ecological scientific journals are full of papers that reveal such relationships: carrying capacity versus nitrate concentration, relationship between the abundance of two populations in competition for space or resources, light

25

intensity and photosynthesis, primary production versus precipitation, etc.

The answer to the question heading this chapter is definitely "yes, urgently". All present indicators point to a continuance of current trends toward a deterioration of the life capacity of our planet. The development unfortunately is only too clear in our minds: decimation of biodiversity and reduction of the ozone shield, which protects life against the life-killing ultraviolet radiation; drastic change in the climate is expected during the coming century due to emission of "greenhouse gases"; an enormous wastage of matter and energy, that may easily cause a lack of important resources in the nearest future. Irreversible ecological damages caused by acid rain; shortage of drinking water of sufficient quality; and human famine....to mention the most pressing problems of humanity today. Where is the science that can ensure sound and planned steering of the harmonious balance and relationship between man and nature?...a relationship and balance, which is absolutely needed, if we want to survive on this planet. Why has the incredible growth of knowledge and understanding realized by Western sciences failed to anticipate and solve all these questions?

We indeed need reductionistic ecology. This book must not be considered an attack on the reductionistic approach. Many of the relationships found in this ecology have served as ideas, perceptions or inspirations for holistic ecology, but because of the pressing global problems we urgently need to think and work much more holistically.

Bohm et al. (1987) theorize that the universe must be fundamentally indivisible, a flowing wholeness, as Bohm calls it, in which the observer cannot be essentially separated from the observed.

We are facing complex, global problems which cannot be analyzed, explained or predicted without a new holistic science that is able to deal with phenomena as complex and multivariate as global changes (Jørgensen et al. 1992) - a science that can deal with systems, that cannot be reduced to component mechanisms without losing the essence of their holism. We are confronted with a need for a new science, that can deal with irreducible systems as ecosystems or the entire ecosphere - systems that cannot be reduced to simple relationships, as we have been used to in mechanical physics.

Ecology deals with irreducible systems (Wolfram 1984 a and b, Jørgensen 1990, 1992, 1992a and Jørgensen et al. 1992). We cannot design simple experiments which reveal a relationship that can in all detail be transferred from one ecological situation and one ecosystem to another situation in another ecosystem. That is possible for instance with Newton's laws on gravity, because the relationship between forces and acceleration is reducible. The relationship between force and acceleration is linear, but growth of living organisms is dependent on many *interacting* factors, which again are functions of time. Feedback mechanisms will simultaneously regulate all the factors and rates and they also interact and are also functions of time, too (Straskraba, 1980).

Table 2.1 shows the hierarchy of regulation mechanisms, that are operating at the same time. From this example the complexity alone clearly prohibits the reduction to simple relationships that can be used repeatedly.

An ecosystem consists of so many interacting components that it is impossible ever to be able to examine all these relationships and even if we could, it would not be possible to separate one relationship and examine it carefully to reveal its details, because the relationship is different when it works in nature with interactions from the many other processes, from when we examine it in a laboratory with the relationship separated from the other ecosystem components.

The observation, that it is impossible to separate and examine processes in real ecosystems, corresponds to that of the examinations of organs that are separated from the organisms in which they are working. Their functions are completely different when separated from their organisms and examined in for instance a laboratory from when they are placed in their right context and in "working" condition.

These observations are indeed expressed in ecosystem-ecology. A known phrase is: "everything is linked to everything" or: "the whole is greater than the sum of the parts" (Allen 1988). It implies that it may be possible to examine the parts by reduction to simple relationships, but when the parts are put together they will form a whole, that behaves differently from the sum of the parts. This statement requires a more detailed discussion of how an ecosystem works.

Allen (1988) claims that the latter statement is correct, because of the evolutionary potential that is hidden within living systems. The ecosystem contains within itself the possibilities of becoming something different, i.e., of adapting and evolving. The evolutionary potential is linked to existence of microscopic freedom, represented by stochasticity and non-average behavior, resulting from the diversity, complexity and variability of its elements.

Underlying the taxonomic classification is the microscopic diversity, which only adds to the complexity to such an extent that it will be completely impossible to cover all the possibilities and details of the observed phenomena. We attempt to capture at least a part of the reality by use of models. It is not possible to use one or a few simple relationships, but a model seems to be the only useful tool when we are dealing with irreducible systems, as will be presented in the next chapters.

**Table 2.1**

The hierarchy of regulating feedback mechanisms, (Jørgensen, 1988).

| Level | Explanation of regulation process | Exemplified by phytoplankton growth |
|---|---|---|
| 1. | rate by concentration in medium | uptake of phosphorus in accordance with phosphorus concentration |
| 2. | rate by needs | uptake of phosphorus in accordance with intracellular concentration |
| 3. | rate by other external factors | chlorophyll concentration in accordance with previous solar radiation |
| 4. | adaptation of properties | change of optimal temperature for growth |
| 5. | selection of other species | shift to better fitted species |
| 6. | selection of other food web | shift to better fitted foodweb |
| 7 | mutations, new sexual recombinations and other shifts of genes. | emergence of new species or shifts of species properties. |

However, one model alone is so far from reality that we need many models, which are simultaneously used to capture reality. It seems our only possibility to deal with the very complex living systems.

This has been acknowledged by the holistic ecology or systems ecology, while the more reductionistic ecology attempts to understand ecological reactions by analysis of one or at the most a few processes, which are related to one or two components. The results of analysis are expanded to be used in the more reductionistic approaches as a basic explanation of observations in real ecosystems, but such an extrapolation is often not valid and leads to false conclusions.

Both ecologies are needed and analysis is a necessary foundation for synthesis, but it may lead to wrong scientific conclusions to stop at the analysis. Analysis of several interacting processes may give a right result of the processes under the analyzed conditions, but the conditions in ecosystems are constantly changing and even if the processes were unchanged (which they very rarely are), it is not possible to overview the analytical results of many simultaneously working processes. Our brain simply cannot overview, what will happen in a system where let us say only 6 interacting processes are working simultaneously.

So, reductionism does not consider that:

1) the basic conditions determined by the external factors for our analysis are constantly changing (one factor is typically varied by an analysis, while all the other are assumed constant) in the real world and the analytical results are therefore not necessarily valid in the system context.

2) the interaction from all the other processes and components may change the processes and the properties of all biological components significantly in the real ecosystem and the analytical results are therefore not valid at all.

3) a direct overview of the many processes simultaneously working is not possible and wrong conclusions may be the result, if it is attempted anyhow.

The conclusion is therefore, that we need a tool to overview and synthesize the many interacting processes. The synthesis may in the first instance just be "putting together" the various analytical results, but afterwards we most often need to make changes to account for an additional effect, resulting from the fact, that the processes are working together and thereby become more than the sum of the parts - they show in other word, a synergistic effect - a symbiosis. In Chapter 8, Section 3 it is demonstrated how important the indirect effects are compared to the direct effects in an ecological network. It is a rigorous quantification of the above-mentioned additional effect of the components and processes working together in a network.

Modelling, which is presented in detail in Chapter 3, is able to meet the needs for a synthesizing tool. It is our only hope that a further synthesis of our knowledge to attain system -understanding of ecosystems will enable us to cope with the environmental problems, that are threatening the survival of mankind.

The basic environmental problem is that mankind has made immense progress, that is unique in our history, but that we have not understood the full consequences on all levels of this progress.

Just think of our present medical knowledge and the possibilities to cure diseases, of our present transport and communication systems and compare them with the corresponding systems and possibilities, that we had 100 years ago - a very short time from an evolutionary point of view. Such progress is favorable for mankind, one would say, but the consequences for the entire ecosphere, for the global conditions, for life including climate and for nature as an entity, were totally overlooked, when the progress was realized.

Today we can see the consequences, but still we do not fully understand them. We therefore have limited possibilities to manage them and change the development in the right direction. What has prevented *Homo Sapiens* to take the necessary measures to prevent the catastrophic and irreversible consequences of his own progress? Was he so fascinated by his own possibilities to make technological progress, that he blindly forgot about nature? Or was he just shortsighted? I do not think that these are the true answers. *Homo Sapiens* evolved in nature, by nature and from nature. No, the answer is rather that in spite of the flattering name Homo Sapiens he can still not deal with systems of enormous complexity; and the living nature has a complexity that is almost impossible to conceive.

A massive scientific effort is needed to teach us how to cope with ecological complexity or even with complex systems in general. Which tools should we use to attack these problems? How do we use the tools with most efficiency? Which general laws are valid for complex systems with many feedbacks and particularly for living systems? Have all hierarchically organized systems with many hierarchically organized feedbacks and regulations the same basic laws? And what do we need to add to these laws for living systems ?

Ulanowicz (1986) calls for holistic descriptions of ecosystems. Holism is taken to mean a description of the system level properties of an ensemble, rather than simply an exhaustive description of all the components. It is thought that by adopting a holistic viewpoint, certain properties become apparent and other behaviors are made visible that otherwise would be undetected.

It is however clear from this discussion that the complexity of ecosystems has set the limitations for our understanding and for the possibilities of proper management. We cannot capture the complexity as such with *all* its details, but we can understand how ecosystems are complex and we can set up a realistic strategy for how to get sufficient knowledge about the system - not knowing all the details, but still understanding and knowing the mean behavior and the important reactions of the system. It means that we can only try to reveal the basic properties *behind* the complexity.

The next section will therefore attempt to understand in which ways the ecosystems are complex and the following section will deal with realistic limitations in our approaches - i.e., an application of quantum mechanic thinking in ecology.

30

We have no other choice than to go holistic. The results from the more reductionistic ecology are essential in our effort "to go to the root" of the system properties of ecosystems, but we need systems ecology, which consists of many new ideas, approaches and concepts, to follow the route to the roots of the basic system properties of ecosystems. The idea may also be expressed in another way: we cannot find the properties of ecosystems by analyzing all the details, because they are simply too many, but only by trying to reveal the system properties of ecosystems by examination of the entire systems.

## 2.2. Complexity of Ecosystems

The complexity of an ecosystem is formed not only by a high number of interacting components; the complexity is far more complex.

The complexity will be reviewed in this section by a survey of the many different forms of complexity of ecosystems:

**1) The number of organisms and species on earth is very high and they are all different.**

We have in other words many different components. We are able to classify all organisms into groups called species. There are many millions of species on earth and there are in the order of $10^{20}$ organisms (the number is, of course, very uncertain). Organisms belonging to the same species have a high extent of similarity, but every organism is nevertheless different from all other organisms, as each *Homo Sapiens* is different from his neighbor.

Complexity certainly increases as the number of components increases, but the number of components is not the only measure of complexity. One mole consists of $6.62 * 10^{23}$ molecules. Yet physicists and chemists are able to make predictions related to pressure, temperature and volume not in spite of, but because of the large numbers of molecules. The reason is, that all the organisms are different, while the molecules are essentially identical (there may be a few different types of molecules: oxygen, nitrogen, carbon dioxide and so on). Interactions of molecules are random and overall system averages are easily performed. We are therefore able to apply statistical methods on the molecules but not to the much lower number of very different organisms. The individual motions of the more than $10^{23}$ molecules are unknowable, but in thermodynamics it is allowed to average out the motions of all the molecules, and that makes predictions possible. When such averaging is impossible, the problem becomes insoluble. The so-called 'three bodies' problem (the influences of three bodies on each other's orbits) is already extremely complex.

Ecosystems or the entire ecosphere are "medium number systems." They include most systems and are characterized by an intermediate number of components and structured interrelationships among these components.

**2) The high number of species gives an extremely high number of possible connections and different relations.**

However, a model with many components and a high number of connections is not necessarily more stable than a simple one, see May (1981). Numerical (Gardner and Ashby, 1970, McMurtrie, 1975) and analytical (May, 1972) studies of food webs involved three parameters: the number of species, S, the average connections of the web, C, and the average magnitude of the interaction between linked species, b. If all self-regulatory terms are taken to be $b_{ii} = -1$, for large S, these systems tend to be stable if

$$b * \sqrt{(S*C)} < 1 \qquad\qquad\qquad\qquad (2.1)$$

This statement is consistent with Margalef and Gutierrez (1983) and Margalef (1991): the product SxC falls in the range between 2 and 12 and remains in most cases around 4. Better precision is achieved if one writes $A = C*S^E$ and $C*2^H$, where $E = H / \log_2 S$ is evenness and H is diversity (Shannon's index). A will be among 2 and 4 and in a large number of electric circuits, it was around 3.5. The limits and regularities that have been observed in connectivity are not surprising and are a consequence of the actual values, which tend to fall around the center of the available range. Actual values of connectivity may be relevant for the functionality of the system, and as an expression of the internal stresses and the interactions that configure them. Margalef (1991) has suggested, that the degree of connection or interaction between two elements is not necessary 0 or 1, but rather a value in between. It means on the one side, that the network of ecosystems is not complicated by a huge number of connections, but that on the other side the complexity is increased by introduction of a degree of connection.

These studies contribute to the intense discussion of stability and diversity of ecosystems in the sixties and seventies. It is now the governing theory that there is no (simple) relation between stability and diversity. It is possible in nature to find very stable and simple ecosystems and it is possible to find rather instable very diverse ecosystems. May (1972 and 1981) claims, that r-selection is associated with a relatively unpredictable environment and simple ecosystems, while K-selection is associated with a relatively predictable environment and a complex biologically crowded community.

It may be concluded that only a few - relatively to the number of species - direct connections exist in ecosystems. As will be discussed in Chapter 8, indirect effects are very important. We may assume, that many direct connections are not needed to render the system stable and too many direct connections may even increase the possibilities for instability, as can be shown by modelling studies.

Figures 2.1 and 2.2 give two different conceptual diagrams, which have been used to demonstrate the increased sensitivity to the selected parameters by an increasing number of connections. Figure 2.1 shows a model consisting of four state variables: soluble phosphorus (ps), phytoplankton phosphorus (pp), zooplankton phosphorus (pz) and detritus phosphorus (pd). The processes are uptake of phosphorus by phytoplankton, grazing, mortality and mineralization. A steady input of soluble phosphorus takes place and it implies a corresponding outflow of soluble ps, pp and pd, but not of pz. Figure 2.2 includes in addition to the processes in Fig. 2.1 a connection between pp and pd (faeces and mortality) and between pz and ps (excretion). The function temperature in both diagrams gives the variation of the temperature over the year (a sine function) and its influence on various rates. The simulations by application of the two (simple) models give approximately the same results by a proper selection of parameters, but the sensitivity of the parameters in model number two (Fig. 2.2) is significantly higher. It means that model number two easily gets instable by selection of another set of parameters.

Table 2.2 gives the results of a sensitivity analysis (for an explanation of this concept see Section 3.3) for the grazing rate on pp and pz for the two models and it is obvious that model two demonstrates a higher sensitivity, see the definition equation (3.1). It is clear from these results, that many connections - at least in these examples - will cause a higher sensitivity and thereby as sensitivity is inverse buffer capacity; see the definition of this concept later in this Section; lower buffer capacity and higher probability of instability due to slight changes in the parameters, which is consistent with May's theory presented above.

In the next chapter the selection of model complexity will be discussed and here it will be shown that the selection of model complexity, both measured by the number of state variables and the number of connections, is a matter of balance. A certain number of connections are needed to obtain a certain recirculation of matter, but the recycling is hardly increased if the number of connections are increased beyond a certain point. So, more pragmatic modelling experience is consistent with the ecological theoretical considerations given above.

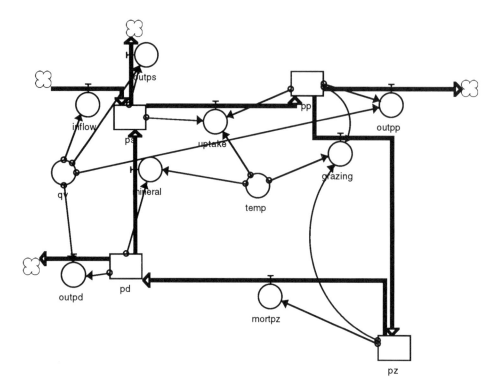

**Figure 2.1.** Conceptual diagram of a model, used to examine the relationship between the number of connections and the stability. The model consists of four state variables: soluble phosphorus (ps), phytoplankton phosphorus (pp), zooplankton phosphorus (pz) and detritus phosphorus (pd).

Reactions of ecosystems to perturbations have been widely discussed in relation to the stability concepts. However, this discussion has in most cases not considered the enormous complexity of regulation - and feedback mechanisms.

The stability concept resilience is understood as the ability of the ecosystem to return "to normal" after perturbations. This concept has more interest in a mathematical discussion of whether equations may be able to return to steady state, but the shortcomings of this concept in real ecosystem context are clear:

An ecosystem is a soft system that will *never* return to the same point again. It will be able to maintain its functions on the highest possible level, but never with exactly the same biological and chemical components in the same concentrations again. The species composition or the foodweb may have changed or may not have changed, but at least it will not be the same organisms with the same properties.

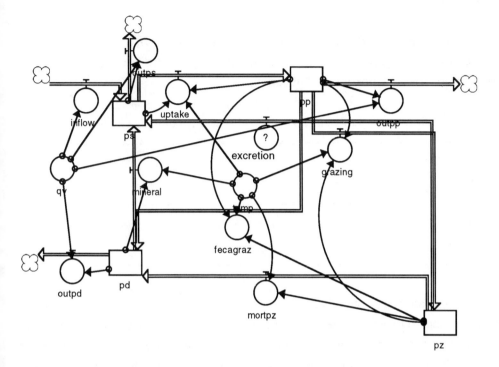

**Figure 2.2.** Conceptual diagram of a model used for examination of the relationship between number of connections and stability. The model contains the same number of state variables as Figure 2.1., but has connections between pp and pd and between pz and ps.

In addition, it is unrealistic to consider that the same conditions will occur again. We can observe that an ecosystem has the property of resilience in the sense that ecosystems have a tendency to recover after stress, but a complete recovery understood as exactly the same situation will appear again will never be realized. The combination of external factors - the impact of the environment on the ecosystem - will never appear again and even if they would, the internal factors - the components of the ecosystem -have meanwhile changed and can therefore not react in the same way as the previous internal factors did. The concept of resilience is therefore not a realistic quantitative concept. If it is used realistic, it is not quantitative and if it is used quantitatively for instance in mathematics, it is not realistic. Resilience to a certain extent covers the ecosystem property of elasticity, but in fact, the ecosystem is more flexible than elastic. It will change to meet the challenge of changing external factors,

35

not try to struggle to return to exactly the same situation.

**Table 2.2.**

**The average sensitivity of the maximum grazing rate, $\mu z$, on phytoplankton, pp, and zooplankton, pz, found on the basis of simulations over a period of 365 days.**

|  | Sensitivity coeff. $\mu z$ versus pp | Sensitivity coeff. $\mu z$ versus pz. |
|---|---|---|
| Model 1 Figure 2.1. | 0.42 | 1.6 |
| Model 2 Figure 2.2. | 1.2 | 6.1 |

Resistance is another widely applied stability concept. It covers the ability of the ecosystem to resist changes, when the external factors are changed. This concept needs, however, a more rigorous definition and needs to be considered multidimensionally to be able to cope with real ecosystem reactions. An ecosystem will always be changed, when the conditions are changed; the question is what is changed and how much?

Webster (1979) examined by use of models the ecosystem reactions to the rate of nutrient recycling. He found that an increase in the amount of recycling relative to input resulted in a decreased margin of stability, faster mean response time, greater resistance (i.e., greater buffer capacity, see the definition below) and less resilience. Increased storage and turnover rates resulted in exactly the same relationships. Increases in both recycling and turnover rates produced opposite results, however leading to a larger stability margin, faster response time, smaller resistance and greater resilience.

Gardner and Ashby (1970) examined the influence on stability of connectance (defined as the number of food links in the food web as a fraction of the number of topologically possible links) of large dynamic systems. They suggest that all large complex dynamic systems may show the property of being stable up to a critical level of connectances and then as the connectance increase further, the system suddenly goes unstable.

36

O'Neill (1976) examined the role on heterotrophs on the resistance and resilience and found that only small changes in heterotroph biomass could reestablish system equilibrium and counteract perturbations. He suggests, that the many regulation mechanisms and spatial heterogeneity should be accounted for, when the stability concepts are applied to explain ecosystem responses. The role of the variability in space and time will be touched upon many times and discussed further below as point 6.

These observations explain why it has been very difficult to find a relationship between ecosystem stability in its broadest sense and species diversity. Compare also with Rosenzweig (1971), where almost the same conclusions are drawn.

It is observed that increased phosphorus loading gives decreased diversity, (Ahl and Weiderholm, 1977 and Weiderholm, 1980), but very eutrophic lakes *are* very stable. Figure 2.3. gives the result of a statistical analysis from a number of Swedish lakes. The relationship shows a correlation between number of species and the eutrophication, measured as chlorophyll-a in µg/l. A similar relationship is obtained between the diversity of the benthic fauna and the phosphorus concentration relative to the depth of the lakes.

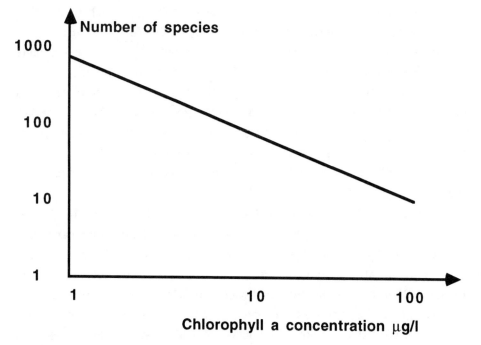

**Fig 2.3.** Weiderholm (1980) obtained the relationship shown for a number of Swedish lakes between the number of species and eutrophication, expressed as chlorophyll-a in µg/l.

Therefore it seems appropriate to introduce another but similar concept, named buffer capacity, ß. It is defined as follows: (Jørgensen 1988 and 1992 a)

$$\text{ß} = 1 / (\partial \text{ (State variable)} / \partial \text{ (Forcing function)}) \tag{2.2}$$

Forcing functions are the external variables that are driving the system such as discharge of waste water, precipitation, wind and so on, while state variables are the internal variables that determine the system, for instance the concentration of soluble phosphorus, the concentration of zooplankton and so on.

As seen the concept of buffer capacity has a definition which allows us to quantify for instance in modelling and it is furthermore applicable to real ecosystems, as it acknowledges that *some* changes will always take place in the ecosystem as response to changed forcing functions. The question is how large these changes are relatively to changes in the conditions (the external variables or forcing functions).

The concept should be considered multidimensionally, as we may consider all combinations of state variables and forcing functions. It implies that even for one type of change there are many buffer capacities corresponding to each of the state variables. Rutledge (1974) defines ecological stability as the ability of the system to resist changes in the presence of perturbations. It is a definition very close to buffer capacity, but it is lacking the multidimensionality of ecological buffer capacity.

The relation between forcing functions (impacts on the system) and state variables indicating the conditions of the system are rarely linear and buffer capacities are therefore not constant. It may therefore in environmental management be important to reveal the relationships between forcing functions and state variables to observe under which conditions buffer capacities are small or large, compare with Figure 2.4.

Model studies (Jørgensen and Mejer, 1977 and Jørgensen, 1986) have revealed that in lakes with a high eutrophication level, a high buffer capacity is obtained by a relatively small diversity. The low diversity in eutrophic lakes is consistent with the above-mentioned results by Ahl and Weiderholm (1977) and Weiderholm (1980). High nutrient concentrations favor large phytoplankton species. The specific surface does not need to be large, because there are plenty of nutrients. The selection or competition is not on the uptake of nutrients but rather on escaping the grazing by zooplankton and here greater size is an advantage. The spectrum of selection becomes in other words more narrow, which means reduced diversity. It demonstrates that a high buffer capacity may be accompanied by low diversity.

If a toxic substance is discharged to an ecosystem, the diversity will be reduced. The species most susceptible to the toxic substance will be extinguished, while other species, the survivors, will metabolize, transform, isolate, excrete, etc., the toxic substance and thereby decrease its concentration. We observe a reduced diversity, but simultaneously we maintain a high buffer capacity, which means that there will be small changes, caused by the toxic substance. Model studies of toxic substance discharge to a lake (Jørgensen and Mejer, 1977 and 1979) demonstrate the same inverse relationship between buffer capacity and diversity.

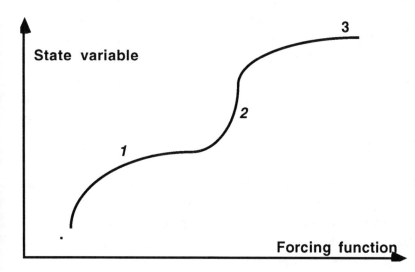

**Figure 2.4.** The relation between state variables and forcing functions is shown. At point 1 and 3 the buffer capacity is high; at point 2 it is low.

Ecosystem stability is therefore a very complex concept (May, 1977) and it seems impossible to find a simple relationship between ecosystem stability and ecosystem properties. Buffer capacity seems to be the most applicable stability concept, as it is based:

1) on an acceptance of the ecological complexity - it is a multidimensional concept ; and

2) on reality, i.e., that an ecosystem will never return to exactly the same situation again.

Another consequence of the complexity of ecosystems mentioned above should be considered here. For mathematical ease, the emphasis has been - particularly in population dynamics - on equilibrium models. The equilibrium conditions may be used as an attractor for the system, but the equilibrium will never be attained. Before the equilibrium should have been reached, the conditions, determined by the external factors and all ecosystem components, have changed and a new equilibrium, and thereby a new attractor, is effective. Before this attractor point has been reached, new conditions will again emerge and so on. A model based upon the equilibrium state will therefore give a wrong picture of ecosystem reactions. The reactions are determined by the present values of the state variables and they are different from those in the equilibrium state. We know from many modelling exercises that the model is sensitive to the initial values of the state variables. These initial values are a part of the conditions for further reactions and development. Consequently, the equilibrium models may give other results than the dynamic models and it is therefore recommended to be very careful, when drawing conclusions on the basis of equilibrium models. We must accept the complication, that ecosystems are dynamic systems and will never attain equilibrium. We therefore need to apply dynamic models as widely as possible and it can easily be shown that dynamic models give other results than static ones; see Section 4.4.

**3) The number of feedbacks and regulations is extremely high and makes it possible for the living organisms and populations to survive and reproduce in spite of changes in external conditions.**

These regulations correspond to level 3 and 4 in Table 2.1. Numerous examples can be found in the literature. If the actual properties of the species are changed the regulation is named adaptation.

Phytoplankton is for instance able to regulate its chlorophyll concentration according to the solar radiation. If more chlorophyll is needed because the radiation is insufficient to guarantee growth, more chlorophyll is produced by the phytoplankton. The digestion efficiency of the food for many animals depends on the abundance of the food.

The same species may be of different sizes in different environments, depending on what is most beneficial for survival and growth. If nutrients are scarce, phytoplankton becomes smaller and vice versa. In this latter case the change in size is a result of a selection process, which is made possible because of the distribution in size as illustrated in Fig. 2.5.

**4) The feedbacks are constantly changing,** i.e., the adaptation is adaptable in the sense that if a regulation is not sufficient another regulation process higher in the hierarchy of feed-backs - see Table 2.1 - will take over. The change in size within the same species is for instance only limited. When this limitation has been reached, other species will take over. It implies that not only the processes and the components, but also the feedbacks can be replaced, if it is needed to achieve a better utilization of the available resources. This further supports the application of dynamic models instead of steady-state or equilibrium models, as discussed above. See furthermore Chapter 11.

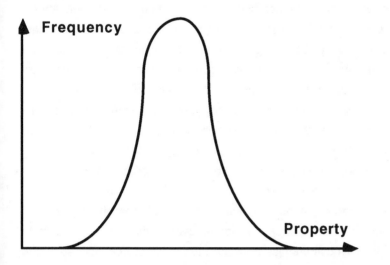

**Figure 2.5.** Typical Gaussian frequency distribution of size within the same species.

**5) The components and their related processes are organized hierarchically.**

This is the well-known hierarchy: genes, cells, organs, organisms, populations and communities. On each level in this hierarchy processes and regulations will take place. Each level works as a unit, which however can be influenced (controlled), however, from a level higher and lower in the hierarchy.

The hierarchy is established because an increased complexity at a certain level passes through a natural boundary and forms a selfsustainable subunit; see Fig. 2.6, which illustrates the relation between the complexity and the level of organization. The buffer capacity will follow the level of organization, because formation of a unit will imply that a higher level of regulations, adaptations and feedback mechanisms will occur.

Three different concepts have been used to explain the functioning of ecosystems.

*1. The individualistic or Gleasonian concept* assumes populations to respond

41

independently to an external environment.

2.*The superorganism or Clementsian concept* views ecosystems as organisms of a higher order and defines succession as ontogenesis of this superorganism, see e.g., on selforganization of ecosystems, Margalef (1968).

Ecosystems and organisms are different, however, in one important aspect. Ecosystems can be dismantled without destroying them; they are just replaced by others, such as agroecosystems or human settlements, or other successional states. Patten (1991) has pointed out that the indirect effects in ecosystems are significant compared to the direct ones, while in organisms the direct linkages will be most dominant. An ecosystem has more linkages than an organism, but most of them are weaker. It makes the ecosystem less sensitive to the presence of *all* the existing linkages. It does not imply that the linkages in ecosystems are insignificant and does not play a role in ecosystem reactions. The ecological network is of great importance in an ecosystem, but the many and indirect effects give the ecosystem buffer capacities to deal with minor changes in the network. The description of ecosystems as superorganism therefore seems insufficient.

3. *The hierarchy theory* (Allen and Star 1982) insists that the higher-level systems have emergent properties, that are independent of the properties of their lower-level components. This compromise between the two other concepts seems to be consistent with our observations in nature.

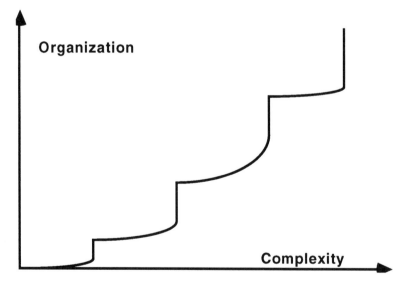

**Figure 2.6.** Organization versus complexity. At certain levels of complexity a step-wise increase of the organization takes place.

The hierarchical theory is a very useful tool to understand and describe such complex "medium number" systems as ecosystems, see O' Neill et al. (1986).

During the last decade a debate has arisen on whether "bottom-up" (limitation by resources) or "top-down" (control by predators) effects primarily control the system dynamics. The conclusion of this debate seems to be that both effects control the dynamics of the system. Sometimes the effect of the resources may be most dominant, sometimes the higher levels control the dynamics of the system and sometimes both effects determine the dynamics of the system.

This conclusion is nicely presented in "Plankton Ecology" by Sommer (1989). In this volume it is clearly demonstrated that the physical conditions (Reynolds, 1989), the resources (Sommer, 1989), the grazers (Sterner, 1989), the predation on zooplankton (Gliwicz and Pijanowska, 1989), and the parasites (Van Donk, 1989) may all be controlling the phytoplankton community and its succession. The more general conclusion of this excellent contribution to plankton ecology is, that ecosystems are very complex and you should be careful in making too broad, general simplifications. Each case should be carefully examined before you make your simplifications, which are only valid for the considered case. Everything in an ecosystem is dependent on everything. A profound understanding of ecosystems is only possible if you accept this property of ecosystem complexity. This is the initial condition for modelling and therefore you can only make simplifications on the basis of a profound knowledge of the particular case, comprising the specific ecosystem and the specific problem in focus.

Network theory will be further discussed in Chapter 7, but as will be shown here the network is a result of a hierarchical interpretation of ecosystem relations. The ecosystem and its properties emerge as a result of many simultaneous and parallel focal-level processes, as influenced by even more remote environmental features. It means that the ecosystem itself will be seen by an observer to be factorable into levels. Features of the immediate environment are enclosed in entities of yet larger scale and so on. This implies that the environment of a system includes historical factors as well as immediately cogent ones (Patten, 1982a). The history of the ecosystem and its components is therefore important for the reactions and further development of the ecosystem. It is one of the main ideas behind Patten's indirect effect that the indirect effect accounts for the "history," while the direct effect only reflects the immediate effect. The importance of the history of the ecosystem and its components emphasizes the need for a dynamic approach and supports the idea that we will never observe the same situation in an ecosystem twice. The history will always be "between" two similar situations. Therefore, as already mentioned above, the equilibrium models may fail in their conclusions, particularly when we want to look into reactions on the system level.

### 6) Ecosystems show a high degree of heterogeneity in space and in time.

An ecosystem is a very dynamic system. All its components and particularly the biological ones are steadily moving and their properties are steadily modified, which is why an ecosystem will never return to the same situation again.

Every point is furthermore different from any other point and therefore offering different conditions for the various life forms.

This enormous heterogeneity explains why there are so many species on earth. There is, so to say, an ecological niche for "everyone" and "everyone" may be able to find a niche where he is best fitted to utilize the resources.

Ecotones, the transition zones between two ecosystems, offer a particular variability in life conditions, which often results in a particular richness of species diversity. Studies of ecotones have recently drawn much attention from ecologists, because ecotones have pronounced gradients in the external and internal variables, which give a clearer picture of the relation between external and internal variables.

Margalef (1991) claims that ecosystems are anisotropic, meaning that they exhibit properties with different values, when measured along axes in different directions. It means that the ecosystem is not homogeneous in relation to properties concerning matter, energy and information, and that the entire dynamics of the ecosystem works toward increasing the differences.

These variations in time and space make it particularly difficult to model ecosystems and to capture the essential features of ecosystems. However, the hierarchy theory, see Section 6.3, applies these variations to develop a natural hierarchy as framework for ecosystem descriptions and theory. The strength of the hierarchy theory is that it facilitates studies and modelling of ecosystems.

### 7) Ecosystems and their biological components, the species, evolve steadily and in the long term perspective toward higher complexity.

Darwin's theory describes the competition among species and states that the species, that are best fitted to the prevailing conditions in the ecosystem will survive. Darwin's theory can, in other words, describe the changes in ecological structure and

44

the species composition, but cannot directly be applied quantitatively e.g. in ecological modelling; see, however Chapters 6 and 11.

All species in an ecosystem are confronted with the question: how is it possible to survive or even grow under the prevailing conditions? The prevailing conditions are considered as *all* factors influencing the species, i.e., all external and internal factors including those originating from other species. This explains the coevolution, as any change in the properties of one species will influence the evolution of the other species.

All natural external and internal factors of ecosystems are dynamic - the conditions are steadily changing, and there are always many species waiting in the wings, ready to take over, if they are better fitted to the emerging conditions than the species dominating under the present conditions. There is a wide spectrum of species representing different combinations of properties available for the ecosystem. The question is, which of these species are best able to survive and grow under the present conditions and which species are best able to survive and grow under the conditions one time step further and two time steps further and so on? The necessity in Monod`s sense is given by the prevailing conditions - the species must have genes or maybe rather phenotypes (meaning properties) which match these conditions, to be able to survive. But the natural external factors and the genetic pool available for the test may change randomly or by "chance".

Steadily new mutations (misprints are produced accidentally) and sexual recombinations (the genes are mixed and shuffled) emerge and give steadily new material to be tested toward the question: which species are best fitted under the conditions prevailing just now?

These ideas are illustrated in Fig. 2.7. The external factors are steadily changed and some even relatively fast - partly at random e.g. the meteorological or climatic factors. The species of the system are selected among the species available and represented by the genetic pool, which again is slowly, but surely changed randomly or by "chance". The selection in the Figure 2.7 includes the level 4 of Table 2.1. It is a selection of the organisms, that possess the properties best fitted to the prevailing organisms according to the frequency distribution; see Fig. 2.5. What is named ecological development is the changes over time in nature caused by the dynamics of the external factors, giving the system sufficient time for the reactions .

Evolution, on the other hand, is related to the genetic pool. It is the result of the relation between the dynamics of the external factors and the dynamics of the genetic pool. The external factors steadily change the conditions for survival and the genetic pool steadily comes up with new solutions to the problem of survival.

Darwin's theory assumes that populations consist of individuals, who:

1) On average produce more offspring than is needed to replace them upon their death - this is the property of high reproduction.

2) Have offspring which resemble their parents more than they resemble randomly chosen individuals in the population - this is the property of inheritance.

3) Vary in heritable traits influencing reproduction and survival (i.e., fitness) - this is the property of variation.

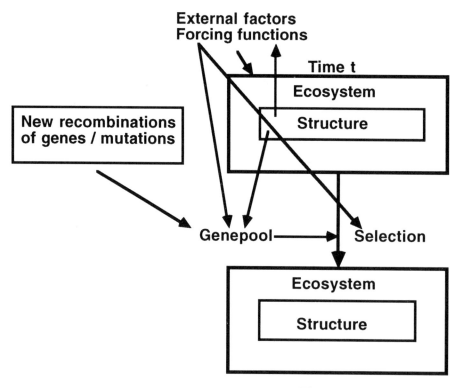

**Figure 2.7.** Conceptualization of how the external factors steadily change the species composition. The possible shifts in species composition are determined by the gene pool, which is steadily changed due to mutations and new sexual recombinations of genes. The development is, however, more complex. This is indicated by 1) arrows from " structure" to "external factors" and "selection" to account for the possibility that the species are able to modify their own environment (see below) and thereby their own selection pressure; 2) an arrow from "structure" to "gene pool" to account for the possibilities that the species can to a certain extent change their own gene pool.

All three properties are part of the presentation in Fig. 2.7. The high reproduction is needed to get a change in the species composition caused by changes in external factors. The variability is represented in the short and long term changes in the genetic pool and the inheritance is needed to see an effect of the fitness test in the long run.

Without the inheritance every new generation would start from the same point and it would not be possible to maintain the result of the fitness test. The evolution is able to continue from the already obtained results.

The species are continuously tested against the prevailing conditions (external as well as internal factors) and the better they are fitted, the better they are able to maintain and even increase their biomass. The specific rate of population growth may even be used as a measure for the fitness (see e.g. Stenseth 1986). But the property of fitness must of course be inheritable to have any effect on the species composition and the ecological structure of the ecosystem in the long run.

Natural selection has been criticized for being a tautology: fitness is measured by survival and survival of the fittest therefore mean survival of the survivors. However, the entire Darwinian theory including the above mentioned three assumptions, cannot be conceived as a tautology, but may be interpreted as follows: the species offer different solutions to survival under given prevailing conditions and the species that have the best combinations of properties to match the conditions, have also the highest probability of survival and growth.

Man-made changes in external factors, i.e., anthropogenic pollution have created new problems, because new genes fitted to these changes do not develop overnight, while most natural changes have occurred many times previously and the genetic pool is therefore prepared and fitted to meet the natural changes. The spectrum of genes is able to meet most natural changes, but not all of the man-made changes, because they are new and untested in the ecosystem.

The evolution moves toward increasing complexity in the long run; see Fig. 2.8. The fossil records have shown a steady increase of species diversity. There may be destructive forces - for instance man-made pollution or natural catastrophes - for a shorter time, but the probability that

    1) new and better genes are developed; and

    2) new ecological niches are utilized

will increase with time. The probability will even - again excluding the short time perspective - increase faster and faster, as the probability is roughly proportional to the amount of genetic material on which the mutations and new sexual recombinations can be developed.

47

It is equally important to note that a biological structure is more than an active non-linear system. In the course of its evolution, the biological structure is continuously changed in such a way that its structural map is itself modified. The overall structure thus becomes a representation of all the information received. Biological structure represents through its complexity a synthesis of the information with which it has been in communication (Schoffeniels 1976).

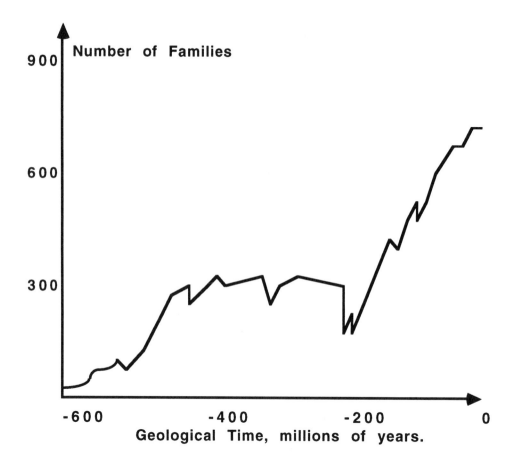

**Fig. 2.8.** Changes in species diversity over geological time. Redrawn from Raup and Sepkowski (1982).

Evolution is maybe the most discussed topic in biology and ecology and millions of pages have been written about evolution and its ecological implications.

Today the basic facts of evolution are taken for granted and the interest has shifted to more subtle classes of fitness / selection, i.e., toward an understanding of the complexity of the evolutionary processes. One of these classes concerns traits that influence not only the fitness of the individuals possessing them, but also the entire

48

population. These traits overtly include social behaviors, such as aggression or cooperation, and activities that through some modification of the biotic and abiotic environment feed back to affect the population at large, for instance pollution and resource depletion.

The following terms are used to cover the various forms of selections (Wilson 1980):

**1. Individual selection:** The component of natural selection that operates on the differential fitness of individuals within local and homogeneous populations.

**2. Group selection:** The component of natural selection that operates on the differential productivity of local populations within a more global population.

**3. Selfishness:** All traits promoted by individual selection $d > r$ in linear selection modelling, where d is the effect on the fitness of the individual itself and r is the effect on every other member of the local population.

**4. Weak altruism:** All nonselfish traits selections, where $0 < d < r$ in linear selection models

**5. Strong altruism:** All nonselfish traits selections, where $0 > d$, when r is sufficiently great in linear selection models.

It can be shown that all these types of selections actually take place in nature and that many observations support the various selection models, that are based on these types of selections. Kin selection has been observed with bees, wasps and ants (Wilson, 1978). Prairie dogs endanger themselves (altruism) by conspicuously barking to warn fellow dogs of an approaching enemy (Wilson 1978) and a parallel behavior is observed for a number of species.

The coevolution explains the interactive processes among species. It is difficult to observe a coevolution, but it is easy to understand that it plays a major role in the entire evolution process. The coevolution of herbivorous animals and plants is a very illustrative example. The plants will develop toward a better spreading of seeds and a better defense towards herbivorous animals. This will in the latter case create a selection of the herbivorous animals that are able to cope with the defense. Therefore the plants and the herbivorous animals will coevolve.

Coevolution means that the evolution process cannot be described as reductionistic, but that the entire system is evolving. A holistic description of the evolution of the system is needed.

The Darwinian and Neodarwinian theories have been criticized from many sides. It has for instance been questioned whether the selection of the fittest can explain the relatively high rate of the evolution. Fitness may here be measured by the ability to grow and reproduce under the prevailing conditions. It implies that the question raised according to the Darwinian theories ( see the discussion above) is: "which species have the properties that give the highest ability for growth and reproduction?" The topic will be further discussed in Section 6.3. We shall not go into the discussion in this context - it is another very comprehensive theme - but just mention that the complexity of the evolution processes is often overlooked in this debate. Many interacting processes in the evolution may be able to explain the relatively high rate of evolution that is observed.

Seven examples are used to illustrate that many processes 1) interact; 2) accelerate the rate of evolution; and 3) increase the complexity of the evolutionary processes.

1) A mother tiger is an excellent hunter and therefore she is able to feed many offsprings and bring her good "hunting genes" further in the evolution. Her tiger kittens have a great probability to survive because they get sufficient food. But in addition she can teach them her hunting strategy and will have more time to care for them in general, because of her successful hunting. So, the kittens not only survive, i.e., the genes survive, but also a better nursing and hunting strategy survives from one tiger generation to the next. We can say in our "computer age" that not only the hardware (the genes) but also the software (the know how) survives.

2) McClintock has observed by working with maize, that genes on chromosomes actually move around or transpose themselves; they even appear to change in relation to environmental stress-factors. He proposes the idea that the genetic program is not necessarily fixed in each one. Other geneticists have found what have been dubbed "jumping genes" and to a certain extent confirm this idea. Jumping genes are often named transposons and many workers have labeled them "selfish DNA" (Dawkins 1989). These discoveries may form the basis for a revolution in biological thinking: the reductionist image of a genetic blueprint may be false.

3) Cairns et al. (1988) showed that when bacteria lacking an enzyme for metabolizing lactose were grown in a lactose medium, some of them underwent a mutation that subsequently enabled them to produce the enzyme. This mutation violated the long-held central dogma of molecular biology, which asserts that information flows only one way in the cell - from genes to RNA to protein and enzyme. Here the information was obviously going in reverse. An enzyme coded for by a particular gene was feeding back to change that gene itself.

4) A problem of mutations with large effects on development is that they are usually selectively disadvantageous. The general connection between magnitude of

effect and probability of being selectively advantageous is shown in Fig. 2.9, curve a. However, Augros and Stanciu (1987) claim that a subsidiary peak occurs at the right hand of the diagram through a different and novel mechanism, which may be explained by a mutation of the D-genes, that control the development of the organism.

5) Symbiosis is generally very well developed in nature. Polycellular organisms are a result of symbiotic relationships among many unicellular organisms according to Lynn Margulis, as can be recognized from the endosymbiosis in all organisms. It may explain the jumps in the evolution: two or more "properties" are suddenly united and create a symbiotic effect; see Mann (1991).

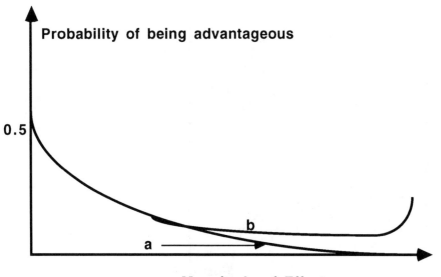

**Fig. 2.9.** The probability of being advantageous is plotted versus the magnitude of effect. a represent the common relationship, while b represents a possible relationship, when mutations on D-genes determining the development of the organism are involved.

6) Fischer and Hinde (1949) describe how the habit of opening milk bottles has spread among blue and great tits. Milk bottles were left on the doorsteps of households and were raided by these songbirds, which open them by tearing off their foil caps. The birds then drink the cream from the top of the bottles. The habit has probably spread through some type of social learning or social enhancement. A novel and learned behavior appears to have modified these birds' environments in ways that have subsequently changed the selection pressures that act back on the bird

themselves (Sherry and Galef 1984). None have shown any genetic response to these altered selection pressures.

This last example illustrates what Odling-Smee and Patten (1992) call ecological inheritance, which they assert works parallel to the genetic inheritance; see Fig. 2.10. The ecological inheritance is a result of the species' ability to change their environment and thereby to a certain extent modify the selection pressure on themselves.

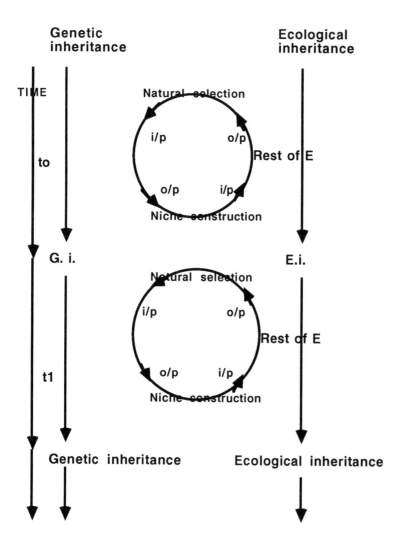

**Fig. 2.10.** Two successive cycles of ecogenetic evolution. 1/p is input and o/p is output. Reproduced from Odling-Smee and Patten (1992).

Nobody dealing with evolution would deny these possibilities of the species to modify their own environment, but the influence of this ability on the evolution process has most probably been underestimated. Odling-Smee and Patten attempt to emphasize the importance by introduction of the concept "envirotype" as supplement to genotype and phenotype.

A total image of the evolution will require a holistic approach to account for the many simultaneously interacting processes. The evolution is a result of many simultaneous processes that are interacting in a very complex way. Figure 2.11 tries to capture the complexity and interactions which may be able to explain the relatively high rate of evolution.

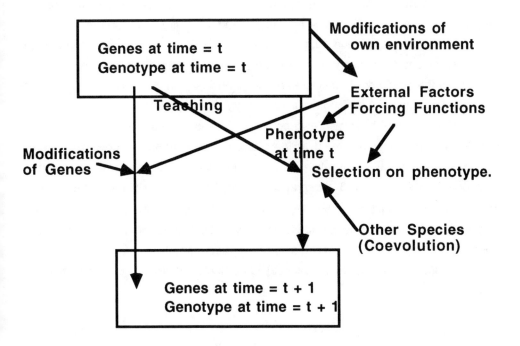

**Complexity of Evolution Processes.**

**Fig. 2.11.** The Figure illustrates that many interacting processes are active in the evolution of species. The core process is the selection, which is influenced by external factors, other species, teaching of offspring by parents and the phenotype, which again is dependent on the genotype and the environment. Notice that the species are able to influence their own environment, and that they are thereby also able to a certain extent to influence their own selection.

7) A further complication is the so-called morphogenes or D-genes, which are

not included in Fig. 2.11. The developmental processes, as mentioned in the fourth example above, are obviously extremely important for the evolution processes, but it would not be possible to go into more detail in this context. Further information can be found in Augros and Stanciu (1987), and Dawkins (1982 and 1989).

## 2.3. Ecology and Quantum Theory

How can we describe such complex systems as ecosystems in details? The answer is that it is impossible, if the description must include all details, including all interactions between all the components in the entire hierarchy and including all details on feedbacks, adaptations, regulations and the entire evolution process.

Jørgensen (1988 and 1990) has introduced the application of the uncertainty principles of quantum mechanics in ecology. In nuclear physics the uncertainty is caused by the observer of the incredibly small nuclear particles, while the uncertainty in ecology is caused by the enormous complexity of ecosystems.

For instance, if we take two components and want to know all the relations between them, we would need at least three observations to show whether the relations were linear or non-linear. Correspondingly, the relations among three components will require $3*3$ observations for the shape of the plane. If we have 18 components we would correspondingly need $3^{17}$ or approximately $10^8$ observations. At present this is probably an approximate, practical upper limit to the number of observations which can be invested in one project aimed for one ecosystem. This could be used to formulate a practical uncertainty relation in ecology, see also Jørgensen (1988):

$$10^{5} * \Delta x / \sqrt{3^{n-1}} \leq 1 \qquad (2.3)$$

where $\Delta x$ is the relative accuracy of one relation, and n is the number of components examined or included in the model.

The 100 million observations could, of course, also be used to give a very exact picture of one relation. Costanza and Sklar (1985) talk about the choice between the two extremes: knowing 'everything' about 'nothing' or 'nothing' about 'everything'. The first refers to the use of all the observations on one relation to obtain a high accuracy and certainty, while the latter refers to the use of all observations on as many relations as possible in an ecosystem.

How we can obtain a balanced complexity in the description will be further discussed in the next chapter.

Equation (2.3) formulates a practical uncertainty relation, but, of course, the possibility that the practical number of observations may be increased in the future cannot be excluded. Ever more automatic analytical equipment is emerging on the market. This means that the number of observations that can be invested in one project may be one, two, three or even several magnitudes larger in one or more decades. However, a theoretical uncertainty relation can be developed. If we go to the limits given by quantum mechanics, the number of variables will still be low, compared to the number of components in an ecosystem.

One of Heisenberg's uncertainty relations is formulated as follows:

$$\Delta s * \Delta p \geq h/2\pi \qquad (2.4)$$

where $\Delta s$ is the uncertainty in determination of the place, and $\Delta p$ is the uncertainty of the momentum. According to this relation, $\Delta x$ of equation (2.3) should be in the order of $10^{-17}$ if $\Delta s$ and $\Delta p$ are about the same. Another of Heisenberg's uncertainty relations may now be used to give the upper limit of the number of observations:

$$\Delta t * \Delta E \geq h/2\pi \qquad (2.5)$$

where $\Delta t$ is the uncertainty in time and $\Delta E$ in energy.

If we use all the energy that that earth has received during its lifetime of 4.5 billion years we get:

$$173 * 10^{15} * 4.5 * 10^9 * 365.3 * 24 * 3600$$
$$= 2.5 * 10^{34} J, \qquad (2.6)$$

where $173 * 10^{15}$ W is the energy flow of solar radiation. $\Delta t$ would, therefore, be in the order of $10^{-69}$ sec. Consequently, an observation will take $10^{-69}$ sec., even if we use all the energy that has been available on earth as $\Delta E$, which must be considered the most extreme case. The hypothetical number of observations possible during the lifetime of the earth would therefore be:

$$4.5 * 10^9 * 365.3 * 3600/10^{-69} = \sim \text{of } 10^{85} \qquad (2.7)$$

This implies that we can replace $10^5$ in equation (2.3) with $10^{60}$ since

$$10^{-17}/\sqrt{10^{85}} = {\sim}10^{-60}$$

If we use $\Delta x = 1$ in equation (2.3) we get:

$$\sqrt{3^{n-1}} \leq 10^{60} \tag{2.8}$$

Or     $n \leq 253$.

From these very theoretical considerations we can clearly conclude that we shall never be able to get enough observations to describe even one ecosystem in all detail. These results are completely in harmony with the Niels Bohr's complementarity theory. He expressed it as follows: "It is not possible to make one unambiguous picture (model) of reality, as uncertainty limits our knowledge." The uncertainty in nuclear physics is caused by the inevitable influence of the observer on the nuclear particles; in ecology it is caused by the enormous complexity and variability.

No map of reality is completely correct. There are many maps (models) of the same piece of nature, and the various maps or models reflect different viewpoints. Accordingly, one model (map) does not give all the information and far from all the details of an ecosystem. In other words, the theory of complementarity is also valid in ecology.

The use of maps in geography is a good parallel to the use of models in ecology. As we have road maps, airplane maps, geological maps, maps in different scales for different purposes, we have in ecology many models of the same ecosystems and we need them all, if we want to get a comprehensive view of ecosystems. A map can furthermore not give a complete picture. We can always do the scale larger and larger and include more details, but we cannot get all the details...for instance where all the cars of an area are situated just now, and if we could the picture would few seconds later be invalid because we want to map too many dynamic details at the same time. An ecosystem also consists of too many dynamic components to enable us to model all the components simultaneously and even if we could, the model would be invalid few seconds later, where the dynamics of the system has changed the "picture."

In nuclear physics we need to use many different pictures of the same phenomena to be able to describe our observations. We say that we need a pluralistic view to cover our observations completely. Our observations of light for instance require that we consider light as waves as well as particles. The situation in ecology is similar. Because of the immense complexity we need a pluralistic view to cover a description of the ecosystems according to our observations. We need many models covering different viewpoints. It is consistent with Gödel's Theorem from 1931 (see Gödel, 1989) , that the infinite truth can never be condensed in a finite theory. There are limits to our insight, or, we cannot produce a map of the world with all possible details, because that would be the world itself.

Furthermore, ecosystems must be considered as irreducible systems (see also Section 1.4) in the sense that it is not possible to make observations and then reduce the observations to more or less complex laws of nature, as is true of mechanics for instance. Too many interacting components force us to consider ecosystems as irreducible systems. The same problem is found today in nuclear physics, where the picture of the atoms is now "a chaos" of many interacting elementary particles. Assumptions on how the particles are interacting are formulated as models, which are tested towards observations. As it will be further discussed in the next chapter, we draw upon exactly the same solution to the problem of complexity in ecology. It is necessary to use what is called experimental mathematics or modelling to cope with such irreducible systems. Today, this is the tool in nuclear physics, and the same tool is increasingly used in ecology. Modelling in ecology is therefore treated as the central topic in the next chapter.

Quantum theory may have an even wider application in ecology. Schrödinger (1944) suggests, that the "jump like changes" you observe in the properties of species are comparable to the jump-like changes in energy by nuclear particles. Schrödinger was inclined to call De Vries' mutation theory (published in 1902), the quantum theory of biology, because the mutations are due to quantum jumps in the gene molecule.

Patten (1982a) defines an elementary "particle" of the environment, called an environ - previously he used the word holon - as a unit which is able to transfer an input to an output. Patten suggests, that a characteristic feature of ecosystems is the connectances. Input signals go into the ecosystem components and they are translated into output signals. Such a "translator unit" is an environmental quantum according to Patten. The concept is borrowed from Koestler (1967), who introduced the word "holon" to designate the unit on a hierarchic tree. The term comes from Greek "holos" = whole, with the suffix "on" as in proton, electron and neutron to suggest a particle or part.

Stonier (1990) introduces the term infon for the elementary particle of information. He envisages an infon as a photon, whose wavelength has been stretched to infinity. At velocities other than c, its wavelength *appears* infinite, its frequency zero. Once an infon is accelerated to the speed of light, it crosses a threshold, which allows it to be perceived as having energy. When that happens, the energy becomes a function of its frequency. Conversely at velocities other than c, the particle exhibits neither energy nor momentum - yet it could retain at least two information properties: its speed and its direction. In other words at velocities other than c, a quantum of energy becomes converted into a quantum of information - an infon.


## 2.4. Holism versus Reductionism

Holism and reductionism are two different approaches to reveal the secrecies of nature.

**Holism** attempts to reveal the properties of complex systems such as ecosystems by studying the systems as a whole. According to this approach the system - properties cannot be found by a study of the components separately and therefore - although it is far more difficult - it is required that the study be on the system level. This does *not* imply that a good knowledge of the components and their properties is redundant. The more we know about the system on all levels, the better we are able to extract the system properties. But it *does* imply, that a study of the components of ecosystems will never be sufficient, because such a study will never reveal the system properties. The components of ecosystems are coevolutionary coordinated to such an extent, that ecosystems work as indivisible unities.

**Reductionism** attempts to reveal the properties of nature by separating the components from their wholeness to simplify the study and to facilitate the interpretation of the scientific results. This scientific method is indeed very useful to find governing relationships in nature - for instance primary production versus radiation intensity, mortality versus concentration of a toxic substance, etc. But the method has obvious shortcomings, when the functions of entire ecosystems are to be revealed. A human being cannot be described on basis of the properties of all the cells of the body. The function of a church cannot be found through studies of the bricks, the columns, etc. There are numerous examples of the need for holistic approaches.

The conclusion from these considerations is clear: we need both approaches, but because it is much easier to apply the reductionistic method, analytical work has been overwhelming synthetic work in science, particularly during the period from 1945 to 1975. The last 15 years of ecological research have shown with increasing clarity that the need for the holistic approach is urgent. Many ecologists feel that a holistic ecosystem theory is a necessary basis for a more comprehensive understanding of the ecosphere and the ecosystems and for a solution to all threatening global problems.

The need for a more holistic approach increases with the complexity, integration, number of interactions, feedbacks and regulation mechanisms. A mechanical system - a watch for instance - is divisible, while an ecosystem is indivisible, because of the well developed interdependence. The ecosystem has developed this interdependence during billions of years. All species have evolved step by step by selection of a set of properties which consider all the conditions - i.e., all external factors and all other species. All species are to a certain extent influenced by all other biological and non-biological components of the ecosystem. All species are therefore confronted with the question: "which of the possible *combinations* of properties will give the best chance for survival and growth, considering all possible factors, i.e., all forcing functions and all other components of the ecosystem?" That combination will be selected and that will be the combination that gives the best benefit in the long run to the entire system, as all the other component try to optimize the answer to the same question. This game has continued for billions of years. A steady refinement of the properties has taken place, and it has been possible through this evolution to consider ever more factors, which means that the species have become increasingly integrated with the system and ever more interactions have developed.

Patten (1991) expresses numerically the direct and the indirect effect. The direct effect between two components in an ecosystem is the effect of the direct link between the two components. The link between phytoplankton and zooplankton is for instance the grazing process. The indirect effect is the effect caused by all relationships between two components except the direct one. The grazing of zooplankton has for instance also a beneficial effect on phytoplankton, because the grazing will accelerate the turnover rate of the nutrients. It is difficult mathematically to consider the total indirect effect to be able to compare it with the direct effect. This problem will be treated in Chapter 8, Section 3, but it can already be revealed in this context that Patten has found that the indirect effect is often larger than the direct one. It implies that a separation of two related components in an ecosystem for examination of the link between them will not be able to account for a significant part of the total effect of the relationship. The conclusion from Patten's work is clearly that it is *not* possible to study an ecosystem on the system level, taken all interrelations into account by studying the direct links only. An ecosystem is more than the sum of its parts.

Lovelock (1979) has taken a full step in the holistic direction, as he considers our planet as one cooperative unit. Its properties cannot be understood in his opinion without an assumption of a coordinated coevolution of the approximately four billion species on earth.

Lovelock (1988) was struck by the unusual composition of the atmosphere. How could methane and oxygen be present simultaneously? Under normal circumstances these two gases would react readily to produce carbon dioxide and water. Looking further he found, that the concentration of carbon dioxide was much smaller on earth than if the atmospheric gases had been allowed to go into equilibrium. The same is true for the salt concentration in the sea. Lovelock concluded that the planet's persistent state of disequilibrium was a clear proof of the life activities and that the regulations of the composition of the spheres on earth have coevolved over time. Particularly the cycling of essential elements has been regulated to the benefit of life on earth. Lovelock believes that innumerable regulating biomechanisms are responsible for the homeostatis or steady-state far-from-equilibrium of the planet. Three examples will be mentioned here to illustrate this challenging idea further.

Ocean plankton emits a sulfurous gas into the atmosphere. A physical-chemical reaction transforms the gas into aerosols on which water vapor condenses, setting the stage for cloud formation. The clouds then reflect back into space a part of the sunlight. If the earth becomes too cool, the number of plankton is cut back by the chill. The cloud formation is thereby reduced and the temperature rises. The plankton operates like a thermostat to keep the earth's temperature within a certain range.

The silica concentration of the sea is controlled by the diatoms. Less than 1% of the silica transported to the sea is maintained at the surface. Diatoms take up the silica and when they die they settle and remove the silica from the water to the sediment. The composition of the sea is maintained far from the equilibrium known from salt lakes without life, due to the presence of diatoms. Life - the diatoms - controls that life conditions are maintained in the sea.

Sulfur is transported from the lithosphere into the sea causing an unbalance. If there were no regulations, the sulfur concentration of the sea would be too high and sulfur would be lacking in the lithosphere as an essential element. However, many aquatic organisms are able to get rid of undesired elements by methylation processes. Methyl compounds of mercury, arsenic and sulfur are very volatile, which implies that these elements are transported from the hydrosphere to the atmosphere by methylation processes. *Polysiphonia fastigiata,* a marine alga, is capable of producing a huge amount of dimethylsulphide (Lovelock, 1979). This biological methylation of sulfur seems able to explain that the delicate balance of essential elements between the spheres is maintained.

The Gaia hypothesis presumes that the components of the ecosphere and therefore also of the ecosystems cooperate more than they compete, when we contemplate the effects from a system's view point. This point will be further treated in Chapter 8, but is illustrated here by an example which shows how symbiosis can develop and lead to new species. The example is described by Barlow (1991) and the event was witnessed and described by Kwang Jeon. Kwang Jeon had been raising amoebas for years, when he received a new batch for his experiments. The new batch spreaded a severe illness and the amoebas refused to eat and failed to reproduce. Many amoebas died and the few that grew and divided did so reluctantly. A close inspection revealed that about 100,000 rod-shaped bacteria, brought in by the new amoebas, were present in each amoeba. The surviving bacterized amoebas were fragile. They were easily killed by antibiotics and oversensitive to heat and starvation. For some five years, Jeon nurtured the infected amoebas back to health by continuously selecting the tougher ones. Although they were still infected they started to divide again at the normal rate. They had not got rid of their bacteria, but they were adapted. and cured of their disease. Each recovered amoeba contained about 40,000 bacteria and they have adjusted their destructive tendencies in order to live and survive inside other living cells.

From friends Jeon reclaimed some of the amoebas that he had sent off before the epidemic. With a hooked glass needle he removed the nuclei from the infected and uninfected organisms and exchanged them, The infected amoebas with new nuclei survived, while the uninfected amoebas supplied with nuclei from cells that had been infected for years struggled for about four days and then died. The nuclei were unable to cope with an uninfected cell. To test this hypothesis Jeon injected uninfected cells with nuclei from infected amoebas with a few bacteria, just before they died. The bacteria rapidly increased to 40,000 per cell and the amoebas returned to health. Obviously, a symbiosis had been developed.

The amoeba experiment shows that cooperation is an important element in evolution. An ultimate cooperation of all components in the ecosystems leads inevitably to a Gaia perception of ecosystems and the entire ecosphere.

It is interesting that Axelrod (1984) demonstrates through the use of game theory that cooperation is a beneficial long-term strategy. The game anticipates a trade situation between you and a dealer. At mutual cooperation both parties earn two points, while at mutual defection both earn zero points. Cooperating while the other part defects stings: you get minus one point while the "rat" gets something for nothing and earns four points. Should you happen to be a rat, while the dealer is cooperative, you get four points and the dealer loses one. Which strategy should you follow to gain most? Two computer tournaments have given the result that the following so-called "tit-for-tat" strategy seems to be winning: start with a cooperative choice and thereafter does what the other player did in the previous move. In other words be open for cooperation unless the dealer is not. But only defect one time after the dealer has defected.

It may be possible to conclude that the acceptance of the Gaia hypothesis does not involve that mysterious, unknown, global forces are needed to be able to explain these observations of homeostatis. It seems to be possible to explain the hypothesis by an evolution based upon five factors:

1. Selection (steadily ongoing test of which properties give the highest chance of survival and growth) from a range of properties, offered by the existing species.

2. Interactions of randomness (new mutations and sexual genetic recombinations are steadily produced) and necessity, i.e., to have the right properties for survival under the prevailing conditions, resulting from all external factors and all other components of the ecosystem.

3. A very long time has been available for this ongoing "trial and error" process, which has developed the ecosphere step-wise toward the present, ingenious complexity, where all components have unique and integrated properties.

4. The ability of the biological components to maintain the results already achieved (by means of genes) and to build upon these results in the effort to develop further.

5. As the complexity of the ecosystems and thereby of the entire ecosphere develops, the indirect effect becomes more and more important; see Chapter 8 for further explanations. It implies that the selection based upon the "effects" on the considered component will be determined by the entire ecosystem and that this selection process will assure that all components of the ecosystem will evolve toward being better and better fitted to the entire ecosystem. It means that the system will evolve toward working more and more as a whole - as an integrated system and that the selection will be more and more beneficial for the entire system.

# 3. MODELS IN ECOLOGY

## 3.1. Modelling in Ecology

A model can be considered as a synthesis of elements of knowledge about a system. The quality of the model is therefore very dependent on the quality of our knowledge elements and the available data. If our knowledge and data of a given problem are poor, it must *not* be expected that the model of the system can fill the holes in our detailed knowledge or repair a poor set of data. On the other hand, models are able to provide new knowledge about the reactions and properties of the entire system. The model represents a synthesis of knowledge and data and can consequently provide results particularly about the system properties. Furthermore, when we put the results of many different models covering different viewpoints together, we get a more comprehensive overall picture of the ecosystem, because we can, as discussed in Chapters 1- 2, only cover our observations completely by use of a pluralistic view. Modelling is a very useful tool in our effort to achieve the best possible pluralistic view.

Science uses analysis of problems as a powerful tool and has until now not made wide use of the synthesis of knowledge as a tool to reveal the secrets of nature. However, the emergence of the very complex environmental and ecological problems has provoked the development of ecological and environmental modelling as a powerful synthesizing tool, where reactions and properties of systems are in focus.

Models are first of all a synthesizing tool, but it should not be forgotten that models may also be used to analyze the properties of the *entire* system at the system level. In ecology, therefore, we do not only use models to overview the problems, but also to reveal the reactions of the entire system for instance to the impact from emissions. We use models, in other words, to reveal the holistic properties.

As such, the use of models is not new, but models have been used generally by mankind as a "simplified picture of reality" to solve problems. Newton's laws may for instance be considered as models of the impact of gravity on bodies. Models used as a synthesizing tool will, of course, not contain *all* features of the real system, because then it would be the real system itself and thereby too complex. But it is important to extract the knowledge *essential* to the problem or viewpoint being solved or described.

An ecological model should therefore contain the features of interest for the management or scientific problem. This statement is very important, as ecological models may very easily become too complex to develop for practical use.

Models may either be physical or mathematical. Physical models contain the main components of the real system whereby the processes and reactions of the complex system are deduced by using observations on the simpler system - the physical model. If, for instance, we want to study the interactions between a toxic substance and a system of plants, insects and soil in nature, we may construct a simplified system containing these components and make our observations on the simpler system and thereby facilitate our interpretation of the data. Physical models are often named 'microcosmos', as they contain all major components of the larger system, but on a smaller scale.

Models in this book are understood as mathematical models based on mathematical formulations of the processes that are most important for the problem under consideration. It will be emphasized if physical models are considered.

The field of environmental modelling has developed very rapidly during the last two decades, due to essentially two factors:

1. The development of computer technology, which has enabled us to handle very complex mathematical systems.

2. A general understanding of pollution problems, including the problems, that are related to ecology and ecosystems.

The ideas behind the application of models in environmental management are illustrated in Fig. 3.1. Emissions are released from the man-made or man-controlled systems to the environment (ecosystems), where they interfere with the living organisms and may change the reactions, the function, or even the structure of the entire system. Complete elimination of all emissions is impossible for post-industrial man with a global human population of more than 5 billion to feed. But if we can relate an emission with its ecological implications in the environment, we should be able to make recommendations on which emissions to eliminate, or reduce, and how much they have to be reduced to guarantee no, or almost no, adverse effects. The idea behind the use of a model is to come up with the best possible estimation for the relation between emission and ecological consequences by synthesizing all the knowledge - or the most important parts of this knowledge - to be able to obtain an overview of the problem in focus.

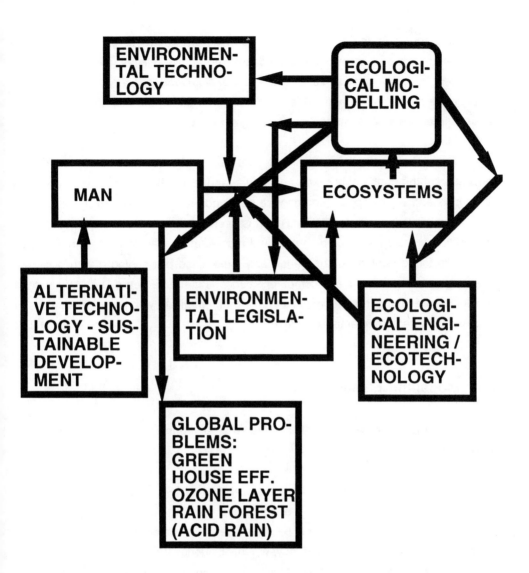

**Fig. 3.1.** The idea behind the use of environmental models in environmental management. The environmental management of today is very complex and must apply environmental technology, alternative technology and ecological engineering or ecotechnology. In addition the global environmental problems play an increasing role. Environmental models are used to select environmental technology, environmental legislation and ecological engineering.

The resulting recommendations may be either in the form of emission limitations or in the form of a more general legislation on the type of emission in question. This is, of course, a political decision, because - even if the model may give a rather clear answer - there are always economical aspects involved in such decisions. It is possible in some instances to construct *ecological-economic* models, which also consider the economic consequences of the various problem solutions, but these models are not yet sufficiently developed to give reliable guidelines in more than a very limited number of cases. However, *ecological-economic* models will most probably be further developed in the near future and during the next decade they will be used in environmental management to a greater extent.

The difficult part of modelling is not the mathematical formulation or the translation of the mathematics into a computer language. The introduction of personal computers and easily applicable software has made it much easier to handle these steps of modelling. The more difficult part is to provide the necessary knowledge and be able to estimate which components and processes to include in the model. It will require profound ecological knowledge and experience. An ecologist with a certain knowledge of mathematics and computer science is therefore better fitted to construct ecological and environmental models than a mathematician with a certain knowledge of ecology and environmental science.

## 3.2 Modelling Elements

In its mathematical formulation a model in environmental sciences consists of five components:

**1. Forcing functions, or external variables,** which are functions or variables of an external nature that influence the state of the ecosystem. In a management context the problem to be solved can often be reformulated as follows: if certain forcing functions are varied, how will this influence the state of the ecosystem? The model is used to predict what will change in the ecosystem, when forcing functions are varied with time. The forcing functions under our control are often called **control functions.** The control functions in ecotoxicological models are for instance inputs of toxic substances to the ecosystems and in eutrophication models the control functions are inputs of nutrients. Other forcing functions of interest could be climatic variables, which influence the biotic and abiotic components and the process rates. They are not controllable forcing functions.

**2. State variables** describe, as the name indicates, the state of the ecosystem. The selection of state variables is crucial to the model structure, but in many cases the choice is obvious. If, for instance, we want to model the bioaccumulation of a toxic substance, the state variables should be the organisms in the most important food chains and concentrations of the toxic substance in the organisms. In eutrophication models the state variables will be the concentrations of nutrients and phytoplankton. When the model is used in a management context, the values of state variables predicted by changing the forcing functions can be considered as the results of the model, because the model will contain relations between the forcing functions and the state variables.

**3. Mathematical equations** are used to represent the biological, chemical and physical processes. They describe the relationship between the forcing functions and state variables. The same type of process may be found in many different environmental contexts, which implies that the same equations can be used in different models. This does not imply, however, that the same process is always formulated by use of the same equation. First, the considered process may be better described by another equation because of the influence of other factors. Second, the number of details needed or wanted to be included in the model may be different from case to case due to a difference in complexity of the system or/and the problem. Some modellers refer to description and mathematical formulation of processes as submodels. A comprehensive overview of submodels may be found in Jørgensen (1988) and Jørgensen et al. (1991).

**4. Parameters** are coefficients in the mathematical representation of processes. They may be considered constant for a specific ecosystem or part of an ecosystem. In causal models the parameter will have a scientific definition, e.g., the excretion rate of cadmium from a fish. Many parameters are not indicated in the literature as constants but as ranges, but even that is of great value in the parameter estimation, as will be discussed further in the following text. In Jørgensen et al. (1979) and (1991) a comprehensive collection of parameters in environmental sciences and ecology can be found. Our limited knowledge of parameters is one of the weakest points in modelling as will be touched on many times throughout the book. Furthermore, the applications of parameters as constants in our models are unrealistic due to the many feed-backs in real ecosystems, see Section 2.3. The flexibility of ecosystems is inconsistent with the application of constant parameters in the models. A new generation of models which attempts to use parameters varying according to some ecological principles seems to be a possible solution to the problem, but a further development in this direction is absolutely needed before we can achieve an improved modelling procedure reflecting the processes in real ecosystems. This topic will be further discussed in Chapter 11.

**5. Universal constants,** such as the gas constant and atomic weights, are also used in most models.

Models can be defined as formal expressions of the essential elements of a problem in mathematical terms. The first recognition of the problem is often verbal. This may be recognized as an essential preliminary step in the modelling procedure, which will be treated in more detail in the next Section. The verbal model is, however, difficult to visualize and it is, therefore, more conveniently translated into a **conceptual diagram,** which contains the state variables, the forcing function and how these components are interrelated by mathematical formulations of processes.

Figure 3.2 illustrates a conceptual diagram of the nitrogen cycle in a lake. The state variables are nitrate, ammonium (which is toxic to fish in the unionized form of ammonia), nitrogen in phytoplankton, nitrogen in zooplankton, nitrogen in fish, nitrogen in sediment and nitrogen in detritus.

The forcing functions are: out- and inflows, concentrations of nitrogen components in the in- and outflows, solar radiation (here indicated by the arrow PHOTO), and the temperature, which is not shown on the diagram, but which influences all the process rates. The arrows in the diagram illustrate the processes, and they are formulated by use of mathematical expressions in the mathematical part of the model.

Three significant steps in the modelling procedure should be defined in this Section. They are calibration, verification and validation:

**Calibration** is an attempt to find the best accordance between computed and observed data by variation of some selected parameters. It may be carried out by trial and error, or by use of software developed to find the parameters giving the best fit between observed and computed values. In some static models and in some simple models, which contain only a few well-defined, or directly measured, parameters, calibration may not be required.

**Verification** is a test of the *internal logic* of the model. Typical questions in the verification phase are: Does the model react as expected? Is the model stable in the long run? Does the model follow the law of mass conservation? Verification is largely a subjective assessment of the behavior of the model. To a large extent the verification will go on during the use of the model before the calibration phase, which has been mentioned above.

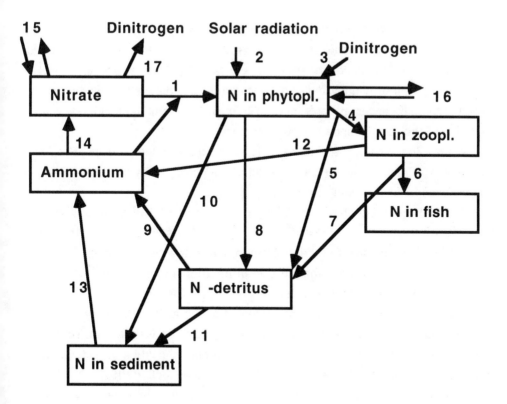

**Figure 3.2.** The conceptual diagram of a nitrogen cycle in an aquatic ecosystem. The processes are: 1) uptake of nitrate and ammonium by algae; 2) photosynthesis; 3) nitrogen fixation; 4) grazing with loss of undigested matter; 5), 6) and 7) are predation and loss of undigested matter; 8) mortality; 9) mineralization; 10) settling of algae; 11) settling of detritus; 12) excretion of ammonium from zooplankton; 13) release of nitrogen from the sediment; 14) nitrification; 15) and 16) are inputs/outputs; and 17) denitrification.

**Validation** must be distinguished from verification. Validation consists of an objective test on how well the model outputs fit the data. The selection of possible objective tests will be dependent on the scope of the model, but the standard deviations between model predictions and observations and a comparison of observed and predicted minimum or maximum values of a particularly important state variable are frequently used. If several state variables are included in the validation, they may be given different weights.

Further detail on these important steps in modelling will be given in the next Section where the entire modelling procedure will be presented.

## 3.3 The Modelling Procedure

A tentative modelling procedure is presented in this Section. The author of this volume has used this procedure successfully several times and strongly recommends that all the steps of the procedure are used very carefully. Other scientists in the field have published other slightly different procedures, but detailed examination will reveal that the differences are only minor. The most important steps of modelling are included in all the recommended modelling procedures.

Always, the initial focus of research is the definition of the problem. This is the only way in which the limited research resources can be correctly allocated instead of being dispersed into irrelevant activities.

The first modelling step is therefore a **definition of the problem** and the definition will need to be bound by the constituents of **space, time and subsystems.** The bounding of the problem in space and time is usually easy, and consequently more explicit, than the identification of the ecotoxicological - subsystems to be incorporated in the model.

Figure 3.3 shows the procedure presented by the author, but it is important to emphasize that this procedure is unlikely to be correct in the first attempt, so there is no need to aim at perfection in one step. The procedure should be considered as an iterative process and the main requirement is to get started (Jeffers, 1978).

It is difficult, at least in the first instance, to determine the optimum number of subsystems to be included in the model for an acceptable level of accuracy defined by the scope of the model. Due to lack of data it will often become necessary at a later stage to accept a lower number than intended at the start or to provide additional data for improvement of the model.

It has often been argued that a more complex model should be able to account more accurately for the reactions of a real system, but this is not necessarily true. Additional factors are involved. A more complex model contains more parameters and increases the level of uncertainty, because parameters have to be estimated either by more observations in the field, by laboratory experiments, or by calibrations, which again are based on field measurements. Parameter estimations are never completely without errors, and the errors are carried through into the model and will thereby contribute to its uncertainty.

The problem of selecting **the right model complexity** will be further discussed in Section 3.5. It is a problem of particular interest for modelling in ecology.

A first approach to the data requirement can be given at this stage, but it is most likely to be changed at a later stage, once experience with the verification, calibration, sensitivity analysis and validation has been gained.

In principle, data for all the selected state variables should be available; in only a few cases would it be acceptable to omit measurements of selected state variables, as the success of the calibration and validation is closely linked to **the quality and quantity of the data.**

Once the **model complexity**, at least at the first attempt, has been selected, it is possible **to conceptualize the model** as, for instance, in the form of a diagram as shown in Fig. 3.2. It will give information on which state variables, forcing functions and processes are required in the model.

It is ideal to determine which data are needed to develop a model according to a conceptual diagram, i.e., to let the conceptual model or even some first more primitive mathematical models determine the data at least within some given economic limitation, but in real life, most models have been developed *after* the data collection as a compromise between model scope and available data. There are developed methods to determine the ideal data set needed for a given model to minimize the uncertainty of the model, but unfortunately the applications of these methods are rather limited.

The next step is a formulation of the processes as **mathematical equations.** Many processes may be described by more than one equation, and it may be of great importance for the results of the final model that the right one is selected for the case under consideration.

Once the system of mathematical equations is available, the **verification** can be carried out. As pointed out in Section 3.2 it is an important step, which unfortunately is omitted by some modellers. It is recommended at this step that answers to the following questions are at least attempted:

1.    **Is the model stable in the long term?** The model is run for a long period with the same annual variations in the forcing functions to observe whether the values of the state variables are maintained at approximately the same levels. During the first period state variables are dependent on the initial values for these and it is recommended that the model is  also run with initial values corresponding to the long-term values of the state variables. The procedure can also be recommended  for finding the initial values if they are not measured or known by other means. This question presumes that real ecosystems are stable in the long run, which is not necessarily the case.

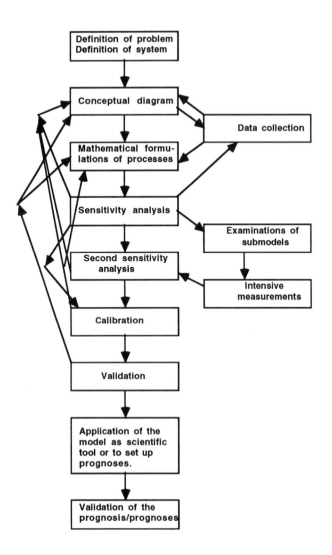

**Fig. 3.3.** A tentative modelling procedure is shown. It is ideal , as mentioned in the text, to determine the data collection on the basis of the model, not the other way round. Both possibilities are shown, because models in practice have often been developed from available data. It is indicated in the diagram that examinations of submodels and intensive measurements should follow after the first sensitivity analysis. Unfortunately many modellers have not had the resources to do so, but have had to bypass these two steps and even the second sensitivity analysis. It must strongly be recommended to follow the sequence of sensitivity analysis, examinations of submodels and intensive measurements and second sensitivity analysis. Notice that there are feedback arrows from sensitivity analysis, calibration, and validation to the mathematical formulation and the conceptual diagram. It indicates that modelling must be considered an iterative process.

**2. Does the model react as expected?** If the input of for instance toxic substances is increased, we should expect a higher concentration of the toxic substance in the top-carnivore. If this is not the case, it indicates that some formulations may be wrong and these should be corrected. This question assumes that we actually know at least some of the reactions of ecosystems, which is not always the case.

In general, playing with the model is recommended at this phase. Through such exercises the modeller gets acquainted with the model and its reactions to perturbations. Models should generally be considered an experimental tool. The experiments are carried out to compare model results with observations and changes of the model are made according to the modeller's intuition and knowledge of the reactions of the models. If the modeller is satisfied with the accordance between model and observations, he accepts the model as a useful description of the real ecosystem at least within the framework of his observations.

**Sensitivity analysis** follows verification. Through this analysis the modeller gets a good overview of the most *sensitive components of the model.* Thus, sensitivity analysis attempts to provide a measure of the sensitivity of either parameters, or forcing functions, or submodels to the state variables of greatest interest in the model. If a modeller wants to simulate a toxic substance concentration in, for instance, carnivorous insects as a result of the use of insecticides, he will obviously choose this state variable as the most important one, maybe in addition to the concentration of the toxic substance concentration in plants and herbivorous insects.

In practical modelling the sensitivity analysis is carried out by changing the parameters, the forcing functions or the submodels. The corresponding response on the selected state variables is observed. Thus, the sensitivity, S, of a parameter, P, is defined as follows:

$$S = [\, \partial x/x \,]\,/\,[\, \partial P/P \,],\tag{3..1}$$

where x is the state variable under consideration.

The relative change in the parameter value is chosen on the basis of our knowledge of the certainty of the parameters. If, for instance, the modeller estimates the uncertainty to be about 50%, he will probably choose a change in the parameters at ±10% and ±50% and record the corresponding change in the state variable(s). It is often necessary to find the sensitivity at two or more levels of parameter changes as the relation between a parameter and a state variable is rarely linear.

A sensitivity analysis on submodels (process equations) can also be carried out. In this case the change in a state variable is recorded when the equation of a submodel is deleted from the model or changed to an alternative expression, for instance, with more details built into the submodel. Such results may be used to make structural changes in the model. If the sensitivity, for instance, shows that it is crucial for the model results to use a more detailed given submodel, this result should be used to change the model correspondingly. The selection of the complexity and the structure of the model should therefore work hand in hand with the sensitivity analysis. This is shown as a response from the sensitivity analysis to the data requirements in Fig. 3.3.

A sensitivity analysis of forcing functions gives an impression of the importance of the various forcing functions and tells us which accuracy is required of the forcing function data.

The scope of the **calibration** is to improve the parameter estimation. Some parameters in causal ecological models can be found in the literature, not necessarily as constants but as approximate values or intervals.

To cover all possible parameters for all possible ecological models including ecotoxicological models, we need, however, to know more than one billion parameters. It is therefore obvious that in modelling there is a particular need for the use of **parameter estimation methods.** This will be discussed further in Chapters 5, 11 and 12. In all circumstances it is a great advantage to be able to give even approximate values of the parameters before the calibration gets started, as already mentioned above. It is, of course, much easier to search for a value between 1 and 10 than to search between 0 and $+\infty$.

Even where all parameters are known within intervals  either  from the literature or from estimation methods, it is usually necessary to calibrate the model. Several sets of parameters are tested by the calibration and the various model outputs of state variables are compared with measured values of the same state variables. The parameter set that gives the best  agreement between model output and measured values is chosen.

The need for the calibration can be explained by use of the following characteristics of ecological models and their parameters:

1.    Most parameters in environmental science and ecology  are not known as exact values. Therefore all literature values for parameters (Jørgensen et al. 1991) have  a certain uncertainty. For parameter estimation methods,

74

particularly in ecological and ecotoxicological models, see, for instance, Jørgensen (1988 and 1990). In addition we must accept that parameters are not constant, as mentioned above. This particular point will be discussed further in Chapter 11.

2.     All models in ecology and environmental sciences are simplifications of nature. The most important components and processes may be included, but the model structure does not account for every detail. To a certain extent the influence of some unimportant components and processes can be taken into account by the calibration. This will give values for the parameters slightly different from the real, but unknown, values in nature, but the difference may partly account for the influence from the omitted details.

3.     By far the most models in environmental sciences and ecology are 'lumped models', what implies that one parameter represents the average values of several species. As each species has its own characteristic parameter value, the variation in the species composition with time will inevitably give a corresponding variation in the average parameter used in the model. Adaptation and shifts in species composition will require other approaches as touched on. This will be discussed in more detail in Chapter 11.

A calibration cannot be carried out randomly if more than a couple of parameters have been selected for calibration. If, for instance, ten parameters have to be calibrated and the uncertainties justify the testing of ten values for each of the parameters, the model has to be run $10^{10}$ times, which of course is an impossible task. Therefore, the modeller will have to learn the behavior of the model by varying one or two parameters at a time and observing the response of the most crucial state variables. In some (few) cases it is possible to separate the model into a number of submodels, which can be calibrated approximately independently. Although the calibration described is based to some extent on a systematic approach, it is still a trial-and-error procedure.

However, procedures for automatic calibration are available. Table 3.1 gives the characteristics of a piece of software, named PSI, intended for automatic calibration. This does not mean that the trial-and-error calibration described above is redundant. If the automatic calibration should give satisfactory results within a certain frame of time, it is necessary to calibrate only 4-8 parameters at the same time. In any circumstances it will become easier to find the optimum parameter set, the smaller the uncertainties of the parameters are, before the calibration gets started.

**Table 3.1**

**Automatic calibration by use of the PSI software.**

---

The user gives:
1.   Initial guesses for parameter
2.   Ranges of parameter variations
3.   A set of measured state variable
4.   An acceptable maximum value for the standard deviation between modelled and measured values

The software tests various combinations of parameters and calculates the standard deviation. The combinations are selected by use of the Marquardt method that combines the Gauss-Newton method and steepest-descent method. It continues until the acceptable maximum value for the standard deviation has been achieved.

---

In the trial-and-error calibration the modeller has to set up, somewhat intuitively, some calibration criteria. For instance, you may want to simulate rather accurately the minimum oxygen concentration for a stream model and/or the time at which the minimum occurs. When you are satisfied with these model results, you may then want to simulate the shape of the oxygen concentration versus time curve properly, and so on. You calibrate the model step by step to achieve these objectives step by step.

If an automatic calibration procedure is applied, it is necessary to formulate objective criteria for the calibration. A possible function would be based on the term for the calculation of the standard deviation:

$$Y = [\, (\Sigma\, ((\, x_c - x_m )^2 /\, x_{m,a} )\, /n\, ]^{1/2} \tag{3.2}$$

where $x_c$ is the computed value of a state variable, $x_m$ is the corresponding measured value, $x_{m,a}$ is the average measured value of a state variable, and n is the number of measured or computed values.

Y is followed and computed during the automatic calibration and the goal of the calibration is to obtain as low a Y-value as possible.

In many cases, the modeller is, however, more interested in a good agreement between model output and observations for one or two state variables, while he is less interested in a good agreement with other state variables. In that case he may choose weights for the various state variables to account for the emphasis he puts on each state variable in the model. For a model of the fate and effect of an insecticide he may put emphasis on the toxic substance concentration of the carnivorous insects and he may consider the toxic substance concentrations in plants, herbivorous insects and soil to be of less importance. He may, therefore, choose a weight of ten for the first state variable and only one for the subsequent three.

If it is impossible to calibrate a model properly, this is not necessarily due to an incorrect model, but may be due to poor quality of the data. The quality of the data is crucial for calibration. It is, furthermore, of great importance that **the observations reflect the dynamics of the system.** If the objective of the model is to give a good description of one or a few state variables, it is essential that the data are able to show the dynamics of just these internal variables. The frequency of the data collection should therefore reflect the dynamics of the state variables in focus. This rule has unfortunately often been violated in modelling.

It is strongly recommended that the dynamics of all state variables are considered before the data collection program is determined in detail. Frequently, some state variables have particularly pronounced dynamics in specific periods - often in spring - and it may be of great advantage to have a dense data collection in this period in particular. Jørgensen et al. (1981) show how a dense data collection program in a certain period can be applied to provide additional certainty for the determination of some important parameters.

From these considerations recommendations can now be drawn up as to the feasibility of carrying out a calibration of a model in ecology:

1.     Find **as many parameters as possible from the literature; see Jørgensen et al. (1991).** Even a *wide* range for the parameters should be considered very valuable, as approximate initial guesses for all parameters are urgently needed.

2.     If some parameters cannot be found in the literature, which is often the case, the **estimation methods** mentioned in Jørgensen (1988 and 1990b) should be used. For some crucial parameters it may be better to determine them by experiments *in situ* or in the laboratory.

3.     A **sensitivity analysis** should be carried out to determine which parameters are most important to be known with high certainty.

4.     The use of **an intensive data collection program** for the most

important state variables should be considered to provide a better estimation for the most crucial parameters.

5.    First at this stage the **calibration** should  be carried out by use of the data not yet applied. The most important parameters are selected and the calibration is limited to these, or, at the most, to eight to ten parameters. In the first instance, the calibration is carried out by using the trial-and-error method to get acquainted with the model reaction to changes in the parameters. An automatic calibration procedure is used afterwards to polish the parameter estimation (see Table 3.1.)

6.    These results are used in **a second sensitivity analysis**, which may give results different from the first sensitivity analysis.

7.    **A second calibration** is now used on the parameters that are most important according to the second sensitivity analysis.  In this case, too, both the above mentioned calibration methods may be used. After this final calibration the model can be considered calibrated and we can go to the next step: validation.

The calibration should always be followed by a **validation.** By this step the modeller tests the model against an independent set of data to observe how well the model simulations fit these data. It must, however, be emphasized that the validation only confirms the model behavior under the range of conditions represented by the available data. Consequently, it is preferable to validate the model using data obtained from a period in which condition other than those of the period of data collection for the calibration prevail. For instance when a model of  eutrophication is tested, it should preferably have data sets for the calibration and the validation, which differ by the level of eutrophication. If an ideal validation can not be obtained, it is, however, still of importance to validate the model.

The method of validation is dependent on the objectives of the model. A comparison between measured and computed data by use of the objective function (3.2) is an obvious test. This is, however, often not sufficient, as it may not focus on *all* the main objectives of the model, but only on the general ability of the model to describe correctly the state variables of the ecosystem. It is necessary, therefore, to translate the main objectives of the model into a few validation criteria. They cannot be formulated generally, but are individual for the model and the modeller. For instance, if we are concerned with the eutrophication in an aquatic ecosystem in carnivorous insects, it would be useful to compare the measured and computed *maximum concentrations* of phytoplankton.

The discussion of the validation can be summarized by the following issues:

1. **Validation is always required** to get a picture of the reliability of the model.

2. Attempts should be made to get data for the validation, which are **entirely different from those used in the calibration.** It is important to have data from a **wide range of forcing functions** that are defined by the objectives of the model.

3. The validation criteria are formulated on the basis of **the objectives of the model** and **the quality of the available data.**

## 3.4 Types of Models

It is useful to distinguish between various types of models and briefly discuss the selection of model types. A more comprehensive treatment of this topic can be found in Jørgensen (1988).

Pairs of models are shown in Table 3.2. The first division of models is based on the application: **scientific and management models.** The next pair is: **stochastic and deterministic models.** A stochastic model contains stochastic input disturbances and random measurement errors, as shown in Fig. 3.4. If they are both assumed to be zero, the stochastic model will reduce to a deterministic model, provided that the parameters are not estimated in terms of statistical distributions. A deterministic model assumes that the future response of the system is completely determined by a knowledge of the present-state and future measured inputs. Stochastic models are rarely applied in ecology today.

The third pair in Table 3.2 is **compartment and matrix models.** By some modellers compartment models are understood as models based on the use of compartment in the conceptual diagram, while other modellers distinguish between the two classes of models entirely by the mathematical formulation as indicated in the table. Both types of models are applied in environmental chemistry, although the use

79

of compartment models is far more pronounced.

The classification of **reductionistic and holistic models** is based upon a difference in the scientific ideas behind the model. The reductionistic modeller will attempt to incorporate as many details of the system as possible to be able to capture its behavior. He believes that the properties of the system are the sum of the details.

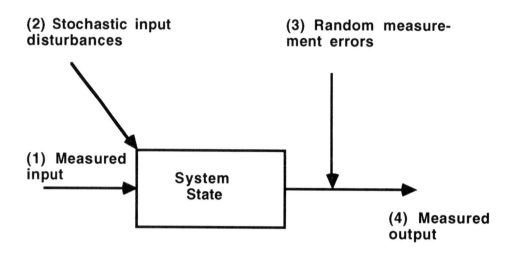

**Fig. 3.4:** A stochastic model considers (1) (2) and (3), while a deterministic model assumes that (2) and (3) are zero.

The holistic modeller, on the other hand, attempts to include in the model system properties of the ecosystem working as a system by use of general principles. In this case, the properties of the system are not the sum of all the details considered, but, the holistic modeller presumes that the system possesses additional properties because the subsystems are working as a unit. Both types of models may be found in ecology, but, in general, the environmental chemist must adopt a holistic approach to the problems to be able to get an overview, because the problems in environmental chemistry are very complex.

Most problems in environmental sciences and ecology may be described by using a **dynamic model**, which uses differential or difference equations to describe the system response to external factors. Differential equations are used to represent continuous changes of state with time, while difference equations use discrete time steps. The steady state corresponds to the situation when all derivatives equal zero.

The oscillations round the steady state are described by use of a dynamic model, while steady state itself can be described by use of a **static model.** As all derivatives are equal to zero in steady states the static model, is reduced to *algebraic equations.*

**Table 3.2**

**Classification of Models (pairs of model types)**

| Type of models | Characterization |
| --- | --- |
| Research models | Used as a research tool |
| Management models | Used as a management tool |
| Deterministic models | The predicted values are computed exactly |
| Stochastic models | The predicted values depend on probability distribution |
| Compartment models | The variables defining the system are quantified by means of time-dependent differential equations |
| Matrix models | Use matrices in the mathematical formulation |
| Reductionistic models | Include as many relevant details as possible |
| Holistic models | Use general principles |
| Static models | The variables defining the system are not dependent on time |
| Dynamic models | The variables defining the system are a function of time (or perhaps of space) |
| Distributed models | The parameters are considered functions of time and space |
| Lumped models | The parameters are within certain prescribed spatial locations and time, considered as constants |
| Linear models | First-degree equations are used consecutively |
| Non-linear models | One or more of the equations are not first- degree |
| Causal models | The inputs, the states and the outputs are interrelated by use of causal relations |
| Black-box models | The input disturbances affect only the output responses. No causality is required |
| Autonomous models | The derivatives are not explicitly dependent on the independent variable (time) |
| Non-autonomous models | The derivatives are explicitly dependent on the independent variable (time) |

Some dynamic systems have no steady state; for instance, systems that show *limit cycles.* This fourth state possibility obviously requires a dynamic model to describe the system behavior. In this case the system is always non-linear, although there are non-linear systems that have steady states.

A **static model** assumes, consequently, that all variables and parameters are independent of time. The advantage of the static model is its potential for simplifying subsequent computational effort through the elimination of one of the independent variables in the model relationship, but as will be discussed in Section 4.4 static models may give unrealistic results because oscillations caused for instance by seasonal and diurnal variations may be utilized by the state variables to obtain by higher average values.

A **distributed model** accounts for variations of variables in time and space. A typical example would be an advection-diffusion model for transport of a dissolved substance along a stream. It might include variations in the three orthogonal directions. The analyst might, however, decide on the basis of prior observations that gradients of dissolved material along one or two directions are not sufficiently large to merit inclusion in the model. The model would then be reduced by that assumption to a lumped parameter model. Whereas the **lumped model** is frequently based upon ordinary differential equations, the distributed model is usually defined by *partial differential equations.*

**The causal, or internally descriptive, model** characterizes the manner in which inputs are connected to states and how the states are connected to each other and to the outputs of the system, whereas **the black-box model** reflects only what changes in the input will affect the output response. In other words, the causal model describes the internal mechanisms of process behavior. The black-box model deals only with what is measurable: the input and the output. The relationship may be found by a statistical analysis. If, on the other hand, the processes are described in the model by use of equations, which cover the relationship, the model will be causal.

The modeller may prefer to use black-box descriptions in the cases where his knowledge about the processes is rather limited. The disadvantage of the black box model is, however, that it is limited in application to the ecosystem under consideration or at least to a similar ecosystem, and that it cannot take into account changes in the system.

If general applicability is needed it is necessary to set up a causal model. The latter type is much more widely used in environmental chemistry than the black-box model, mainly due to the understanding that the causal model gives the user the function of the system including the many chemical, physical and biological reactions.

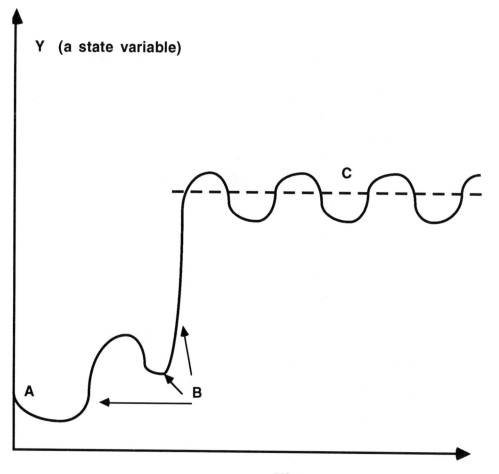

**Y (a state variable)**

**Time**

**Fig. 3.5:** Y is a state variable expressed as a function of time. A is the initial state, B transient states and C oscillation round steady state. The dotted line corresponds to the steady state which can be described by use of a static model.

**Autonomous models** are not explicitly dependent on time (the independent variable):

$$dy/dt = a^*y^b + c^*y^d + e \qquad (3.3)$$

**Non-autonomous models** contain terms, g(t), that make the derivatives dependent on time, for instance:

$$dy/dt = a*y^b + c*y^d + e + g(t) \qquad (3.4)$$

Table 3.3 shows another classification of models. The differences among the three types of models are the choice of components used as state variables. If the model aims for a description of a number of individuals, species or classes of species, the model will be called **biodemographic.** A model that describes the energy flows is named **bioenergetic** and the state variables will typically be expressed in kW or kW per unit of volume or area. The **biogeochemical models** consider the flow of material and the state variables are indicated as kg or kg per unit of volume or area. This model type is mainly used in ecology.

**Table 3.3**
**Identification of Models**

| Type of models | Organization | Pattern | Measurements |
|---|---|---|---|
| Biodemographic | Conservation of genetic information | Life cycles of species | Number of species or individuals |
| Bioenergetic | Conservation of energy | Energy flow | Energy |
| Biogeochemical | Conservation of mass | Element cycles | Mass or concentrations |

## 3.5 Complexity of Models

The literature of environmental modelling contains several methods which are applicable to the selection of model complexity. A rather comprehensive discussion is presented in Jørgensen (1988), where references are given to the following papers devoted to this question: Halfon (1983) and (1984), Halfon et al. (1979), Costanza and Sklar (1985), Bosserman (1980) and (1982) and Jørgensen and Mejer (1977).

It is clear from the previous discussions in this chapter that selection of the model complexity is *a matter of balance.* On the one hand, it is necessary to include the state variables and the processes essential for the problem in focus. On the other hand, it is - as already pointed out - of importance not to make the model more complex than the data set can bear. Our knowledge of processes and state variables together with our data set will determine the selection of model complexity. If our knowledge is poor, the model will be unable to give many details and will have a relatively high uncertainty. If we have a profound knowledge of the problem we want to model, we can construct a more detailed model with a relatively low uncertainty. Many researchers claim that a model cannot be developed before one has a certain level of knowledge and that it is wrong to attempt to construct a model in a data poor situation. In my opinion, this is wrong, because the model can always assist the researcher by synthesis of the present knowledge and by visualization of the system. But the researcher must, of course, always present the shortcomings and the uncertainties of the model, and not try to pretend that the model is a complete picture of reality in *all* its details. A model will often be a fruitful instrument to test hypotheses in the hand of the researcher, but only if the incompleteness of the model is fully acknowledged.

It should not be forgotten that models have always been applied in science. The difference between the present and previous models is only that today, with modern computer technology, we are able to work with very complex models. However, it has been a temptation to construct models that are too complex - it is easy to add more equations and more state variables to the computer program, but much harder to get the data needed for calibration and validation of the model.

Even if we have very detailed knowledge about a problem, we shall never be able to develop a model that will be capable of accounting for the complete input-output behavior of a real ecosystem and be valid for all frames (Zeigler 1976). This model is named 'the base model' by Zeigler, and it would be very complex and require such a great number of computational resources that it would be almost impossible to simulate. The base model of a problem in ecology will never be fully known, because of the complexity of the system and the impossibility to observe all states. However, given an experimental frame of current interest, a modeller is likely to find it possible to construct a relatively simple model that is workable in that frame.

It is according to this discussion that, up to a point, a model may be made more realistic by adding ever more connections. Additions of new parameters after that point do not contribute further to improved simulation; on the contrary, more parameters imply more uncertainty, because of the possible lack of information about the flows which the parameters quantify. Given a certain amount of data, the addition of new state variables or parameters beyond a certain model complexity does not add to our ability to model the ecosystem, but only adds to unaccountable uncertainty.

These ideas are visualized in Figure 3.6.

The relationship between knowledge gained through a model and its complexity is shown for two levels of data quality and quantity. The question under discussion can be formulated with relation to this figure: **How can we select the complexity and the structure of the model to assure the optimum for knowledge gained or the best answer to the question posed by the model?**

We shall not here discuss the methods available to select a good model structure, but again refer to the publications mentioned at the start of this section. If a rather complex model is developed, the use of one of the methods presented in these publications is recommended, but for simpler models it is often sufficient to go for a model of balanced complexity, as discussed above.

Costanza and Sklar (1985) have examined 88 different models and they were able to show that the more theoretical discussion behind Fig. 3.6, is actually valid in practice. Their results are summarized in Fig. 3.7, where effectiveness is plotted versus articulation (= expression for model complexity). Effectiveness is understood as a product of how much the model is able to tell and with what certainty, while articulation is a measure of the complexity of the model with respect to number of components, time and space. It is clearly seen by comparison of Figs. 3.6 and 3.7, that they show the same relationship.

Selection of the right complexity is of great importance in environmental and ecological models as already stated. It is possible by use of the methods presented in Jørgensen (1988) to select by a rather objective procedure the approximately correct level of complexity of models. However, the selection will always require that the application of these methods is combined with a good knowledge of the system being modelled. The methods must work hand in hand with an intelligent answer to the question: Which components and processes are most important for the problem in focus? Such an answer is even of importance in the right use of the mentioned methods. The conclusion is therefore: Know your system and your problem before you select your model, including the complexity of the model.

It should not be forgotten in this context, that the model will always be an extreme simplification of nature. It implies that we cannot make a model of an ecosystem, but we *can* develop a model of some aspects of an ecosystem.

A parallel to the application of maps can be used again: we cannot make a map (model) of a state with all its details  for instance, but only show some aspects of the geography on a certain scale. There lies our limitation, as touched on in Section 2.3, which is due to the immense complexity of nature. We have to accept this limitation or we cannot produce any model or get any picture of a natural system at all. But as some kind of map is always more useful than no map, some kind of model of an ecosystem is better than no model at all. As the map will become better, the better our techniques and knowledge are, so will the model of an ecosystem become better, the more experience we gain in modelling and the more we improve our ecological knowledge. We do not need all details to get a proper overview and a holistic picture. We need some details and we need to understand how the system works on the system level.

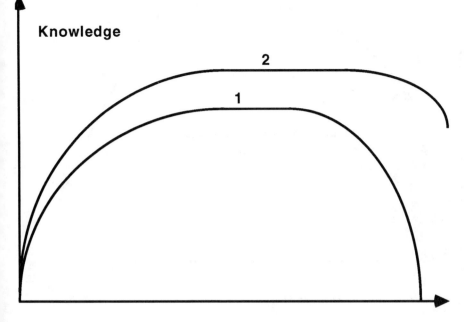

**Fig. 3.6:** Knowledge plotted versus model complexity measured, for instance, by the number of state variables. The knowledge increases up to a certain level. Increased complexity beyond this level will not add to the knowledge gained about the modelled system. At a certain level the knowledge might even be decreased due to uncertainty caused by too high a number of unknown parameters. (2) corresponds to an available data set, which is more comprehensive or has a better quality than (1). Therefore the knowledge gained and the optimum complexity is higher for data set (2) than for (1). Reproduced from Jørgensen (1988).

The conclusion is, therefore, that although we can never know all, that is needed to make a complete model, - i.e., with inclusion of all details - we can indeed produce good workable models which can expand our knowledge of the ecosystems, particularly of their properties as systems. This is completely consistent with Ulanowicz (1979). They point out that the biological world is a sloppy place. Very precise predictive models will inevitably be wrong. It would be more fruitful to build a model which indicates the general trends and take into account the probabilistic nature of the environment.

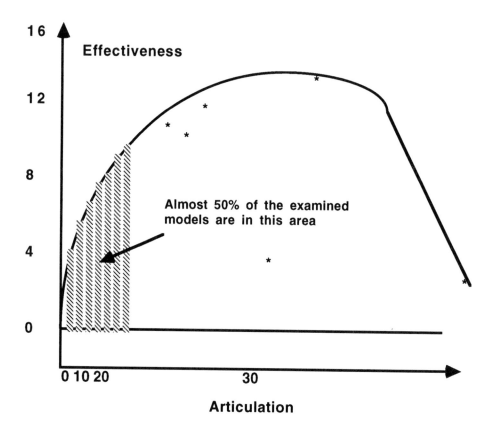

**Fig. 3.7:** Plot of articulation index versus effectiveness = articulation*certainty for the models reviewed by Costanza and Sklar (1985). As almost 50% of the models were not validated, they had an effectiveness of 0. These models are not included in the figure, but are represented by the line effectiveness = 0. Notice that almost another 50% of the models have a relatively low effectiveness due to too little articulation and that only one model had too high articulation, which implies that the uncertainty by drawing the effectiveness frontier as shown in the figure is high at articulations above 25. The figure is reproduced from Costanza and Sklar (1985).

Furthermore, it seems possible at least in some situations to apply models as management tool, see for instance Jørgensen (1986 and 1988). All in all models should be considered as tools - tools to overview complex systems, where already a few interactive state variables make it impossible to overview how the system reacts to perturbations or other changes - and tools to obtain a picture of the systems properties on the system level.


## 3.6. Modelling Constraints

A modeller is very much concerned about the application of the right description of the components and processes in his models. The model equations and their parameters should reflect the properties of the model components and processes as correctly as possible. The modeller must, however, also be concerned with the right description of the system properties and too little research has been done in this direction. A continuous development of models as scientific tool will need to consider to apply constraints on models according to the system properties.

The conservation principles are often used as modelling constraints; see Section 4.1. Biogeochemical models must follow the conservation of mass and bioenergical models must equally obey the laws of energy and momentum conservation. These are the classical principles which are imposed on models of engineering systems, too.

Boundary and initial conditions are imposed on models as mathematical constraints, based upon system properties.

Many biogeochemical models are given narrow bands of the chemical composition of the biomass. Eutrophication models are either based on a constant stoichiometric ratio of elements in phytoplankton or on an independent cycling of the nutrients, where for instance the phosphorus content may vary from 0.4% to 2.5 %, the nitrogen content from 4% to 12% and the carbon content from 35% to 55%.

Some modellers have used the second law of thermodynamics and the concept of entropy to impose thermodynamic constraints on models; see for instance Mauerberger (1986), who has used this constraint to assess process equations, too. This approach together with other uses of thermodynamics in system ecology will be presented in Chapters 5 and 6.

Ecological models contain many parameters and process descriptions and at least some interacting components, but the parameters and processes can hardly be given unambiguous values and equations, even by use of the already mentioned model constraints. It means that an ecological model in the initial phase of development has many degrees of freedom. It is therefore necessary to limit the degrees of freedom to come up with a workable model, which is not doubtful and undeterministic.

Many modellers use a comprehensive data set and a calibration to limit the number of possible models. This is, however, a cumbersome method, if it is not accompanied by some realistic constraints on the model. The calibration is therefore often limited to giving the parameters realistic and literature-based intervals, within which the calibration is carried out, as mentioned in Section 3.3.

But far more would maybe be gained, if it were possible to give the models more ecological properties and/or test the model from an ecological point of view to exclude the editions of the model, that are not ecologically possible. How could for instance the hierarchy of regulation mechanisms presented in Table 2.1 be accounted for in the models? Straskraba (1979 and 1980a) classifies models according to the number of levels, that the model includes from this hierarchy. He concludes that we need experience with the models of the higher levels to be able to develop structural dynamic models. This is the topic for Chapter 11.

We know that the evolution has created very complex ecosystems with many feedbacks, regulations and interactions. The coordinated coevolution means that rules and principles for the cooperation among the biological components have been imposed. These rules and principles are the governing laws of ecosystems, which is the focus of this book, and our models should of course as broadly as possible follow these principles and laws.

It seems also possible to limit the number of parameter *combinations* by use of what could be named "ecological" tests. The maximum growth rates of phytoplankton and zooplankton may for instance have realistic values in a eutrophication model, but the two parameters do not fit to each other, because they will create chaos in the ecosystem, which is inconsistent with the actual or general observations. Such combinations should be excluded at an early stage of the model development. This will be discussed further in Chapter 10.

Figure 3.8 summarizes the considerations of using various constraints to limit the number of possible values for parameters, possible descriptions of processes and possible models to facilitate the development of a feasible and workable model.

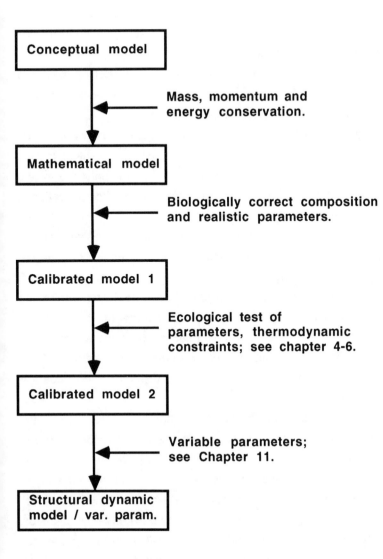

**Fig. 3.8.** Considerations on using various constraints by development of models. Particularly the range of parameter values is limited by the procedure shown.

## 3.7. Application of Models as Scientific, Experimental Tools

The focus of this volume is on ecosystem theory and not on ecological modelling, which is treated comprehensively in other books, for instance Jørgensen (1988), Grant (1986) and Swartzmann and Kaluzny (1987). However, modelling is an important tool, when we want to reveal system properties of ecosystems. Modelling has therefore been presented in this chapter in some detail and will be mentioned in several other chapters because of its power as scientific tool. Modelling may to a certain extent be considered a tool for the examination of system properties, just as statistics is a tool for performing general scientific examinations.

It is clear from the presentation of modelling in this chapter that we can *not* construct a model of all details or components of an ecosystem. We have to limit ourselves to include the components and processes which are of importance for the system properties that we want to investigate. This is consistent with the application of the quantum mechanical ideas in ecology; see Section 2.3.

It is anticipated that we have been able to define a specific problem and the components of the ecosystem of importance for that problem. It implies that we are able to construct a model which to certain extent can be used as a representation for the ecosystem in the context of the focal problem. The model has during the construction phase already been used as a scientific, experimental tool. If the verification, calibration and validation are not running satisfactorily, we will of course ask ourselves: "Why?" and the answer may be that we need to include more feedbacks, a state variable more or less, or change a process description, because it is too primitive in its present form.

When the verification, calibration and validation have been accepted, the model is ready to be used as a scientific tool on the next level. The idea is to ask "scientific questions" to the model about system properties. Patten (1991) uses models in this sense, asking: what is the ratio between direct and indirect effects? Jørgensen (1991) gives another example. The questions are here: If we test which combination of properties currently give the best survival and growth of phytoplankton, are we then able to describe the change and the composition of phytoplankton species? Or in other words: Can we express the survival / growth thermodynamically and quantitatively (which is the idea pursued in the paper) and thereby account for the changes in species and their properties, as observed in the case study examined in Jørgensen (1990 and 1991)?

As will be illustrated several times throughout the volume, we can use models to test the hypothesis of ecosystem behavior, such as for instance the principle of maximum power presented by H.T. Odum (1983), the concepts of ascendancy presented by Ulanowicz (1986), the various proposed thermodynamic principles of ecosystems and the many tests of ecosystem stability concepts.

The certainty of the hypothesis test by use of models is, however, not on the same level as the tests used in in the more reductionistic science. If a relation is found here between two or more variables on the basis of, for instance, use of statistics on available treatment of data, the relationship is afterwards tested on a number of additional cases to increase the scientific certainty. If the results are accepted, the relationship is ready to be used to make predictions and it is examined whether the predictions are wrong or right. If the relationship still holds, we are satisfied and a wider scientific use of the relationship is made possible.

When we are using models as scientific tools to test hypotheses, we have a "double doubt". We anticipate that the model is correct in the problem context, but the model is a hypothesis of its own. We therefore have four cases instead of two (acceptance/non-acceptance):

1. The model is correct in the problem context, and the hypothesis is correct .
2. The model is not correct, but the hypothesis is correct.
3. The model is correct, but the hypothesis is not correct.
4. The model is not correct and the hypothesis is not correct.

To omit 2 and 4 only very well examined and well accepted models should be used to test hypotheses on system properties, but our experience today in modelling ecosystems unfortunately is limited. We do have some well examined models today, but we are not completely certain that they are correct in the problem context and we would generally need a wider range of models. A wider experience in modelling may therefore the prerequisite for further development in ecosystem research.

The use of models as a scientific tool in the sense described above is not only known from ecology; other sciences use the same technique, when complex problems and complex systems are under investigation. There are simply no other possibilities, when we are dealing with irreducible systems (Wolfram l984a and 1984b). Nuclear physics has used this procedure to find several new nuclear particles. The behavior of protons and neutrons has given inspiration to models of their composition of smaller particles, the so-called quarks. These models have been used to make predictions on the results of planned cyclotron experiments, which have often given inspiration to further changes of the model.

The idea behind the use of models as scientific tools, may be described as an iterative development of a pattern. Each time we can conclude that case 1 (see above for the four cases) is valid, i.e., both the model and the hypothesis are correct, we can add one more "piece to the pattern." And that of course provokes the question: Does the piece fit into the overall pattern?, which signifies an additional test of the hypothesis. If not, we can go back and change the model and/or the hypothesis, or we may be forced to change the pattern, which of course will require more comprehensive investigations. If the answer is "yes", we can use the piece at least temporary in the pattern, which is then used to explain other observations, improve our models  and make other predictions, which are tested. This procedure is used repeatedly to proceed step-wise toward a better understanding of nature on the system level. Figure 3.9 illustrates the procedure in a conceptual diagram.

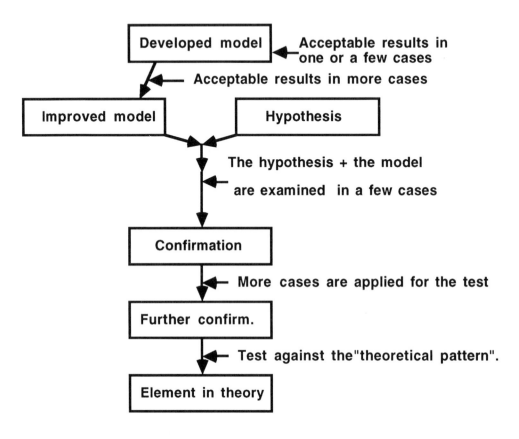

**Fig. 3.9.** The diagram shows how it is required  to use several test steps, if a model must be  used to test a hypothesis about ecosystems, as a model may be considered a hypothesis of its own.

We are not very far in the application of this procedure today in ecosystem theory. We need, as already mentioned, much more modelling experience, and we also need a more comprehensive application of our ecological models in this direction and context.

The ecosystem theory presented in this volume is  partly based on the use of this  procedure to  develop a pattern step-wise. The entire ecosystem theory presented in this volume must therefore be considered as the first approach to construct such a pattern. It should indeed be expected that the pattern will be changed and expanded during the coming years, but we do have sufficient results already today to be able to make the first tentative pattern to have a framework for our further work on ecosystem theory.

It should be considered the primary scope of the volume to present this first pattern for as wide a spectrum of readers as possible in the hope that more scientists will contribute to further development of a sound scientifically founded "pattern" of an ecological ecosystem theory.

# 4. ENERGY AND ECOLOGY

## 4.1 Conservation of Energy and Matter

Energy and matter are conserved according to basic physical concepts which are also valid for ecosystems. This means that energy and matter are neither created nor destroyed.

The expression "energy and matter" is used, as energy can be transformed into matter and matter into energy. The unification of the two concepts is possible by the use of Einstein's law:

$$E = mc^2 \quad (ML^2T^{-2}),$$
(4.1)

where E is energy, m mass and c the velocity of electromagnetic radiation in vacuum (= $3*10^8$ m sec-1). The transformation from matter into energy and vice versa is only of interest for nuclear processes and does not need be applied on ecosystems on t earth. We might therefore break the proposition down to two more useful propositions, when applied in ecology:

1.    **Ecosystems conserve matter,**
2.    **Ecosystems conserve energy.**

The conservation of matter may mathematically be expressed as follows:

$$dm/dt = \text{input - output} \quad (MT^{-1}),$$
(4.2)

where m is the total mass of a given system. The increase in mass is equal to the input minus the output. The practical application of the statement requires that a system is defined, which implies that the boundaries of the system, must be indicated.

Concentration is used instead of mass in most models of ecosystems:

$$V\, dc/dt = \text{input - output} \quad (MT^{-1})$$
(4.3)

where V is the volume of the system under consideration and assumed constant.

97

If the law of mass conservation is used for chemical compounds that can be transformed to other chemical compounds the equation (4.3) must be changed to:

$$V * dc_i / dt = \text{input - output + formation - transformation} \quad (MT^{-1}) \qquad (4.4)$$

The principle of mass conservation is widely used in the class of ecological models called biogeochemical models. The equation is set up for the relevant elements, e.g., for eutrophication models for C, P, N and perhaps Si (see Jørgensen, 1976, Jørgensen et al., 1978 and Jørgensen, 1982a).

For terrestrial ecosystems mass per unit of area is often applied in the mass conservation equation:

$$A * dm_a / dt = \text{input - output + formation - transformation} \quad (MT^{-1}) \qquad (4.5)$$

where
A  = area
ma  = mass per unit of area.

The Streeter-Phelps model (Streeter and Phelps, 1925) is a classical model of an aquatic ecosystem which is based upon conservation of matter and first-order kinetics. The model uses the following equation:

$$dD/dt + K_a{}^*D = Lo * K_1{}^*K_T{}^{(T-20}{}^*e^{-K*t} \quad (ML^{-3}T^{-1}) \qquad (4.6)$$

where
D      $= C_s - C(t)$
$C_s$    = concentration of oxygen at saturation
C(t)   = actual concentration of oxygen
t        = time
$K_a$    = reaeration coefficient (dependent on the temperature)
Lo     = BOD5 at time = o
$K_1$    = rate constant for decomposition of biodegradable matter.
$K_T$    = constant of temperature dependence.

The equation states that change (decrease) in oxygen concentration + input

98

from reaeration is equal to the oxygen consumed by decomposition of biodegradable organic matter according to a first-order reaction scheme.

Equations according to (4.4) are also used in models describing the fate of toxic substances in the ecosystem. Examples can be found in Thomann (1984) and Jørgensen (1979 and 1990b).

The mass flow through a food chain is mapped by use of the mass conservation principle. The food taken in by one level in the food chain is used in respiration, waste food, undigested food, excretion, growth and reproduction. If the growth and reproduction are considered as the net production, it can be stated that

net production = intake of food - respiration - excretion - waste food      (4.7)

The ratio of the net production to the intake of food is named the net efficiency. The net efficiency is dependent on several factors, but is often as low as 10-20%. Any toxic matter in the food is unlikely to be lost through respiration and excretions, because it is much less biodegradable than the normal components in the food. This being so, the net efficiency of toxic matter is often higher than for normal food components, and as a result some chemicals, such as chlorinated hydrocarbons including DDT and PCB, will be magnified in the food chain.

This phenomenon is called biological magnification and is illustrated for DDT in Table 4.1. DDT and other chlorinated hydrocarbons have an especially high biological magnification, because they have a very low biodegradability and are only excreted from the body very slowly, due to dissolution in fatty tissue.

These considerations can also explain why pesticide residues observed in fish increase with the increasing weight of the fish (see Fig. 4.1).

As man is the last link of the food chain, relatively high DDT concentrations have been observed in the human body fat (see Table 4.2)

The understanding of the principle of conservation of energy, called the first law of thermodynamics, was initiated in 1778 by Rumford. He observed the large quantity of heat that appeared when a hole is bored in metal. Rumford assumed that the mechanical work was converted to heat by friction. He proposed that heat was a type of energy that is transformed at the expense of another form of energy, in this case mechanical energy. It was left to J.P. Joule in 1843 to develop a mathematical relationship between the quantity of heat developed and the mechanical energy dissipated.

Two German physicists J.R. Mayer and H.L.F. Helmholtz working separately, showed that when a gas expands the internal energy of the gas decreases in proportion to the amount of work performed. These observations led to the first law of thermodynamics: energy can neither be created nor destroyed.

Table 4.1

Biological magnification (data after Woodwell et al., 1967)

| Trophic level | Concentration of DDT (mg/kg dry matter) | Magnification |
|---|---|---|
| Water | 0.000003 | 1 |
| Phytoplankton | 0.0005 | 160 |
| Zooplankton | 0.04 | ˜ 13,000 |
| Small fish | 0.5 | ˜ 167,000 |
| Large fish | 2 | ˜ 667,000 |
| Fish-eating birds | 25 | ˜ 8,500,000 |

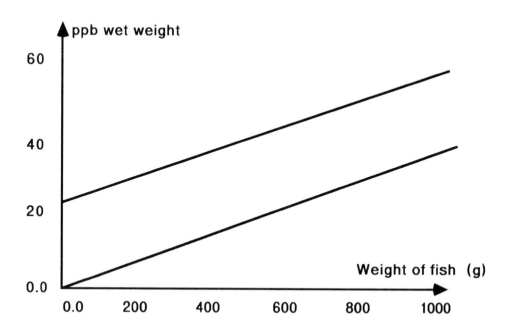

**Fig. 4.1.** Increase in pesticide residues in fish as weight of the fish increases. Top line = total residues; bottom line = DDT only. (After Cox, 1970).

**Table 4.2.**

**Concentration of DDT (mg per kg dry matter)**

| | |
|---|---|
| Atmosphere | 0.000004 |
| Rain water | 0.0002 |
| Atmospheric dust | 0.04 |
| Cultivated soil | 2.0 |
| Fresh water | 0.00001 |
| Sea water | 0.000001 |
| Grass | 0.05 |
| Aquatic macrophytes | 0.01 |
| Phytoplankton | 0.0003 |
| Invertebrates on land | 4.1 |
| Invertebrates in sea | 0.001 |
| Fresh-water fish | 2.0 |
| Sea fish | 0.5 |
| Eagles, falcons | 10.0 |
| Swallows | 2.0 |
| Herbivorous mammals | 0.5 |
| Carnivorous mammals | 1.0 |
| Human food, plants | 0.02 |
| Human food, meat | 0.2 |
| Man | 6.0 |

If the concept internal energy, dU, is introduced:

$$dQ = dU + dW \qquad (ML^2T^{-2}) \qquad (4.8)$$

where

dQ  = thermal energy added to the system
dU  = increase in internal energy of the system
dW  = mechanical work done by the system on its environment.

Then the principle of energy conservation can be expressed in mathematical terms as follows:

U is a state variable which means that $\int_1^2 dU$ is independent on the pathway 1 to 2.

The internal energy, U, includes several forms of energy: mechanical, electrical, chemical, and magnetic energy, etc.

The transformation of solar energy to chemical energy by plants conforms with the first law of thermodynamics,: (see also Fig. 4.2):

Solar energy assimilated by plants = chemical energy of plant tissue growth + heat

$$\text{energy of respiration} \tag{4.9}$$

For the next level in the food chains, the herbivorous animals, the energy balance can also be set up:

$$F = A + UD = G + H + UD, \qquad (ML^2T^{-2}) \tag{4.10}$$

where

F     = the food intake converted to energy (Joule)

A     = the energy assimilated by the animals

UD   = undigested food or the chemical energy of faeces

G     = chemical energy of animal growth

H     = the heat energy of respiration.

These considerations pursue the same lines as those mentioned in context with equation (4.7), where the mass conservation principle was applied. The conversion of biomass to chemical energy is illustrated in Table 4.3. The energy content per g ash-free organic material is surprisingly uniform, as is illustrated in Table 4.3. Table 4.3D indicates $\Delta H$, which symbolizes the increase in enthalpi, defined as : $H = U + p^*V$.

Biomass can be translated into energy (see Table 4.3), and this is also true of transformations through food chains. This implies that the short food chains of 'grain to human' should be preferred to the longer and more wasteful 'grain to domestic animal to human'. The problem of food shortage can, however, not be solved so simply, since animals produce proteins with a more favorable amino acid composition for human food (lysine is missing in plant proteins) and eat plants that cannot all be used as human food today. But food production can to a certain extent be increased by making the food chains as short as possible.

**Table 4.3.**

**A - Combustion heat of animal material**

| Organism | Species | Heat of combustion (kcal/ash-free gm) |
|---|---|---|
| Ciliate | Tetrahymena pyriformis | -5.938 |
| Hydra | Hydra littoralis | -6.034 |
| Green hydra | Chlorohydra viridissima | -5.729 |
| Flatworm | Dugesia tigrina | -6.286 |
| Terrestrial flatworm | Bipalium kewense | -5.684 |
| Aquatic snail | Succinea ovalis | -5.415 |
| Brachiipode | Gottidia pyramidata | -4.397 |
| Brinc shrimp | Artemia sp.(nauplii) | -6.737 |
| Cladocera | Leptodora kindtii | -5.605 |
| Copepode | Calanus helgolandicus | -5.400 |
| Copepode | Trigriopus californicus | -5.515 |
| Caddis fly | Pycnopsyche lepido | -5.687 |
| Caddis fly | Pycnopsyche guttifer | -5.706 |
| Spit bug | Philenus leucopthalmus | -6.962 |
| Mite | Tyroglyphus lintneri | -5.808 |
| Beetle | Tenebrio molitor | -6.314 |
| Guppie | Lebistes reticulatus | -5.823 |

**B. Energy values in an Andropogus virginicus Old - Field Community in Georgia**

| Component | Energy value (kcal/ash-free gm) |
|---|---|
| Green grass | -4.373 |
| Standing dead vegetation | -4.290 |
| Litter | -4.139 |
| Roots | -4.167 |
| Green herbs | -4.288 |
| Average | -4.251 |

# Table 4.3. (continued)

## C. Combustion heat of migratory and non-migratory birds

| Sample | Ash-free material (kcal/gm) | Fat ratio (% dry weight as fat) |
|---|---|---|
| Fall birds | -8.08 | 71.7 |
| Spring birds | -7.04 | 44.1 |
| Non-migrants | -6.26 | 21.2 |
| Extracted bird fat | -9.03 | 100.0 |
| Fat extracted: fall birds | -5.47 | 0.0 |
| Fat extracted: spring birds | -5.41 | 0.0 |
| Fat extracted: non-migrants | -5.44 | 0.0 |

## D. Combustion heat of components of biomass

| Material | $\Delta H$ protein (kcal/gm) | $\Delta H$ fat (kcal/gm) | $\Delta H$ carbohydrate (kcal/gm) |
|---|---|---|---|
| Eggs | -5.75 | -9.50 | -3.75 |
| Gelatin | -5.27 | -9.50 | |
| Glycogen | | | -4.19 |
| Meat, fish | -5.65 | -9.50 | |
| Milk | -5.65 | -9.25 | -3.95 |
| Fruits | -5.20 | -9.30 | -4.00 |
| Grain | -5.80 | -9.30 | -4.20 |
| Sucrose | | | -3.95 |
| Glucose | | | -3.75 |
| Mushroom | -5.00 | -9.30 | -4.10 |
| Yeast | -5.00 | -9.30 | -4.20 |

Source Morowitz, (1968).

These relationships can also be illustrated by means of so-called ecological pyramids that can either represent the number of individuals, the biomass (or energy content) or the energy flows on each level in the food chains or foodweb. Only the energy flow forms a true pyramid according to the first law of thermodynamics. The pyramids based on numbers are affected by variation in size and the biomass pyramids by the metabolic rates of individuals. However, as will be demonstrated in Section 8.2, energy in ecosystems is cycles like mass, if we consider the chemical energy carried by biomass. It will, however, make the interpretation of trophic levels more complicated.

Ecological energy flows are of considerable environmental interest as calculations of biological magnifications are based on energy flows.

Ecological efficiency should also be mentioned here; see Table 4.4, where some useful definitions are listed and efficiency values are exemplified.

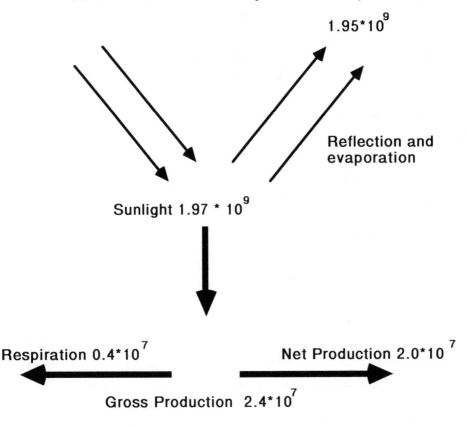

$1.95*10^9$

Reflection and evaporation

Sunlight $1.97 * 10^9$

Respiration $0.4*10^7$    Net Production $2.0*10^7$

Gross Production  $2.4*10^7$

**Fig. 4.2.** Fate of solar energy incident upon the perennial grass-herb vegetation of an old field community in Michigan. All values in $J\ m^{-2}\ y^{-1}$.

There is a close relationship between energy flow rates and organism size and some of the most useful of these relationships are illustrated in Jørgensen (1988 and 1990b). See furthermore Peters (1986). Any self sustaining ecosystem will contain a wide spectrum of organisms ranging in size from tiny microbes to large animals and plants. The small organisms account in most cases for most of the respiration (energy turnover), whereas the larger organisms comprise most of the biomass.

**Table 4.4a.**

Ecological efficiency. Abbreviations: I: input of indigested food, ND:non-digested food, A:assimilated food, R:respiration, P:net production, E=excretion, G:growth, n=trophic level. $I=ND+A$ and $A=P+R$ and $P=G+E$.

| Concept | Definition |
|---|---|
| Lindeman's efficiency | Ratio of energy intake level n to n-1: $I_n/I_{n-1}$ |
| Trophic level assimilation efficiency | $A_n/A_{n-1}$ |
| Trophic level production efficiency | $P_n/P_{n-1}$ |
| Tissue growth efficiency | $P_n/A_n$ |
| Ecological growth efficiency | $P_n/I_n$ |
| Assimilation efficiency | $A_n/I_n$ |
| Utilization efficiency | $I_n/ND_{n-1}$ |

**Table 4.4b.**

**Assimilation efficiency (A/I) for selected organisms** (after various authors)

| Taxa | A/I value |
|---|---|
| Internal parasites | |
|     Entomophagous Hymenoptera / | |
|     *chneumon* sp. | 0.90 |

| Taxa | A/I value |
|---|---|
| Carnivores | |
| Amphibian (*Nectophrynoides occidentalis*) | 0.83 |
| Lizard (*Mabuya buettneri*) | 0.80 |
| Praying mantis | 0.80 |
| Spiders | 0.80 to 0.90 |
| Warm- and cold-blooded herbivores | |
| Deer (*Odocoileus* sp.) | 0.80 |
| Vole (*Microtus* sp.) | 0.70 |
| Foraging termite (*Trinervitermes* sp.) | 0.70 |
| *Impala* antelope | 0.60 |
| Domestic cattle | 0.44 |
| Elephant (*Loxodonta*) | 0.30 |
| Pulmonate mollusc (*Cepaea* sp.) | 0.33 |
| Tropical cricket (*Orthochtha brachycnemis*) | 0.20 |
| Detritus eaters | |
| Termite (*Macrotermes* sp.) | 0.30 |
| Wood louse (*Philoscia muscorum*) | 0.19 |
| Soil-eating organisms | |
| Tropical earthworm (*Millsonia anomala*) | 0.07 |

**Table 4.4c.**

**Tissue Growth Efficiency (P/A) for selected organisms** (after various authors)

| Taxa | P/A value |
|---|---|
| Immobile, cold-blooded internal parasites | |
| *Ichneumon* sp. | 0.65 |
| Cold-blooded, herbivorous and detritus-eating organisms | |
| Tropical cricket (*Orthochtha brachycnemis*) | 0.42 |
| Other crickets | 0.16 |
| Pulmonate mollusc (*Cepaea* sp.) | 0.35 |

| Taxa | P/A value |
| --- | --- |
| Termite (*Macrotermes* sp.) | 0.30 |
| Termite (*Trinervitermes* sp.) | 0.20 |
| Wood louse (*Philoscia muscorum*) | 0.16 |
| Cold-blooded, carnivorous vertebrates and invertebrates | |
| Amphibian (*Nectophrynoides occidentalis*) | 0.21 |
| Lizard (*Mabuya buettneri*)0.14 | |
| Spiders | 0.40 |
| Warm-blooded birds and mammals | |
| Domestic cattle | 0.057 |
| *Impala* antelope | 0.039 |
| Vole (*Microtus* sp.) | 0.028 |
| Elephant (*Loxodonta*) | 0.015 |
| Deer (*Odocoileus* sp.) | 0.014 |
| Savanna sparrow (*Passerculus* sp.) | 0.011 |
| Shrews | Even lower values |

**Table 4.4d.**

**Ecological Growth Efficiency (P/I) for selected organisms** (after various authors)

| Taxa | P/I value |
| --- | --- |
| Herbivorous mammals | |
| Domestic cattle | 0.026 (0.44 x 0.057) |
| *Impala* antelope | 0.022 (0.59 x 0.039) |
| Vole (*Microtus* sp.) | 0.020 (0.70 x 0.285) |
| Deer (*Odocoileus* sp.) | 0.012 (0.80 x 0.014) |
| Elephant (*Loxodonta*) | 0.005 (0.30 x 0.015) |
| Birds | |
| Savanna sparrow (*Passerculus* sp.) | 0.010 (0.90 x 0.011) |

| Taxa | P/I value |
| --- | --- |
| Herbivorous invertebrates | |
| Termite (*Trinervitermes* sp.) | 0.140 (0.70 x 0.20) |
| Tropical cricket (*Orthochtha brachycnemis*) | 0.085 (0.20 x 0.42) |
| Other crickets (New Zealand taxa) | 0.050 (0.31 x 0.16) |
| Pulmonate mollusc (*Cepaea* sp.) | 0.130 (0.33 x 0.30) |
| Detritus-eating and soil-eating invertebrates | |
| Termite (*Macrotermes* sp.) | 0.090 (0.30 x 0.30) |
| Wood louse (*Philoscia muscorum*) | 0.030 (0.19 x 0.16) |
| Tropical earthworm (*Millsonia anomala*) | 0.005 (0.076 x 0.06) |
| Carnivorous vertebrates | |
| Lizard (*Mabuya* sp.) | 0.100 (0.80 x 0.14) |
| Amphibian (*Nectophrynoides occidentalis*) | 0.180 (0.83 x 0.21) |
| Carnivorous invertebrate | |
| Spiders | 0.350 (0.85 x 0.42) |
| Internal parasites | |
| *Ichneumon* sp. | 0.580 (0.90 x 0.65) |

## 4.2. Energy Flows in Ecosystems.

Ecological Modelling often focuses on the energy or mass flows in the ecosystem, because these flows determine the further development of the system and characterize the present conditions of the system. H.T. Odum has developed an energy language, see Fig. 4.3., which is a useful tool to incorporate much information into an energy flow diagram. The symbols used allow to consider not only the flows, but also the feed back mechanisms and the rate regulators.

Figure 4.4 shows the application of the energy language symbols on a farm. Comparison of the diagram with real farms suggests many different ways to draw the diagram, showing more or fewer details, including other factors and aggregating more or less.

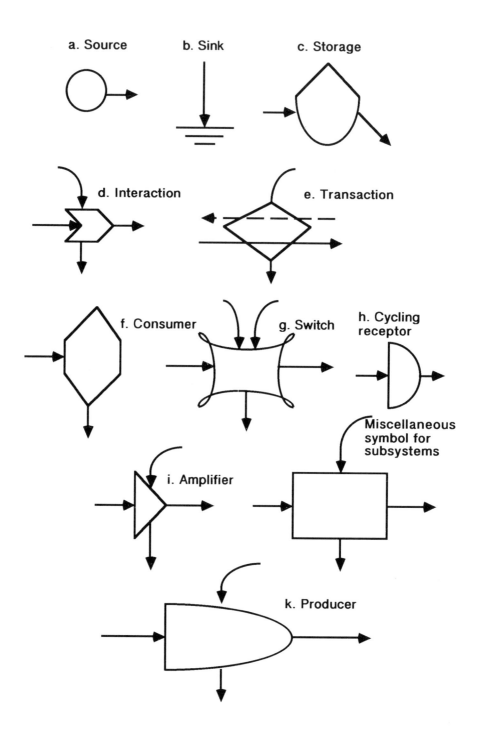

**Fig. 4.3.** Diagrammatic Energy Circuit Language, developed by H.T. Odum (1971, 1972 and 1983).

The pathway line is like the usual electrical current in a wire with the driving force, X, balanced by a frictional force that develops almost in proportion to the rate of flow, J, so that there is a balance of forces:

$$X = R * J \qquad\qquad (4.11)$$

where R is the resistance. Equation (4.11) is, as seen, a parallel to Ohm's law. L = 1/R may be denoted conductivity, and equation (4.11) may be reformulated to (Onsager, 1931, who stated that $L_{ij} = L_{ji}$).

A.

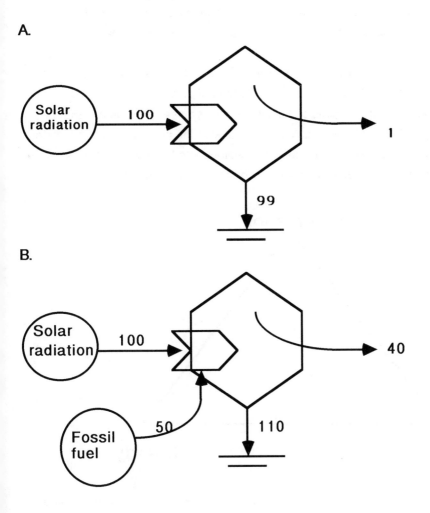

B.

Fig. 4.4. The application of the Energy Circuit Language on (A) Animal Husbandry without fossil fuel; (B) Animal husbandry with fossil fuel. Notice the difference in yield: 1 versus 40. Unit: kcal/ $m^2$*day.

$$J = L * X \qquad\qquad (4.12)$$

Ecological processes may be described in the same manner, for instance the metabolism J of a population N:

$$J = L * N \qquad\qquad (4.13)$$

The ecosystem also has a flow of mass under the driving influence of a thermodynamic force. The flux is the flow of food through a food chain, expressed in units such as carbon per square meter of ecosystem area per unit of time. The force is some function of the concentration gradient of organic matter and biomass.

Energy is the driving factor of ecosystems, see Fig. 4.4. The various energy flows, however, are of different quality with different ratios of solar calories required in the world web to generate a calorie of that type of energy, see H.T. Odum (1983).
It is the strength of Odum's approach that he includes the importance of self design, also called feedback design or autocatalytic reactions into his energy diagrams to be able to consider the role of these mechanisms on the utilization of energy.

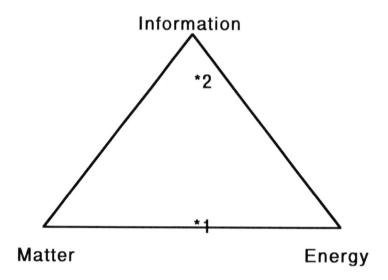

Fig. 4.5. The conceptual triangle of matter, energy and information. Point 1 corresponds to input of matter and energy, e.g., organic matter in form of detritus. Point 2 will corresponds to immigration of new species carrying genes and thereby information. It is accompanied by an input of matter and energy, but as shown in the diagram it is relatively minor.

**Table 4.5**

Differences between initial stage and mature stage are indicated.

| Properties | Early stages | | Late or mature stage |
|---|---|---|---|
| **A**    **Energetic** | | | |
| P/R | >>1 | <<1 | Close to 1 |
| P/B | High | | Low |
| Yield | High | | Low |
| Specific entropy | High | | Low |
| Entropy production per unit of time | Low | | High |
| Exergy | Low | | High |
| Information | Low | | High |
| | | | |
| **B**    **Structure** | | | |
| Total biomass | Small | | Large |
| Inorganic nutrients | Extrabiotic | | Intrabiotic |
| Diversity, ecological | Low | | High |
| Diversity, biological | Low | | High |
| Patterns | Poorly organized | | Well organized |
| Niche specialization | Broad | | Narrow |
| Size of organisms | Small | | Large |
| Life cycles | Simple | | Complex |
| Mineral cycles | Open | | Closed |
| Nutrient exchange rate | Rapid | | Slow |
| | | | |
| **C**    **Selection and homeostatis** | | | |
| Internal symbiosis | Undeveloped | | Developed |
| Stability (resistance to external perturbations) | Poor | | Good |
| Ecological buffer capacity | Low | | High |
| Feedback control | Poor | | Good |
| Growth form | Rapid growth | | Feedback controlled growth |

The developments and reactions of ecosystems in general are not only a question of the energy flow, as will be touched upon many times in this volume. Matter and information also play a major role. A conceptual triangle of matter, energy and information is shown in Fig. 4.5. No transfer of energy is possible without matter and information and the higher the levels of information, the higher the utilization of matter and energy for further development of ecosystems away from the thermodynamic equilibrium; see also Sections 5.2 and 6.2.

The conservation laws of energy and matter set limits to the further development of "pure" energy and matter, while information may be amplified (almost) without limit.

A major design principle observed in natural systems is the feed back of energy from storages to stimulate the inflow pathways as a reward from receiver storage to the inflow source (H.T. Odum, 1971). By this feature the flow values developed reinforce the processes that are doing useful work. Feedback allows the circuit to learn. A wider use of the self-organization ability of ecosystems in environmental or rather ecological management has been proposed by H.T. Odum (1988).

E.P. Odum has described the development of ecosystems from the initial stage to the mature stage as a result of continuous use of the self-design ability (E.P. Odum, 1969 and 1971) See the significant differences between the two types of systems listed in Table 4.5. and notice that the major differences are on the level of information. The content of information increases in the course of an ecological development, because an ecosystem encompasses an integration of all the modifications, that is imposed on the environment. Thus it is on the background of genetic information that systems develop which allow interaction of an informational nature with the environment. Herein lies the importance in the feedback organism - environment, that means that an organism can only evolve in an evolving environment

The differences between the two stages include entropy and exergy, which will be discussed later in Chapters 5 and 6.


## 4.3. The Maximum Power Principle

Lotka (1925) formulated the maximum power principle. He suggested that systems prevail that develop designs that maximize the flow of *useful* energy and Odum uses this principle to explain much about the structure and processes of ecosystems (Odum and Pinkerton, 1955). Boltzmann (1905) said that the struggle for existence is a struggle for free energy available for work, which is a definition very close to the maximum exergy principle introduced in Chapter 6. This principle asserts that systems that are able to gain most exergy under the given conditions, i.e., to move most away from the thermodynamic equilibrium prevail. Exergy is defined as the free energy, i.e., useful or available energy, of the system relatively to the environment.

Such systems will gain most biogeochemical energy available for doing work and therefore have most energy stored to be able to struggle for their existence. There seems to be a certain parallelism therefore, between the three formulations of principles. However, the differences between the maximum power principle and the exergy principle will be further discussed in Chapter 11. The maximum power principle will be presented here in more detail and Chapter 6 will present further aspects of the maximum exergy principle.

Power for electrical current is the product of voltage and current. Similarly, the product of J and X, see the equations (4.11) and (4.12), is power (H.T. Odum et al. 1960).

The organic matter accumulated in the biomass of an ecosystem may be defined as the ecopotential, E, equal to the free energy, F, per unit of carbon. Thus, the ecopotential is a function of the concentration of biomass and organic matter. The product of ecopotential and ecoflux has the dimensions of power:

$$\text{Power} = E * J = \sum \Delta F * dC / (C * dt), \qquad (ML^2T^{-3}) \qquad (4.14)$$

where C is the concentration of biomass. Power, as seen, is the increase in biomass concentration per unit of time converted to free energy.

H.T. Odum (1983) defines the maximum power principle as a maximization of *useful* power. It implies that equation (4.14) is applied to the ecosystem level by summing up all the contributions to the *total* power that are useful. It means, that non-useful power is not included in the summation. The difference between useful and non-useful power will be further discussed in Chapter 11, because the emphasis on *useful* power is perhaps the key to understand Odum's principle and to utilize it to interpret ecosystem properties.

A major unsolved question is the role of oscillating forcing functions for the development of ecosystems and their ability to maximize power and/or exergy. Richardson and Odum (1981) found an optimal frequency for maximum power in a general model of production, consumption and recycling.

It may be assumed that the overall properties of ecosystems are adapted to the oscillations of temperature and radiance on earth, and that therefore oscillations are beneficial to the present ecosystems on earth. Figure 2.2 shows a model that was applied to test the influence of oscillations on ecosystem development. The temperature was either oscillating according to a sine function or constantly equal to 1. The difference between superimposing constant or oscillating forcing functions (the average being the same as the constant forcing functions) on the model is presented in Figs. 4.6 and 4.7. It is clear from these results that the oscillating forcing function will give a higher overall biomass of the system. With a constant forcing function the zooplankton and detritus get a lower concentration. In addition, the model is not given flexible parameters that would correspond better to reality, where species better fitted to the spring situation will dominate during the spring and species fitted to the summer situation will dominate during the summer and so on. If the model simulated these natural conditions, the biomass would be even higher, because better fitted species would be available all the time.

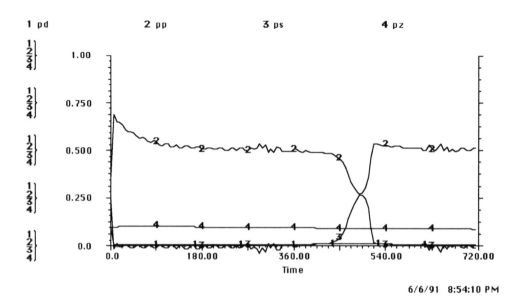

6/6/91  8:54:10 PM

**Fig. 4.6.** Simulations by use of the model in Fig. 2.2. An oscillating temperature function is applied. pd, pp, ps and pz are expressed in mg/l and time in days.

The concepts of ecological niche, territoriality and of different species at the same site are examples of spatio-temporal distributions. Despite the random environment, populations develop according to a heterogeneous spatial structure with a certain life span. This is the so-called patchiness effect, i.e. a spatial distribution of populations according to various geometrical figures. An explanation of this effect by use of models has been given by Dubois (1975). His results show that the spatial heterogeneity provokes an additional organization (the patchiness) that contributes to an increased stability and a better utilization of the resources.

These results should be kept in mind, when results of steady-state models are interpreted - they may *not* represent the real ecosystem. The relation of biomass to maximum useful power and exergy will be discussed further in Chapter 11.

The increase in biomass is one of the products of the net production early in succession; see also Table 4.5. As respiratory requirement accumulates for the maintenance of more structure, the increase of net production is reduced. More

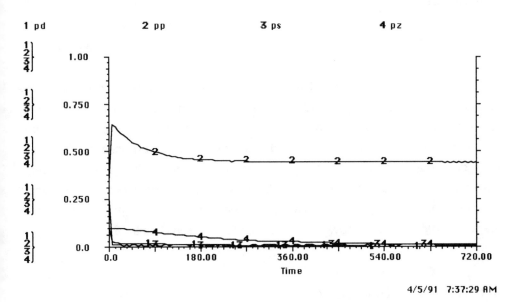

**Fig. 4.7.** Simulation by use of the model in Fig. 2.2. A constant temperature is applied.

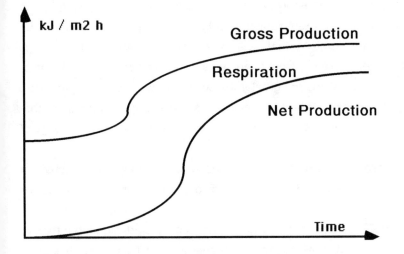

**Fig. 4.8.** Development of gross and net production and respiration in an ecosystem.

117

biomass is then maintained for less respiration per unit of biomass (Margalef 1963 and E.P. Odum 1969); see also the discussion in Section 5.7. and Fig. 4. 8.

H.T. Odum (1983) claims that if the maximum power principle holds, it requires maximization of respiration from both production and import income in the steady-state balance:

$$P + I = R + E + f \quad (ML^2T^{-3}) \tag{4.15}$$

Here P is the production, I the import, E the export, R the respiration and f is the feedback mechanism, all expressed in the unit of energy per unit of time. R may represent power, but it is hard to see how it can represent the maximum *useful* power. However, H.T. Odum (1972 and 1988) here touches an essential feature by ecosystem development by including f. f may be included in the maximum *useful* power and is rooted in some kind of structure, which will contribute to the overall biogeochemical energy of the system (and therefore to the exergy, see the above-mentioned definition of exergy, and to the ascendancy, see Chapter 8 ).

## 4.4. Embodied Energy/Emergy.

This concept was introduced by H.T. Odum (1983) and attempts to account for the energy required in formation of organisms in different trophic levels. Energies of different types are converted into equivalents of the same type by multiplying by the energy transformation ratio. For example fish, zooplankton and phytoplankton can be compared by multiplying their actual energy content by their solar energy transformation ratios. The more transformation steps there are between two kinds of energy, the greater the quality and the greater the solar energy required to produce a unit of energy (J) of that type. When one calculates the energy of one type, that generates a flow of another, this is sometimes referred to as the embodied energy of that type.

Figure 4. 9 presents the concept of embodied energy in a hierarchical chain of energy transformation and Table 4.6. gives embodied energy equivalents for various types of energy.

H.T. Odum (1983) reasons that surviving systems develop designs that receive as much energy amplifier action as possible. The energy amplifier ratio is defined in Fig. 4.10 as the ratio of output B to control flow C. H.T. Odum (1983) suggests that in surviving systems the amplifier effects are proportional to embodied energy, but full empirical testing of this theory still needs to be carried out in the future.

**Table 4.6.**

**Embodied Energy Equivalents for various Types of Energy**

| Type of Energy | Embodied Energy Equivalents. |
|---|---|
| Solar Energy | 1.0 |
| Winds | 315 |
| Gross Photosynthesis | 920 |
| Coal | 6800 |
| Tide | 11560 |
| Electricity | 27200 |

One of the properties of high-quality energies is their flexibility. Whereas low-quality products tend to be special, requiring special uses, the higher-quality part of a web is of a form that can be fed back as an amplifier to many different units throughout the web. For example, the biochemistry at the bottom of the food chain in algae and microbes is diverse and specialized, whereas the biochemistry of top animal consumer units tends to be similar and general, with services, recycles and chemical compositions usable throughout.

Hannon (1973, 1979 and 1983) and Herendeen (1981) applied energy intensity coefficients as the ratios of assigned embodied energy to actual energy to compare systems with different efficiencies. This will be touched on in Chapter 11.

The difference between embodied energy and power, see equation (4.14), simply seems to be a conversion to solar energy equivalents of the free energy $\Delta F$. The increase in biomass, in equation (4.14), is a conversion to the free energy flow and the definition of embodied energy is a further conversion to solar energy equivalents.

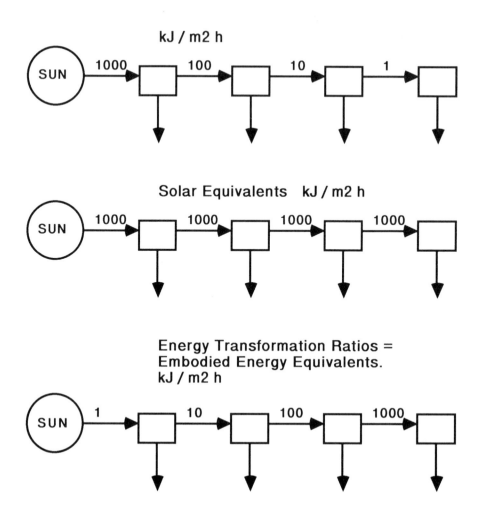

**Fig. 4.9.** Energy flow, solar equivalents and energy transformation ratios= embodied energy equivalents in a food chain.

Embodied energy is, as seen, from these definitions, the biogeochemical energy *flow* into an ecosystem component, measured in solar energy equivalents. It is therefore very close to the concept of exergy. As will be discussed in Chapters 6 and 11, the exergy for trophic levels 2, 3 and 4 would have a more improbable thermodynamic equilibrium concentration and therefore it could be accounted for by setting the thermodynamic equilibrium concentration 10, 100 and 1000 times smaller, respectively. The exergy is defined as the free energy of the system relatively to the environment. As thermodynamic equilibrium is often used as the "environment", the exergy for zooplankton, plantivorous fish and topcarnivorous fish thereby becomes 10,

100, and 1000 times greater by a calculation of the biogeochemical energy of these components, relatively to the thermodynamic equilibrium. This approach would eliminate the difference between emergy (= embodied energy) and increase in exergy, although a more thermodynamically correct approach to the calculation of exergy for different trophic levels will be presented in Chapter 11.

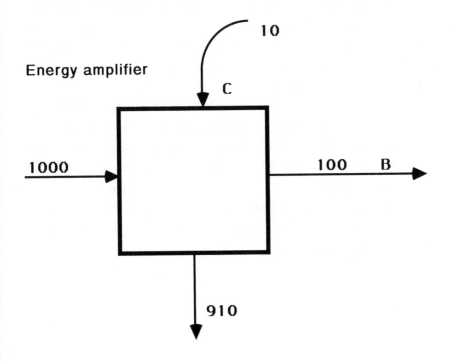

**Fig. 4.10** The Energy Amplifier Ratio, R, is defined as the ratio of output B to control flow C. It means that R = 10 in this case.

The remaining difference between the two concepts may be summarized as follows:

1) Emergy has no clear reference state, which is not needed as it is a measure of energy flows, while exergy is defined relatively to the environment (see also Chapter 6).

2) The two concepts will not give the same results in for instance the number of J per m$^2$. The parallelism will rather be that the ratios of exergy and emergy between two different ecosystems will be approximately the same, i.e., the comparisons between two different situations / systems will give the same

results.

3) Exergy is better anchored in thermodynamics and therefore has a wider theoretical basis.

4) Emergy is based upon flows and increase/decrease of exergy upon changes of state variables with time. In general our knowledge of state variables of ecosystems is better than our knowledge of flows. Ecologists measure the components of an ecosystem but only rarely the flows - simply because it is easier to measure the components as function of time than the flows. Therefore it will be easier in most cases to determine the exergy than the emergy as a function of time.

5) Exergy is easier to compute than emergy from a model study, as the contributions to exergy of the same state variable are independent of the sources of flows/inputs to the state variables, while different flows to the same state variable may have different solar energy ratios, which must be reflected in the emergy computation.

Section 8.2. will illustrate how complicated it is to determine the trophic level n, where $10^n$ is the factor used for emergy calculation. It implies that the calculations of emergy become ambiguous.

# 5.Entropy and Ecology

## 5.1. The Second Law of Thermodynamics Applied to Ecosystems

Spontaneous changes are always accompanied by a degradation into a more dispersed chaotic form of the ecosystem, as gas expands to fill the available volume and a hot body cools to the temperature of its surroundings.

The first law led to the introduction of internal energy of the system and it identifies the permissible changes (see Chapter 4), while the second law of thermodynamics leads to the concept of entropy, S, which identifies the natural (or spontaneous) changes among the permissible changes.

The second law of thermodynamics is expressed mathematically by application of the entropy concept, S:

$$dS = \partial Q / T \quad (ML^2T^{-2}) \tag{5.1}$$

Entropy has the property for *any* process in an isolated system that:

$$dS \geq 0 \tag{5.2}$$

where > refers to real, i.e., non-equilibrium processes and = refers to all equilibrium processes. Notice that S is a state variable: $\int_1^2 dS$ is independent of the path from 1 to 2.

In nature we can distinguish two processes: spontaneous processes, which occur naturally without an input of energy from outside, and non-spontaneous processes, which require an input of energy from outside. These facts are included in the second law of thermodynamics, which states that processes involving energy transformations will not occur spontaneously, unless a degradation of energy from a non-random to a random form occurs, or from a concentrated into a dispersed form. In other words, all energy transformations will involve energy of high quality being degraded to energy of lower quality, e.g., potential energy to heat. The quality of energy is measured by means of the thermodynamic state variable entropy (high quality = low entropy).

123

From a physical standpoint the environmental crisis is an entropy crisis, as pollution creates disorder. An example of this is given in Fig. 5.1 which illustrates the concentration of lead in the Greenland ice pack from the year 1700 to the present. This steady increase demonstrates, that lead released to the atmosphere is distributed worldwide and entropy is increased correspondingly. That entropy is increased by dispersion of the pollutants, can be shown by a simple model consisting of two bulbs of equal volume, connected with a valve. One chamber contains one mole of a pure ideal gas (it means that p v = R T (5.3)) and the second one is empty. If we open the valve between the two chambers, and assume that $\Delta U = 0$ and T is constant, an increase in entropy will be observed:

$$\Delta S = \int_{1}^{2} \partial Q / T = Q / T = W = R^* \ln V_2 / V_1 = R \ln 2 , \qquad (5.4)$$

where $\Delta S$ = the increase in entropy and $V_2$ is the volume occupied by the model of gas after the valve was opened, while $V_1$ is the volume before the valve was opened.

Thus, paradoxically, the more we attempt to maintain order, the more energy we require and the greater stress (entropy) we inevitably put on the environment, as all energy transformations from one form to another imply production of waste heat and entropy according to the second law of thermodynamics.

We cannot escape the second law of thermodynamics, but we can minimize energy waste:

1. **By keeping the energy chain as short as possible,** compare Fig. 5.2.

2. **By increasing the efficiency**, i.e., the ratio of useful energy output to the total energy input,

3. **By wasting as little heat to the surroundings as possible**, e.g., by insulation, and by using heat produced by energy transfer (heat produced at power stations can be used for heating purposes).

Organisms, ecosystems and the entire ecosphere possess the essential thermodynamic characteristic of being able to create and maintain a high state of internal order or a condition of low entropy (entropy can be said to measure disorder, lack of information on molecular details, or the amount of unavailable energy). Low entropy is achieved by a continuous dissipation of energy of high utility - light or food - to energy of low utility - heat. Order is maintained in the ecosystem by respiration that

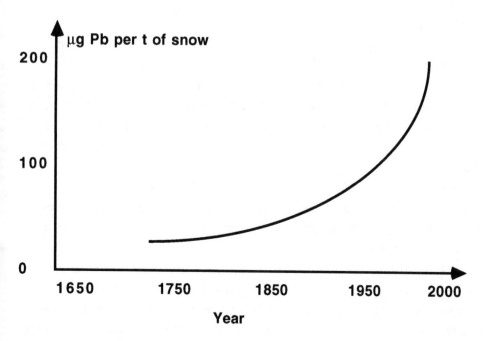

**Fig. 5.1.** Accumulation of lead in the Greenland ice pack from about 1700 to the present. (After Chemistry, 1968.)

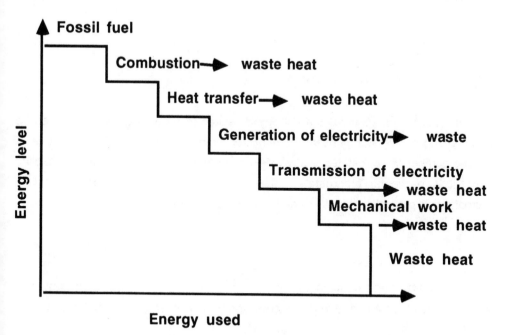

**Fig. 5.2** shows an energy chain that illustrates the transformation of chemical energy in fossil fuel through electricity to mechanical work.

125

continually produces disorder (heat).

The second law of thermodynamics may also explain why and how ecosystems can maintain organization and order. A system tends to move spontaneously toward increasing disorder (or randomness), and if we consider the system as consisting of an ecosystem and its surroundings, we can understand that order (negative entropy) *can* be produced in the ecosystem *if* and *only if* - according to the second law of thermodynamics - more disorder (entropy) is produced in its surroundings.

Thermodynamics often solely considers dissipation of energy. However, dissipation of matter accompanies dissipation of energy, and dissipation of information is based ultimately on degradation of "the energy matter makers", upon which information is always carried.

It is obvious from the second law of thermodynamics that the state in which matter, energy and information are spread uniformly throughout the volume of the system is more likely to occur than any other configuration, and is in particular much more probable than the state in which all matter, energy or information is concentrated within a smaller region. Alternatively, we may assert that the equilibrium state is the most probable state.


## 5.2. Information and Entropy

In statistical mechanics the entropy is related to probability. A system can be characterized by averaging ensembles of microscopic states to yield the macrostate. If W is the number of microstates that will yield one particular macrostate, the probability P that this particular macrostate will occur as opposed to all other possible macrostates is proportional to W. It can further be shown that:

$$S = k * \ln W \hspace{4cm} (5.5)$$

where k is Boltzmann's constant, $1.3803 * 10^{-23}$ J/(molecules*deg). The entropy is a logarithmic function of W and thus measures the total number of ways that a particular macrostate can be constituted microscopically.

S may be called thermodynamic information, meaning the amount of information needed to describe the system, which must not be interpreted as the information, that we actually possess. The more microstates there are and the more disordered they are, the more information is required and the more difficult it will be to describe the system.

Entropy of information is frequently applied to social and biological problems. Although entropy of information is analogous to thermodynamic entropy, it is not the same thing, since thermodynamic entropy is derived from physical laws only.

Shannon and Weaver (1949 and 1963) have introduced a measure of information <which is widely used as a diversity index by ecologists under the name of Shannon's index:

$$H = - \sum_{i=1}^{n} p_i \log_2 (p_i) \qquad (5.6)$$

where $p_i$ is the probability distribution of species.

Shannon's index of diversity (Shannon and Weaver, 1963) is sometimes called entropy, but should not be confused with thermodynamic information. The symbol H is used to avoid confusion. The use of Shannon's index should be limited to a measure of diversity and communication, although as mentioned above, the two concepts to a certain extent are parallel. Both S and H increase with an increasing number of possible (micro)states.

If an ecosystem is in thermodynamic equilibrium, the entropy, Seq., is higher than in non-equilibrium. The excess entropy may be denoted the thermodynamic information and is also defined as the negentropy NE:

$$I = Seq - S = NE \qquad (5.7)$$

In other words, a decrease in entropy will imply an increase in information and erasion or loss of information implies increase of entropy, as pointed out by Landauer; see for instance Landauer (1991). Further, the principle of the second law of thermodynamics corresponds to a progressive decrease of the information content. An isolated system can evolve only by degrading its information.

I also equals Kullbach's measure of information (Brillouin, 1956):

$$I = k * \sum_j p_j^* \ln ( p_j^* / p_j) \qquad (5.8)$$

127

where $p_j^*$ and $p_j$ are probability distributions, a posteriori and a priori to an observation of the molecular detail of the system, and k is Boltzmann's constant. It means that I expresses the amount of information that is gained as a result of the observations. If we observe the system described on p. 124, which consists of two connected chambers, we expect the molecules to be equally distributed in the two chambers, i.e., $p_1 = p_2$ is equal to 1/2. If we, on the other hand, observe that all the molecules are in one chamber, we get $p_1^* = 1$ and $p_2 = 0$. As seen we get the same entropy by application of equation (5.8) as we did on page 124, since $R = k^*A$, where A is Avogadro's number, and there is proportionality to the number of molecules.

Schrödinger (1944) formulated Boltzmann's equation (5.4) as follows:

$$S = k \ln D, \qquad\qquad (5.9)$$

where S is the entropy, k is Boltzmann's constant, and D is the quantitative measure of the atomic disorder. D partly covers the heat motion and partly random mixing of atoms and molecules. Furthermore 1/D may be defined as order, Or. Equation (5.9) may therefore be reformulated:

$$- S = k * \ln (1/D) = k * \ln ( Or ) \qquad\qquad (5.10)$$

In other words negative entropy is a measure of order.

It is interesting in this context to draw a parallel with the discussion of the development of entropy for the entire Universe. The classical thermodynamic interpretations of the second law of thermodynamics predict that the Universe will develop toward "the heat death", where the entire Universe will have the same temperature, no changes will take place and final overall thermodynamic equilibrium will be the result. This prediction is based upon the steady increase of the entropy according to the second law of thermodynamics: the thermodynamic equilibrium is the attractor. It can, however, be shown (see Frautschi, 1988, Layzer, 1988 and Jørgensen et al., 1992b) that the thermodynamic equilibrium is moving away at a higher rate than the rate with which the Universe is moving toward the thermodynamic equilibrium due to the expansion of the Universe. The situation is the same in the ecosystem. Due to the incoming energy of solar radiation the system is able to move away from the thermodynamic equilibrium - i.e., the system evolves, obtains more information and order. The ecosystem must produce entropy for maintenance, but the low-entropy energy flowing through the system may be able to more than cover this production of disorder, resulting in an increased order or information of the ecosystem, see also Section 5.6.

Figure 5.3 shows the relationship, as presented by Brooks et al. (1989), Brooks and Wiley (1986), Wiley (1988) and Layzer (1976). H-max corresponds to the entropy of the ecosystem if it were in thermodynamic equilibrium, while H-obs is the actual entropy level of the system. The difference covers the information or order. It means that:

$$H\text{-max} = \log W, \tag{5.11}$$

where W is the number of microstates available to the system. H-obs is defined according to the following equation:

$$H\text{-obs} = -\sum_{i=1}^{n} p_i \ln (p_i) \tag{5.12}$$

Brooks and Wiley have interpreted this development of entropy in a variety of ways:

1. H-obs is interpreted as complexity - the higher the complexity, the more energy is needed for maintenance and therefore wasted as heat. The information in this case becomes the macroscopic information.

2. H-obs is translated to realization, while H-max becomes the total information capacity. Information may in this case be called constraints. Notice, however, that the strict thermodynamic interpretation of H-max is H at thermodynamic equilibrium, which does not develop (change) for an ecosystem on earth.

3. H-obs represents the observed distribution of genotypes and H-max is any genotype equally likely to be found. The information becomes the organization of organism over genotypes.

Brooks and Wiley's theory seems inconsistent with the general perception of ecological development: order increases - entropy therefore decreases at the cost of entropy production of the environment; see for instance Nicolis and Prigogine (1989). The misinterpretation lies probably in the translation of order to information. By increasing order, the amount of information needed decreases. Note that entropy in this context covers the amount of information needed. The relation of this theory to other thermodynamic approaches will be discussed in Sections 5.7, 6.5 and Chapter 12.

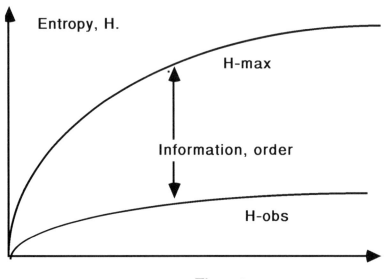

**Fig. 5.3.** H-max and H-obs are plotted versus time. The difference between H-max and H-obs represents I, which increases with time, t (Brooks and Wiley ,1986).

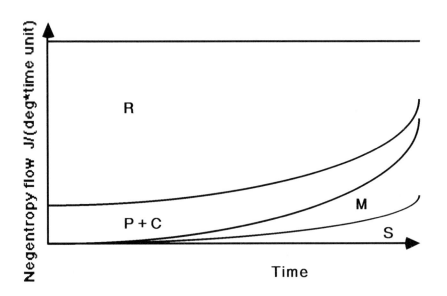

**Fig. 5.4.** The figure shows a tentative development due to the biological evolution in the application of the negentropy flow (solar radiation) on earth versus time. The negentropy is 1) not used, but reflected, R; 2) used by physical and chemical processes on earth, P + C, 3) used for maintenance of the biological structure, M; or 4) used to construct biological structure, S.

Figure 5.4 attempts to give a different, but tentative picture of the development in application of the negentropy flow (= the solar radiation) on earth due to the evolution. The negentropy flow is considered approximately constant, although the solar radiation has shown some (relatively minor) changes. Four different applications of negentropy are considered: unused negentropy (reflection of the radiation), negentropy used for physical and chemical processes, negentropy used for maintenance of life (respiration) and negentropy used for construction of biological structures. The latter two increase at the expense of the other two, particularly at the expense of reflection. It has been widely discussed whether ecosystems attempt to maximize H-obs, negentropy = Information = H-max - S-obs. The difference between biological and thermodynamic entropy is also subject of discussion (Collier, 1988).

## 5.3   Ecosystems Generate Entropy

A number of processes take place in an ecosystem, such as transport of matter and heat, caused by diffusion and external forces and an overwhelming number of biogeochemical processes. They are all irreversible and therefore generate entropy.

Gibbs function, G = free energy, is most commonly used for the description of chemical reactions. It is defined as:

$$G = H - TS \qquad\qquad (ML^2T^{-2}) \qquad\qquad (5.13)$$

where H is the state variable enthalpi, defined as $U + pV$.

To determine whether a chemical reaction will tend to go in a particular direction (the pressure and temperature being constant and no matter flow across the boundaries), we must determine $\Delta G$ for the reaction:

$$\Delta G = G_{product} - G_{reactants} \quad (ML^2T^{-2}) \qquad\qquad (5.14)$$

If this $\Delta G$ is negative, then the reaction has a natural tendency to move spontaneously from reactants to products. If $\Delta G$ is positive the reaction will not proceed spontaneously, but the reverse reaction will be the spontaneous one.

The interpretation of reactions as tending to sink down the slope of the Gibbs function until they attain equilibrium at the minimum is the same as for all spontaneous processes. In this case the apparent driving force is a tendency to move towards lower enthalpi and a higher entropy, but the real interpretation in classical thermodynamics is towards maximum entropy of the Universe, the heat death; see Section 5.2, where a more optimistic interpretation is presented.

The chemical energy released by spontaneous chemical processes is, of course, conserved and can be found somewhere else in the system. The decomposition processes of cells and organisms are called catabolic reactions. They involve decomposition of more complex chemical compounds in the food to simpler organic or inorganic compounds. These reactions are, of course, irreversible and generate heat and entropy.

The ecosystem catabolism is the catabolic processes of all organisms and cells in the ecosystem. The energy released by the catabolic processes firstly is used by the organisms and cells to maintain a "status quo" situation. If the law of mass conservation is used on the feeding of an organism, a part of the feed will not be assimilated but lost as feces. Another part will be used in catabolic processes to keep the organism alive; this means that the energy released is used for the life processes and for maintaining a temperature different from the environment. The energy needed corresponds to the minimum food intake. Poikilothermic animals and hibernators reduce energy needs by reduction of activity and body temperature at low environmental temperature.

The catabolic processes involve the decomposition of food components into more simple molecules, and are in this respect equated with combustion. It differs, however, from combustion in several other respects. Unlike combustion it proceeds at ordinary temperature without the sudden liberation of large amounts of heat. The total amount of energy released from a given decomposition process is the same - regardless of whether combustion or catabolism is involved in the process. The difference lies in the fact that the catabolic process is ordered, catalyzed by enzymes, and consists of many integrated step reactions, whereas combustion is an uncontrolled, disordered series of reactions proceeding at high temperature.

At ordinary temperature most organic compounds are relatively stable, also in the presence of atmospheric oxygen. At high temperature the rate of collision between molecules is increased and the internal chemical bonds are weakened. As a result the compounds decompose most often by reaction with oxygen, and heat is released in the process.

One of the major functions of enzymes in cells and organisms is to eliminate the necessity for high temperature by removing the requirement for a high energy of activation. The combination of an enzyme with its substrate, the chemical changes that occur in the enzyme-bound substrate, and the release of the end product are all reactions that have a low energy of activation. The entire sequence of processes involved in catabolism can therefore proceed spontaneously at ordinary temperature and catalysis is achieved.

Another essential function of enzymes is to provide for an orderly step-wise decomposition of organic nutrients. The third essential function of the enzyme is to make part of the energy that is available from the catabolic processes useful for the cells and organisms. The multiplicity of the reactions and the energetic coupling between them prevent the release of very large amounts of heat in any one step and permit the accumulation of chemical bond energy, in the form of ATP within the cell.

As seen from this overview of catabolic pathways, the basic features, the energy carrier ATP, and to a certain extent also the enzymes, are the same for the various catabolic process chains. The life conditions are, however, different for the different cells and organisms. This implies that in an ecosystem that offers a certain spectrum of life conditions, all or almost all pathways will be represented, resulting in an overall breakdown of the organic compounds to inorganic molecules with very low chemical energy (cf. Fig. 5.5). The ultimate products of organics will be carbon dioxide, water, nitrate, phosphate and sulfate, which corresponds to a complete use of the chemical energy available in the organic compounds.

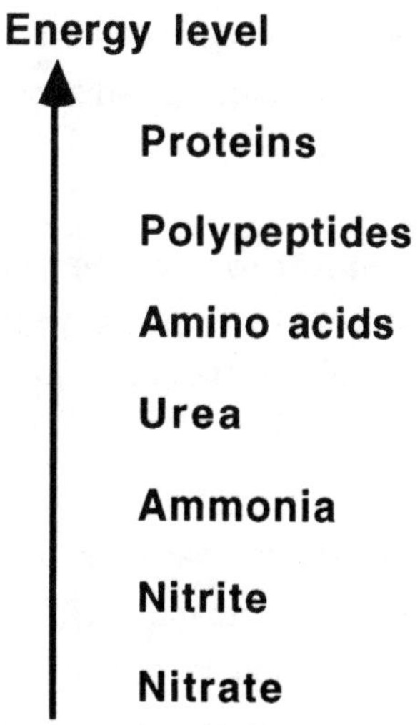

**Energy level**

↑

**Proteins**

**Polypeptides**

**Amino acids**

**Urea**

**Ammonia**

**Nitrite**

**Nitrate**

**Fig. 5.5.** The level of free energy per mole for various nitrogen compounds.

The catabolic reactions are the source of energy for maintenance of life in the ecosystem. These reactions generate heat and entropy that must be transferred, however, to the environment to prevent a constant increase in the temperature of the ecosystem. The ecosystem must therefore be non-isolated - a very important property, to which the next section is devoted.


## 5.4  Ecosystems Are Non-isolated Systems

Let us summarize the conclusions from the previous section: The life processes in ecosystems are maintained by use of catabolism in ecosystems. These processes are spontaneous as they work towards equilibrium and generate entropy (and heat), which causes a dissipation of energy, matter and information. This implies that an ecosystem must be open to be able to transfer the produced entropy (and heat) to the environment - ultimately from the entire ecosphere to the Universe.

If an ecosystem were isolated it would be subject to a series of processes tending toward equilibrium. In statistical terms it will tend to move from the very improbable state of order which characterizes the ecosystem to one of the very probable states associated with the thermodynamic equilibrium. To prevent this drift towards equilibrium, it is constantly necessary to do work to move the system back into the improbable state of order. The necessary condition for this is that the system is connected to a low-entropy energy source and a high-tropy energy sink, which for the ecosystem on earth is ultimately the solar radiation and long wave outgoing radiation. It might also be expressed chemically as follows:

**An ecosystem constantly decomposes organic matter to provide the needed energy for the life processes by catabolism. This implies that new organic matter must be formed, which requires input of low-entropy energy.**

In other words, ecosystems exchange energy with the environment and are therefore non-isolated systems. Most ecosystems are furthermore open to matter.

This has already been assumed by the practical application in ecological modelling of the principles of matter and energy conservation mentioned in Section 4.1, but here we can state that openness is an *absolute* condition for ecosystems.

Or,  expressed more elaborately:

**A low-entropy source and high-entropy sink of energy are necessary to maintain the order, that characterizes the ecosystem.**

The properties of the necessary input and output environment will be examined here before we turn to the crucial question of whether a source  and sink of energy are also *sufficient* to establish order and ultimately life.

As an ecosystem is non-isolated, the entropy changes during a time interval, dt can be decomposed into the entropy flux due to exchanges with the environment, $d_eS$, and the entropy production due to the irreversible processes inside the system such as diffusion, heat conduction and chemical reactions, $d_iS$.

It can be expressed as follows:

$$dS/dt = d_eS/dt + d_iS/dt \qquad (5.16)$$

For an isolated system $d_eS = 0$, and the second law of thermodynamics yields:

$$dS = d_iS \geq 0 \qquad (5.17)$$

In other words $d_iS$, the internal entropy production (increase) can never be negative, while $d_eS$ does not have a definite sign.

Equation (5.16) - among other things - shows that systems can only maintain a non-equilibrium steady state (dS/dt = 0) by compensating the internal entropy production ($d_iS/dt > 0$) with a negative entropy influx ($d_eS/dt < 0$). Such an influx induces order into the system. In ecosystems the ultimate negative entropy influx comes from solar radiation, and the order induced is, e.g., biochemical molecular order.

A special case of non-equilibrium systems is the steady state, where the state variable does not evolve in time. This condition implies that

$$d_eS = -d_iS < 0 \qquad (5.18)$$

Thus, to maintain a steady non-equilibrium state, it is necessary to pump a negative flow of entropy of the same magnitude as the internal entropy production continuously into the system.

If $d_eS > d_iS$ the system has surplus negative entropy, which may be utilized to construct further order in the system. The system will thereby move further away from the thermodynamic equilibrium. The evolution shows that this situation has been valid for the ecosphere on a long-term basis. In spring and summer ecosystems are in the typical situation that $-d_eS$ exceeds $d_iS$.

If $-d_eS < dSi$, the system cannot maintain the order already achieved, but will move closer to the thermodynamic equilibrium, i.e., it will lose order. This may be the situation for ecosystems during fall and winter.

An ecosystem will contain a great number of chemical compounds, which are spontaneously degrading to other compounds with lower energy by the production of entropy. The processes are irreversible and therefore the amount of entropy will increase, as mentioned in Section 5.3.

Figure 5.5 demonstrates the energy level of nitrogen compounds, which can all be found in an ecosystem. Proteins have the highest energy and they will spontaneously decompose to polypeptides, which will decompose to amino acids that will oxidize to carbon dioxide, water and ammonium, which through nitrite is oxidized to nitrate. For each of these steps, energy is released and dispersed throughout the system.

Similarly, starch and other high-energy components of ecosystems will spontaneously  decompose to components with lower energy by the release of energy.

These processes are vital for the ecosystem because they are the energy source or the fuel of ecosystems.

An ecosystem left alone (isolated from the rest of the world) will degrade to an inorganic soup, which will contain the degradation products uniformly spread throughout the volume of the system.

The ecosystem maintains a certain concentration of high energy components, however, because the ecosystem is *not*  isolated, but steadily receive energy and thereby negentropy (negative entropy) from outside. On earth the solar radiation is the main source of this input of energy and negentropy.

Ecosystems have a global attractor state, the thermodynamic equilibrium, but will never  reach this state as long as they are not isolated but receives negentropy from outside to combat the decomposition of its compounds. As ecosystems have an energy through-flow,  the attractor in nature becomes the steady state, where the formation of new biological compounds is in balance with the decomposition processes.

The results of the processes may be illustrated as follows:

Energy (mainly solar radiation) is transferred to high molecular components with high energy.  They decompose by generation of energy, which can be utilized by the ecosystem.

or

Negentropy (mainly solar radiation) is utilized for production of components with high energy. They decompose by generation of entropy.

or

High energy components tend to decompose and move towards the

136

thermodynamic equilibrium by irreversible processes. Formation of new high energy components takes place due to input of energy from external source. The thermodynamic equilibrium is therefore never reached by an open ecosystem with through-flow of energy. A steady state, where the two tendencies balance each other, may occur, however.

The decomposition processes, as mentioned in Sections 5.1 and 5.2, are spontaneous and irreversible. A number of processes take place in the ecosystem such as biogeochemical processes including the above-mentioned decomposition processes, and transport of matter and heat caused by diffusion and external forces.

To summarize: ecological processes are all irreversible and they generate therefore entropy. High energy components can be maintained and produced in the ecosystem due to input of negentropy, but notice that according to the second law of thermodynamics the overall result will be a generation of entropy corresponding to the generation of heat; see equation (5.1). The total entropy is *not preserved* but will steadily increase according to generation of heat.

Equation (5.15) may be used to find $\Delta G$ for biogeochemical processes in ecosystems, as G for various compounds may be found in physical-chemical handbooks. As $- R^*T^* \ln K = \Delta G$, it is possible to find the equilibrium constant K. If the concentrations of the reactants are known, it is then possible to determine the corresponding concentrations in equilibrium, which is the global attractor state.
For instance, the process:

Protein + oxygen = carbon dioxide + water + ammonium + energy

has a very high equilibrium constant, corresponding to relatively high concentrations of the product compounds and a low concentration protein, as oxygen is present in the atmosphere at a constant concentration. This does however not imply that it is impossible to form proteins against this decomposition tendency, but that formation of protein does not happen spontaneously (except in an extremely low concentration corresponding to the thermodynamic equilibrium). Formation of protein will require a coupling to another process that is able to deliver the energy needed for this process, namely the photosynthesis.

The energy released by the spontaneous, catabolic processes; see Section 5.3, is, of course, conserved according to the first law of thermodynamics. It can be found elsewhere in the system and is used in one way or another.

The catabolic processes attract the system toward the steady state, which gives the ecosystem the property of resilience stability, i.e., the ability to return to equilibrium or rather steady state. Some authors use the expression "normal" after a disturbance or stress period. Orians (1975) calls this concept elasticity and Holling (1973) calls it stability, but as discussed in Section 2.2, the system will never return to the very same situation again.

Due to the input of energy (solar radiation) the following reaction chain is valid; compare with the processes given above:

Solar radiation ---- construction of complex molecules ---- catabolism ---- energy utilized in the system ---- generation of energy (entropy) ---- dissipation of energy --- heat transfer to the environment.

It has also been observed that a system subject to time-independent constraints reaches a steady state after sufficient time. Ecosystems will, however, always have time-dependent constraints. It can be shown, see Nicolis and Prigogine (1977) that entropy production in *linear* systems, where linear thermodynamics is adopted, at steady non-equilibrium state, becomes a minimum, compatible with the constraints applied to the system. This theorem guarantees the stability of a steady non-equilibrium state, but is not directly applicable to living systems that are *non-linear*. Prigogine's theorem is, however, dependent on seven assumptions (Kay, 1984), which are not valid for ecosystems:

1. Local equilibrium thermodynamics applies.

2. The fluxes can be expressed as a linear combination of the flows obeying the Onsager's Reciprocity Relationship.

3. The fluxes are time-independent.

4. The boundary conditions are time-independent.

5. The system is isothermal.

6. The medium is isotropic.

7. The system is in mechanical and thermal equilibrium with its environment. Only mass flows occur across the boundary.

It is completely consistent with Prigogine et al (1972 and 1972a) and Prigogine (1980): "The theorem of minimum entropy production is strictly valid only in the neighborhood of equilibrium and for many years great efforts were made to extend this theorem to systems farther from equilibrium. It came as a great surprise when it was shown that in systems far from equilibrium the thermodynamic behavior could be quite different - in fact, even directly opposite, that predicted by the theorem of minimum entropy."

Mauersberger (1982, 1983 and 1985) has used the second law of thermodynamics and irreversible thermodynamics to limit the feasible expressions for crucial processes in ecosystems. He shows, for instance, that the logistic growth expression seems to be a proper description of primary production and grazing (Mauersberger, 1982).


## 5.5. Energy Sources and Sinks Establish Order

It has been stated that it is necessary for an ecosystem to be able to transfer the generated entropy to the environment and to be able to receive energy from the environment for formation of organic matter which is the energy basis for maintenance of the life processes. We may now return to the question: will energy source and sink also be *sufficient* to initiate formation of organic matter, which can be used as source for entropy combating processes?

The answer to this question is "Yes." It can be shown by the use of simple model systems and basic thermodynamics; see Morowitz (1968), who shows that a flow of energy from sources to sinks leads to an internal organization of the system and to the establishment of element cycles. The type of organization is, of course, dependent on a number of factors: the temperature, the elements present, the initial conditions of the system and the time available for the development of organization. It is characteristic for the system, as pointed out above, that the steady state does *not* involve chemical equilibrium.

An interesting illustration of the creation of organization as a result of an energy flow through ecosystems concerns the possibilities to form organic matter from the inorganic components which were present in the primeval atmosphere. Since 1897 many simulation experiments have been performed to explain how the first organic matter was formed on earth from inorganic matter. All of them point to the conclusion that energy interacts with a mixture of gases to form a large set of randomly synthesized organic compounds. Most interesting is perhaps the experiment performed by Stanley Miller and Harold Urey at the University of Chicago in 1953, because it showed that amino acids can be formed by sparking a mixture of $CH_4$, $H_2O$, $NH_3$ and $H_2$; corresponding approximately to the composition of the primeval atmosphere.

The apparatus used is shown in Fig. 5.6. The gas mixture was bled into the reaction chamber after it was evacuated. Boiling water provided water vapor and the condenser served to circulate the gas mixture through the vessel, where the spark discharge electrodes were located. After continuous sparking at 60,000 Volt for several days - an energy input comparable to that of some $4000*10^6$ years ago on the primeval earth - the water phase was analyzed for synthesized organic compounds. Table 5.1 lists some of the compounds. The mixture contained an extensive variety of small organic molecules such as several amino acids and lactic acids, which are involved in biological utilization.

It is hardly possible to write the chemical equations corresponding to the results of such experiments, which attempt to simulate how energy interacts with the primeval atmosphere. The difficulties are that each chemical reaction equation represents a single clean isolated set of observations. The reality is, however, entirely different because the atmosphere was a very complex mixture of gases, interacting with each other and with products in all possible combinations and permutations.

Since 1953 numerous workers have performed experiments to those of Miller and Urey, varying input gases and energy sources. Spark discharges represent only one form of energy input in the primeval environment. Other possible forms are ultraviolet radiation, beta and gamma radiation, cosmic rays and shock waves, see Table 5.2.

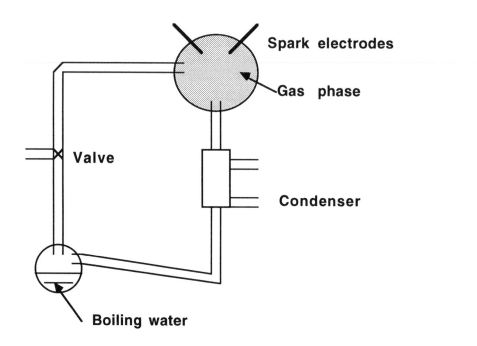

**Fig 5.6.** The apparatus used by Stanley Miller and Harold Urey to simulate reactions in the primeval atmosphere.

Edward Ander's group at the University of Chicago has studied Fischer-Tropsch-type reactions that involve heating gas mixture (900-1200 K) in closed containers in the presence of various metallic catalysts to simulate reaction between the primeval atmosphere and lava flows. Table 5.3 lists the results compiled from such experiments.

It should be noted that not only amino acids are formed but also hydrocarbons, nucleic acid bases, fatty acids and some reactive intermediates. It can be concluded that these reaction circumstances can result in  the formation of biologically important compounds.

**Table  5.1**

**Types and yields of simple organic compounds obtained from sparking a mixture of $CH_4$, $H_2O$, $NH_3$ and $H_2$. (Yields in weight are relative to formic acid = 1000.)**

| Compound | Relative  yield |
|---|---|
| Glycine | 270 |
| Sacrosine | 21 |
| Alanine | 145 |
| N-Methylalanine | 4 |
| ß-alanine | 64 |
| Alpha-amino-n-butyric acid | 21 |
| Alpha-amino-isobutyric acid | 2 |
| Aspartic acid | 2 |
| Glutamic acid | 2 |
| Iminodiacetic acid | 66 |
| Imino-propionic acid | 6 |
| Lactic acid | 133 |
| Formic acid | 1000 |
| Acetic acid | 64 |
| Propionic acid | 56 |
| Alpha-hydroxybutyric acid | 21 |
| Succinic acid | 17 |
| Urea | 8 |
| N-methyl urea | 6 |

Other experiments have shown that applying solar energetic ultraviolet radiation to a mixture of primitive gases that were present in the primeval atmosphere, such as nitrogen, hydrogen, water and carbon oxides resulted in the synthesis of amino acids, several reactive organic intermediates and what is important: polymers.

Melvin Calvin's group at Berkeley has demonstrated that beta and gamma radiation upon a mixture of $CH_4$, $NH_3$ and $H_2O$ is able to synthesize adenine, which is a component of ATP.

All these series of experiments point in the same direction: interplay of all forms of energy with gaseous carbon, nitrogen, water and hydrogen, which were present in the primeval atmosphere, leads to the formation of reactive intermediates, which interact to form a large set of biological components, including polymers. No single experiment is representative of the primitive earth, but all of them together might be.

**Table 5.2.**

**Source of energy for chemical synthesis in the primitive atmosphere.**

| Source | $10^5$ kJ / (m$^2$ y) |
| --- | --- |
| Total solar radiation | 110 |
| Ultraviolet radiation | |
|     300-250 nm | 1.2 |
|     250-200 nm | 0.22 |
|     200-150 nm | 0.017 |
|     < 150 nm | 0.00081 |
| Corona discharge | 0.0013 |
| Natural radioactivity | 0.0012 |
| Lightning | 0.00042 |
| Shock and pressure waves | 0.0004 |
| Solar wind | 0.00008 |
| Volcanic heat | 0.00006 |
| Cosmic Rays | 0.0000006 |

The conditions at the earth's beginning, some 4500 million years ago, can probably be described as follows: shallow lakes and ponds of fresh rainwater, murky with volcanic ash. Surface temperature about 25°C. Intense volcanic activity, thunderstorms and energetic solar ultraviolet radiation (no protective ozone layer yet). Energy of all forms was abundant. The major gases in the atmosphere were nitrogen, carbon monoxide, hydrogen and water vapor. Figure 5.7 represents the probable chemical evolution on the primeval earth resulting from the energy flow through the system.

The volatile components such as hydrogen cyanide and formaldehyde largely remained in the atmosphere, while amino acids and nucleic acid base were mainly dissolved in the water. Hydrocarbons and long-chain fatty acids floated on the water surface as scum.

Since all energy sources including solar ultraviolet radiation continued their input, the synthesis or organic compounds continued and so did consequently their degradation. This lead to a steady state, characterized by a cycling of components:

$$H_2 + CO + N_2 + H_2O \text{ ------ organic compounds and} \qquad (5.19)$$
$$\text{organic compounds ------ } H_2 + CO + N_2 + H_2O$$

**Table 5.3.**

**Some organic compounds formed from Fischer-Tropsch Reactions, in which CO, H2 and NH3 gases are heated to 900 K by presence of metallic catalysts.**

_____

**Biological amino acids:** Glycine, alanine, valine, leucine, isoleucine, aspartate, glutamate, tyrosine, proline, ornithine, lysine, histidine, arginine.

**Biological nitrogen bases:** adenine, guanine, xanthine, thymine, uracil.

**Non-biological nitrogen bases:** melamine, ammeline, cyanuric acid, guanyl urea.

**Fatty acids:** all varieties from C-12 to C-20.

**Hydrocarbons:** A wide variety resembling that isolated from carbonaceous meteorites.

**Non-biological amino acids:** N-methyl glycine, ß-alanine, alpha-amino-isobutyrate, alpha amino-n-butyrate, ß-amino-isobutyrate, gamma-aminobutyrate.

**Small reactive molecules:** Hydrogen cyanide, formaldehyde, formic acid, acetic acid, urea and related compounds, guanidine and related compounds.

_____

The cycles were driven by the energy input and allowed the matter, or rather the elements, to be used repeatedly. As energy cannot be separated from matter, cycling of matter implies a simultaneous cycling of biochemical energy, carried by the matter.

Process (5.19) represents a non-biological cycle of matter driven by a flow of energy. Such non-biological cycles exist in many forms on earth, for example: oxygen is formed by photo dissociation of water and can react with volcanic hydrogen to appear as water again.

## An overall view of the products formed in chemical evolution experiments

**GASES:**

$H_2O$    CO    $CO_2$    $H_2$        $CH_4$        $N_2$    $CH_4$

**React and form**

**REACTIVE   INTERMEDIATES**

HCN  (hydrogen cyanide)

HCOH (formaldehyde)

$HCO_2H$ (formic acid)

$HN(CN)_2$ (dicyanamide)

$HOCH_2CHO$ (glycoaldehyde)

$CH_3CO_2H$ (acetic acid)

**SMALL  ORGANIC  COMPOUNDS**

| | |
|---|---|
| Amino Acids: | several hundred, including the biological subset of 20 |
| Fatty acids: | all varieties from C-12 to C-20 |
| Hydrocarbons: | a complex "random" mixture |
| Nitrogenous bases: | uracil, cytosine, thymine, adenine, guanine, xanthine, hypoxanthine, trazines |
| Other small organic compounds: | |
| | urea and derivatives, guanidine and derivatives, acids and diacids |
| Polymer | |

---

**Fig. 5.7.** An overall view of the products formed in the chemical evolution experiment.

Process (5.20) is also a part of a cycle, as aldehydes and oxygen undergo a chain reaction giving carbon dioxide and water, among other products. The overall reaction scheme is:

$$
\begin{array}{ll}
& \text{energy} \\
CO_2 + H_2O \; \text{-------} & \text{aldehydes} + O_2 \text{ and} \qquad\qquad (5.20) \\
\text{aldehydes} + O_2 \; \text{------} & CO_2 + H_2O + \text{energy}
\end{array}
$$

The chemical compounds that take part in these cycle processes are very dependent on the level of the energy flow through the system. As the energy flow increases, higher and higher energy levels become more and more accessible and ever more chemical possibilities become available to the system. At a certain level, however, the molecules start to dissociate and form free radicals and ions. The system proceeds toward increasingly chaotic states at the molecular level. Reaction rates become extremely high and stable compounds cannot be maintained. Finally, the system passes into a dense plasma, defined as follows: The dynamic behavior of the gas is dominated by electromagnetic forces acting on the free radicals and electrons. The system gets other properties that are described by introduction of the name "plasma" to denote a gas in such a highly ionized state.

The very high energy state is accompanied by a high temperature, which measures the velocity of the molecules. The conclusion from these considerations is therefore that the biological compounds mentioned can only exist in a certain range of energy flux.

If the energy flux is below this range the biological active compounds cannot be formed and if the energy flux is above this range these compounds will dissociate.

As the temperature of the system is determined by the energy flux, this proposition also implies that the ecosystems on earth with their characteristic biochemistry can only exist in a certain temperature range. So, the ecosystem has the property of antientropic growth to be able to compensate for the decomposition.

As mentioned, the ecosystem energy flow is sufficient to produce closed energy and matter cycles. The overall cycle that is closed in ecosystems is illustrated in Fig. 5.8.

The driving energy is, of course, solar radiation. Growth might be directly based on solar radiation as for photosynthesis, where the overall process is

$$
6CO_2 + hv + 6H_2O = C_6H_{12}O_6 \qquad\qquad (5.21)
$$

145

However, the process is step-wise, as the catabolic processes. The growth might also be indirect, as the material produced by the photosynthesis can be used by other organisms (called herbivorous organisms) as feed, and the herbivorous organisms can again be used as feed for carnivorous organisms. 4-5 levels can be maintained in this way, but the overall process is that the energy needed to combat the decomposition of organic matter - energy which is lost as heat to the environment - is provided from solar radiation and used for growth to compensate for the organic matter decomposed.

However, growth does not necessarily compensate exactly for respiration (decomposition) but might for a given period be larger or smaller than the decomposition. The difference between growth and respiration is called net production. Gross production is equal to growth. Ecosystems in steady state have no net production but balance between gross production or growth and respiration or decomposition; compare Section 4.4 and Fig. 4.8.

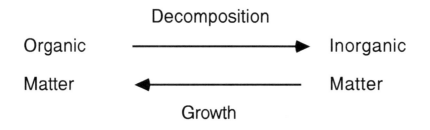

**Fig. 5.8.** The cycle of matter in ecosystems, driven by solar energy.

Growth of the ecosystem implies that an ecosystem can apply an energy flow (receive energy and give it away again) to maintain the system organized and away from equilibrium.

To summarize: An ecosystem establishes entropy combating processes due to the energy flux - from a low-entropy energy source to a high-entropy energy sink - through the system. Entropy is generated by decomposition of organic matter steadily formed as a result of the energy flux. This implies that an ecosystem is maintained organized away from equilibrium, as it "lies" in an energy flow and receives energy from one system and gives it away again.

## 5.6. Self-organization.

Prigogine and his colleagues have shown that open systems that are exposed to an energy through-flow exhibit coherent self-organization behavior and are known as dissipative structures. Formations of complex organic compounds from inorganic matter as mentioned in Section 5.5 are typical examples of self-organization. Such systems can remain in their organized state by exporting entropy outside the system, see equations (5.16-5.18). Organized systems are dependent on outside energy fluxes to maintain their organization, as was already mentioned and emphasized in Section 5.5.

Ferracin et al. (1978) identify two distinct characteristics of self-organization: organization of structure and organization of function; compare with the definition of organization in Section 1.5.

Glansdroff and Prigogine (1971) have shown that the thermodynamic relationship of far from equilibrium dissipative structures is best represented by coupled non-linear relationships, i.e., autocatalytic positive feedback cycles.

Two physical-chemical examples of self-organizations should be mentioned to illustrate the formation of dissipative structure:

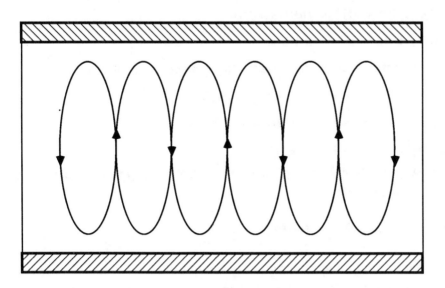

**Fig. 5.9.** Formation of convection cells in a so-called Benard cell.

1. Imagine a layer of water between two horizontal parallel plates, whose dimensions are much larger than the width of the layer. It is called a *Benard cell* after the French physicist Benard, who carried out the experiment in 1900. Left to itself the fluid will rapidly tend towards a homogeneous state in which all its parts will be identical. We can induce a flow of energy, say from below. The temperature of the lower plate becomes higher than the temperature of the upper plate : $\Delta T > 0$. Suppose that the constraint is weak, i.e., $\Delta T$ is small. The system will adopt a simple and unique `state in which heat is transported from the lower to the upper plate by conduction. If we move the system farther and farther from equilibrium by increasing $\Delta T$ suddenly at a value of $\Delta T$, that may be called critical the fluid begins to perform bulk movement and becomes structured in a series of small convection cells: see Fig. 5.9. The fluid is now in the regime of convection. See for instance Nicolis and Prigogine (1989).

2. *The so-called BZ-reaction* shows a similar tendency to self-organization. Cerium (IV) sulfate, malonic acid and potassium bromate react in sulfuric acid. The evolution of the processes can be followed visually since an excess of Ce(IV)-ions gives a pale yellow color, whereas an excess of Ce(III)-ions leaves the solution colorless. The three chemicals are pumped into a reaction chamber, which is well mixed.

**With enough Br⁻:**

$$BrO_3^- + Br^- + 2H^+ = HBrO_2 + HOBr$$

$$HBrO_2 + Br^- + H^+ = 2\ HOBr$$

**With small quantities of Br⁻ left, Ce⁺³ is oxidized according to:**

$$BrO_3^- + HBrO_2 + H^+ = 2\ BrO_2^\cdot + H_2O$$

$$BrO_2^\cdot + Ce^{+3} + H^+ = HBrO_2 + Ce^{+4}$$

$$HBrO_2 = BrO_3^- + HOBr + H^+$$

**The first step is rate limiting, whereas HOBr disappears quickly by combining with malonic acid.**

**Fig. 5.10.** The individual processes of the BZ-reaction.

This experimental setup allows easy control over the rates at which the chemicals are pumped into or out of the system, i.e., we can vary the residence times of these substances within the reaction vessel. Long residence times essentially result in a closed system and we expect the system to reach equilibrium-like behavior. Conversely, by short residence times we expect the system to manifest non-equilibrium` behavior. This is according to what the experiment shows. For long residence times, the concentrations of chemicals remain constant. If we reduce the residence time, we suddenly encounter a different pattern. A pale yellow color emerges, indicating an excess of Ce (IV)-ions. Later the solution becomes colorless, indicating now an excess of Ce (III)-ions. The process will go on as a chemical clock: yellow, colorless, yellow, colorless, and so on.

The amplitude depends only on the experimental parameters. The chemical reactions responsible for the observations are shown in Fig. 5.10. and they can - as can be seen from the figure - be explained by the presence of autocatalysis.


## 5.7. The Maximum Entropy or Maximum Energy Dissipation Theory

Wicken (1976,1978, 1978a, 1979 and 1980) suggests that the second law of thermodynamics dictates the emergence of "chemical factories" in a system bombarded with solar energy. The factories degrade (utilize) the solar energy, i.e., increase the entropy. As time goes on, the "chemical factories" become stable and they evolve mechanisms to stabilize their internal chemical processes and to maintain the function of the system in spite of environmental changes. The degradation of the solar energy would then be assured. This expectation would be justified by the second law of thermodynamics alone, but is reinforced by Prigogine's findings regarding the emergence of stable dissipative structures; see Section 5.6.

Kay (1983) has - as continuation of Wicken's work - presented two hypotheses about ecosystem development, which enable us to understand the thermodynamics behind the selection processes in the evolution of ecosystems.

The first hypothesis asserts that ecosystems will organize themselves to maximize the degradation of the available work, i.e., the maximum work which can be extracted from stored energy (Keenan, 1951) = exergy (Brzustowski and Golem, 1978 and Ahern, 1980; see furthermore Sections 6.1 and 6.2). A corollary is that material flow cycles will tend to be closed (see also Morowitz, 1968). The hypothesis implies not only that $\Delta S > 0$ (the second law of thermodynamics), but that the system will be organized to maximize $\Delta S$. Therefore the hypothetical law is named the restated Second Law of Thermodynamics.

The second hypothesis is a consequence of the first and it states that ecosystems will evolve and adapt to maximize the potential for the ecosystem and its component systems to survive. Such behavior will assure the continued degradation

149

adaptation, selection and evolution, must be offset by the gain in energy degrading ability of the ecosystem. Also, each compartment will not be able to maximize its own survival because it would be done at the expense of other components. Thus the maximization process is constrained and represents a thermodynamic and system optimization.

The thermodynamic and more theoretical support of these hypotheses is given in Kay (1984). Some illustrative physical, chemical and biological examples (Schneider, 1988, Schneider and Kay, 1990 and Kay and Schneider, 1992) of the application of these hypotheses are given below. They give a better picture of this interesting approach and its relations to living systems and the other thermodynamic approaches mentioned in the Chapters 4-6. As entropy is not defined rigorously far from equilibrium, Kay and Schneider prefer to talk about maximum energy dissipation or maximum exergy destruction and avoid the expression "maximum entropy production."

The theory can be applied to the Benard cell, mentioned in Section 5.6. Brown (1973) has conducted carefully designed experiments to study the formation of self-organization. When the temperature difference between the lower and upper plate is low, the energy transfer is by conduction, i.e., molecule-to-molecule interaction. The transition to a dissipative structure occurs at a certain critical value of the temperature gradient and this coherent kinetic structuring increases the rate of heat transfer. The temperature gradient destruction is thereby increased, too. From a classical thermodynamic perspective the emergence of such a structure should not occur, but it is consistent, as shown by Kay and Schneider (1990) and Schneider and Kay (1990), with the restated version of the second law of thermodynamic, given above. They have studied the original data sets of Brown and found that the Rayleigh number (Ra), a dimensionless measure of the applied gradient, is directly proportional to $\Delta$ T. The transition to coherent behavior occurs at Ra = 1708. In Fig. 5.11 the heat transfer rate versus Ra is shown. The curve labeled "conduction" is the dissipation that would occur without emergence of self-organization. The difference between the curves labeled "total" and "conduction" is the increase in dissipation due to the dissipative structure. It can be seen from the figure that there is a dramatic increase in the heat transfer across the fluid. Furthermore, the amount of free energy necessary to increase the temperature gradient increases steeply as the temperature gradient increases; see Fig. 5.12. It is consistent with the maximum exergy principle, which will be presented in Sections 6.2-6.4. At higher temperature gradients, there are a number of further transitions at which the system step-wise gets even more self-organized and for each step the cost of increasing the temperature gradient escalates even more quickly. The

150

step the cost of increasing the temperature gradient escalates even more quickly. The point of this example, according to Kay and Schneider, is that the new emergent structures are better able to resist the application of an external gradient. The more the system is moved from thermodynamic equilibrium, the more sophisticated its mechanisms for resisting further movement away from equilibrium, as also expected from the restated second law of thermodynamics.

The development of temperature gradients between a warm earth and a cooler overlying atmosphere results in highly organized convective cloud patterns, which reduce the temperature gradient. The formation of tornadoes is a self-organizing structure of high ability to dissipate rapidly strong temperature - and barometric gradients. Hurricanes are other examples of such mesoscale dissipative meteorological structures.

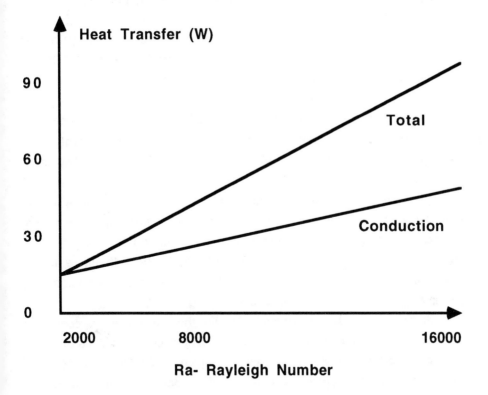

**Fig 5.11.** Dissipation in a Benard cell after self-organization occurs. The curve labeled "conduction" is what would have occurred if the dissipative structure had not emerged, while the curve labeled " total" gives the total heat transfer. Ra is a non-dimensional measure of the temperature gradient. As seen, the formation of a dissipative structure implies that the heat transfer is increased.

The earth is an open thermodynamic system with a large gradient impressed on it by the sun, and **this system will, according to Kay and Schneider strives, to reduce this gradient by all physical and chemical processes available, and life exists on earth as another (sophisticated) means of dissipating the solar-induced gradient.**

This hypothesis presents no contradiction with the modernized Neodarwinian theory, but would play down the importance of the selfish gene as the only process in selection.

The hypothesis imposes constraints on the genes, which are not allowed to develop completely without limitations. In this context life is not an isolated event, but represents the emergence of yet another class of processes (although the most sophisticated till now), whose goal is dissipation of thermodynamic gradients.

The thesis is that growth, development and evolution occur to assure a better degradation of the incoming solar energy (Kay, 1984 and Schneider, 1988).This provides a criterion for evaluating growth and development: the better dissipator will win.

The hypothesis is consistent with Brooks and Wiley's theory, presented in` Section 5.2. S-obs is simply translated to entropy production generated for maintenance of the structure (information)  already developed corresponding to S-max minus S-obs.

It is impossible to prove the presented hypothesis in the mathematical-physical sense, particularly when we are dealing with such complex systems as ecosystems. However, we can assume the hypothesis and then support it or falsify it by confrontation with our observations and models of nature. We are furthermore able to examine how this theory fits into the ecosystem theory pattern, that we are attempting to construct in this volume; compare also Section 3.7, Fig. 3.9.

It is  furthermore possible to examine whether the hypotheses are consistent with a pattern of an ecosystem theory which we are trying to  construct piece by piece. The latter test of the hypotheses will be discussed again in Chapter 12, while some general observations will be examined in relation to the hypotheses in this chapter.

Living systems develop in a way that minimizes *their specific* entropy production; but the total entropy production increases  (Zotin, 1978 and 1984). It is illustrated in Figure 5.13, where the total entropy production and specific entropy production during the ontogenesis of salamanders are shown. The figure is redrawn from Kay and Schneider and data were calculated from the experimental results of

Zotin and Lamprecht (1978). The observations are consistent with the viewpoints of several authors: Odum and Pinkerton (1955), Morowitz (1968), Ulanowicz (1986), Wicken (1980), Kay (1984 and 1991) and Schneider (1988).

Plant growth is another attempt to capture solar energy and dissipate the gradient it causes. The gradient-capturing aspects of plants can be seen in phototropisms and their shapes, designed to capture and thereby degrade sunlight. The energy budgets of terrestrial plants show that most of their energy capture is involved in evapotranspiration. Data synthesized by Currie and Paquin (1987) demonstrates that the large scale biogeographical distribution of species richness of trees is strongly correlated with realized annual evapotranspiration and available energy. Lieth (1976) showed that there exists a strong correlation between primary productivity and evapotranspiration and asserted that the latter process is stabilizing the temperature regime. Lieth (1976 and 1976a) considers this stabilization as extremely important, as the ecosystems according to his theory optimize the temperature stability. The role of evapotranspiration for the energy budget of the ecosphere is under all circumstances underestimated and it is significant for the amount of energy dissipated.

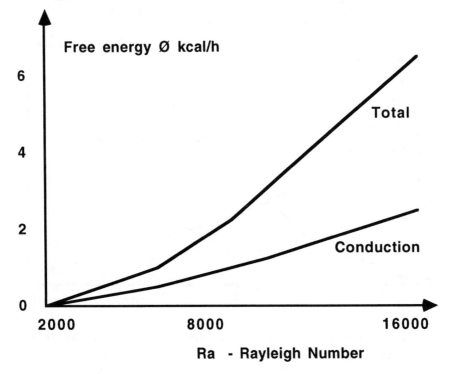

**Fig. 5.12.** The free energy Ø needed to maintain the gradient in the presence of the dissipative structure is plotted versus the Rayleigh number.

Sellers and Mintz (1986) have recently calculated the mean surface energy budget for four large regions of the earth for 50 days in the summer. The regions are:

a) The Amazon basin, which is uniformly covered by rain forest

b) Central and Eastern United States, which consists mainly of cultivated land, grasslands and some mixed forest.

c) Asia a heterogeneous mix of tropical rain, forest, cultivated land and desert.

d) The Sahara Desert.

Their data were obtained from the satellite-derived Earth Radiation Budget Experiment and have been applied by Kay and Schneider as support for their theory. They measured insolation, albedo, net long- and short-wave energy absorbed at the earth surface, net radiation or available energy and calculated important heat fluxes by modelling physiological and biological processes which influence radiation, momentum, mass and heat transfer of the vegetation surface to atmosphere. The results are presented in Table 5.4.

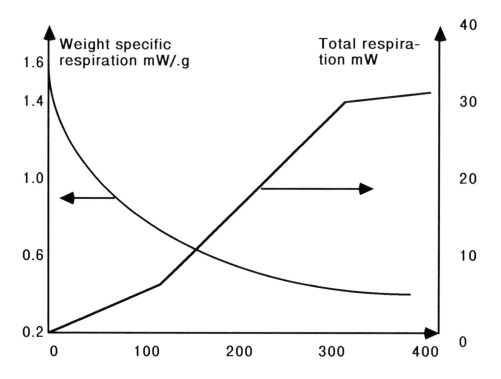

**Fig. 5.13.** Experimental data on changes in total respiration, mW, and weight specific respiration, mW/g, during the ontogenesis of salamanders.

The reradiated long-wave radiation and the sensible heat flux represent the energy that has not been degraded to the ambient, while evapotranspiration represents energy that is dissipated and will no longer cause disequilibrium. The hypotheses developed by Kay and Schneider are consistent with the results in Table 5.4, as evapotranspiration increases with ecosystem development, while long-wave radiation and sensible heat flux decrease. More developed systems are better dissipators.

Zotin (1984) has studied the bioenergetic trends of the evolution of organisms and noted that evolution has progressed with increasing dissipation rates, i.e., respiratory intensity: see Fig. 5.14. *Homo Sapiens* is currently the most sophisticated example in the evolutionary process and has also developed the best mechanism for dissipation of gradients, as he has learned to use fossil gradients created in past geological epochs. Future survival will depend on building systems that rely on externally maintained gradients, i.e., solar energy or by discovering new gradients to dissipate (Schneider and Kay 1990).

More illustrations supporting this theory will be presented in Section 8.3., where examples of the application of this theory and the theory of ascendency are presented in parallel.

**Table 5.4.**

**Energy absorbed (W/m$^2$) at the surface of varied ecosystems, and the percentage of this energy, which is remitted into space.**

| Ecosystem | Energy absorbed | Energy reradiated | Sensible Heat Flux | Evapotrans- piration |
|-----------|-----------------|-------------------|--------------------|----------------------|
| Amazon    | 184.7           | 16%               | 15%                | 69%                  |
| USA       | 220.2           | 18%               | 20%                | 62%                  |
| Asia      | 223.4           | 24%               | 26%                | 50%                  |
| Sahara    | 202.0           | 41%               | 57%                | 2%                   |

The possibilities to place this hypothesis in the overall pattern of ecosystem

155

theories will be discussed in Chapter 12, but it is possible to assert at this stage that Kay and Schneider's theory represents the longest step away from classical thermodynamics by formulation of a restated second law of thermodynamics. The step is so long even, that it seems unnecessary to link it with the second law of thermodynamics, as it is not a direct consequence of this law, but contains its own independent assertion.

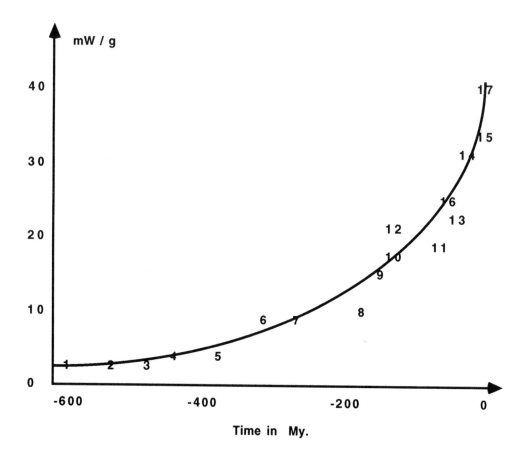

**Fig. 5.14.** Change in respiration intensity (a in the equation rate of respiration $= a^*W^b$, where a and b are allometric constants and W is the weight) or the rate of dissipative capacity of animals over the course of evolution. a in mW/g is plotted versus time in My. The numbers cover the following species: 1: Coelenterata, 2: Crustacea, 3: Mollusca, 4: Teleostei, 5: Amphibia, 6: Insects, 7: Reptilia, 8-15: Mammalia, 16-17: Aves. Data from Zotin (1984). Redrawn from Schneider and Kay (1990).

# 6. EXERGY AND ECOLOGY

## 6.1. The Application of Exergy in Ecological Thermodynamics

The cells that form the basic units of ecosystems are a result of a long evolution from organic soup to protobiont, to protocells and further on to ever more complex cells with very complex anabolic (synthesizing) and information development processes. A wide spectrum of biochemical compounds with specific functions is produced in the cells. This ability is preserved by use of a very sophisticated genetic function and code to assure that no significant information is lost. The first part of the evolution after the appearance of the "inorganic soup," which characterized the earth some 3600 to 4000 million years ago, was based on randomly produced organic compounds. Repeated use of "trial and error" found new pathways to create organization and move further away from the thermodynamic equilibrium, corresponding to the inorganic soup. The system was moving further and further away from equilibrium, due to an average net negentropy gain per unit of time, utilized for development of new pathways.

Exergy is a central concept in this context, as it expresses energy with a built-in measure of quality. Exergy accounts natural resources (Erikson et al., 1976) and can be considered as fuel for any system that converts energy and matter in a metabolic process (Schrödinger 1944). Ecosystems consume energy, and an exergy flow through the system is necessary to keep the system functioning. Exergy measures the distance from the "inorganic soup" in energy terms, as will be further explained below.

Exergy, Ex, is defined by the following equation:

$$Ex = T_o * NE \tag{6.1}$$

and may be introduced and related to other thermodynamic concepts as follows:
Consider an ecosystem, A, in a surrounding system, Ao, which is assumed to be homogeneous and large, in comparison with A (Fig. 6.1). The environment can be characterized by its intensive variables (= variable not dependent on the size of the system) $T_o$, $p_o$, $\mu_{oc}$ (temperature, pressure and chemical potentials). The ecosystem is correspondingly characterized by T, p and $\mu_c$. The extensive variables (= variables dependent on the size of the system) for the two systems are 1) energy, 2) volume, 3) entropy and 4) the number of molecules of different chemical species: U, V, S and $N_i$ for

A and Uo, Vo, So and Nio for Ao.

The combined system A + Ao is assumed to be isolated (no exchange of matter or energy with the external world) apart from work W extracted from A. This means:

$$dU + dUo + dW = 0 \qquad (6.2)$$
$$dV + dVo = 0 \qquad (6.3)$$
$$dNi + dNio = 0 \qquad (6.4)$$

Interaction between A and Ao can take place in a controlled way through the boundary surface of A. Since A is small, compared with Ao, this will not change the intensive parameters of Ao.

We have

$$dTo = 0$$
$$dpo = 0 \qquad (6.5)$$
$$d\mu oc = 0$$

The entropy differential of the environment Ao is:

$$dSo = \frac{1}{To} (dUo + po{*}dVo - \sum (\mu oc {*}dNio) = \qquad (6.6)$$
$$- \frac{1}{To} (-dU + po * dV - \sum_{c} \mu oc * dNi) - \frac{dW}{To}$$

Correspondingly, the total entropy differential can be found:

$$dS(tot) = dSo + dS = \qquad (6.7)$$

$$- \frac{1}{To} ( dU + po{*}dV - To{*}dS - \sum_{c} (\mu oc{*}dNio) - \frac{dW}{To} ,$$

which might be written as:

$$dS(tot) = - \frac{1}{To} (dEx + dW) \qquad (6.8)$$

158

where we have introduced the concept exergy, Ex:

$$Ex = U + p_o * V - T_o * S - \sum_c (\mu_{oc} * N_i) \qquad (6.9)$$

## Environment Ao

**Intensive variables: To, po, $\mu_{oc}$**
**Extensive variables: Uo, Vo, So , Nio**

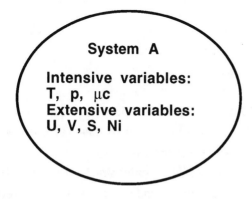

**System A**

**Intensive variables:
T, p, $\mu_c$
Extensive variables:
U, V, S, Ni**

**Fig. 6.1.** Definition of exergy.

If the following relation is used:

$$U = TS - p * V + \sum_c (\mu_c * N_i) \qquad (6.10)$$

in (6.9) it leads to:

$$Ex = S(T - T_o) - V(p - p_o) + \sum_c N_i(\mu_c - \mu_{oc}) \qquad (6.11)$$

As seen, Ex vanishes by equilibrium ($T = T_o$, $p = p_o$, $\mu_c = \mu_{oc}$), as expected. Note that Ex is not a state variables, as it is dependent on the state of the environment.

If A evolves towards the equilibrium with its environment Ao without doing any work (dW = 0), the exergy, Ex, is then changed from Ex to O and the total entropy is changed from S to Seq.

By integration of the equation (6.8) the following is obtained:

$$S_{eq} - S = -1^* (-Ex) / To \qquad (6.12)$$

and thus:

$$Ex = To^* (S_{eq} - S) \qquad (6.13)$$

which leads to; see equation (5.7):

$$Ex = To^* NE = To^* I \qquad (6.14)$$

or, Ex of A is To multiplied with the negentropy for A.

It can be shown (Evans, 1969) that exergy differences can be reduced to differences of other, better known, thermodynamic potentials, see Table 6.1, which may facilitate the computations of exergy in some relevant cases.

As seen the exergy of the system measures the contrast - it is the difference in free energy if there is no difference in pressure, as may be assumed for an ecosystem and its environment - against the surrounding environment. If the system is in equilibrium with the surrounding environment the exergy is zero.

Since the only way to move systems away from equilibrium is to perform work on them, and since the available work in a system is a measure of the ability, we have to distinguish between the system and its environment or thermodynamic equilibrium alias the inorganic soup. Therefore it is reasonable to use the available work, i.e., the exergy, as a measure of the distance from thermodynamic equilibrium.

As we know that the ecosystem due to the through-flow of energy has the tendency to develop away from thermodynamic equilibrium losing entropy or gaining negentropy and information as presented in Section 5.6, we can put forward the following proposition, which can be considered just another formulation of the major results of Chapter 5:

**Ecosystems attempt to develop toward a higher level of exergy.**

**Table 6.4**

**Relations between differences in exergy and in other thermodynamic potentials**

---

| Case | Relevant thermodynamic potentials, which may be equal to Ex | | |
| --- | --- | --- | --- |
| | Potential | Definition | Usually named |
| $\Delta Ni = 0$ | $\Delta Go$ | $Go = U + po^*V - To^*S$ | |
| $\Delta Ni = 0, \Delta V = 0$ | $\Delta Fo$ | $Fo = U - To^*S$ | |
| $\Delta Ni = 0, \Delta S = 0$ | $\Delta Ho$ | $Ho = U + po^*V$ | |
| $\Delta Ni = 0, T = To$ | | | |
| $p = po$ | $\Delta G$ | $G = U + p^*V - T^*S$ | Gibb's free energy |
| $\Delta Ni = 0, \Delta V = 0$ | | | |
| $T = To$ | $\Delta F$ | $F = U - T^*S$ | Helmholtz's free energy |
| $\Delta Ni = 0, \Delta S = 0$ | | | |
| $p = po$ | $\Delta H$ | $H = U + p^*V$ | Enthalpi |

---

In this context it may be interesting to consider the case of a system A in a local environment AL, which in its turn is embedded in a global environment. We may then define a local exergy:

$$ExL = U + pL * V - TL *S - \sum_c (\mu cL * Ni) \qquad (6.15)$$

which is related to the global exergy, equation (6.9), through:

$$Ex = ExLo + ExL \qquad (6.16)$$

ExLo gives the contribution due to the deviation of the local environment from the global one:

$$ExLo = S(TL - To) - V(pL - po) + \sum_c Ni(\mu cL - \mu oc) \qquad (6.17)$$

which is the exergy expression for  A  with the intensive parameters of AL replacing those of  A.

In other words, the exergy can be said to be an energy measure of the contrast of a system against an average gray background.


## 6.2. Exergy and Information

It is also of importance that exergy is closely related to information theory.

As seen, a high local concentration of a chemical compound, for instance, with a biochemical function that is rare elsewhere, carries exergy <u>and</u> information; see equation (6.1) and Section 5.2.

On the more complex levels, information may still be strongly related to exergy but in more indirect ways. Information is also a convenient measure of physical structure (see Fig. 6.2). A certain structure is chosen out of all possible structures and defined within certain tolerance margins (Berry, 1972 and Thoma, 1977)

Biological structures maintain and reproduce themselves by transforming energy, and thereby also information, from one form to another. Thus, the exergy of the radiation from the sun is used to build the highly ordered organic compounds. The information lay down in the genetic material is developed and transferred from one generation to the next.

The chromosomes of one human cell have an information storage capacity corresponding to 2 billion  K-bytes! This would require 1000 km of standard magnetic tape to store on a macro computer! When biological materials are used to the benefit of mankind it is in fact the organic structures and the information contained therein that are of  advantage, for instance, when using wood.

The exergy can theoretically be measured as demonstrated in Fig. 6.3. The system is characterized by the state variables S, U, V, N1, N2, ..... The system is coupled to a reservoir by a shaft, but the system + the reservoir is a closed system. The system develops toward thermodynamic equilibrium and is simultaneously able to release entropy-free energy to the reservoir. During this process the volume of the system is constant, as the entropy-free energy must be transferred through the shaft only.

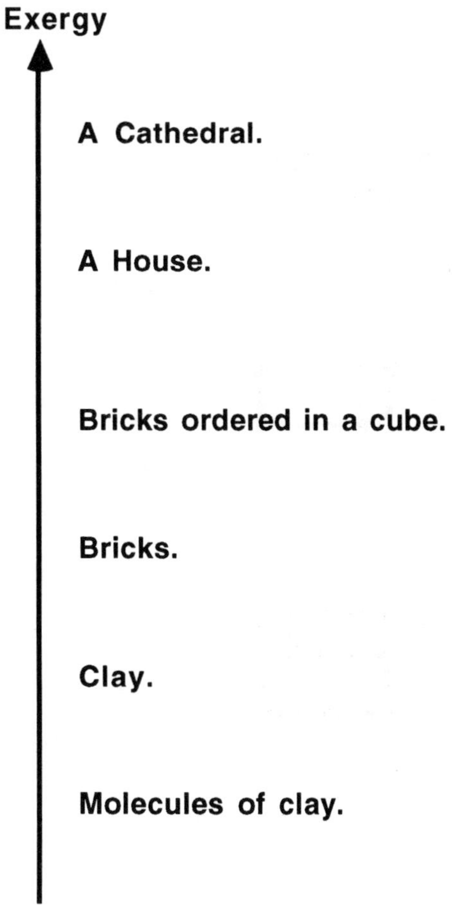

**Exergy**

A Cathedral.

A House.

Bricks ordered in a cube.

Bricks.

Clay.

Molecules of clay.

Fig. 6.2. Illustration of the relation between exergy and physical structure.

**The total transfer of entropy-free energy is in this case the exergy of the system.**

However, the total system - consisting of the system plus the reservoir - must be adiabatically isolated from the environment during the measurement, otherwise exchange of mass, heat or volume with the environment would be able to cause transfer of exergy from the environment to the reservoir. **From these considerations as from the definition it is seen that exergy is dependent on the state of the total system (= system + reservoir) and not dependent entirely on the state of the system. Exergy is not a state variable.**

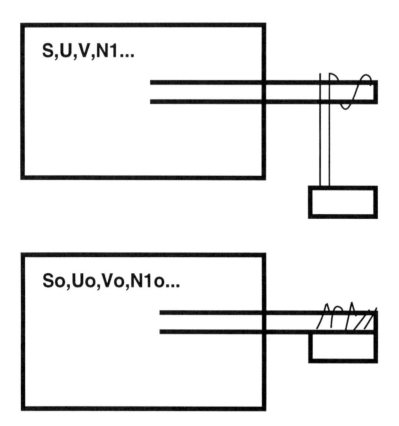

**Fig. 6.3.** Illustration of how exergy could be measured theoretically.

In accordance with the first law of thermodynamics

$$U - U_0 = \Delta U = E_{m,R} \tag{6.18}$$

where $E_{m,R}$ is the increase of energy in the reservoir, and according to the definition of exergy:

$$Ex = E_{-m,R} \tag{6.19}$$

Many authors prefer the physical or thermodynamic information as a measure for the development of ecosystems - or the ontogenetic order. Exergy has been introduced here as a better measure, because it has a few but pronounced advantages compared with the thermodynamic information:

1)     **Exergy contains a level, or an intensive term, the temperature of the environment, and an extensive term, the negentropy.** This is consistent with all other descriptions of energy concepts. It is a descriptive advantage in several contexts to use a term with energy units as a measure for the development of ecosystems, for instance, when the allocation of energy to an ecosystem between maintenance and growth or development is considered. Mauersberger (1979) describes the role of balance equations for mass, momentum and energy as the bookkeepers, while the entropy, like the director, determines the further development of the system. Here, it would be more consistent to replace entropy with exergy.

2)     **Exergy is not a state variable, but is dependent on the state of the environment,** which makes this function more suited to describe the actual situation of the ecosystem.

3)     **The exergy is conserved by transformation of entropy-free energy.** If, for example, two reservoirs exchange entropy-free energy, it is obvious that the resulting thermodynamic information is changed:

$$I_1 + I_2 = \Delta Ex_1 / T_1 + \Delta Ex_2 / T_2 \neq 0 \qquad (6.20)$$

However, the resulting exergy $\Delta(Ex_1 + Ex_2) = 0$.

4)     **One bit of information corresponds to  k * T * ln2 in exergy.** (k is Boltzmann's constant; see p. 126). In other words, the temperature is of importance for the information. Information from a system of high temperature can cause more constructive changes in the environment than information from a low temperature system at the same negentropy level. The exergy is directly measuring the amount of order (work) that the system is able to induce on  other systems. By introduction of equations (5.7) and (5.8) into equation (6.1), we obtain a direct relationship between exergy and probabilities, a posteriori and a priori.

5) **Entropy is not clearly defined for far-from-equilibrium systems, particularly living systems;** see Kay (1984), while exergy has a clear definition also for far-from-equilibrium systems (see Section 6.1. and Fig. 6.3).

Exergy is spent in any energy, mass or information conversion process, which goes at a finite rate. When a structure is built, some exergy is spent in the structure and some is spent in the conversion processes.

The concept of physical information, defined as $Ex/k'*To$, where $k' = k \ln 2$ and $k$ is Boltzmann's constant, is introduced. One can now define a characteristic temperature of an information transfer:

$$T_{transfer} = Ex/k'l, \qquad (6.21)$$

$T_{transfer}$ must be large enough so that sufficient energy is dissipated to ensure irreversibility. This implies that $T_{transfer}$ must be large compared to To in the sense that (Brillouin, 1962):

$$\exp(-T_{tranfer}/To) \ll 1 \qquad (6.22)$$

Note that this condition is quite favorable since $T_{transfer}/To$ appears in a decreasing exponential. In Table 6.2 the characteristic temperatures of various information transfers are shown, and in Fig. 6.4 an information rate (frequency)-power plot is made for different types of information transfer. As seen, the human eye functions close to the quantum mechanical limit, while the computer memory has a $T_{transfer}$ about 106 times the temperature of sight. The computer has, however, a speed of resolution that is about 106 times better than the eye.

On the other hand the biosynthesis of the cells is still several orders of magnitude more efficient than the computer. The biosynthesis of protein falls very close to the critical line of the room temperature (see Fig. 6.4), which is possible because of the fact that in every elementary transfer 2.3 bits of information are exchanged. Electronics is the best technology mankind has achieved, from an exergy-economic point of view. Still, life itself is much more efficient in its use of exergy in constructing biological material.

An allosteric enzyme, which is a protein specialized in molecular engineering, has a weight of $10^{-17}$ g, while an electronic component with the same logical properties will weigh $10^{-3} - 10^{-2}$ g. Further development in electronic engineering might reduce the weight 1-2 magnitudes, but still the allosteric enzyme will be $10^{12}$ times lighter.

Allosteric enzymes control and carry out the biosynthesis spontaneously, fast and at low temperature due to formation of stereospecific complexes with the substrate. They may almost be perceived as Maxwell's demons, who can prevent certain molecules to pass from one container to another.

**Table 6.2.**

**Efficiency in information transfer (expressed in characteristic temperature (Tribus and McIrvine, 1971), and Lehninger, 1970).**

| Type of information transfer | Log ($T_{transfer}$) (K) |
|---|---|
| Typewriter | 23 |
| Radio | 19.7 |
| Television | 18.3 |
| Computer memory | 11 |
| Human speech | 7 |
| Human ear | 6 |
| Human eye | 5.7 |
| Protein synthesis in a cell | 2.65 |

Other examples of effective transfer of information may be found among pheromones. A few molecules ($10^{-17}$ g ) of the sex pheromone bombycol are sufficient to act on the receptor localized on the antenna of the male *Bombyx mori* to cause a stimulus, which activates male behavior.

However, Leon Brillouin (1949) gave the solution to this paradox: all use and storage of information, whether it is the "Maxwell's demons" or the allosteric enzymes, requires energy (or even more correctly expressed: exergy). Landauer (1989) has later shown that it is rather "to get rid of all this redundant information again", that costs energy.

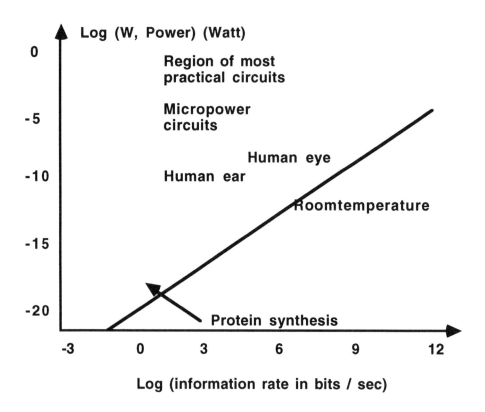

**Fig. 6.4.** Frequency-power diagram of information transfer. (Erikson et al. 1976).

The second law of thermodynamics is not violated but it is anyhow remarkable that a molecule of about $10^{-17}$ g with correspondingly low exergy cost can contain so much information, available for biological construction work. It shows that nature has developed toward a very effective storage of information per unit of mass. The mass available for an ecological development away from thermodynamic equilibrium is limited. Further development in this direction has therefore been dependent on an increased content of information per unit of mass.

The high efficiency in the use of exergy by ecosystems at the present "room temperature" on earth works hand in hand with the chemical stability of the chemical species characteristic of life on earth. Macromolecules are subject to thermal denaturation. Among the macromolecules proteins are most sensitive to thermal effects, and this constant breakdown of proteins leads to a substantial turnover of amino acids in the organisms. According to biochemistry an adult man synthesizes

168

and degrades approximately 1 g of protein nitrogen per kilo of body weight per day. This corresponds to a protein turnover of about 7.7 % per day for a man with a body temperature of 37°C. Figure 6.5 shows the rate constant as function of the temperature for denaturation of average proteins and the corresponding daily protein turnover. Considering that protein anabolism requires energy, it is obvious that organisms utilizing the most commonly found proteins would have difficulties in homeostasis at temperatures much above the mid forties. Most animals which possess some temperature regulation, such as mammals and birds therefore have a temperature of homeostatis between 30 and 46°C (see Fig. 6.5).

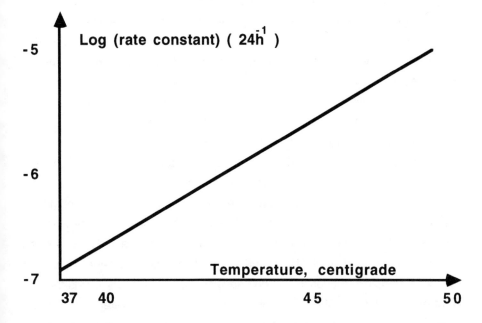

**Fig. 6.5**. Rate constant of protein denaturation versus temperature.

Microbial species which appear to grow at higher temperatures synthesize proteins with higher heat stability at rapid rate so that the 24-hour protein replacement load is not a limiting factor.

On the other hand, the overall process:

nutrients converted to cells and waste products

requires a certain temperature to proceed at a sufficient rate.

This implies that life has a lower temperature limit, at least in the form it has on earth. Animals that possess temperature regulation would otherwise lose too much heat by thermal conduction, whereas organisms without temperature regulation - and that includes all the most primitive forms of life - will obviously require a certain ambient temperature.

## 6.3. Application of Exergy in Ecosystem Theory

Ecosystems are soft systems in the sense that they are able to meet changes in external factors or impacts with many varying regulations processes on different levels; see Chapter 2, Sections 1-2. The results are that only minor changes are observed in the function of the ecosystem, despite the relatively major changes in environmental conditions. It means that the state variables - but not necessarily the species - are maintained almost unchanged, in spite of changes in external factors.

It has been widely discussed during the last years (H.T. Odum, 1983, Straskraba, 1980 and Straskraba and Gnauck, 1983) how it is possible to describe these regulation processes, particularly those on the ecosystem level - i.e., the changes in ecological structure and the species composition.

The Neodarwinian theory expanded to include 1) coevolution, 2) transfer of knowledge (information) from parents to children, 3) the ability of organisms to regulate their environment and thereby the selection pressure on them, 4) modernized concepts according to Brooks et al. (1988) and Wiley (1988) and 5) D-genes, is able to describe the very complex competition among species. Darwin's theory states that the species, that are best fitted to the prevailing conditions in the ecosystem will survive. As discussed in Section 2.2, this formulation may be interpreted as a tautology. We should therefore prefer the following formulation: Life is a matter of survival and growth. Given the conditions, determined by the external and internal functions, the question is: which of the available species (and there are more available species than needed) have the combinations of properties to give the highest probability for survival and growth? Those species, or rather this combination of species, may be denoted the fittest and will be selected. Darwin's theory may in other words, be used to describe the changes in ecological structure and species composition, but can not be directly applied quantitatively with the present formulation, for instance in ecological modelling.

The problem of describing the ecological structural changes and the changes species composition by quantitative methods, developed by translation of "survival of the fittest" into thermodynamics terms, will be discussed further in Chapter 11. It is presented in this context as a hypothetical theory, which will attempt to unite Darwin's, Monod's (Monod 1972) and Prigogine's theories (Prigogine et al. 1972 and 1972a) in the explanation of ecosystem development and evolution by application of exergy.

These ideas are illustrated in Fig. 2.6 and discussed in Section 2.6. What is named ecological development is the changes with time in nature caused by the dynamics of the external factors, giving the system sufficient time for the reactions. Note that the ideas behind this figure are analogous with Wiley (1988), Brooks et al. (1988), Ulanowicz (1980) and (1990) and Wicken (1988). They claim that the following is characteristic for the evolution from a thermodynamic point of view:

1. **Dollo's Law of an irreversible evolution** - the same species will never reappear - **is valid**, because we will never reach the same situation again with the same forcing functions and state variables.

2. **The entire ecosystem is evolving**, because everything is linked to everything. It explains the strength in the ascendency concept.

3. **The history of the system is important**, because that will determine which genes are available to find the best solution to the problem of survival. The history also determines the initial conditions, which are of great importance for the development of the system - compare also the indirect effect in Section 8.3.

4. **The selection is based upon the given condition in the entire ecosystem** and is separated from the evolution of the genetic pool. Evolution is on the other hand related to the genetic pool. **It is the result of the relation between the dynamics of the external factors and the dynamics of the genetic pool.** The external factors steadily change the conditions for survival and the genetic pool steadily comes up with new solutions to the problem of survival.

5. **The most complex ecosystem does not necessarily give the best answer to the problem of survival** (Olmsted 1988). Therefore - maybe - we cannot find any relationship between complexity and stability. It does not exist as underlined by May; see also Chapter 2.

Let us turn to the translation of Darwin's theory into thermodynamics (see the presentation in Section 2.2. pp. 44-47), applying exergy as the basic concept - see the definition in Section 6.1. Survival implies maintenance of the biomass, and growth means increase of biomass. It has cost exergy to construct biomass and it therefore possesses exergy, which is transferable to support other exergy (energy) processes. Survival and growth can therefore be measured by use of the thermodynamic concept exergy, which may be understood as *the free energy relative to the environment;* see equations (6.8) and (6.13) and Table 6.1.

Darwin`s theory may therefore be reformulated in thermodynamic terms as follows: **The prevailing conditions of an ecosystem steadily change and the system will continuously select the species that can contribute most to the maintenance or even growth of the exergy of the system.**

Ecosystems are open systems, see Section 5.3, and receive an inflow of solar energy. It carries low entropy, while the radiation from the ecosystem carries high entropy.

If the power of the solar radiation is W and the average temperature of the system is $T_1$, then the exergy gain per unit of time, $\Delta Ex$ is (Erikson et al. 1976):

$$\Delta Ex = T_1 * W (1/T_0 - 1/T_2), \tag{6.23}$$

where $T_0$ is the temperature of the environment and $T_2$ is the temperature of the sun. This exergy flow can be used to construct and maintain structure far away from equilibrium.

Notice that the thermodynamic translation of Darwin's theory requires that populations have the above mentioned properties of reproduction, inheritance and variation. The selection of the species that contribute most to the exergy of the system under the prevailing conditions requires that there are enough individuals with different properties that a selection can take place - it means that the reproduction and the variation must be high and that once a change has taken place due to better fitness it can be conveyed to the next generation.

Notice furthermore that the change in exergy is not necessarily $\geq 0$, it depends on the changes of the resources of the ecosystem. The proposition claims, however, that the ecosystem attempts to reach the highest possible exergy level under the given circumstances and with the available genetic pool ready for this attempt (Jørgensen and Mejer, 1977 and 1979). Compare Fig. 6.6, where the reactions of exergy to an increase and a decrease in nutrient concentrations are shown.

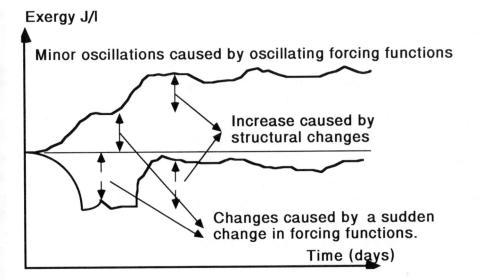

**Exergy J/l**

Minor oscillations caused by oscillating forcing functions

Increase caused by structural changes

Changes caused by a sudden change in forcing functions.

Time (days)

**Fig. 6.6.** Exergy response to increased and decreased nutrient concentration.

It is not possible to measure exergy directly - but it is possible to compute it, if the composition of the ecosystem is known. Mejer and Jørgensen (1979) have shown by the use of thermodynamics that the following equation is valid for the components of an ecosystem:

$$Ex = RT \sum_{i=1}^{i=n} (C_i * \ln (C_i/C_{eq,i}) - (C_i - C_{eq,i})), \qquad (6.24)$$

where R is the gas constant, T the temperature of the environment (Kelvin), while $C_i$ represents the i'th component expressed in a suitable unit, e.g., for phytoplankton in a lake $C_i$ could be milligrams of a focal nutrient in the phytoplankton per liter of lake water, $C_{eq,i}$ is the concentration of the i'th component at thermodynamic equilibrium, which can be found in Morowitz (1968) and n is the number of components. $C_{eq,i}$ is, of course, a very small concentration of organic components, corresponding to the probability of forming a complex organic compound in an inorganic soup (at thermodynamic equilibrium). Morowitz (1968) has calculated this probability and found that for proteins, carbohydrates and fats the concentration is about $10^{-60}$ mg /l, which may be used as the concentration at thermodynamic equilibrium.

For more complex compounds such as uni-cell organism, it will be even smaller

173

and these compounds would therefore even if they are present in a very small concentration, also contribute significantly to the exergy. Morowitz (1968) has estimated the probability of forming one coli bacterium to be $10^{-110}$.

The probability of forming multi-cell organisms at thermodynamic equilibrium is even lower, because additional exergy is required to aggregate the cells to form an organism. The additional exergy may be estimated by means of equation (5.3) by multiplication with the temperature. If we consider, that the aggregation of the ca. 100,000 cells of zooplankton correspond to a reduction in volume of a factor of about 1000 (100, 000 cells in an aquatic ecosystem are for instance found in 100 ml and the volume of zooplankton is about 100 µl), the difference in exergy will be $R^*T \ln 1000$, and the probable concentration of zooplankton at thermodynamic equilibrium (in an inorganic soup) must therefore be 3 magnitudes lower to be able to account for the decreased probability for the aggregation of 100,000 cells to form zooplankton. $C_{eq,i}$ for zooplankton therefore becomes $10^{-113}$ mg/l by a total concentration of 1 mg/l. A fish has about 10 millions cells. If we have a 100 g fish per 100,000,000 l, the aggregation to 100 ml fish corresponds to a factor 1000,000 smaller probability to find a fish with 10 millions of cells than to find one cell at thermodynamic equilibrium. $C_{eq,i}$ for fish therefore becomes $10^{-116}$ mg/l by a total concentration of 1 mg/l. This implies that the biomass of zooplankton will contribute 1000 times more to the exergy per unit of biomass than one- cellular organisms and that fish will contribute 1000, 000 times more than one-cellular organisms. As indicated above these figures are only estimates. They could in principle be calculated for each individual case, but for first estimates, where only levels of exergy are compared, it is acceptable to use these round figures. Notice that the factors are two magnitudes more than used by calculations of emergy; see Section 4.4, where a factor 10 is applied for a trophic level one step higher. This difference between exergy and emergy is not surprising because emergy accounts for the energy costs in solar equivalents, while exergy takes the energy costs of organization into account.

The term $(C_i * \ln (C_i/C_{eq,i})$ corresponds to the theoretical minimum work (free energy) to be done on the ecosystem to change its concentration relative to the reference level and the term $(C_i - C_{eq,i})$ is the work done by the constant-concentrations' surroundings. Jørgensen et al. (1992) show that equation (6.24) implies that exergy is always non-negative, independent of whether the system is more or less concentrated than the reference state. In practice the system is more concentrated than the surroundings and the second term becomes negligible, except for the inorganic components, where the equilibrium concentration will correspond to

174

the total concentration.

The equation is valid for systems with an inorganic net inflow and passive outflow. It can be derived from basic thermodynamic equations, see for instance Mejer and Jørgensen (1979). The equation presented above presumes, however, the validity of ideal liquid solution. Aoki (1992) has therefore proposed to accept the expression as a macroscopic measure of ecological systems, rather than to assert that it expresses the exergy. He shows that equation (6.24) is the sum of Kullback's information and Wiener entropy and proposes to improve the expression by replacement of the Wiener entropy with a scale-independent quantity. It is importto underline that *all* computations of exergy have the following shortcomings:

1). The computations will be based upon a model and will therefore not be more correct than the model. The results of the computations are therefore more appropriate for finding a *relative* difference in exergy by a comparison of an ecosystem under different conditions by use of the model.

2). The calculations - as all calculations in thermodynamics - are based upon approximations and assumptions. But as we draw conclusions on the basis of the differences in exergy rather than on the basis of absolute values, the results may be applicable in ecosystem theoretical context.

The theory behind the application of exergy may be correct - but should of course be considered a hypothesis at this stage - , but the practical application of the theory to real ecosystems will suffer from the above mentioned shortcomings. This implies that the exergy computations could to a certain extent, as proposed by Aoki (1992) be considered a determination of an index, which is a valuable indicator of the healthiness or integrity of the ecosystem. Further experience should, however, be gained with such computations before a more widely reliable use of indices is introduced.

The exergy computations of an ecosystem should, nevertheless, be illustrated by the use of an example. It will demonstrate the shortcomings of the exergy computations, but it will also show that the calculations are relatively simple and can be used as relative terms. Let us consider an algae pond, which only contains one species. The phosphorus concentration of algae is 1 mg/l and in the form of orthophosphate 0.6 mg/l. The temperature is 300K. If we are concerned only with the contribution to the exergy from the phosphorus compounds, $Ex_p$, we find by use of the above equation:

$$Ex_p = 8.31*300(1/31(\ln(1/10^{-110}))-(1/31-10^{-110}/31)$$
$$+(0.6/31(\ln(0.6/1.6))-(0.6/31-1.6/31))$$
$$= 20346 \text{ mJ/l} \tag{6.25}$$

Note that only the algae concentration contributes significantly to the exergy. Similarly, it is possible to calculate the contribution to exergy for nitrogen and *all* other relevant compounds, including the contribution originating from the more complex compounds such as genes and hormones. The theoretical definition of exergy would imply that we must find the concentration of all components, calculate the contribution to the exergy of every component and add all these contributions to get the total exergy. In practice, however, we cannot find the concentrations of all components, but if we are only concerned with the changes caused by for instance phosphorus, it is sufficient to make the computations shown to see the *relative changes* in exergy. Calculations of exergy are carried out in relation to an ecological model and in that case the result will, of course, give the exergy of the model ecosystem and not of the real ecosystem. If the model is used in two different situations, i.e., two different sets of external factors are imposed on the ecosystem (model), the computations of exergy will be able to give some good indications of the differences in exergy of the real ecosystem in the two different situations, provided that the model is able to capture the essential features of the ecosystem in relation to the changes in external factors. Notice that exergy is defined as the free energy of the system relative to the environment and if we define the environment as the inorganic soup on earth 4 billion years ago, we will have the indicated - see equation (6.25) - low concentrations of biological components in the inorganic soup.

If zooplankton is introduced to the algae pond more phosphorus will most probably be bound in the organic form and we will therefore find more exergy. If for instance the allocation of the phosphorus will be 0.9 mg/l in phytoplankton, 0.26 mg/l in zooplankton and the remaining 0.36 mg/l in the form of orthophosphate, it can be calculated that the exergy will increase to 23710 mJ/l, using $10^{-113}$ mg/ l as concentration for zooplankton at thermodynamic equilibrium.

Jizhong et al. (1992) use exergy computations to set up exergy balances for plants and animals. They distinguish between exergy and anexergy, which is the non-exergetic part of the energy. Jizhong et al. compute the exergy efficiency as the ratio between out- put exergy + exergy change of the system and exergy input. They propose to use exergy efficiency as objective function in optimization of an ecosystem, i.e. the organisms that have higher efficiency in the use of exergy will be selected.

Shieh and Fan (1982) have suggested the estimations of exergy contents in structurally complicated material in kcal / kg under standard conditions (a pressure of 1 atm. and 298.15 K) as : 8177.79 [C] + 5.25 [N] +27892.63 [H] + 4364.33 [S] - 3173.66 [O] + 5763.41 [F] + 2810 [Cl] + 1204.3 [Br] + 692.5 [I] - $S_{ash}$ *T* $W_{ash}$ + 0.15[O] *( 7837.667 [C] + 33888.889 [H] + 3828.75 [S] - 4236.10 [O] + 4447.37 [F] + 1790.9 [Cl] + 681.97 [Br] + 334.86 [I] ), where [C] , [H], etc. refer to the content in kg per kg of structurally complicated material of the respective elements. $S_{ash}$ refers to the specific entropy of ash. It is assumed to have a value of 0.17152 kcal/ (kg ash*K). $W_{ash}$ refers to the weight of ash expressed as kg per kg of structurally complicated material and T is the absolute temperature. If the composition of an organic material under consideration is known, the equation shown above can be used in a straightforward manner. Such calculations will, however, not take exergy stored as information, and neither does equation (6.24). The application of exergy calculations will therefore require that a model, containing all the focal information for the specific problem, is used simultaneously. It implies as already underlined, that the results will be dependent on the model as well as on the exergy computations.

We can distinguish between two changes in exergy: a change caused directly by the external factors directly and a change caused by the response of the living organisms to the external factors. The former is related to the available resources in the ecosystem. If the phosphorus concentration is increased or decreased, the exergy will also increase or decrease. The latter change in exergy is caused by the effort of the organisms to survive and reproduce and will therefore reflect the many regulation mechanisms that an ecosystem and its organisms possess. Any change in the species composition or the ecological structure will therefore imply that the new structure and composition are better fitted to the emerging conditions of the ecosystem.

In other words, whenever the external factors are changed, we observe a change in exergy, ΔEx, which can be expressed as:

$$\Delta Ex = \Delta Ex_E + \Delta Ex_I \qquad (6.26)$$

where the subscript E refers to the changes caused by the external factors directly, while the subscript I represents the effort of the organisms by adaptation to the new conditions (including those waiting in the wings) to get the best possible growth and reproduction out of the circumstances. $\Delta Ex_E$ may be negative or positive, while **$\Delta Ex_I$ will always be $\geq$ 0 and the species giving the highest value will win (= be selected).**

The two contributions to exergy have previously (see Jørgensen 1988) been mentioned as contributions coming from changes in resources and from structural changes. The reformulation is a result of a discussion with R. Herendeen - see also Herendeen (1989) and (1990). If we consider stocking an aquatic ecosystem with fish, we add to the exergy of the resources as well as to exergy of the structure. If we distinguish between external and internal changes, it becomes clear that stocking with fish corresponds to external changes, and the proposition presented above also becomes valid in this case.

Herendeen (1989) has been able to distinguish between the contribution to exergy coming from the resources (a size term), representing the overall concentration of the system's stock relative to that of the reference level, and from the structure, representing the distribution of stocks among the compartments relative to that of the reference level:

$$Ex = RT\, C_0 \{ \ln\, (C_0/C_{eq,0}) - (1 - (C_{eq,0}/C_0)) + \sum_{i=1}^{i=n} X_i \ln\, (X_i / X_{eq,i})\}, \qquad (6.27)$$

where $X_i$ is $C_i/C_0$, $C_0$ being the total concentration $= \sum C_i$.

Herendeen (1990) rewrites equation (6.27) in the following manner:

$$Ex = \text{Size term ( concentration term + structure term )}. \qquad (6.28)$$

The change in exergy due to the change in external factors $\Delta Ex_E$ may give changes in all three terms, while the changes in $\Delta Ex_I$ mainly imply change in the structure term. Changes in other terms may, however, occur due to for instance a modified effect of external factors on the ecosystem after a reallocation of the structure, i.e., the biomass has taken place. The proposition given above may now be reformulated as follows:

The change in internal exergy is always non-negative and may (with some exceptions, where the influence of external factors on exergy is dependent on the structure) be calculated by the use of the structure term as follows:

$$R^*T^*C_0^*\Delta[\sum_{i=1}^{i=n} X_i \ln\, (X_i / X_{eq,i})]/\Delta t = \Delta E_I \geq 0 \qquad (6.29)$$

178

Notice that $C_0$ is constant and that the *structural* changes in exergy, caused by external factors are omitted, because only the internal changes, *after* a perturbation has taken place, are considered. $\Delta t$ should be selected according to the dynamics of the components considered. Equation (6.29) expresses the ability of the system to recover after perturbations.

It implies that if for instance the fish stock is increased by external inputs, it is considered entirely an increase in the size term. In this case only the change in exergy after external inputs have taken place ($C_0$ has increased or decreased) is accounted for in the use of (6.29).

Furthermore, if for instance an aquatic ecosystem is covered by a black sheet, the photosynthesis is eliminated and the plant organisms and those organisms having only plants as food items are therefore completely eliminated by external factors and should therefore be omitted in the use of equation (6.29). It means that (6.29) should only account for *recovery* of the system after the impact has affected the system.

The idea with this formulation is that all externally caused changes may give any possible change in the exergy, but **the effort of the ecosystem to "get the best" out of the situation including recovery after a stress situation always gives a contribution to exergy $\geq 0$, and among the possible sets of $X_i$ values the set giving the highest $\Delta E_I$ will be selected. $E_I$ may therefore be considered a measure of health or ecological indicator of the system.**

Notice that $\Delta E_I = 0$ will correspond to the rare situation, where the previous components of the system in exactly the same concentrations are the best one for coping with the new situation.


## 4. Exergy and Modelling

The most crucial application of exergy and the presented proposition is maybe in practical development of models which are able to *predict changes* in the species composition and/or in the ecological structure or at least indicate the changes of the important properties of the dominant species to account for ecosystem reactions to changes in external factors. This application of exergy in practical modelling will be further touched on in Chapter 11.

At this stage it can only be considered a hypothesis that ecosystems react according to the presented proposition. On the other hand it might be considered a strong support for the hypothesis, if ecological models were able to describe the changes observed. As mentioned above, since ecosystems are irreducible systems there seems not to be any other way to examine a hypothesis on the system level than to test the hypothesis on models, that have been verified, calibrated and validated. Therefore it has been considered of great importance to test such models with dynamic structure against real observations; see the discussion in Section 3.7. It is, however, not sufficient to test the reactions of a few models, but it is necessary to try many models of various ecosystems and in various situations, compare model reactions with observations and try to build up a pattern piece by piece, examining whether each piece fits into to the over-all pattern. It is a troublesome stepwise procedure, but it is the only possible way to go.

Realistic models have been developed as a basis for the test of the hypothesis according to the considerations above. Three models were applied in the analysis: a eutrophication model, a toxic substance model and a stream model.

The eutrophication model has been used in 18 case studies - with modification from case to case according to the ecosystem characteristics; see also Chapter 3. In one of the case studies the investigations have been carried out over a period of several years and the model has been calibrated, validated and even the prognosis previously published has been validated with a fully acceptable result - for further details on these investigations; see Jørgensen (1976) and Jørgensen et al. (1978, 1981, 1986 and 1986a). Figure 3.2 gives the conceptual diagram for the nitrogen cycle of this model. Similar cycles are included for carbon and phosphorus and even silica, if diatoms are of importance.

The toxic substance model considers the effect of ionic copper on a lake ecosystem. The conceptual diagram is shown Fig. 6.7. It represents the foodweb, and the model includes a formulation of uptake of copper from water and food and the effects, that the concentration of copper in the organisms has on the growth and mortality. For further details on this model see Jørgensen (1979 and 1984), Kamp Nielsen et al. (1983) and Jørgensen (1990b).

The stream model is conceptualized in Fig. 6.8. The results have not been published but the characteristic features are consistent with a few widely used river models, see Armstrong (1977) and Wat. Res. Eng. (1973). It is noticeable that the model includes how the growth of aerobic microorganisms, phytoplankton and zooplankton is affected by the oxygen concentration below a certain threshold value.

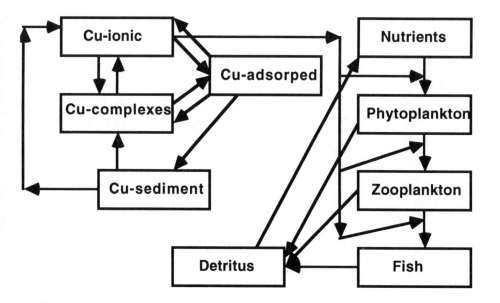

**Fig. 6.7.** Conceptual diagram of the copper model applied in test of the presented hypothesis on development in exergy.

Perturbations were imposed on these three models. Observations on model reactions were made. Changes in exergy and buffer capacities were observed and the model results were finally compared with the ecological observations.

The results may be summarized in the following points:

1. The immediate reaction of exergy to changes in external factors may be either toward a higher or a lower level according to the changes in available resources, see also Fig. 6.6. Afterwards when the species composition has had sufficient time to react to the changes, the exergy will always increase. If for instance the phosphorus concentration is suddenly decreased, the available resources are reduced and the exergy is decreased accordingly, but the changes in species composition, which is a consequence of the new situation - the water contain less nutrient and is therefore less eutrophic - , cause an increase in exergy again, because those species which are better fitted to deal with the new situation, i.e., better able to move away from the thermodynamic equilibrium, will take over.

2) The buffer capacities *related* to the changes are always increased. If phosphorus input is changed, ß-P is increased, while other buffer capacities may be reduced.

3) It was found by a statistical analysis of the results that there is a

181

relationship between exergy and the buffer capacities:

$$Ex = \sum a_j * \beta_j \quad , \tag{6.30}$$

where $a_j$ represents regression coefficients and $\beta_j$ represents the buffer capacities found by the computations. Some buffer capacities may be reduced even when the exergy increases, as mentioned under point 2` above, but it is more than compensated by the increase of other buffer capacities. This observation explains why it has been very difficult to find a relationship between ecosystem stabilities in the broadest sense and species diversity, see the discussion in Chapter 2, Section 2. It is observed that increased phosphorus loading gives decreased diversity; see Fig. 6.9, which is based on the results found by the use of the eutrophication model and is furthermore consistent with Weiderholm (1980) and Ahl and Weiderholm (1977). Stability in its broadest ecological sense is in other words a multidisciplinary concept and the relation between species is diversity and stability is therefore not simple and can be revealed only by a multidimensional relation. If species diversity decreased, the stability - represented by the buffer capacity - may be decreased in some directions, but will increase in others. It may be formulated as follows:

If the system can offer a better survival, i.e., a better buffer capacity in relation to the changing forcing function by decreasing the diversity, the system will not hesitate to react accordingly.

4) It has been emphasized above that it is important that the model used for these investigations is realistic. All three models have been examined carefully and are supported by good data. The reactions of the models were furthermore according to general ecological observations, for instance the eutrophication model shows reactions similar to those illustrated in Fig. 6.9.

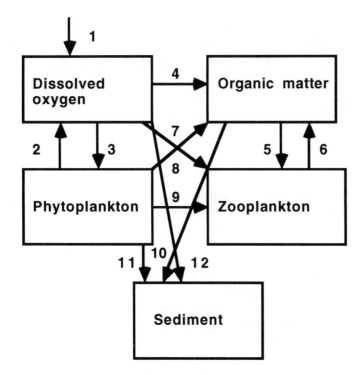

The processes are: 1 reaeration, 2 photosynthesis, 3 respiration 4 biological oxygen consumption, 5 detritus used by zooplankton as feed, 6 mortality, 7 respiration, 8 mortality, 9 grazing, 10 and settling, 12` oxygen consumption by sediment.

**Fig. 6.8.** Conceptual diagram of the river model applied to test of the presented hypothesis on development in exergy.

It would be obvious - with the above-mentioned results in mind - to ask why ecosystems react to the perturbations in the way they do. It may be explained by reference to Darwin's theory: all species do their very best to survive and grow under the prevailing conditions, which include external and internal factors. The species with the properties best fitted to give survival and growth will win. Darwin's theory may be applied quantitatively by use of the exergy concept, as discussed above.

It would be possible to express these explanations in a different way: systems with biological / ecological properties will always react in this way. Biological / ecological properties are here understood as:

**1) All matter cycle.**

**2) There are many positive and negative feedback mechanisms, organized hierarchically.**

**3) The living components are able to grow and reproduce.**

**4) Ecosystems and their living components attempt to maintain the level of information achieved and even to raise this level.**

It is of importance that these ecological properties are reflected in the model used as experimental tool, when ecosystem-theoretical results are tested. All three models mentioned above possess these properties.

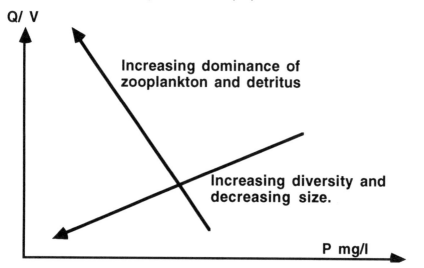

**Fig. 6.9.** Reactions of lakes to change in phosphorus loading and retention time (Q/V). The reactions are according to observations as well as to model results.

More support for the hypothesis may be taken from Prigogine and Stengers (1979). They describe the population dynamic development by use of the logistic equation:

$$dN / dt = r*N*(K - N )/ K - mN, \qquad (6.31)$$

where N is the number of individuals in a population, r is the reproduction rate, K is the carrying capacity and m is the mortality. This equation corresponds to an increase in exergy up to the level of species 1 in Fig. 6.10.

184

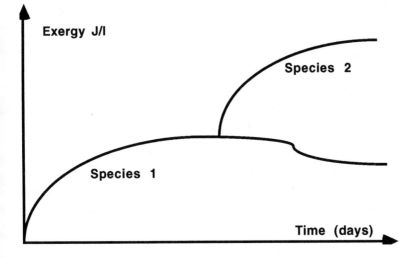

**Fig. 6.10.** Exergy is plotted versus time. The figure illustrates the utilization of an ecological niche.

However, when for instance an ecological niche is going to be exploited by organisms, r, K and m should not be considered as constants forever. The various species will be able to adapt better to the conditions and therefore the constants will develop towards more advantageous values. The constants do not have the same values for all organisms of a species, but may for instance be normally distributed around an average value. Those organisms with the best fitted values will be more dominant and thereby the constants will change to their values.

Such development of species could correspond to the increase in exergy from the level of species 1 to the level of species 1 and 2. In addition many other species may come to the niche and try to utilize the resources available. This may imply that the first species will be reduced in number as shown in Fig. 6.10. and thereby in contribution to the exergy, but together will the two or more species now populating the ecological niche will contribute to a higher level of exergy. This is shown in Fig. 6.10, which illustrates the development in an ecological niche. The same figure, but with numbers on the y-axis, is shown in Prigogine and Stengers (1979).

Fränzle (1981) has studied the structure of plants and animals in ecotones. They show a very high diversity (compare also the results by Maarel (1976)) and stability, which correspond to a high negentropy (exergy). Furthermore there seems to be a relationship between the negentropy (exergy) of the system and its structural and physiological diversity.

185

In all it seems a workable hypothesis to use exergy as a measure or indicator for the development of ecosystem structure and for changes in species composition. Structural exergy should be considered as a particularly appropriate measure of ecological integrity.

The propositions should not be interpreted as saying that as ecosystems have set up goals to maximize the exergy, but rather that exergy is conveniently used to quantify Darwin's theory and to account for the results of the many regulating processes and feed- back mechanisms that are present in an ecosystem. It may be expressed in another way: exergy is an embodied holistic property of ecosystems and it seems feasible to cover the reactions on the system level, resulting from the many properties including the hierarchy of regulations (see Chapter 2, Section 1-2), by application of exergy.

## 6.5. The Fourth or Ecological Law of Thermodynamics

It now seems feasible to formulate a fourth or ecological law of thermodynamics, which may be considered a core law of ecosystem ecology:

**If a system has a through-flow of exergy, it will attempt to utilize the flow to increase *its exergy* , i.e., to move farther away from thermodynamic equilibrium; if more combinations and processes are offered to utilize the exergy flow, the organization that is able to give the system the *highest exergy under the prevailing conditions and pertubations* will be selected.**

We could call this law the fourth law of thermodynamics, but to underline its parti-cular applicability on ecosystems, which are characterized by many methods of organization, it might be preferable to name it **The Ecological Law of Thermodynamics (abbreviated ELT),** or the thermodynamic law of ecology.

The first "exergy" in the formulation of the Ecological Law of Thermodynamics shown above may be replaced by "low-entropy energy." Some may like to replace it by "negentropy," bus as the classical thermodynamic expressions cannot be rigorously defined for systems far from equilibrium, preference should go toward using either exergy.

The second "exergy" (written in italics), may eventually be replaced by "order, information, maximum power, dissipation of energy or exergy, or dissipation of gradients."

Some may again prefer to use "negentropy" or "maximum production of entropy", but as explained above entropy is not unambiguously defined far from equilibrium and therefore it is recommended to apply some of the other formulations.

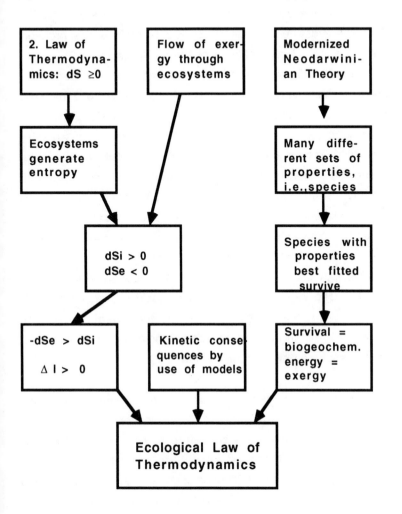

**Fig 6.11.** A flow chart of the arguments applied in Chapters 4-6 to develop "The Ecological Law of Thermodynamics."

The difference between the maximum exergy theory and Kay and Schneider's application of the maximum dissipation of energy, exergy or gradients is not crucial, but should rather be seen as two sides of the same coin. Both theories assert, that the ecosystem develops toward the highest possible organization, which implies both that the system moves furthest away from thermodynamic equilibrium and that due to requirement for maintenance of very developed organization it will dissipate most energy or exergy.

The ascendency concept will be introduced in Section 8.4. It measures the organization both qualitatively and quantitatively, but presumes the application of network representation for the ecosystems. Ascendency could therefore most probably also replace "exergy" in italics in the Ecological Law of Thermodynamics.

The law is consistent with Chapters 4-6. Figure 6.11. shows a flow chart of the most crucial inferences from these three chapters. It is not possible to prove the basic thermodynamic laws, including the Ecological Law of Thermodynamics. A fundamental law must, however, be supported from many sides and be a workable "model" in many contexts. It means that a fundamental law should facilitate the explanation of our observations, simplify and fit the overall scientific pattern and be consistent with all other laws. The tentative Ecological Law of Thermodynamics (ELT) seems to fulfill these requirements. In addition, it has been possible to show analytically in some specific ecosystem cases, that exergy follows the proposition given above (Jørgensen et al. 1992a). It furthermore bridges the gap between thermodynamics and Darwin's theory, which is considered an important feature of the law. ELT therefore has a strong support, but should be considered only tentatively anyhow. The coming years will reveal, if the ELT fits into the overall ecosystem-theoretical pattern, that will result from further research and development in the field. That is the real and needed test for a new fundamental law.

The energy flow through an ecosystem renders it possible to realize processes that require energy, as for instance construction of complex biochemical compounds: energy and simple inorganic compounds are converted to complex biochemical molecules. This is completely according to the first and second law of thermodynamics. However, nature offers many pathways for such processes that are competing and ELT is concerned with the selection process under the prevailing conditions, which are continuously changed.

Energy is in most cases not limiting (but not in all cases!), which may be deduced from the low efficiency of photosynthesis: only 2% of the solar radiation. Shading may, of course, play a role and the shape of many plants and trees can be explained by an effective way to escape shading.

The question is which of the many biochemical pathways will win, or rather, which combinations of pathways will win? The different pathways compete, however, in a very complex way, because the processes are many and complex and are therefore dependent on many factors:

1) at least 20 inorganic compounds, of which some may be limiting,

188

2) competition from the other pathways,

3) temperature,

4) light (for photosynthetic pathways only),

5) ability to utilize the combined resources.

The conditions are furthermore varying in time and space. This implies that the history of the system also plays a role in selection of the organization that gives the highest exergy. Two systems with the same prevailing conditions will consequently not necessarily select the same species and food web, because the two systems most probably have a different history.

Decomposition rates are of great importance, as they determine not only the ability of the different products (organisms) to maintain their concentrations, but also at which rate the inorganic compounds are recycled and can be reused.

It is not surprising from this description that:

1. **There is room for "survival" of many pathways**, considering the heterogeneity in time and space, the many simultaneously determining factors and the many developed mechanisms to utilize different resources in the ecosystems.

2. **The competition is very complex and there are many possible pathways**. The description of the selection will therefore be very complex, too.

3. As **everything is linked to everything** in an ecosystem, it is necessary to look at the entire system, i.e., to ask which *combination* of pathways is best able to utilize the resources? This implies that we have to find the combination of pathways - among the possible ones - that are able to move the entire system furthest away from the thermodynamic equilibrium - and the distance from thermodynamic equilibrium is measured by the exergy of the total system. Because everything is linked to everything, it is obvious that every component in an ecosystem must consider the influence of all other components. The selection pressure comes from the forcing functions as well as from the other components. This explains the coevolution and the development of Gaia; see Section 2.4.

It is not surprising that the highest exergy also means the highest ability to dissipate gradients and produce entropy, (see Section 5.7), because the most developed system will require the most energy / exergy for maintenance, i. e., respiration. This makes the ecological law of thermodynamics consistent with Kay and Schneider's theory presented in Section 5.7.

4. **Maintenance and development of biomass is extremely**

189

important for storage of the information level already achieved, i.e., to work on the "shoulders" of previous results. Without the ability to store information already gained it would be impossible to explain the rate of evolution or, rather, there wouldn't have been evolution at all. The role of storing the already achieved level of information may be illustrated by a simple example. This book contains about 900,000 signs. If a chimpanzee should write the book by touching a keyboard (of, let us say, 50 different keys) randomly with a rate of let us say 900 000 signs per day, the probability that the book would be finished in one day would be 50 $^{(-900\,000)}$. Even if the chimpanzee had worked since the Big Bang 15 billions years ago, the probability would still be less than 0.000 (more than 1.5 million zeros)...1. If on the other hand we preserve each time the chimpanzee has tried to type the book ( 900,000 signs) the signs correctly placed and next time let the chimpanzee only try to find randomly the incorrect signs and so on, there would be a probability close to one that the book would be finished in about 200 days!! The test on what is right and wrong in nature is carried out by the selection of the properties guaranteeing survival and growth and the genes preserve the results already achieved. The development of a mechanism to maintain information already gained has been crucial for the rate of evolution.

The concepts of competition / selection may be experimented, illustrated and presented by the application of models. The model in Fig. 6.12. has been used as an experimental tool to illustrate the factors that are essential for competition. The model is considered a very simplified edition of a real ecosystem. Two plants are competing for one resource (nutrient). The resource is recycled by a mineralization process carried out by microorganisms (micro). The factors determining the competition / selection in this simple system are: the rate of nutrient uptake, the half-saturation constant for uptake, i.e., the ability of the plants to pursue the uptake at very low concentrations, and the mortality of the plants, i.e., the ability to maintain the biomass. In a real ecosystem the competition is, of course, much more complex and many more factors determine the final result. In addition, the species are able to adapt, i. e., change their properties within a certain range to give better probability of survival under the prevailing conditions. Models that consider these properties of adaptation will be applied as scientific tools in Chapter 11. It will be demonstrated here that the selection and adaptation follow the Ecological Law of Thermodynamics. The examinations resulting from the use of the model in Figure 6.12 do not include exergy but will demonstrate how elementary properties (parameters) of the biological components may interact in the competition / selection process.

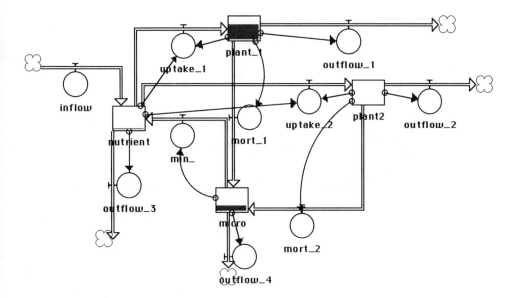

**Fig. 6.12.** The model used to illustrate competition/ selection.

Figure 6.13. gives the results of model simulations, when plant 1 has an uptake rate of 1.8, a half-saturation constant of 0.5 and a mortality rate of 0.35, while plant 2 has an uptake rate of 0.9, a mortality rate of 0.175 and the same half-saturation rate. As seen, the plants can coexist, but plant 1 achieves the highest biomass.

Figure 6.14 shows the results in the case where plant 2 is given the same mortality rate as plant 1 but still keeps the uptake rate of 0.9. As seen plant 2 is now almost out of competition and is kept on a low biomass level, corresponding to the very low level, when the mortality is set to zero.

Figure 6.15 shows the situation where a sine variation in uptake rates and mineralization rates is imposed on the system. The same rates as used for Fig. 6.14 are otherwise maintained. As seen, plant 2 is not able to utilize the improved conditions, when the sine function is at maximum.

The equations in computer program code for this latter case are given in Table 6.5. The plant species applied in the model simulations up to now have been r-strategists: rapid growth and rapid mortality. If a K-strategist is introduced the result will be different.

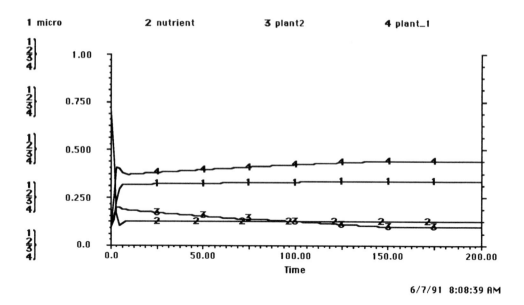

**Fig. 6.13.** Results of model simulations, when plant 1 has twice the uptake rate and mortality of plant 2, while the half-saturation constant is the same. Units: mg/l.

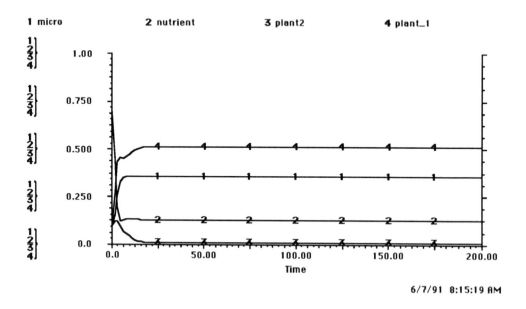

**Fig. 6.14.** Model simulation based upon the same mortality for the two plant species, while plant 1 has twice the uptake rate of plant 2. Units: mg/l.

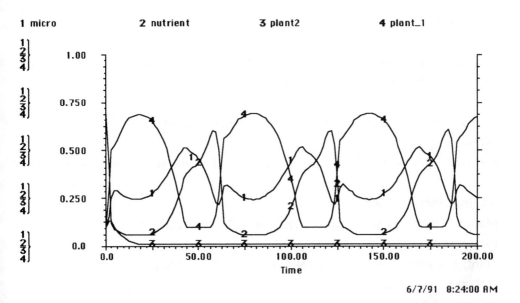

6/7/91  8:24:00 AM

**Fig.6.15.** Results in mg/l of model simulations, applying sine oscillations for uptake and mineralization rates.

This is illustrated in Fig. 6.16, where plant 2 was given a low uptake rate, namely 0.05 compared to plant 1's 1.8, but the mortality rate is decreased even more to 0.00035. In this case the slow growing is very competitive, because it is able to maintain the already gained biomass, as seen in Fig. 6.15.

It can furthermore be seen that the K-strategist, plant 2, is able to utilize the sine oscillation better than the r-strategist, because it maintains the gained biomass in the period of fast growth without losing it again in the period of slow growth.

The interpretation of the proposed fourth or ecological law of thermodynamics by use of models and reaction kinetics is a parallel to Dawkins' "Selfish Gene" (Dawkins 1989). The selfish gene produces survival machines to be able to protect the information stored in the gene and thereby maintains the level of information (exergy / biogeochemical energy) already achieved.

**Table 6.5.**

Source Code used for the model in Fig. 6.12. The version corresponding to the simulations presented in Fig. 6.15 is given.

```
micro = micro + dt * ( mort_2 + mort_1 - min_ - outflow_4 )
INIT(micro) = 0.1
nutrient = nutrient + dt * ( inflow - uptake_1 - uptake_2 + min_ - outflow_3
)
INIT(nutrient) = 0.7
plant2 = plant2 + dt * ( uptake_2 - mort_2 - outflow_2 )
INIT(plant2) = 0.1
plant_1 = plant_1 + dt * ( uptake_1 - mort_1 - outflow_1 )
INIT(plant_1) = 0.1
inflow = 0.01
min_  = 0.5*micro*(1+SIN(0.1*TIME))
mort_1 = IF plant_1 < 0.1 THEN 0 ELSE 0.35*plant_1
mort_2 = IF plant2 < 0.01 THEN 0 ELSE 0.35*plant2
outflow_1 = 0.01*plant_1
outflow_2 = 0.01*plant2
outflow_3 = 0.01*nutrient
outflow_4 = 0.01*micro
uptake_1  = 1.8*plant_1*nutrient/(0.5+nutrient)*(1+SIN(0.1*TIME))
uptake_2  = 0.9*plant2*nutrient/(0.5+nutrient)*(1+SIN(0.1*TIME))
```

---

Dawkins uses the expression "replicator" to underline the importance of the replication process and talk about the gradual improvement by the replicators to ensure their own continuance in the world. There is no contradiction to the Gaia hypothesis. The selfish replicators are not surprising, when we consider that cooperation is generally more beneficial than competition and it is probably true that the more complex the system becomes, the more beneficial the cooperation is.

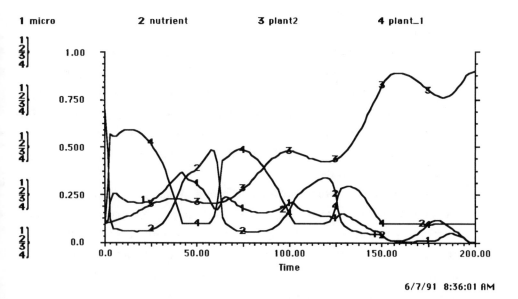

**1 micro**  **2 nutrient**  **3 plant2**  **4 plant_1**

6/7/91 8:36:01 AM

**Fig. 6.16.** Simulation using the model presented in Fig. 6.11. In this case plant 2 was given parameters corresponding to a K-strategist, i.e., a relatively slow uptake rate and mortality rate.

The next obvious question may be: Which factors determine the ability of the system to move further away from the thermodynamic equilibrium, in order to obtain a higher level of information and more structural biogeochemical energy (exergy)? The evolution of ecosystems has created ever more possibilities to utilize the opportunity offered to the ecosystems by input of energy from solar radiation. The factors of importance in this context will be listed and commented on below.

This book does not focus on the evolution, as already mentioned in Chapter 2, but is entirely devoted to the systems ecology of ecosystems. However, the evolutionary capacity of the ecosystem is a major feature of ecosystems and in this context evolution is covered and will be included in the listing below.

The abilities of the ecosystems to utilize the through-flows of energy or exergy are rooted in the following properties:

**1. The variety of the gene pool.** The more genes, the more possibilities are given to find a better solution to obtain even more exergy. Furthermore, the more genes, the more mutations and sexual recombinations will occur and the more new possibilities the system will get to move further away from the equilibrium. It implies that the gene pools do not only determine the possibilities to get the highest possible exergy today but also determine how to get even better possibilities in the future.

**2. The chemical composition of the ecosystem.** The better the chemical composition of the ecosystem matches the needs of the biological components, the better the ecosystem will be able to utilize the energy flow. This may explain why the tropical rain forest has an enormous diversity. The chemical composition (and the temperature, see point 4) in tropical rain forests is almost ideal for growth, including the presence of the most important compound on earth: water.

**3. The temperature pattern.** The rate of utilization of the energy flow is dependent on the temperature, see for instance also the role of temperature, mentioned in Section 6.2. Compare furthermore Figs. 6.14 and 6.15. The closer the temperature pattern matches the optimum for growth and reproduction and vice versa, the higher the rate of utilization and the faster the system will be able to move away from thermodynamic equilibrium.

**4. Fluctuations and other changes of the forcing functions.** The changes of forcing functions will steadily pose new questions for the ecosystem: how to get the best survival and growth under the prevailing conditions just now? This challenge, provided that the system is not brought outside its framework of ability, will create new information. The natural fluctuations of the forcing functions have been governing (with some exceptions, of course) for billions of years. The genes have therefore been able to cope with these fluctuations and even understand to benefit from them by moving further away from the thermodynamic equilibrium - compare the role, that fluctuations may play on the overall biomass (exergy); see Chapter 4, Section 4.

A dissipative structure is so organized that it increases its internal exergy and dissipates more efficiently the flow of exergy, which traverses it. This implies a maximum accumulation of exergy in the system, expressed biologically in the law of growth of an organism and in population dynamics.

Population dynamics deals with the spatio-temporal evolution of living species in relation to each other. The concepts of ecological niche, territorially and of different species at the same site are examples of spatio-temporal populations. An example in point is afforded by the study of populations of plankton in the ocean (Dubois 1974). Plankton lives and develops in an environment which is submitted to currents and turbulent diffusion. Despite this random environment these populations develop according to a heterogeneous spatial structure over distances of 5 to 100 km with a life span of several weeks. This is the so-called patchiness effect (see also Section 4.3), a spatial distribution of populations according to various geometrical figures. This order is remarkable, considering how water is constantly disturbed; a disturbance which will lead to a homogeneous spreading of the populations. Moreover, there is no correlation between this phenomenon and the chemical and physical properties of the environment such as nutrients, oxygen, salinity, light and temperature.

Dubois (1975) theoretically explains the emergence of patchiness. He suggests a competition between ecological interactions and the environment. In this approach a non-linear interaction of the prey and predator competes with transport phenomena by advection due to residual current and turbulent diffusion. The initiation of the patchiness effect is the result of the instabilities created by the advection

If mankind on the other hand changes the forcing functions outside the natural limits for the ecosystems, the challenge may be too difficult to meet for the ecosystem in spite of its well developed structure. It is what we experience today as the consequences of all the pollution problems.

Moving away from thermodynamic equilibrium may take the form of increasingly complicated chemical and physical structures, but a further antientropic movement requires that what has been already achieved is maintained, stored and built upon for further improvements. Therefore information and storages of information are so important. The great steps forward in evolution tool place, when the genes were developed, when the coordination among more cells to form organisms was developed and when learning processes became an integrated part of the species properties. Pathways with the ability to accelerate the exchange of information among them were formed.

The corresponding steps forward for mankind were
1) the development of a language (it became possible to convey experience in a much simpler fashion),
2) when writing was invented to facilitate the spreading of information further,
3) when printing was invented to multiply the distribution of information and
4) when the computer was invented to facilitate the storage of and the access to the entire pool of information.

It is noticeable that information creates exergy / negentropy and that through information the system will be able to move further away from the thermodynamic equilibrium. The more information the more pathways are available to increase exergy.

Information has (see also Sections 5.2, 5.5 and 6.2) a very low cost of energy. Developments of physical and chemical structures will increase the exergy, but how high an exergy level we are able to achieve is limited by energy and matter. Information does not have these limitations, because information can be multiplied almost infinitely, since it does not, or rather hardly consume energy and matter.

It is therefore not surprising that information has been used as the method of ecosystem and society to increase the level of exergy. Ecosystems by development of ever more species with an ever increasing ability made it possible to coordinate the functions of many cells, organs and organisms simultaneously.

This could be interpreted as the ecosystems' aim toward higher and higher complexity, but complexity may not be interchanged for information. A more complex ecosystem may be unable to cope with a given combination of forcing functions, which a simpler system can manage - for instance, a very eutrophic lake may have a simpler food web than an oligotrophic lake.

The crucial question in this context is not "which structure is most complex?", but "which structure gives the highest level of useful information storage?"

This is the third time in this volume that we meet the disaccord between complexity (diversity) and stability, which is consistent with ecological concepts of today.

On the other hand it is important to emphasize that the diversity / complexity / the gene pool is important for the ability to create new possibilities for moving further away from the thermodynamic equilibrium and attain higher buffer capacities for the ecosystem. Therefore it is of great importance that we maintain the existing gene pool and maintain natural ecosystems for developments of new genes.

The exergy principle has been presented as a tentative thermodynamic law, which may be used as a hypothesis in our effort to find a pattern for the presented ecosystem theories. It will be shown in Chapter 12 that it *is* possible to find such a pattern, and that there are relationships between the different theories. The presented tentative law or hypothesis fits furthermore nicely into basic concepts of the other thermodynamic laws. The first law states the limitations in all possible processes by the conservation principles. The second law makes further limitations by introduction of the entropy concept and states that it is only possible to realize processes moving toward a higher entropy level in an isolated system. The fourth or ecological law of thermodynamics asserts further limitations and indicates which processes are biologically feasible, namely those (among many possible ones), which give the highest exergy under the prevailing conditions and perturbations in their widest sense. It will require a through-flow of exergy to realize these processes and thereby to combat the entropy production according to the second law of thermodynamics. The applicability of the law is therefore of particular interest for ecosystems, as these systems are characterized by many possible pathways and a through-flow of exergy.

# 7. NETWORK AND HIERARCHICAL CONCEPTS OF ECOSYSTEMS

## 7.1. Networks in Ecology

This book is about recent developments and enrichments in ecosystem ecology and as the network concepts of ecology have contributed significantly to this part of ecology, inclusion of one or even more chapters on network theories is compulsory.

Ecosystems should be conceived as more than simply a collection of organisms, and more than energy - and mass flows, trophic webs and interacting populations. Ecosystems should be conceived as the full interactive network among coexisting living organisms and their non-biological physical-chemical environment (Higashi and Burns 1991).

One feature of life is that living matter comes in discrete packages called organisms, which are the nodes or junctions in the network, while the flows of energy, mass and information are represented by links between the nodes. Figure 3.2 illustrates the cycling of nitrogen in an aquatic ecosystem and is in principle a network. The state variables are the nodes or junctions, and the processes determine the flows between the state variables. In this modelling approach emphasis has been put on the dynamics of the state variables rather than on the properties of the entire ecological network, which may, however, be considered the core of network theory applied to ecology.

The network conceptualization of nature is widely used in science, for instance to understand blood circulation, nervous systems and transportation in vascular plants. The concepts of resistance, capacitance and inductance, known from electronics, which was perhaps the first discipline to use network thinking, have their counterpart in all dynamic systems that involve flows of mass, energy or information. The overall systematic structure provides a framework for formulating the solution to problems in a rigorously consistent and illuminating manner. Two interesting questions that we will pursue, are: "which properties does such a network have?" and "which properties can be foreseen for ecosystems, because they may be considered as networks?"

The network per se is not hierarchical, but in its application to reality a network model must specify the level to which it belongs. As pointed out by Allen and O'Neill (1991), the network perspectives inherently involve hierarchy and it is indeed possible and useful to explicitly link these two perspectives. The hierarchical concepts of ecosystems are therefore included in this chapter after presentation of the more basal network theory, while Chapter 8 is devoted to further implications of network theory such as indirect effects, utility theory and ascendency.

Network thermodynamics is a relatively new field that uses both classical and non-equilibrium thermodynamics and kinetics in conjunction with graph/network theory. The aim is to provide a unified analysis of highly structured systems as ecosystems and thereby to attempt to reveal underlying properties of the ecological networks. Thermodynamics is, as presented in Chapters 4 and 5, a very useful holistic approach to ecosystem theory. A unification of network - and thermodynamic theories should inevitably lead to new principles in ecosystem theory. Recent results in network thermodynamics are therefore presented in the last section of this chapter.

The network approaches give information on flows and storage and are up to now mainly used in a steady state situation, although there are exceptions. As many of the network computations in static models are rather complex already, the dynamic approach has been omitted in several of the presented network theories; for instance the indirect effects. This must be considered a disadvantage in the interpretation of the results, as the variations and fluctuations in the forcing functions often are of great significance for the response of the ecosystem; see for instance Chapter 4, Section 4.


## 7.2 Network Concepts


Figure 7.1 shows a static five-compartment network model of nitrogen flow in a Puerto Rican tropical rain forest. This model will be used to show the basic concepts of network theory and the related input/output computations.

The dynamics of the state variables can be described by the use of the following equations:

$$d\,x_i/dt = \sum_{\substack{j=0 \\ j \neq i}}^{n} f_{ij}(t) - \sum_{\substack{j=0 \\ j \neq i}}^{n} f_{ji}(t) = z_i + \sum_{\substack{j=1 \\ j \neq i}}^{n} f_{ij}(t) - \sum_{\substack{j=1 \\ j \neq i}}^{n} f_{ji}(t) - y_i \quad i = 1,2..., \quad (7.1.)$$

where $x_i$ represents the storage, i.e., the state variables, while $f_{ij}$ represents flow from compartment j to i and $f_{ji}$ from i to j. The environment of the system is denoted by subscript 0 and $f_{io}$ is named $z_i$, while $f_{oi}$ may be replaced by $y_i$.

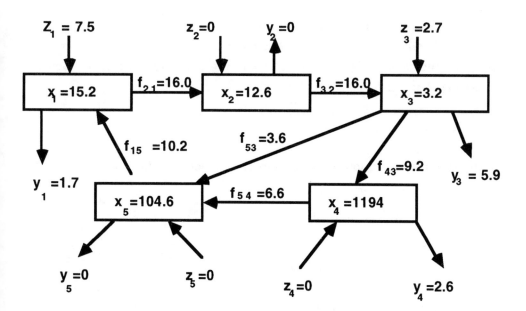

**Fig. 7.1.** Static model of nitrogen flow in a tropical rain forest. Storages, state variables, are $x_i$, i = 1, 2, 3, ....5, are in units of g N m$^{-2}$ and flows are in g N m$^{-2}$ y$^{-1}$. The compartments are 1: leaves and epiphyllae, 2: loose litter, 3: fibrous roots, 4: soil and 5: wood. $z_1$ represents nitrogen dissolved in rainwater and fixation of atmospheric nitrogen by epiphyllous complex, $z_3$ is nitrogen fixation by algae and bacteria associated with fibrous roots. The outputs are: $y_1$ nitrogen release by denitrification, $y_3$ denitrification and run-off associated with fibrous roots and $y_4$ denitrification and run-off associated with soil.

It is possible to set up a linear model by formulating each flow in equation (7.1) as a fraction of its donor compartment:

$$d\,x_i/dt = \sum_{\substack{j=1 \\ j \neq i}}^{n} a''_{ij}(t) * x_j + z_i - \sum_{\substack{j=0 \\ j \neq i}}^{n} a''_{ji}(t) * x_i \,, \tag{7.2.}$$

where a expresses the flows relatively to the donor compartment.

Another linear model can be set up by formulating each flow as a fraction of its recipient compartment:

$$d\,x_i/dt = \sum_{\substack{j=0 \\ j \neq i}}^{n} a'_{ij}(t) * x_i - \sum_{\substack{j=1 \\ j \neq i}}^{n} a''_{ji}(t) * x_j - y_i \,, \tag{7.3.}$$

where a' expresses the flows relatively to the recipient compartment.

These equations are in a static situation (d $x_i$/dt = 0) written in matrix notation in Table 7.1. The model in Fig. 7.1 is presented in Table 7.2 by the use of the equations in (7.2) and (7.3) and in Table 7.1.

**Table 7.1.**

**Matrix notation of equations (7.2) and (7.3) when d $x_i$/dt = $\dot{x}_i$ = 0**

$$\dot{X} = 0 = A'' . x^* + z$$

$$\dot{X} = 0 = - A' . x^* - y = A' . x^* + y$$

where

$$x^* = \begin{pmatrix} x_1 \\ \vdots \\ x_n \end{pmatrix}, \quad \dot{x} = \begin{pmatrix} \dot{x}_1 \\ \vdots \\ \dot{x}_n \end{pmatrix}, \quad z = \begin{pmatrix} z_1 \\ \vdots \\ z_n \end{pmatrix}, \quad y = \begin{pmatrix} y_1 \\ \vdots \\ y_n \end{pmatrix},$$

$$A'' = \begin{pmatrix} a''_{11} & \cdots & a''_{1n} \\ \vdots & & \vdots \\ a''_{11} & \cdots & a''_{nn} \end{pmatrix}, \quad A' = \begin{pmatrix} a'_{11} & \cdots & a'_{1n} \\ \vdots & & \vdots \\ a'_{11} & \cdots & a'_{nn} \end{pmatrix},$$

$$x^* = -\left(A''\right)^{-1} \cdot z$$

$$x^* = -\left(A'\right)^{-1} \cdot y$$

The pattern of interconnections among state variables in a network can be described with an adjacency matrix. If there is a direct link i -j the element $A_{ij}$ = 1, and if no direct link exists $A_{ij}$ = 0. The direct connectivity of a network is the number of ones in the adjacency matrix divided by n, the number of rows or columns.

**Table 7.2.**

**Matrix representation of the model Fig. 7.1.**

$$\mathbf{A''} = \begin{pmatrix} -1.16447 & 0 & 0 & 0 & .09751 \\ 1.05263 & -1.26984 & 0 & 0 & 0 \\ 0 & 1.26984 & -5.84375 & 0 & 0 \\ 0 & 0 & 2.87500 & -.00771 & 0 \\ 0 & 0 & 1.12500 & .00553 & -.09751 \end{pmatrix}$$

$$\mathbf{A'} = \begin{pmatrix} -1.16447 & 1.26984 & 0 & 0 & 0 \\ 0 & -1.26984 & 5.00000 & 0 & 0 \\ 0 & 0 & -5.84375 & .00771 & .03441 \\ 0 & 0 & 0 & -.00771 & .06310 \\ 0.67105 & 0 & 0 & 0 & -.09751 \end{pmatrix}$$

$$-(\mathbf{A''})^{-1} = \begin{pmatrix} 1.69 & 0.92 & 0.92 & 1.21 & 1.69 \\ 1.40 & 1.55 & 0.77 & 1.01 & 1.40 \\ 0.31 & 0.34 & 0.34 & 0.22 & 0.31 \\ 113.86 & 125.95 & 125.95 & 241.46 & 113.86 \\ 9.97 & 11.03 & 11.03 & 14.51 & 20.23 \end{pmatrix}$$

$$-(\mathbf{A'})^{-1} = \begin{pmatrix} 1.69 & 1.69 & 1.45 & 1.45 & 1.45 \\ 0.77 & 1.55 & 1.33 & 1.33 & 1.33 \\ 0.19 & 0.19 & 0.34 & 0.34 & 0.34 \\ 95.46 & 95.46 & 81.68 & 211.46 & 165.66 \\ 11.66 & 11.66 & 9.97 & 9.97 & 20.23 \end{pmatrix}$$

Multi-length links of order k can be studied by looking at the elements of the matrix $A^k$. The recycling measure, c, introduced by Bosserman (1980 and 1982), is the number of ones in the first n matrices of the power series divided by $n^2$, which is equal to the number of possible ones. The recycling measure, c, will therefore vary between 0 and 1, when there are no paths or when all paths are realized, respectively. Halfon (1983) uses c as an index of connectivity and as a criteria for selection of the model structure. Halfon found that a marked change in c is often seen at a certain stage, when adding more links. Figure 7.2 shows a typical relationship between the number of links, n, (including links to the environment) in a network, the direct connectivity, d, and c, (recycling index or measure), and, as seen in this case, c increases significantly at n = 10 and d = approximately 0.3.

Halfon concluded that the network with a number of links corresponding to the marked increase in c, was the minimum and also the approximate right complexity which should be selected for the purpose of modelling the ecosystem under consideration, as the last link (from n = 10 to n= 11) in this case was significant for the recycling of mass or energy. On the other hand a further increase in complexity above n = 11 hardly adds to the description from a recycling point of view at least, because c is only increased slightly from n= 11 to n=12, to n=13 and so on.

General modelling experience supports Halfon's approach, as models can easily become too complex; see Section 3.5. The observations referred to are furthermore consistent with the stability criteria in equation (2.1); see Section 2.2.

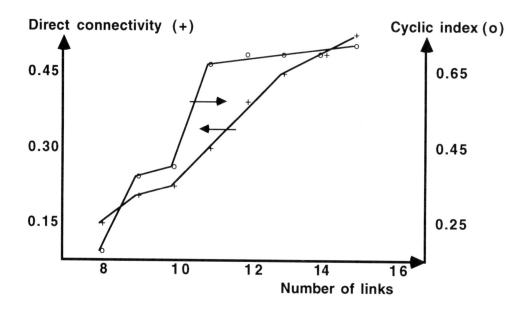

**Fig. 7.2.** d (direct connectivity) and c (cyclic index) are plotted versus the number of links, n.

These observations are furthermore consistent with MacArthur (1971), who argues that stable systems have an intermediate level of connectance, which may be expressed numerically by the use of the concept connectivity; see the definition above. The breakdown of organizational structure, which shows instability, indicates that the system is either underconnected or overconnected. It is on the other hand of crucial importance for ecosystems that they have sufficient connectivity to allow the elements to cycle.

The type of change due to underconnectance is referred to in Paine (1974 and 1980). Many cases of predator removal from the system show this instability. Prey populations begin to grow rapidly and over-exploit their food supply. Allen and Starr (1982) provide a number of examples on how underconnectance leads to instability.

At the other extreme, the system may become unstable due to too high connectance. This is demonstrated by Gardner and Ashby (1970); see also Section 2.2. They showed that increasing the number of direct connections would decrease the probability that the system would remain stable. MacArthur (1972) considered two prey species populations in competition and showed that larger competition and predation terms increase the probability that one of the two prey populations would be driven to extinction;; Levin (1974) demonstrated that the more connections there are in a system, the greater the chance that a positive feedback will emerge and destroy the present organization of the system.

O' Neill et al. (1986) concluded that, because there are two ways that a system can become unstable - either by being overconnected or underconnected -, the addition of a new component can have opposite effects depending on the circumstances. An increase in diversity can stabilize the system either by adding connected components to an underconnected system or by adding disconnected components to an overconnected system. Conversely, increased diversity can decrease stability either by adding a highly connected component to an overconnected system or by adding a disconnected or weakly connected component to an underconnected system.

The conclusion seems to be that it is connectance of the system that plays a role in the complexity-stability relationship rather than the number of components, which is to a certain extent consistent with the earlier insights into system organization; see for instance E.P. Odum (1953) and MacArthur (1955).

The hierarchical theory, which is presented in the next section, Section 7.3, is able to give suggestions on how these observations can be explained in an organizational context.

## 7.3. Hierarchical Theory of Ecosystems

The hierarchical theory has been developed in the context of general systems theory; see for instance Simon (1962,1969 and 1973), Pattee (1969 and 1972), Mesarovic et al. (1970), Allen and Starr (1982) and O'Neill et al. (1986).

The ecological applications are presented by Patten (1978, 1982 and 1985) and Overton (1972 and 1974).

Medium-number systems (see Section 2.2) operate under a very wide range of rates, which causes great difficulties in modelling these systems. However, in most cases the rates can be grouped into classes and if the classes are sufficiently distinct, then the system can be considered as a hierarchical system and dealt with as a small number system. The structure of ecosystems imposed by differences in rates is sufficient to decompose a very complex system into organizational levels and discrete components within each level (Overton, 1974).

Within an organizational level, a hierarchical system may be further decomposed into subsystems or holons (Koestler, 1967 and 1969), based on differences in rates. The theory assumes that components interact strongly within each holon, but only weakly with components of other holons. Each holon should be defined in terms of the boundary that encloses its components and separates them from other components of the system (Allen et al., 1984). The boundary may be visible as the skin of an organism or the shoreline of a lake, or intangible in the case of for instance populations and species. The rates inside the boundary characterize the interactions among components and are relatively rapid and uniform, while rates outside the boundary characterize interactions among holons and are relatively slow and weak.

The possible spectrum of ecological dynamics is illustrated in Figure 7.3. The interactions between biological components occur at many scales, a dilemma that the hierarchical theory can easily resolve. The scale of observation determines the organizational level (O'Neill et al., 1986). Higher-level behaviors occur slowly and appear in the descriptions as constants, while lower-level behaviors occur rapidly and appear as averages or steady state properties in the description - compare  Fig. 7.4. For instance, analyses of annual tree growth need not consider instantaneous changes in stomata's openings, nor long term changes in regional climate.

From a hierarchical perspective the definition of the system depends on the window (O' Neill et al., 1986), through which the world is viewed. If one is looking at the effects of nutrients in a five minute pulse of rain, the relevant components are leaves, litter surface, fungi and fine roots, but if the study is concerned with long-term climatic changes, the relevant components may be large pools of organic matter,  such as the rain forests or the development in agriculture.

It is important to realize that the entities of ecosystems form networks of selective interactions. Possibilities at each level of identification are limited by the variants produced in lower-level processes and constrained by the selective environment of higher levels,; see Fig. 7.4.

An ecological system may also be decomposed on the basis of spatial discontinuities. The hierarchies of space and time share many properties. For example, the spatial hierarchy as the temporal one is nested in the higher level, because the higher level is composed of the lower level; compare Fig. 7.4.

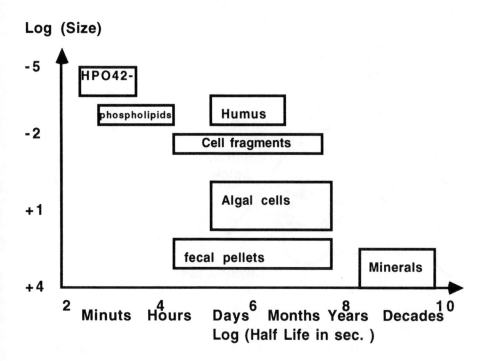

**Fig. 7.3.** The relationship between time and space in a plankton ecosystem (Scavia 1980).

The real advantage of hierarchy theory is that it offers an approach to the medium number systems, which takes advantage of their organized complexity (O'Neill et al. 1986). Ecosystems are very complex systems and we have to decompose them to be able to analyze their behavior, understand their underlying principles, model them for predictive purposes and so on. The hierarchy theory approaches this problem by searching for a structure that is already there; either it is a rate or a spatial structure.

As mentioned in Section 7.2, hierarchy theory is also concerned with the complexity-stability relationship. Hierarchy theory suggests that in a stable system, direct and symmetric connections should be isolated in well-defined holons.

Interactions between components of different holons are rare and thereby the number of strong connections is kept relatively low in spite of the high number of components.

209

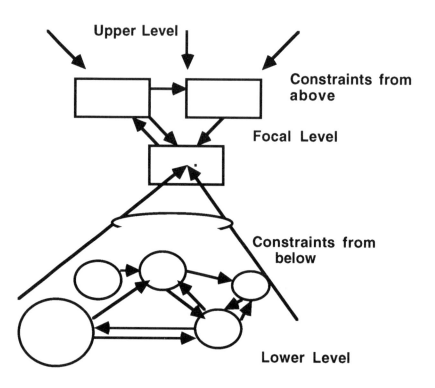

**Fig. 7.4.** A hierarchical network conception of ecological systems. The focal level is assumed to be modelled. The constraints from the upper level occur slowly and are taken into account as constants, while the constraint from the lower levels occur rapidly and are accounted for as averages.

If, for instance, a multi-species community is considered the hierarchy will be arranged with weak interactions among holons of strongly interacting species. Many studies show that very complex systems need not be unstable, if it is organized in this manner (May, 1972 and 1974, and Mc Murtrie, 1975).

De Angelis (1975) has carried out studies on Lyapunov stability and connectance (number of connections). He considered a food web with three trophic levels and ten species and asked what conditions would reverse previous results and favor an increase in stability with increasing connectance. He found that stability would increase in three cases:

1) The consumers were inefficient.

2) The higher trophic levels experience a strong self-dampening force that controls their population growth.

3) There is a bias toward donor dependence in the interactions.

Other studies have emphasized the importance of feedback loops for stability. It is possible (May, 1973) to show that there are limitations on the feedback loops, if the Lyapunov stability criteria should be satisfied. These feedback criteria place certain restrictions on the shape of the food web. The criteria are satisfied by the network in Fig. 7.5, but not for that in Fig. 7.6, which has loops of length greater than two. These results relate to the previously presented influence of overconnection on stability; see Section 7.2.

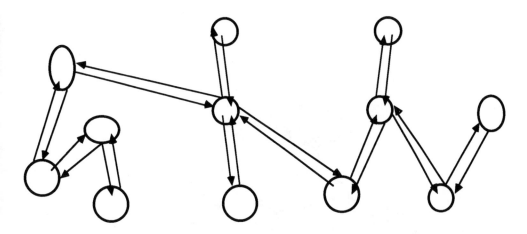

**Fig. 7.5.** A branched - chain structure is shown. It is defined as a structure composed by mutually connected species connected by line segments in a branched-chain form without forming loops.

It would provide great simplifications if all ecological systems were structured in branched-chain forms; see Fig. 7.5. However, we do know that cycling is an important feature of ecosystem functions. Tansky (1978) has attempted to generalize the criteria, to the cases in which loop structure groups exist. The total system may be stable if the overall structure is a branched chain with loop structure groups as points.

Tansky showed that the overall system is insensitive to the fine structure at lower level in the hierarchy as long as that fine structure is contained within a loop structure group; see Figure 7.6. However, these studies have probably not sufficiently considered the need for cycling from a nutrient balance point of view, which must be conceived as a more basic property; see Section 4.1.

There is considerable evidence that food webs are compartmentalized into tightly interacting subsystems with a few species. O'Neill et al. (1986) refer to several of these empirical evidences.

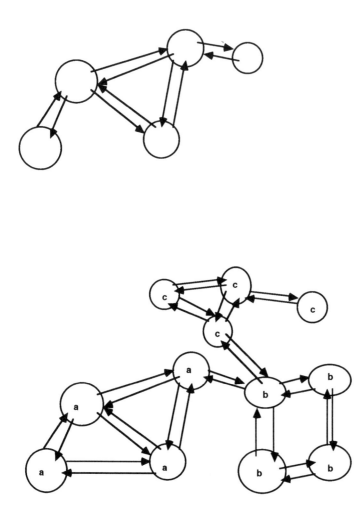

**Fig. 7.6.** The upper figure shows a looped structure that contains feed back loops of length greater than two. The lower figure illustrates an interactive structure in a complex food web. The species interactions can be grouped into a loop structure group (Tansky 1978). Notice that all feedback loops of steps greater than two are isolated within the loop structure group.

The results of multivariant analysis carried out by Allen and Koonce (1973) on phytoplankton data are presented in this context, because they illustrate clearly how species tend to be aggregated into distinct subsystems based upon their physiological characteristics, and how every ecological niche is utilized. Tolerance for low-temperature and needs for high-nutrient concentrations define an early-spring group, while preference for higher-temperature and tolerance for low-nutrient concentrations define a late-summer group. Within the groups there are strong competitive interacti-

# Intertidal algal community

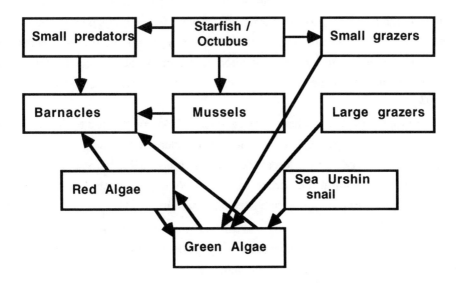

**Fig. 7.7.** Conceptual diagram of the intertidal algal community study by Sousa (1979). Experimental removal of any species in this system resulted in marked changes in the green algal component and in the entire community.

ons and in some years some species will not appear at all. Although there is a certain but small overlap, the seasonal separation results in weak interactions between the two groups.

Figure 7.7 represents an intertidal algal community studied by Sousa (1979), who introduced experimental manipulations of the system. Removal of any one species resulted in marked change in the dynamics of *Ulva* - a green alga - and in the entire community. Murdoch (1979) interpreted these observations as difficulties to sort out subsystems, that are independent on strong interactions outside the subsystem. Paine (1980) on the other hand asserted that strong interactions can encourage the development of subsystems.

Pimm (1980 and 1982) and Pimm and Lawton (1980) have examined several food webs from the ecological literature to determine if compartmentalization exists to a statistically significant degree. They found that partial separation into modules is common; for instance, grazing and detrital chains are often somewhat separated.

It can be concluded from the ecological literature that food webs tend to have internal organization and that species tend to group into subsystems or modules.

The results are a hierarchical structure that enhances the stability according to both analytical and modelling studies.

A perturbation comes from the environment of the system and should therefore be uncontrolled, when viewed from the components of the system. However, as pointed out by Odling-Smee and Patten (1992), the phenotype has at least in some cases the possibilities to modify its environment and thereby influence the selection pressure on the phenotype itself - see also Section 2.2, where some examples are presented.

The rate of carbon fixation is dependent on and constrained by factors such as temperature, light and wind. The short-term fluctuations are outside the control of the trees. If, however, trees form a forest stand, the stand is able to dampen the fluctuations of all tree factors, so that the carbon fixation is no longer affected by the short-term fluctuations in environmental variables; compare Larsen (1922), who found that air temperature under a closed canopy was $10°$ C higher at night and $10°$ C cooler by day than the same area following clear-cutting. By grouping trees a new organization level has emerged and the perturbation has been incorporated.

Perturbations may also be passively incorporated in a spatial framework. Only systems that are large relative to their perturbations maintain a relatively constant structure (Shugart and West, 1981). Figure 7.8 shows the average size of perturbations affecting a variety of ecosystems. For instance the Caribbean Islands are small compared to hurricanes and cannot avoid being constrained by these events. On the other hand, the Appalachian Forests are large compared to the average wildfire and are relatively constant in composition over time.

There are several examples on how fire may be incorporated passively by ecosystems (Mooney et al., 1981). Extensive forests in Western United States, for example are distributed across a very broad and diverse landscape and as some portions of the landscape are not destroyed by a fire, recovery of the entire system can take place.

Section 1.5 touches on the two views of ecosystems: the population ecological view emphasizing individuals organized into populations, guilds and communities and the process-functional view emphasizing productivity, nutrient cycling and other processes. Hierarchy theory provides a framework for understanding the relationship between the two view points, without ranking one area of emphasis higher than the other. Although it is possible to imagine observations where only one of the two views plays a dominant role and may be isolated, constraints from both dimensions are most likely to play a role in most real cases, simply because the function is embodied in the species and all species have a certain function in an ecosystem and are initiators of

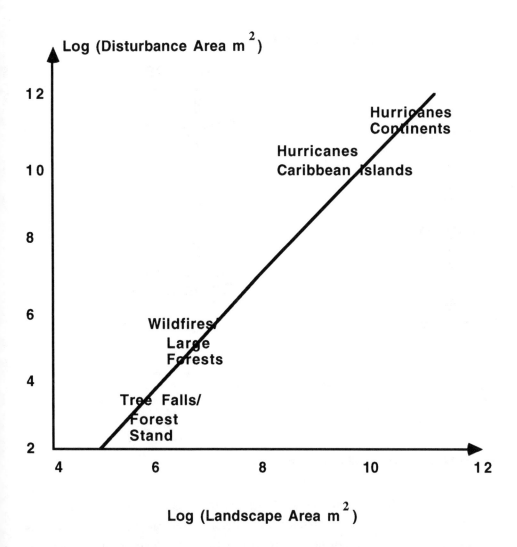

**Fig 7.8.** Size of landscape area is plotted versus size of disturbance. Above the diagonal are disequilibrium systems such as the Caribbean` Islands, which are the same size as or smaller than hurricanes - their characteristic perturbations. Below the line are more constant systems, that are relatively large to their perturbations. Reproduced from Shugart and West (1981).

processes. O Neill et al. (1986) assert therefore that the two views are nicely covered by the use of a dual hierarchy; see Fig. 7.9, and they discuss how the two constraint systems may interdigitate. They assume that the constraints alternate; for instance when the diatoms evolved a silicaceous shell, they freed themselves from a biotic constraint, the predation, but got a new constraint: the mass balance limitation of silica in the sea water.

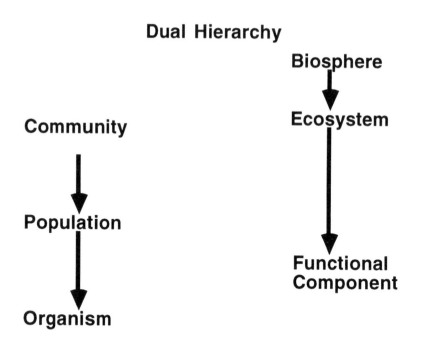

**Dual Hierarchy**

Biosphere

Ecosystem

Community

Population

Functional
Component

Organism

**Fig. 7.9.** The dual hierarchy proposed by O'Neill et al. (1986).

## 7.4. Network Thermodynamics

Network thermodynamics uses all that we know about simple systems and combines it with topology, mainly through graph theory.` Network thermodynamics has been applied to achieve more holistic representations for instance by studies of transport into cells and subsequent metabolism (May and Mikulecky, 1983, and Huf and Mikulecky, 1986) and by the studies of sites of action of hormones (Fidelman and Mikulecky, 1986).

Tellegen (1952) was the first to show that the holistic description of systems resulted in very powerful relations between the flows and forces. Tellegen's theorem is a simple one and was already presented and applied in Section 4.2:

$$J * X = 0 \qquad (7.4)$$

where $J$ is the flow vector and $X$ the force vector. It means that:

$$J_1 * X_1 + J_2 * X_2 + ...J_n * X_n = 0 \qquad (7.5)$$

These equations may be applied on ecological network by use of the following relations (Mikulecky 1991):

$$\text{Flow} = \text{constant} * \text{node concentration on feed side} \qquad (7.7)$$

$$\text{Resistance} = (\text{feed side node value - receiver side node value}) / \text{flow}$$
$$= \Delta \text{ concentration} / \text{flow} \qquad (7.7)$$

$$\text{Conductance} = \text{flow} / \text{feed side node value} \qquad (7.8)$$

Aoki (1987, 1988, 1989 and 1992) has developed network calculations of ecological systems using entropy and exergy and shown how such basic calculations can lead to new conclusions about ecological systems. He applies equations (7.1 - 7.3) on entropy flows and storages, and uses furthermore the concept that the entropy production is non-negative according to the second law of thermodynamics (see, for instance, Nicolis and Prigogine, 1977). The exergy calculations follow the same pattern, using the equations in Section 7.4, to calculate the contributions from each compartment.

Aoki (1988 and 1989) found that an ecological network has the following properties with respect to entropy and exergy flows:

**1. The flow through a compartment and the total system through-flow of entropy and exergy for irreversible processes are always larger than those for reversible processes.** This is of course not surprising when we have the second law of thermodynamic in mind, and may be considered a network version of the second law of thermodynamics.

**2. Irreversibility - activity of the system induces an increase of the flow through a compartment and the total system through-flow of entropy and of exergy.** It may be translated into more ecological concepts: increased activity increased for instance the grazing rate of zooplankton. High food concentration or high concentration gradient (big appetite) will simultaneously increase entropy production and exergy flow. Increased exergy means that the system is moving further away from the thermodynamic equilibrium. This means that the system is getting a higher order or level of information; but it will be at the cost of higher entropy production; see also

Section 5.7. Aoki shows, in other words, that when the developmental process of an ecosystem, meaning the exergy, is increased, an increase in entropy production also takes place. It is shown in Table 4.5, Section 4.2, however, that an ecosystem develops toward bigger organisms which will require less entropy production for the same biomass. The development may lead to a system, which is better able to economize with the exergy by producing less entropy for maintenance per *unit* of biomass, but this development costs entropy production and the *total* entropy production will increase. It is completely consistent with Kay and Schneider's theory, presented in Section 5.7. Aoki's results support a strong relation between the theory of maximum dissipation of energy or exergy and the theory of development toward a higher exergy level.

## 3. Entropy path lengths and entropy cycling index for irreversible processes are dependent on the ecological networks under consideration.

Aoki has also found entropy production and change in total entropy for total ecosystems. The monthly entropy fluxes associated with direct, diffused and reflected solar radiation was calculated for lake ecosystems from the corresponding energy data. Furthermore, the entropy fluxes associated with infrared radiation, evaporation and sensible heat are estimated. The change of entropy content is computed from the change of heat storage and the mean temperature of the lake. From net entropy flow and the change of entropy content the entropy production is calculated.

These calculations show that the net entropy flow into a lake system is negative, which means that a lake absorbs negentropy (and exergy) from its surroundings. A lake, Aoki concludes, can be regarded as a superorganism that has ordered structures and functions, which is completely according to Chapter 5.

The entropy production in Lake Mendota is shown in Fig. 7.10. As seen, the entropy production follows the seasonal variations in solar radiation and as shown in Fig. 7.11, the entropy production and the solar radiation are highly correlated (the correlation coefficient was found to be 0.997).

Aoki has compared the entropy production for different lakes by use of the following expression, relating entropy production, S-prod to solar radiation R-solar (see Fig. 7.11.):

$$S\text{-prod} = a + b^* \, R\text{-solar} \qquad\qquad (7.9)$$

Aoki found that a and b reflect the level of eutrophication, i.e., the level of productivity. Table 7.3 gives the comparison between the more eutrophic Lake Mendo-

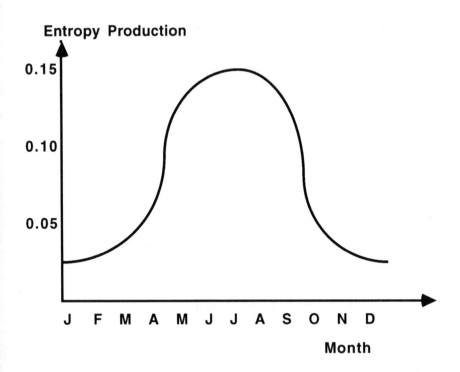

**Fig. 7.10.** The seasonal variations of entropy production (MJ m$^{-3}$ month$^{-1}$ K$^{-1}$) in Lake Mendota.

ta and the oligo-mesotrophic Northern Lake Biwa. Exergy would follow the same trends, as the more productive Lake Mendota, due to the higher concentration of nutrients, is able to construct more biomass and thereby move further away from the thermodynamic equilibrium; compare also Sections 6.4, 8.4 (Table 8.3), and 11.2.

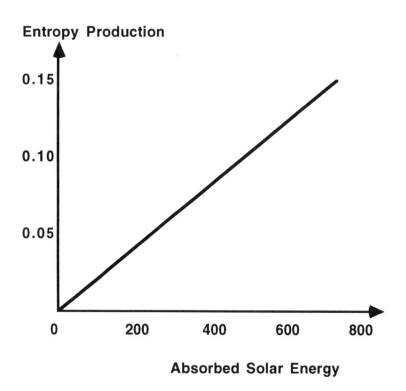

**Fig. 7.11.** Monthly entropy production (MJ m$^{-3}$ month$^{-1}$ K$^{-1}$) is plotted versus the monthly solar energy absorbed by the lake surface. The correlation coefficient for the relationship is 0.997.

**Table 7.3.**

### Comparison of S-prod and E-solar correlations.

| Lake | Total P mg/l | Status | a | b |
|------|--------------|--------|---|---|
| Northern Biwa | 0.01 | oligo-mesotrophic | 0.002 | 0.7 |
| Mendota | 0.14 | eutrophic | 0.007 | 2.3 |

a in units of MJ m$^{-3}$ month$^{-1}$ K$^{-1}$ , b in $10^{-4}$ m$^{-1}$ K$^{-1}$.

# 8. UTILITY THEORY, INDIRECT EFFECT AND ASCENDENCY

## 8.1 Toward a wider Application of Network Theory

The application of networks to describe ecosystems provides means of exploring the interactions among the components and the flows of mass, energy and/or information. The application of the network representation makes it possible to survey the total system in its entity and thereby to observe how the various parts of the system may be influenced by changes in inputs and outputs; see Section 7.1. The obvious next step would, however, be to examine what properties a system, organized in a typical network, possesses. It was for instance mentioned in Section 7.3 (see Figure 7.8), that the removal of any component in this network would radically change the green algae's component and the entire system. This example demonstrates that the components are influencing each other far more than just by the direct link between two adjacent components. Any change in the system will propagate to all components of the network and the network gives information about the pathways that the propagation will follow.

Such considerations lead us to three very obvious questions, which we would like to answer by the use of the network approach. Figure 8.1 demonstrates a network in steady state. It is an intertidal oyster reef compartment model, taken from Patten (1985a). The example has been used in numerous network studies and it is therefore obvious that it is used in this context as well. The questions are presented in detail below and the answers to each of the three questions form the following three sections of this chapter.

**The first question relates to the utilization of the mass and/or energy in the network.** The deposit feeders in Fig. 8.1 have inputs of 0.6609 + 1.2060 + 0.6431 = totally 2.5100 and use 0.4303 for respiration (output to the environment), while the remaining 2.0797 is reused in the system, namely 0.1721 by predators and 1.9076 becomes detritus. It implies that 2.0797*100/2.51 = 82.86 % is reused by the system and is eventually is comes back again to the deposit feeders. These considerations lead to the obvious questions: "by which efficiency is the ecosystem able to utilize the energy?" and "how many times will the energy cycle in the system, before it finally dissipates to the environment as heat?" These questions can be answered by use of a mathematical analysis of networks, and the answer can be found in Patten (1985), Patten et al. (1989 and 1990), Higashi and Patten (1986 and 1989) and Higashi et al. (1989 and 1991).

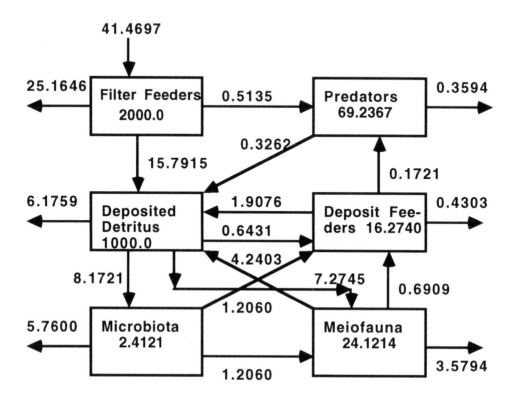

**Fig. 8.1.** Compartmental model of an intertidal oyster reef. Numbers within compartments (state variables) indicate steady-state standing crop energy storages (kcal $m^{-2}$) and those associated with arrows give the energy flows (kcal $m^{-2} d^{-1}$).

**The second question focuses on the role of indirect effects relative to the direct one.** We distinguish between direct effects, where the cause and its effects are adjacent and indirect effects, where the cause and its effects are separated.

From the example in Figure 8.1 referred to above, it is obvious that the effect resulting from the propagation through the network is significant and that any transfer of energy propagates and cycles around many times in the network, before it is finally damped and dissipated as heat to the environment. So, it is not surprising that rather complex calculations are needed to express the role of the indirect effect.

The two questions raised above show clearly that everything is linked to everything in a network and it is therefore important to try to find relationships between the network and its linkage properties, i.e., how firm is the linkage between two non-adjacent components?

The third question concerns the development of a network and a total measure or index for the efficiency of a network. Ulanowicz (1983, 1986, 1989 and 1991) has proposed a measure or index which accounts for size as well as for organization in ecological networks. It is named ascendency. A rise in ascendency therefore represents an increase in system size or organization. It is therefore a measure for growth and development, and a comparison of the ascendency of two different systems tells us which one has the highest efficiency. We may go one step further and use calculations of the ascendency to point the direction of development for the network of the entire ecosystem and possibly indicate which network will be selected among some or many possible networks.

Chapters 4, 5 and 6 present a thermodynamic viewpoint on ecosystems. Several concepts to account for development of ecosystems were defined. How do these thermodynamic concepts fit into the network theoretical approach? Or which of the two approaches should we use? The answer is already given in Section 2.3: an ecosystem is such a complex system that a pluralistic view is needed to cover all possible aspects of an ecosystem and thereby to capture a complete picture of it. We therefore urgently need both viewpoints and they will both contribute to a more comprehensive ecosystem theory. Consequently, a comparison of the results by application of the various approaches would be an interesting exercise to perform. A comparison with the thermodynamic concepts, see Chapters 4, 5 and 6, is therefore included in the presentation of the indirect effects and of ascendency, see furthermore Chapter 12.

## 8.2. Energy Transfer and Utilization Coefficients in Networks

Lindeman (1942) was the first to take an ecosystem approach to trophic interactions and energy transfer. He used Hutchinson's (1941) notion of progressive efficiency of energy transfer between trophic levels as an index of ecosystem's function. Lindeman reduced the ecosystem to a single simple food chain of 4-5 trophic levels connected in series by a one-way flow of energy, see the model representation in Fig. 8.2. This led to a dilemma between two tendencies, which he identified in his data:

1) Increasing progressive efficiencies :

$$E_2/E_1 \; < \; E_3/E_2 \; < ..........$$ (8.1)

2) Increasing respiration-loss ratio:

$$R_1/E_1 \; < \; R_2/E_2 \; < ..........$$ (8.2)

where $R_k$ represents the respiration rate and $E_k$ represents the gross production at the $k$ th trophic level.

These two factual relations are a logical contradiction in the single food-chain model which neglects feedbacks through detrital decomposer compartments and jump-forward flows. Several ecosystem studies have demonstrated the significance of these processes; see for instance Pomeroy (1974 and 1985), Kerfoot and DeMott (1984) and Coleman (1985).

The progressive efficiencies, equation (8.1), may be considered transfer coefficients. However, to evaluate the transfer coefficients for general food networks, we must account for *all* paths from one compartment to another, that do not contain cycles including the latter compartment; see Ulanowicz (1983 and 1986).

If $T_i$ denotes the total flow through a compartment, we get the following expression by the use of the symbols presented in Section 7.2:

$$T_i = \sum_{j=1}^{n} f_{ij} + z_i = \sum_{j=1}^{n} f_{ji} + y_j$$ (8.3)

For any path $\pi$ connecting any two compartment j and i, let $g(\pi)$ denote the product of donor-normalized flows, $g_{kh} = f_{kh}/T_h$ associated with the path $\pi$; for instance, if path $\pi$ is represented by the path j to k to h to i, then:

$$g(\pi) = g_{ih} * g_{hk} * g_{kj} = (f_{ih}/T_h) * (f_{hk}/T_k) * (f_{kj}/T_j)$$ (8.4)

For any path $\pi$ connecting j to i, $g(\pi)$ clearly represents the fraction of $T_j$ that will follow path $\pi$ to i. Thus, the transfer coefficient from j to i, i.e., the fraction of $T_j$ that is transferred to i, is given by $\sum g(\pi)$, where the summation is taken over the entire parallel path $\pi$ from j to i, which are the paths that do not contain cycling including i.

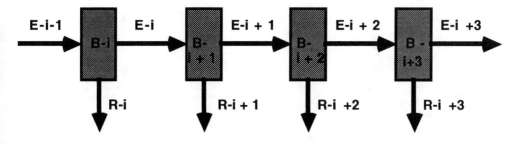

**Fig. 8.2.** The single chain model used by Lindeman (1942) as the theoretical basis for ecosystem trophic dynamics. Compartments are assigned entirely to trophic levels. The symbols are explained in the text.

Patten (1985), Patten et al. (1989), Higashi et al. (1989) and Higashi et al. (1991) have in addition to the transfer coefficient defined a utilization coefficient, which considers *all* paths *including* recycling paths. The utilization coefficient of consumer i with respect to resource $T_j$ is then given by the summation $\Sigma$ g($\pi$) over all paths $\pi$. It may be shown that while the transfer coefficients of course always lie between 0 and 1, utilization coefficients, defined as above, can exceed 1 and may also increase with trophic level along a food chain in the network. This introduction of utility coefficients is in accordance with Ulanowicz and Puccia (1990).

It is clear from the simple computations given in Section 8.1 related to Fig. 8.1 that the deposit feeders in this network will have a utilization coefficient which will even exceed 2, as about 83% of the energy flow to this compartment will come a second time and 0.83*83% = about 69% will even come a third time and 0.83*69% = about 57% will even come a fourth time and so on. The utilization coefficient is seen to account for all the cycled energy *relatively* to only the first input, and a utilization coefficient above 1 does therefore not violate the first law of thermodynamics. If all inputs, including all the cycled energy, are accounted for, the utilization can, of course, not exceed 100%. It implies that the utilization coefficient is a measure for the cycling of energy rather than the utilization of energy as such by particular component in the network.

The application of a more complex food web represented by a network (see for instance Fig. 8.1), implies that an organism may belong to more than one trophic level (Cummins et al., 1966, Riley, 1966 and E.P. Odum, 1968). Higashi et al. (1989) use network unfolding to clarify this question.

Figure 8.3 illustrates two hypothetical food webs and Figure 8.4 shows how the unfolding is able to identify the partitioning along the trophic level axis.

225

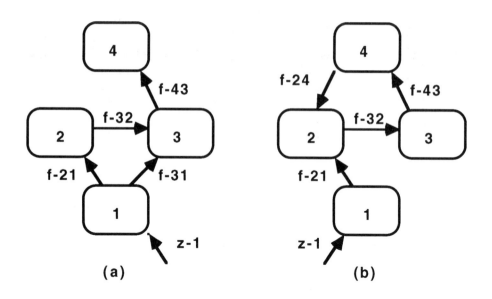

**Fig. 8.3.** Two hypothetical food webs. The unfoldings of these two webs are shown in Fig. 8.4.

The network resulting from unfolding any network is not cyclic but includes the original cycles, because all paths always run toward higher trophic levels. It means that the classical notation by Lindeman (1942) and Hutchinson (1941) is applied in principle.

Figure 8.6 shows a construction of a single macro trophic chain from the trophic network in Fig. 8.5.

The trophic level components $f_{ij}(k)$, $y_j(k)$, $T_j(k)$ and $x_j(k)$, for $k = 1, 2, 3....$defined above or in Section 7.2, correspond to a macro chain based upon gross production rates $E_k$, respiration rates $R_k$, and standing stocks $B_k$, on trophic levels $k = 1, 2...n$
The following relations may be defined:

$$E_k = \sum_{j=1}^{n} T_j(k) = \sum_{j=1}^{n} \left( \sum_{i=1}^{n} f_{ij}(k) + y_j(k) \right) \tag{8.5}$$

$$R_k = \sum_{j=1}^{n} y_j(k) \tag{8.6}$$

$$B_k = \sum_{j=1}^{n} x_j(k) \qquad (8.7)$$

for k = 1, 2...n and

$$E_1 = \sum_{j=1}^{n} z_j \qquad (8.8)$$

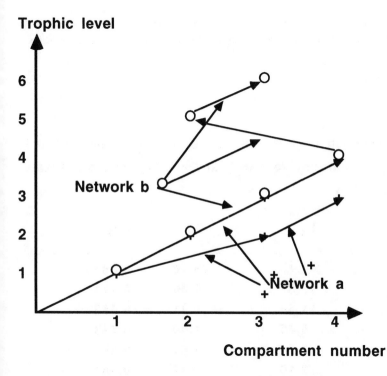

**Fig. 8.4.** The unfoldings of the two food webs shown in Fig. 7.3. The partitioning along the trophic level axis of each compartment's standing stock and the flows in the food webs are shown.

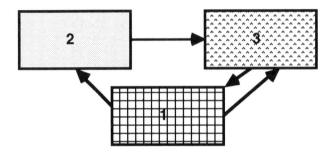

**Fig. 8.5.** A hypothetical food network with only three compartments. For simplicity it is assumed that the turnover rate is equal for all three compartments; that means that the size of standing stock is proportional to that of through-flow.

Table 8.1.

The Values of $B_k$, standing stock in kcal / $m^2$, $E_k$, gross production rate in kcal / $m^2$ day, $R_k$, respiration rate in kcal / $m^2$ day, and progressive efficiency PE $_k = E_{k+1} / E_k$.

| k | $B_k$ | $E_k$ | $R_k$ | $PE_k$ |
|---|---|---|---|---|
| 1 | 2000 | 41.47 | 25.16 | 0.393 |
| 2 | 761 | 16.31 | 4.65 | 0.714 |
| 3 | 30 | 11.66 | 6.41 | 0.450 |
| 4 | 145 | 5.25 | 1.50 | 0.713 |
| 5 | 77 | 3.74 | 1.64 | 0.561 |
| 6 | 34 | 2.10 | 0.87 | 0.584 |
| 7 | 27 | 1.23 | 0.48 | 0.614 |
| 8 | 14 | 0.75 | 0.31 | 0.578 |
| 9 | 9 | 0.44 | 0.18 | 0.597 |

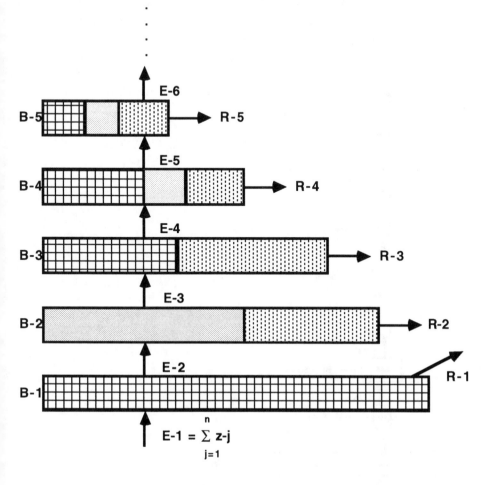

**Fig. 8.6.** The macro trophic chain for the trophic network in Fig. 8.5, obtained by combining those components on the same trophic level to form the gross production rates, respiration rates and standing stocks of the trophic levels $k = 1, 2, 3.....n$.

The macro chain is the structure of the corresponding unfolded network, because it preserves the information regarding inter-level movement of energy and matter in the network, while the information regarding inter-compartmental movement is neglected. It means that for $f_{ij}(k)$ k is preserved, while i and j are neglected.

The progressive efficiency defined according to (8.1) may be extended to any level k for the unfolded food chain and it is clear since $E_k = R_k + E_{k+1}$ that $E_k$ decreases with increasing k, as also asserted by Lindeman (1941).

Figure 8.7 shows the macro trophic chain for the network of Fig. 8.1 and Table 8.1 gives the various indexes for various steps of the macro food chain, based upon

Fig. 8.1. Notice that the food chain has more than 4-5 levels, because of the cycling of matter and energy. Only nine levels have been included in Fig. 8.7 and in Table 8.1, but in principle the food chain may continue infinitely.

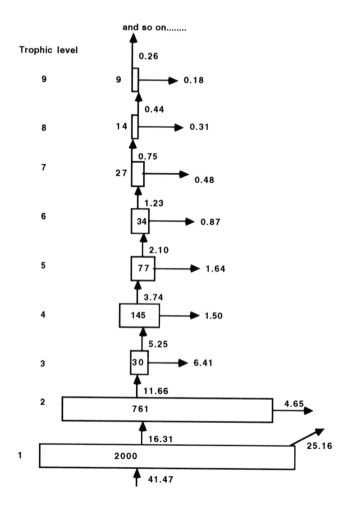

**Fig 8.7.** The macro trophic chain for the food network of the oyster reef ecosystem, presented in Fig. 8.1. Values in boxes are in kcal / m² and those associated with energy transfers are in kcal / m² day.

This is another way of expressing, that the utilization of the energy transfer may exceed 1.0, of course, under the assumption that the efficiency is counted on the basis of the total outputs, while the inputs are only counted once, namely by the first passage. If all inputs are included in calculations of the efficiency, including the inputs coming from the second, third, fourth, etc. cycling of the energy, then the efficiency is of course less than 1.0.

To summarize the results of the presented network analysis, including Ulanowicz's "Structure of Cycling in Ecosystems" ( see Ulanowicz, 1983 and 1986):

1. By use of an unfolding of network and macro food chain it is possible to get the picture of the mass and energy utilization in a network. The single chain model used by Lindeman is a simplification, which does *not* account for the cycling of mass and energy and for the difficulties in determining the trophic level to which any given organism uniquely belongs.

2. The progressive efficiencies and the respiration-loss ratios may or may not follow the tendencies asserted by Lindeman (1942). The decreasing gross production rate by increasing k is according to Lindeman (1942).

3. Energy cycles as mass does and thereby may the utilization coefficient, which accounts for the cycling paths may exceed 1.00, provided that the efficiency is defined as "$\Sigma$outputs of energy - dissipated energy" / 'first input of energy". The utility coefficient should therefore rather be considered as an index for the energy cycling and not as the usual applied coefficients of efficiencies, which of course not can exceed 1.0 due to the first law of thermodynamics.

Ulanowicz (1989) has proposed another trophic aggregation than the method developed by Patten (1985), Higashi et al. (1989) and (1991). The aggregation is similar to the one applied in Fig. 8.4. with the difference that the detrital pool is separated from primary producers, as shown in Fig. 8.8. The productivity of higher trophic levels is overwhelmingly dependent upon the recycling of nutrients and energy. In order to evaluate the trophic efficiencies, Ulanowicz merges the detrital pool with primary producers; see Fig. 8.9. An uniform decrease in trophic efficiencies takes place, which is not necessarily always the case.

Trophic efficiency is defined as that fraction of the total carbon input to a trophic level, which is transmitted to the next higher trophic level; see Fig. 8.9. Notice that the efficiency is a genuine efficiency and not an index that expresses the cycling as the above-mentioned utility coefficient.

The presence of cycling of mass and energy is crucial for ecosystems. Without cycling of mass there would be no life, because the various essential elements would be depleted due to the mass conservation principle. As mass carries energy and energy must be carried by mass, both energy and mass cycles are needed for ecosystems. It is consistent with Morowitz's assertion (1968), that an energy flow through a system will inevitably create cycling. Presumably, cycling points to some form of homeostatic control working to retain materials in the system for reuse.

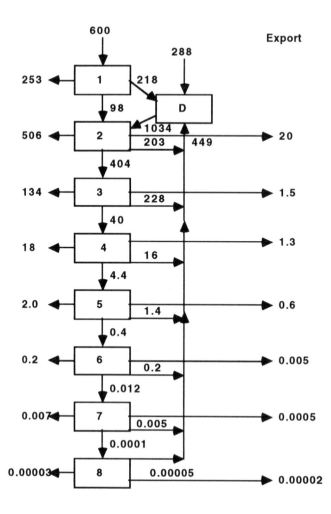

**Fig. 8.8.** The aggregation of the flow web for Chesapeake Bay into eight trophic levels. Flows out of the tops of level 2-7 represent exports. Recycling of non-living material is through compartment D. Flows are given as approximate values in mg / (m$^3$ year).

Ulanowicz (1983) notes how cycles can accompany autocatalytic configurations of processes, that are capable of exerting selection pressure upon their participating components. In the same paper he gives the methodology for analyzing the structure of cycling present in a network.

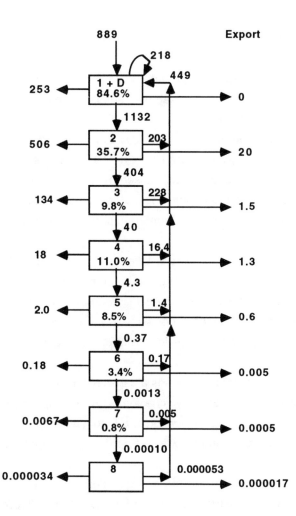

**Fig. 8.9.** The trophic chain of Fig. 8.8. of Chesapeake Bay with primary producers and detritus merged. The percentages in the boxes represent annual trophic efficiencies.

Three major tasks are involved:

    1. The identification and enumeration of all simple cycles.

    2. The collection of cycles into distinct subgrouping, called nexuses, wherein all cycles composing a particular nexus share the same limiting or smallest link.

    3. The successive removal of all nexuses from their supporting tree.

    Two analyses of the structure of cycling according to Ulanowicz are shown in Section 8.4. and the results are compared with other analysis, including calculation of ascendency and entropy production.

## 8.3. The Indirect Effects in Networks

Indirect effects are recognized everywhere and numerous examples can be found in the literature. A few of the most illustrative examples should be mentioned here to show how powerful the indirect effects might be.

Toxic compounds have repeatedly surprised the world due to the indirect effect caused by the biomagnification, see for instance Hurlbert (1975). DDT embrittled the eggshells of falcons and eagles due to the indirect effect caused by biomagnification. Mercury caused the Minamata disease and cadmium the ital-itai disease due to indirect effects: the sediment processes and the biomagnification caused the diseases, not the direct discharge.

The uses of biomanipulation as a tool to restore lakes are another widely accepted application of the indirect effects. By increasing the amount of carnivorous fish, the plantivorous fish will decrease in number, thereby causing an increase in the zooplankton concentration and the final effect being a decrease in the phytoplankton concentration, i.e., a decrease in eutrophication; see for instance Brabrand et al. (1984).

The idea of keystone species (Paine 1974) presumes a capacity for widespread ecosystem changes to follow upon removal of the keystone forms. An example was already mentioned in Section 7.4. Montague (1980), working in a Georgia Salt marsh, found that fiddler crabs altered the productivity and growth of *Spartina* grass by their burrowing activities.

These and many more examples provoke the obvious question: knowing that everything is linked to everything, how is it possible to account for this indirect effect? Are we able to quantify it? Is it possible to set up rules for how a change at one point of the network propagates throughout the network?

Patten and Hagashi (1984) and Patten et al. (1990) have examined the oyster reef model, presented in Fig. 8.1 to compute the number of paths of length n and the energy flows associated with them. The number of paths of length n is simply found as $A^n$, where $A$ is the adjacency matrix. The energy flows corresponding to longer paths are found as $P^n$, where $P$ is the flow matrix. The values for the processes 1 to 2, 4 to 5 and 6 to 5 taken from the first, second, third, tenth and fiftieth order matrices for the oyster reef model as presented in Fig. 8.1, are shown in Table 8.2 as an illustration. It is seen that the number of paths increases very rapidly and although a dissipation of energy will take place, the huge number of paths also increases the influences.

**Table 8.2.**

Values taken from the adjacency (A) and flow matrices (P) of first and higher orders.

| Order | Adjacency matrices | | | Flow matrices | | |
|---|---|---|---|---|---|---|
| | 1 to 2 | 4 to 5 | 6 to 5 | 1 to 2 | 4 to 5 | 6 to 5 |
| 1 | 1 | 1 | 0 | 0.002 | 0.007 | 0 |
| 2 | 3 | 3 | 1 | 0.004 | 0.013 | $1.9*10^{-7}$ |
| 3 | 8 | 9 | 5 | 0.006 | 0.018 | $8.7*10^{-7}$ |
| 10 | 23696 | 27201 | 16169 | 0.019 | 0.039 | $2.0*10^{-5}$ |
| 50 | $2*10^{24}$ | $2*10^{24}$ | $1*10^{24}$ | 0.078 | 0.024 | 0.0004 |
| Cumulative influences over all paths through length 50 | | | | 2.141 | 1.690 | 0.008 |

Figure 8.10 shows the graphic illustration of the resulting relationships between the path length on the one side and the number of paths, the influence, the propagated influence and the influence per path. It is seen from this examination that a network links every component to every other component (directly or indirectly). The cycling of mass and energy again and again implies, furthermore, that the entire network will have more influence on the components than the direct linkages. An ecosystem examination not considering these results will be incomplete and insufficient.

These indirect influences have been important throughout the entire evolution. It means that the prevailing conditions that determine the selection pressure, encompass not only the forcing functions but the entire network (ecosystem).

The examinations by the use of matrices based upon steady state models are of course insufficient to draw the entire history or future of an ecosystem, which we do to a certain extent, by looking into the influences after a certain number of paths.

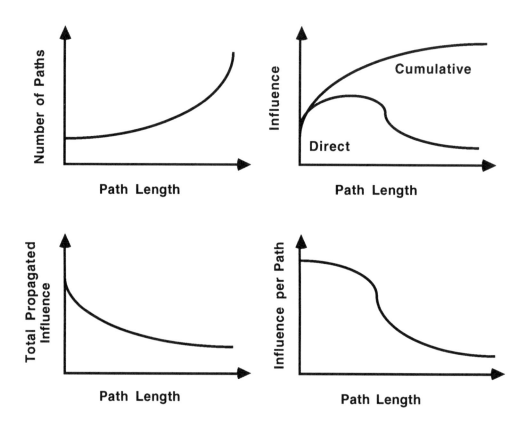

**Fig. 8.10.** Number of paths, influence( including cumulative influence) and propagated influence and influence per path are all plotted versus path length.

This should, however, be considered a computation method, rather than an integration over a long time. So, the results should rather be interpreted as relative contributions to the flows here and now.

The indirect effects hypothesis may be summarized in the following three points (Patten, 1982a,1985 and Patten et al., 1989 and 1990 ):

1. Local interactions do not exclusively determine the dynamics, distributions, abundance, fitness or selection or other ecological characteristics of organisms.

2. Local interactions do serve to structure a global system network to which control passes from the local.

3. Globally propagated indirect effects plus local direct causes jointly determine the ecological properties of organisms.

4. Indirect global effects exceed quantitatively direct, local effects.

236

Higashi and Patten (1986) have shown that it is a mathematical consequence of a network that :

1. The ratio between indirect and direct effect increases with increasing
   a. system order
   b. connectivity
   c. storage
   d. cycling
   e. feedback
   f. direct effects

These results should be interpreted in the context of the thermodynamic hypothesis presented in Chapters 4-6. Indirect effect or the ratio between indirect and direct effect must not be considered an ecological goal function. System order and storage are both closely related to exergy, which may be considered a goal function. Cycling on the other side is a necessity, as mentioned in Chapter 7 and Section 8.2. From modelling exercises (see for instance the discussion on the relation between chaotic behavior and parameters in Section 10.4) we know that the cycling should have a balanced (medium) rate to give the highest possible exergy or biomass or storage. More feedback means better regulation. Increasing strength or numbers of feedbacks will therefore imply that a high exergy (biomass, i.e., survival) is easier to obtain and maintain. The direct effects are related strongly to storage and it is therefore not surprising that a higher direct effect gives a higher storage and therefore a higher I to D ratio.

Connectivity is probably the most difficult of the above-mentioned factors to explain, because many model examinations indicate that the connectivity should be balanced. I / D should not, as mentioned above, be considered a goal function. Therefore the network, that gives the highest growth and survival is selected and it may very well be a network with medium connectivity, because increased connectivity also means more pathways to lose mass and energy. It is, however, still an open question if the very simple networks we are using to imitate the real ecosystems are sufficiently complex to allow the conclusions that we have made. The networks in nature are very complex and flexible in contrast to their computer-built representations.

The conclusion from this discussion could be that it is not surprising that nature has built complex networks with very high indirect influence, because more storage (and thereby more direct effect), more system order, more cycling (up to a certain limit) and more feedback will all give the system more exergy. The connectivity on the other hand finds a balance, which gives the best guarantee for survival and growth

Patten et al. (1989) and (1990), Patten (1991) and Ulanowicz and Puccia (1990)

have presented computational methods to quantify the indirect effect relatively to the direct effect, distinguishing between advantageous and disadvantageous effects. A simple example is presented to illustrate the methods. The results of these computations are maybe the clearest illustration of the assertion: "the whole is more than the sum of the parts."

The network of our simple example is given in Fig. 8.11. The three matrices **A**, based upon the flows, **G**, consisting of the non-dimensional flow intensities $g_{ij}$ measured relatively to the donor flow and **G'** consisting of the non-dimensional flow intensities $g'_{ij}$ relatively to flow of the receiver comes from the input-output analysis; see Leontief (1966) and Hannon (1973). The three matrices are shown in Figure 8.11, where the **D** matrix = **G'**- **G**$^T$ (see Ulanowicz and Puccia, 1990) is shown, too. **G**$^T$ is the transformed matrix of **G** and it is also given in Fig. 8. 12. **D** is named the direct utility matrix, representing the net direct flow from each j to each i in the network, and its elements quantify the single-signed digraph of loop analysis.

The **direct utility index, DUI,** is found from the elements of **D** as "the positive elements"/ I"the negative elements"I  =  2 / 0.6  = 3.333 = DUI.

**D** has the eigenvalues: 0.775 and 0, which satisfy Kawasaki's conditions (all eigenvalues of D < 1) for the convergence:

$$\sum_{m=0}^{\infty} \mathbf{D}^m = (\mathbf{I} - \mathbf{D})^{-1} \equiv \mathbf{U} \qquad\qquad (8.9)$$

and the resulting non-dimensional relative unit integral utility matrix        for    the network is **U,** which is presented together with the other matrices in Fig. 8.12. An **indirect utility index, IUI,**  may be calculated in the same manner as the direct utility index, namely as the "positive elements" in **U** / I"the negative elements" I in **U.** From Fig. 8.12. IUI  is found to be 3.5 / 0.75  = 4. 67 = IUI.

However, each of the elements in the matrices **D** and **U** may be interpreted by a more detailed analysis of the direct and indirect effects. In **D** a unit of input into the first compartment generates positive direct relative utilities at compartment 2 and 3, whereas unit inflows to 2 and 3 cause direct relative disutilities: $d_{12} = - 0.400$ and $d_{13} = - 0.200$ at compartment 1.

In the matrix **U**, however, a unit input into the prey compartment  including all gains and losses generates an equal benefit to all  the three compartments by 0.625. A unit of inflow to compartment 2 produces a benefit to that compartment by 0.750 at a cost of 2 times 0.250 experienced by both prey  and predator 3. Similarly predator 3 generates benefit for that compartment by 0.875, while prey 1 and predator 2 suffer disutilities of 0.125 each.

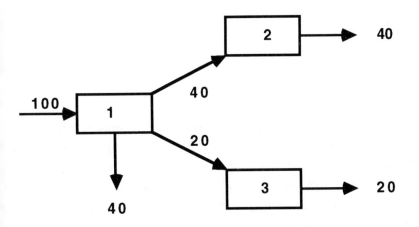

**Fig. 8.11.** A simple model applied to illustrate the calculations of the indirect effect in networks, Ulanowicz and Puccia (1990).

So, all compartments have positive net utilities from the network, while it is not the case for the direct effect. This means that the picture is the same as the one we got by use of the indexes given above: the indirect effect is more significant than the direct one.

Patten (1991) has given several examples, which generally give the same picture: the indirect effect is more significant than the direct one. The point is, however, not so much which of the two classes of effects that is most dominant. The major conclusions of these computations are that the indirect effects are quite significant, which implies that it is not sufficient on the ecosystem level to examine the direct effects. It is necessary to include the indirect effects to capture the entire picture of an ecosystem, which means that you have to work with the entire network / system and observe the reactions of the entire system.

It is furthermore important that the indirect effect in general is beneficial for all the focal components in contrast to the direct effect. Higashi and Patten (1986) have examined the direct and the resulting indirect effect for various relationships between two interacting organisms. A relationship may be interpreted as one of the following nine possibilities: (an ordered pair is given to indicate the interaction type),

Neutralism (0,0)
Anabolism (+,0)
Catabolism (Dissipation) (-,0)

| Commensalism | (0,+) |
|---|---|
| Amensalism | (0,-) |
| Nihilism (Predation) | (+,-) |
| Altruism | (-,+) |
| Mutulism | (+,+) |
| Competition | (-,-). |

They found that in *all* cases the indirect effect changed the interaction types to a more favorable one for *both* organisms. They talk therefore about **network mutalisms**, meaning the benefit that all organisms receive from the network (the cooperation). It is a surprisingly high benefit as we have seen by including the indirect effect in our calculations. Remote components in a network cooperate as seen through the network to the benefit of all components. We may therefore also call it the Gaia-effect, because it can explain why the entire ecosphere is working as a cooperative unit, in spite of only a few direct linkages. The presence of a network with all its important indirect effects can explain why we see a long-distance cooperation between components in the ecosphere.

These results are consistent with the utility coefficients discussed in Section 8.2. Here it was for instance shown that about 83% of the feed to the deposit feeders in Figure 8.1 are recycled. So, 83% of the feed will be able to give indirect effects, and if we assume the same efficiency for the later energy transfer processes, 83% out of the 83% or 69% will be able to give indirect effect a second time and 83% of that again or 59% will be able to give indirect effect a third time and so on. It means that, when we consider the very simple case of same efficiency, tr = 0.83, for each transfer of energy and want to express the indirect effect that one unit of direct effect can exert, we get the following equation:

$$\text{Indirect effect} = \text{direct effect} \left( \sum_{n=1}^{\infty} tr^n \right) \tag{8.10}$$

If tr is, as indicated above, 0.83, we get:

$$\text{Indirect effect} = \text{Direct} * ( 0.83 + 0.69 + 0.59\ldots\ldots )$$
$$> 5 * \text{Direct effect} \tag{8.11}$$

These last computations are, of course, very primitive, compared with those by Patten (1991). They do not take into consideration, that the various steps have different efficiencies and that the energy rapidly propagates over the entire network, but the computations demonstrate the basic meaning behind the assertion that the indirect effect is significant and sometimes greater than the direct one.

$$A = \begin{vmatrix} 0 & 0 & 0 \\ 40 & 0 & 0 \\ 20 & 0 & 0 \end{vmatrix} \qquad G = \begin{vmatrix} 0 & 0 & 0 \\ 0.4 & 0 & 0 \\ 0.2 & 0 & 0 \end{vmatrix}$$

$$G' = \begin{vmatrix} 0 & 0 & 0 \\ 1 & 0 & 0 \\ 1 & 0 & 0 \end{vmatrix}$$

$$G\text{-trans} = \begin{vmatrix} 0 & 0.4 & 0.2 \\ 0 & 0 & 0 \\ 0 & 0 & 0 \end{vmatrix} \qquad D = \begin{vmatrix} 0 & -0.4 & -0.2 \\ 1 & 0 & 0 \\ 1 & 0 & 0 \end{vmatrix}$$

$$U = \begin{vmatrix} 0.625 & -0.250 & -0.125 \\ 0.625 & 0.750 & -0.125 \\ 0.625 & -0.250 & 0.875 \end{vmatrix}$$

**Fig.8.12.** Matrices used in the computation of the indirect effect.

Embodied energy or emergy was introduced in Section 4.4. It is basically the same idea that is behind emergy and indirect effects. The concept emergy multiplies the energy transfer with a factor 10, each time it passes a trophic level - or you may say that each time it gains one step and becomes "one level more indirect" to the solar radiation. The energy is multiplied by a factor 10 to account for the relatively higher utilization of the energy caused by the reuse of the energy on the next trophic level.

The relation between indirect effect and exergy has been examined by use of the model in Fig. 7.1. It was found that additions of more input energy create more exergy, while the direct and indirect effects remain the same as they are based upon the quantitative linkages. If on the other hand an extra linkage is added, for instance between 2 and , the direct and indirect effects are both increased, although the latter more than the former, while the exergy is not changed, provided that the transfer from 2 to 4 is balanced by a corresponding reduction in the transfer 2 to 3 and from 3 to 4. Other examinations of hypothetical models give the same results, namely that there seems to be no relationship between exergy and negentropy on the one side and the indirect and direct effect on the other. However, it has been found that in the case, where a more complex network gives a better utilization of the resources, i.e., more inorganic matter is transferred into biomass, exergy and indirect effects both increase.

Table 8.3 shows the results obtained by the use of the two models :

A. A model consisting of five state variables, namely soluble nutrients, phytoplankton, zooplankton, nutrients in sediment and detritus/bacteria.

B. A model consisting of six state variables, namely the same five as in A + benthic filter feeders, giving transfer of the sediment - nutrients to the detritus and soluble nutrients pools.

The conceptual diagrams of the two models are shown in Figs. 8.13 and 8.14. Both models were run until steady state has been achieved. The steady state situation was used for computation of the direct and indirect effects

The weak relationship between indirect effects and exergy/negentropy is not surprising, because more linkages are not necessarily beneficial for ecosystems, as it has been discussed in Section 2.2. Indirect effect should therefore not be considered a "goal function", to account for development of ecosystem, but rather an excellent method to quantify the role of the entire network relatively to the direct linkage and to understand the nature of ecosystems.

**Table 8.3.**

**Comparison of indirect and direct effects and exergy.**

| Model | $\Sigma$ direct effects | $\Sigma$ indirect effects | Exergy kJ / m$^3$ |
|---|---|---|---|
| A : fig. 7.10 | 1.033 | 2.709 | 492 |
| B: fig. 7.11 | 1.068 | 4.070 | 614 |

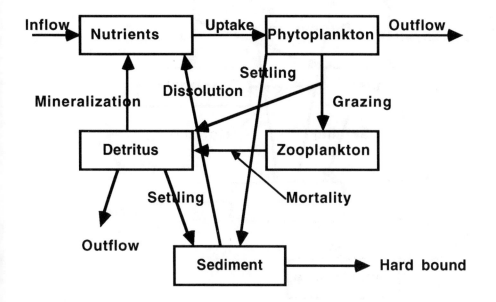

**Fig. 8.13.** Model used for comparison of exergy and indirect/direct effects. The model has five state variables: nutrients, phytoplankton, zooplankton, sediment and detritus.

The theory of indirect effects has been heavily criticized and one of the most substantial criticism concerns the fact that the indirect effect is not indirect but rather a result of a storage in the compartments, which causes a timelag between the input to a compartment and the corresponding output. Storage represents the distance of the system from thermodynamic equilibrium and the exergy of the system and the function

243

of the entire network is embedded in the presence of storages. Storages are the translators of causes to effects. They furthermore  encompass the information that controls the entire system including its processes and they give the system the buffer capacity which is absolutely necessary to level out instant changes.

Therefore it is obvious, that the storages will cause a time-lag and delay the indirect effects, which does not change the fact,  however, that the effects are caused by a non- adjacent cause.

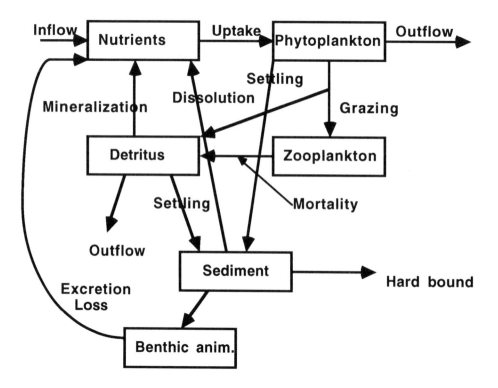

**Fig. 8.14.** Model used for comparison of exergy and indirect/direct effects. The model has six state variables: nutrients, phytoplankton, zooplankton, sediment, benthic animals and detritus.

Higashi and Patten (1989) have been able to distinguish between the indirect effects caused by the storage delayed effects of all orders and the total indirect effects. Their investigations of a number of ecological networks lead to the following hypothesis:

$$p,t\text{-indirect effects} > p\text{-direct, } t\text{-indirect effects} > p,t\text{-direct effects,} \qquad (8.12)$$

where p,t-indirect effects are the indirect effects and p,t-direct effects are the direct effects, used throughout this section, while the p-direct,t-indirect effects are the storage-delayed effects, i.e., the effects caused by a cycling of energy (and therefore they are indirect by nature), but after shorter or longer storage they exert a direct effect. This type of indirect effects accounts, so to say, for the history of the system. The importance of the history is a very dominant feature of an ecosystem. The results by Higashi and Patten: that the "historical" effects are more important than the direct effects here and now, are therefore not surprising. The following points will emphasize the importance of these "historical" effects:

> 1. The storage as mentioned represents above the information and the distance from thermodynamic equilibrium. The storage is a result of the long-term development and the storage-delayed effects are the expressions of this development.

> 2. The absolute and relative sizes of the compartments represent a long experience regarding which sizes are most beneficial for the entire ecosystem. The relative sizes are a result of the history, including the history of the forcing functions.

> 3. Every modeller knows that his model is sensitive to the initial values of the state variables, which just shows that the model is sensitive to/dependent on the history of the system.

A question that remains open, however, is "What is the role of ongoing fluctuations of the forcing functions and the steady variations of the state variables with regard to the relation between direct and indirect effects?" We know from numerous examinations (see for instance Section 4.4), that the fluctuations open up for additional possibilities for the components of an ecosystem to survive and grow. Are these results of fluctuations the cause of a direct or an indirect effect? Future research will certainly be able to answer these question, which need to be answered to complete the theory of indirect effect.

## 8.4. Ascendency

Ascendency is a measure of size and organization (Ulanowicz 1983, 1986 and 1991) in ecological networks and the definition is given in Fig. 8.15, where $T_{ij}$ indicates the flow from i to j. Notice that Patten uses the reverse, which is also applied in Section

7.2 and 8.2. $T_{ij}$ may be averaged over space and time or it may be the instant values. Ascendency may therefore be used dynamically. The ascendency is computed below for the network in Fig. 8.1, which is, however, an instantaneous picture of the ecosystem, so that the calculations are limited to the static attributes of size and organization, while the concept is defined as a measure for growth and development. Therefore a full use of the concept will require that the network is described at more distinct times.

## Ascendency $= T * I$

$$T = \sum_{j=0}^{n} \sum_{i=1}^{n+2} T_{ji}$$

$$I = \sum_{j=0}^{n} \sum_{i=1}^{n+2} (T_{ji} / T) * \log((T_{ji} * T) / (T_j * T_i))$$

**Fig. 8.15.** Definition of the concept ascendency. Notice that Ulanowicz uses $T_{ij}$ to signify the flow from i to j, while Patten and others use the reverse.

As a measure for system size was previously applied "the total amount of flow activities in the system". The total throughput of the oyster reef is the sum of all flows in Fig. 8.1, which amounts to 125.05 kcal m$^{-2}$ day$^{-1}$.

This summation of the flows does, however, not give the location of mass or energy (or information) at any time in a highly articulated system. I (see Fig. 8.15) yields this information by taking the average over all components of the system. It is easy to demonstrate that A is largest when the network is maximally articulated, why no articulation leads to A = 0. All real networks have values in between these extremes.

The ascendency has been calculated for the network in Fig. 8.1; see Ulanowicz (1991). The 49 terms generated by the oyster reef network are arrayed in Fig. 8.16. The various flows are substituted into the equations for A (see Figure 8.14), setting the logarithmic base to 2 to obtain the dimension of flow*bits for A. A was found to be 166.35 kcal-bits $m^{-2}$ day $^{-1}$. It is seen from Fig. 8.15., that the components of the ascendency may be negative or positive, although A always is non-negative. The logarithmic terms may be interpreted as forces, i.e., they express the whole-system level pressure upon their corresponding flows.

**Components of the ascendency of the oyster reef community, Fig. 8.1.**

|   | 0 | 1 | 2 | 3 | 4 | 5 | 6 | 7 |
|---|---|---|---|---|---|---|---|---|
| 0 | 0 | 0 | 0 | 0 | 0 | 0 | 0 | 0 |
| 1 | 66.037 | 0 | 0 | 0 | 0 | 0 | 0 | 0 |
| 2 | 0 | 17.319 | 0 | 0 | 6.317 | 3.994 | 0.463 | 0 |
| 3 | 0 | 0 | 20.346 | 0 | 0 | 0 | 0 | 0 |
| 4 | 0 | 0 | 16.501 | 1.353 | 0 | 0 | 0 | 0 |
| 5 | 0 | 0 | 0.338 | 3.471 | 1.293 | 0 | 0 | 0 |
| 6 | 0 | 0.604 | 0 | 0 | 0 | 0.627 | 0 | 0 |
| 7 | 0 | 21.937 | -1.591 | 6.266 | 1.246 | -0.410 | 0.237 | 0 |

**Fig. 8.16.** Components of the ascendency of the oyster reef community, see Fig. 8.1. Values in kcal-bits $m^{-2}$ day $^{-1}$. Components in row i and column j were generated by the flow from j to i. The 0 represents external inputs, the 7 the combined exports and respirations.

Everything that grows is also constrained by temporal, spatial or material factors. Such constraints serve to keep the system ascendency within its limits. It is helpful to split A into only two terms to be able to observe, how restrictions on A arise (Ulanowicz and Norden, 1990):

$$A = -T \sum_{j=0}^{n+2} \sum_{i=0}^{n+2} (T_{ji}/T) \log (T_{ji}/T) - \left( -T \sum_{j=0}^{n+2} \sum_{i=0}^{n+2} (T_{ji}/T) \log (T_{ji}^2/T_jT_i) \right) \qquad (8.13)$$

The term in brackets in equation (8.13) is a non-negative quantity called the

247

conditional entropy, because it measures the uncertainty remaining after the flow structure has been specified. It is also named the system's overhead; Salines (1986). A in equation (8.13) is written as the difference between two inherently non-negative quantity, which implies that the first term serves as an upper bound on A. This quantity is assigned the symbol C and called the development capacity by Ulanowicz:

$$A = -T \sum_{j=0}^{n+2} \sum_{i=0}^{n+2} (T_{ji}/T) \log (T_{ji}/T) \qquad (8.14)$$

It is evident from the definitions of A and C, that $C \geq A \geq 0$. Therefore the limits on the growth of C will also act as limits on the increase of A. Furthermore, the two factors that limits C are T, i.e., the total system's through-flow, which is ultimately limited by the total amount of inputs, and n, the number of compartments. A greater number of compartments would increase the sum in equation (8.14.) and in fact, a proliferation of species during the early stages of development is often observed. There are, however, practical limits to this trend. As the flows become distributed over more components, the average through-flow per compartment will decrease. Inevitably, some of the compartments will possess through-puts that are so small as they become highly vulnerable to extinction by random perturbations.

It is an old idea that order in the world results from a struggle between countervailing forces, compare Ying and Yang. Growth and development or Size and organization can also be seen to arise from a tension between two seemingly opposing tendencies (Ulanowicz 1986).

Ulanowicz (1986) has used the concept of ascendency phenomenologically, to incorporate into a simple measure all the observations shown in Table 4.5, although not all criteria in this table can be readily interpreted as pertaining to the network. Ulanowicz has therefore found it necessary to translate several of the results in Table 4.5. to flow terminology before they were tested by the theory of ascendency. He found that the development tendencies shown in Table 4.5. are generally consistent with increased ascendency.

Ascendency has furthermore been used in experimental modelling and a few examples will illustrate how ascendency follows changes in ecosystems. Figs. 8.17. and 8.18 show two four-compartment models and while the compartments of Fig. 8.17 are generalists, those in Fig. 8.18. are specialists. The flows were rerouted in the last figure, making the respiration quotients of the four compartments almost the same as in Fig. 8.17. The rerouting resulted in an increase in the total through-flow from 525 to

553 and an even smaller increase (3.7%) in development capacity, C; see equation (8.14). The ascendency, however, rose by 22% from 594.8 to 726.7, while the overhead fell by 23% from 417.9 to 323.3.

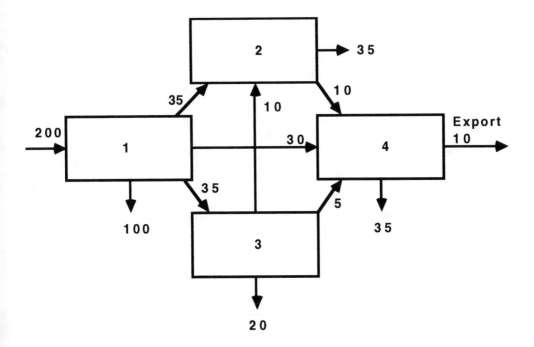

**Fig. 8.17** A network of flows among four compartments, representing generalists.

Fig. 8.19. shows a modification of Fig. 8.17, as cycling is introduced. One would expect that cycling would contribute to the overall ascendency of a system, but it is not generally the case. The system in Fig. 8.19 has almost the same ascendency as the one in Fig. 8.17.

The network in Fig. 8.17. is thrown slightly out of balance by swapping the 1- 3 and 1-4 flows, as shown in Fig. 8.20, while leaving all other flows unchanged. This has created a surplus of inputs to compartment 4 and corresponding deficit into 3, so that the total systems through-flow remains unchanged at 525 flow units and the capacity holds at 1012.7 flow bits. The overall ascendency drops, however, from 594.8 flow bits in the steady-state system to 592 in the marginally out-of-balance network.

Ascendency has been widely used as a tool to state the preference for one particular ecological network among many possible solutions. Pahl-Wostl (1990) uses for instance the ascendency to aggregate species into functional ataxonomic assemblages according to their functional and spatio-temporal characteristics. The basic idea behind her work is that ascendency is able to quantify the influence of the aggregation, which allows her to select the permissible aggregations out of a great number of possible ones.

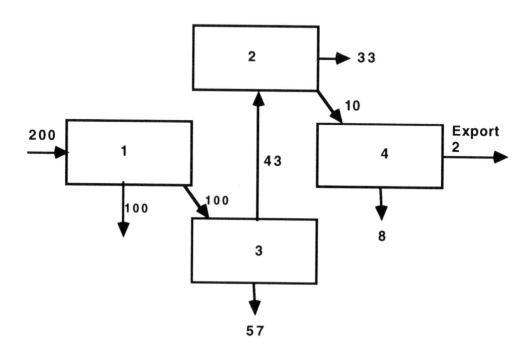

Fig 8.18. A network of flows simplified from the one in Fig. 8.14. by rerouting all flows along the pathway 1-3-2-4. Each component behaves more as a specialist in comparison with its counterpart in Fig. 8.16.

Herendeen (1989 and 1990) has used ascendency together with other concepts as a measure of structural changes. The results of his work will be presented in Chapter 11, which will focus entirely on development of ecosystems, including structural changes , as the different approaches to an ecosystem theory here maybe meet the greatest challenge.

Salomonsen (1992) has compared maximum power, ascendency and exergy for two lakes, an oligotrophic and an eutrophic lake. The results of the comparison are seen in Table 8.4.

The results are interesting first because the three concepts follow the same trends, which is strong support for the pluralistic view of ecosystems. All three measures are approximately a factor ten higher in the eutrophic lake than in the oligotrophic one due to the higher availability of resources (nutrients), which are reflected in the larger compartments of the system (state variables / biomass), while the level of information is unchanged. All three factors follow with other words the size of the biological structure, that is forming the ecosystem.

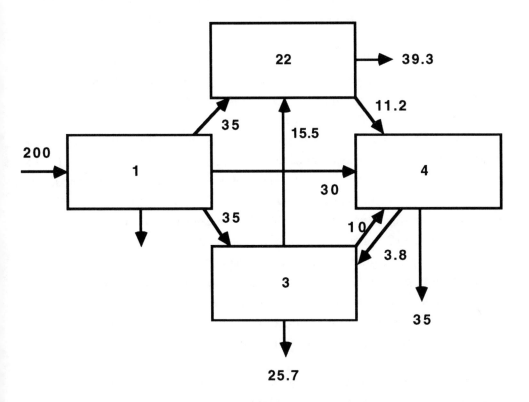

**Figure 8.19.** The network in Figure 8.17. is modified by shunting the export from node 4 back into node 3. Two new cycles are created and the former flow is thereby internalized.

Schneider and Kay (1990) have compared ascendency, length of trophic chain and number of cycles for Chesapeake Bay and the Baltic Sea, using the data from Ulanowicz (1986).

Their assumptions were that every additional step in the food web which can be supported by the ecosystem will result in more exergy destruction - or in terms of the classical second law of thermodynamics - in more entropy production:

1. More and longer cycles in the food web will allow more opportunity for energy degradation at each step as the energy cycles.

2. The effective number of trophic levels will increase. This will allow more opportunity for the degradation of energy, as energy that is passed higher up the food chain will degrade further than energy that is shunted immediately into the detrital subsystem, In order for more trophic levels to exist the efficiency of each trophic level must increase.

3. It will generally allow more and narrower resource niches in the ecosystem, and thereby more pathways for energy degradation will be created.

In short, the structure of the ecosystem will become more articulated as shown by Ulanowicz (1980 and 1986), when more cycling takes place and more steps are added to the food web. In addition, higher entropy production should be expected according to the points 1-3 given above.

The comparison of the two ecosystems, Chesapeake Bay and the Baltic Sea, shows that the Baltic Sea has lower species diversity, its primary production is 1/3 that of Chesapeake Bay, its total system through-flow is 20% of Chesapeake's and it is 33 times bigger. These more traditional measures would normally indicate that, of the two ecosystems, the Baltic Sea is in poorer shape than Chesapeake. However, Wulff and Ulanowicz found that the Baltic Sea was trophically more efficient and possessed a more highly structured array of recycling loop than does the Chesapeake. More mass and energy was passed up in the higher trophic levels in the Baltic Sea. Finally the number of cycles was higher in the Baltic Sea (20 vs. 14) and the length of the cycles was longer in the Baltic; see the comparison Table 8.5. The authors conclude from these analyses that Chesapeake Bay is more stressed than the Baltic Sea.

A similar analysis was carried out for two tidal marsh ecosystems adjacent to a large nuclear power plant at the Crystal River in Florida; see Ulanowicz (1986). The two ecosystems have identical environmental conditions except that one is exposed to hot water effluent from the nuclear power station. The effluent results in a temperature increase of the river water of up to 6° C. The results of this analysis are shown in Table 8.5, too.

Table 8.5. shows clearly that when the number of trophic levels, the number of cycles and nexuses increase, the ascendency will follow the same trends, relatively to the biomass - see the difference in biomass per sq. m in Chesapeake Bay and the Baltic Sea in Table 8.5.

Due to the relations between entropy production and exergy destruction on the one side and the cycling, the number of trophic levels and steps in the food chain; see the three points above, it may be concluded that entropy production / exergy destruction and ascendency (taken relatively to the biomass) express in parallel the development and the stress of ecosystems. As the maximum exergy principle and the exergy consumption due to maintenance are two sides of the same coin, the three theories may be considered three different viewpoints / descriptions of the same properties by ecosystem development.

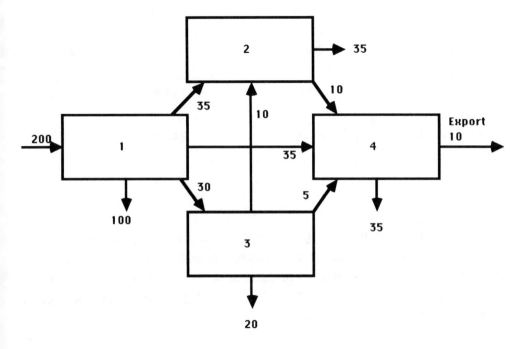

**Fig. 8.20.** A permutation of the flow network in Figure 8.14. obtained by` swapping the magnitudes of flow 1-3 and 1-4. Components 3 and 4 are thereby placed slightly out of balance.

Table 8.4.

Comparison of maximum power, ascendency and exergy.

| Concept (Unit) | A Oligotrophic lake | B Eutrophic lake | Ratio B:A |
|---|---|---|---|
| Max. Power, J $g^{-1}y^{-1}$ | 0.348 | 0.369 | 1.1 |
| Max. Power, J $m^{-3}y^{-1}$ | 0.103 | 1.028 | 10 |
| Exergy, kJ $m^{-3}$ | 6.67 | 64.1 | 9.6 |
| Information, bits | 1311 | 1249 | 0.95 |
| Ascendency kg C $m^{-3}$ $y^{-1}$ | 27.8 | 248.2 | 8.9 |

Table 8.5.

Comparisons of biomass (B) g / sq m/day, number of trophic levels (TL), number of cycles (C), number of nexuses (N) and ascendency (A) for 1) a stressed (s-CR) and unstressed (u-CR) marsh ecosystem at Crystal River, 2) Chesapeake Bay (CB) and the Baltic Sea (BS). The figures are taken from Schneider and Kay (1990).

| Ecosystem | B | TL | C | N | A |
|---|---|---|---|---|---|
| s-CR | 755 | 5 | 69 | 36 | 22,397 |
| u-CR | 1157 | 5 | 142 | 49 | 28,499 |
| CB | 345 | 7 | 14 | 13 | 4,449 |
| BS | 1480 | 8 | 20 | 13 | 15.650 |

# 9. CATASTROPHE THEORY AND ECOLOGY

## 9.1. What is Applied Catastrophe Theory?

Applied catastrophe theory is in a strict sense a theory of equilibria. Thom's classification theorem states (Thom 1972 and 1975) that, a dynamic system, governed by a scalar potential function and dependent on up to five external variables, changes in the equilibrium values of state variables for slow changes in the parameters (caused by the forcing functions). The system can be modelled by one out of seven canonical functions. These functions can be analytically deduced from the actual potential function through coordinate transformations and other mathematical techniques; for further details see Poston and Stewart (1978). A complete list of catastrophe functions can be found in this reference, too. The theory has been applied in several fields including social sciences, medicine, ecology and economy (Zeeman 1982, Poston and Stewart 1978, Kempf 1980 and Loehle 1989)

The usefulness of Thom's theorem lies in the graphical simplicity of catastrophe surfaces for displaying how the behavior of equilibria is influenced by parameter changes. The simplicity is best exemplified by the catastrophe function with the widest application. The canonical potential function is:

$$Y = x^4/4 + a^* x^2/2 + b^*x \qquad (9.1)$$

and the behavior surface is given by the derivate equation:

$$dY/dx = x^3 + x^*a + b, \qquad (9.2)$$

where a and b are the parameters that vary slowly compared with Y. x is a state variable. In a cusp-like system equation (9.2) will be the differential equation of the state variables in canonical coordinates at equilibrium. If b is varied for a in the region less than zero, different types of equilibria will appear, when a and b cross the bifurcation set:

$$4^*a^3 + 27^*b^2 = 0 \qquad\qquad (9.3)$$

The standard cusp behavior surface is shown Figure 9.1, which is derived from equations (9.2 -9.3).

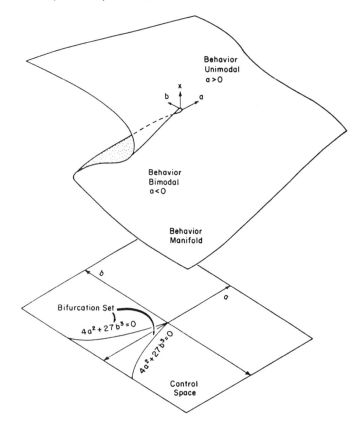

**Fig. 9.1.** The standard cusp behavior surface is shown.

The theory uses 11 elementary catastrophe shapes, of which four are considered in ecology: fold, cusp (most widely used in ecology up to now), swallowtail and butterfly. The fold is a one-dimensional catastrophe. A curve representing equilibria is S-shaped when plotted as response versus control. Dynamic movement along the X-axis results in hysteresis. It is, however, recommended to search for a second control variable, when hysteresis is observed. It may result in a cusp catastrophe.

In the region of two stable states, the cross section of the cusp manifold (see Figure 9.1), is S-shaped. As we move back in the plane in Fig. 9.1, the degree of folding decreases until the surface becomes smooth. The response surface can consist of a series of cusp figures joined. Thus the cusp catastrophe model is not necessarily as simple to picture as in Fig. 9.1.

Two major factors are able to explain the relatively slow development of this theory in ecology according to Loehle (1989):

1) The theory is based upon the highly specialized mathematical field, topology.

2) The procedure to follow is not explained in layman's terms outside the specialized mathematical literature. It is therefore difficult to use for most ecologists.

Catastrophe theory deals with shifts in equilibrium or attractor points on the system level and there is much evidence, that such shifts take place in the ecosystem. Phenomena that other methods would ignore or explain only partially can be described by catastrophe theory.

Typical living systems follow a catastrophic pattern in response to severe environmental stresses. It is therefore natural to include the application of catastrophe theory in a book about ecosystem theory, which is concerned with the behavior and properties of ecosystems. They have developed mechanisms for dealing with stress due to environmental changes. One of these mechanisms is a sudden shift in properties, which may be named a catastrophe. Such catastrophes are therefore not necessarily negative events, as it may be a fast adaptation to a new situation. In addition, many systems take the advantage of severe environmental conditions to test the survivability of the components of the system or eliminate weak ones.

Catastrophes occur typically in cases where two or more non-linear processes are interacting, which is the general case for ecosystems. Catastrophic behavior of ecosystems should, due to the non-linearity of ecological processes be expected much more often in an ecosystem than they are actually observed - a point that will be discussed further in Section 9.5. The emergence of catastrophic behavior by interactions of two or more non-linear, ecological processes is clearly illustrated by Bendoricchio (1988) in his application of catastrophe theory to the eutrophication of the Venice Lagoon. Bendoricchio shows that the interaction between

1) Diffusion described by use of Rabinowitch's (1951) biochemical diffu-

sive model,

2) The net phytoplankton growth obtained as the difference between the overall growth and the mortality and

3) The overall growth related to the nutrient concentration by a Michaelis-Menten equation,

leads to the canonic equation of a cusp catastrophe (see equation 9.2.):

$P^3 + a*P + b = 0$, where P is a transformed variable encompassing the phytoplankton concentration. The observations in the Lagoons of Venice seems consistent with the results of the description by use of the three above mentioned interacting processes (Bendoricchio 1988).

The catastrophe theory is presented in more detail in this chapter by the use of two other typical, ecological examples in the Sections 9.2 and 9.3, followed by an overview of where the theory has been applied up to now in ecology, based on Loehle's excellent review from 1989. Last in this chapter in Section 9.5 there will be a section on the general implication for the ecosystem, and on how the catastrophe theory can be integrated in the other ecological theories presented in this volume.

## 9.2. Application of Catastrophe Theory to Explain Shifts in Oxygen Concentration as Function of Time in a Stream

Catastrophic shifts in the oxygen concentration at spring and fall have been observed in Southern Belgian rivers and Dubois (1979) explained these observations by use of the catastrophe theory.

The change in oxygen concentration can be expressed by the use of the following equation:

dC(t) / dt = Exchange air/water + production by photosynthesis - consumption by respiration (9.4)

The consumption of oxygen, OC, can be given by a Michaelis-Menten equation:

$OC = k_2 * C(t) / ( C(t) + k_1)$, (9.5)

where $C(t)$ is the oxygen concentration at time t, and $k_1$ and $k_2$ are known constants.

The production of oxygen by photosynthesis, PP, may be found by the use of a logistic equation:

$$PP = k_3 * C(t) (1 - q * C(t)),$$
(9.6)

where $k_3$ and q are constants.

The reaeration, RA, is described by the use of the following expression:

$$RA = K_a * (C_s - C(t)),$$
(9.7)

where $K_a$ is the reaeration constant (characteristic for the stream) and $C_s$ is the oxygen concentration at saturation, which is a function of the temperature and barometric pressure.

We now have the following equation:

$$dC(t)/dt = K_a * (C_s - C(t)) + k_3 * C(t) (1 - q * C(t)) -$$
$$k_2 * C(t) / (C(t) + k_1)$$
(9.8)

A transformation of equation (9.8) is carried out by use of the following symbols:

$x = C(t) / k_1$
$x-s = C_s / k_1$
$a(T) = K_a * C_s$, where T is the temperature.
$b = k_3 - K_a$
$c = q * k_3 k_1 / b$
$d = k_2 / k_1$

(9.8) is transformed to the following expression:

$$dx/dt = a(T) + b*x (1 - C*x) - d * x / (1 + x)$$
(9.9)

Figure 9.2 gives the relationship - dx/dt + a(T) for particular values of the constants b, c and d ( b = 1, c = 0.1 and d = 4) versus x. a (T) = 0.5 is shown in the figure, too. a(T) varies with the temperature and as T varies with the seasonal changes.

If we presume that the temperature varies according to a sine function, we can express the a(T) as a function of time, t, by use of the following equation:

$$a(T) = B - G \sin (w^*t), \qquad (9.10)$$

where B, G and w are constants.

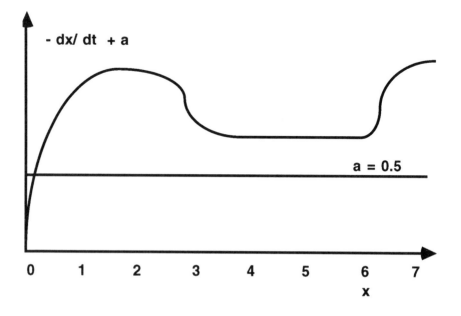

Fig. 9.2.  - dx / dt + a is plotted versus x.

Figure 9.3 shows - dx/ dt for six different a-values which occur at six different times of the year. For a = 0.5 there exists only one attractor point corresponding to - dx / dt = 0 and x = S.  For a = 1, there are two attractor points, x= S and x = Q, but x will still remain in S. For a = 1.2, x will jump to the second attractor point Q. For a = 1.3 or above the attractor point Q will be the only one. For a = 1, there are again two attractor points, but now x will remain in Q. At a = 0.75, x will jump back to attractor point S. So, the jump will take place by increasing a (T) (i.e., during the spring months) at a = 1.2, while the jump back takes place at a = 0.75, i.e., by decreasing a. This explains the observed hysteresis effect; see Fig. 9.4, which illustrates the relationship between x and a.

The model (see the equations 9.9 -9.10) was constructed by the use of

260

the software STELLA. The results are shown Figs. 9.5 and 9.6. The model was run for 1000 days. The oxygen is plotted versus the time in Fig. 9.5 and the temperature in Fig. 9.6.

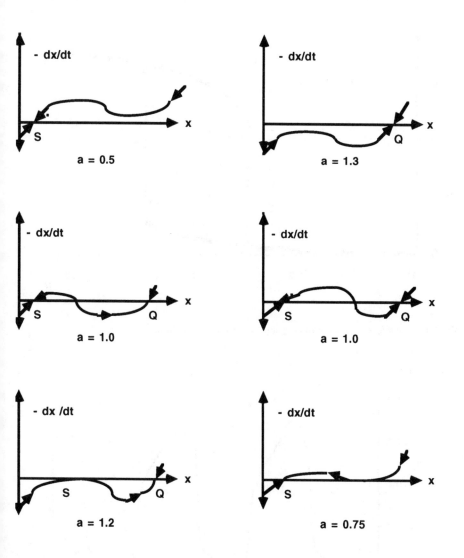

**Fig. 9.3.** dx/ dt is plotted versus x for six different a-values. S and Q are attractor points. Arrows indicate how x will evolve. Notice that the 6 different a -values correspond to 6 different time points.

Comparing the two curves, it is possible to observe the hysteresis. By increasing temperature the oxygen will already jump from a high to a low level

261

at about 6° C, while the jump from the high to low oxygen concentration takes place at 18 ° C, when the temperature is decreasing.

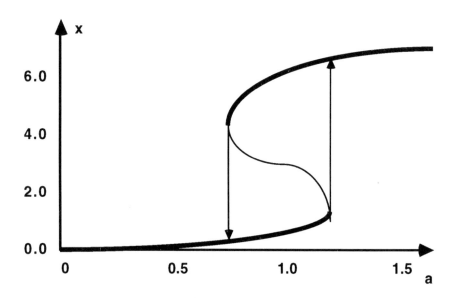

**Fig. 9.4.** Stable x-values are plotted versus a. Note the hysteresis effect.

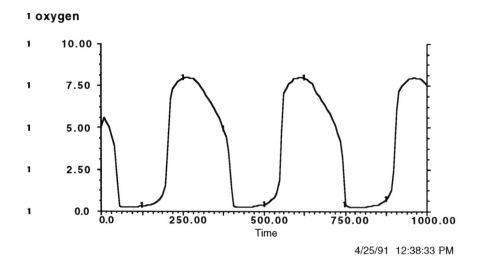

4/25/91  12:38:33 PM

**Fig. 9.5.** Oxygen concentration (mg/l) (x] is plotted versus time (days). Results of the model in Fig. 9.7.

It implies that the hysteresis effect can be found in this case by selecting temperature as a control variable, i.e., plotting x versus T, but Figure 9.5 should already give the observer the idea to examine the possibilities of using the catastrophe theory to explain the observations, when two distinct levels of oxygen are seen in Fig. 9.5.

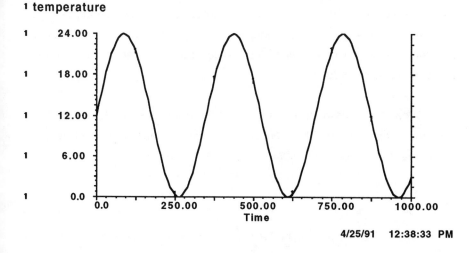

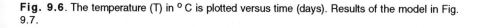

**4/25/91   12:38:33  PM**

**Fig. 9.6.** The temperature (T) in $^\circ$ C is plotted versus time (days). Results of the model in Fig. 9.7.

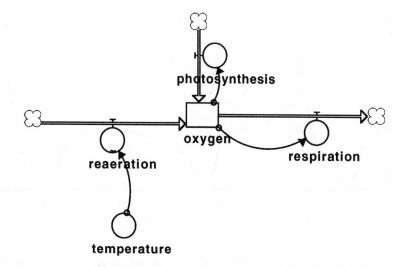

**Fig. 9.7.** Oxygen model used for the simulations given in Figs. 9.5, 9.6 and 9.8.

The model used for the computations leading to Figs. 9.5 and 9.6, is shown in Fig. 9.7

As already mentioned the obtained results in Fig. 9.5 are realistic in the light of measurements in very polluted Belgian rivers. If the loading of organic biodegradable matter is high, the water has constantly a high consumption of oxygen and becomes extremely susceptible to the input of new oxygen by the reaeration process, which again is very much dependent on the oxygen saturation concentration, which is very much dependent on the temperature. If the water was less polluted, the consumption of oxygen would have been less and thereby the susceptibility of the oxygen concentration to the reaeration process would be reduced.

What happens in the water can be further illustrated by use of the concept buffer capacity. The most obvious buffer capacity to use would be the oxygen-temperature buffer capacity, which is defined as:

$$\beta = \partial T / \partial x \qquad (9.11)$$

Figure 9.8 shows the buffer capacity versus the time for the first 440 days. It is seen that the low buffer capacities coincide, as expected with the jumps in oxygen concentration, whenever the jump is toward higher or lower oxygen concentration. It is also seen that every second time the buffer capaci-

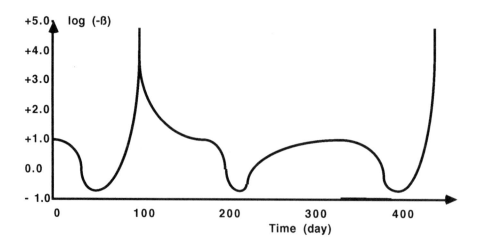

**Fig. 9.8.** $\beta$ is plotted versus time. The results are taken from simulations by the use of the model conceptualized in Fig. 9.7.

264

ty is low, the buffer capacity afterwards increases to extremely high values. This is the summer situation: the oxygen concentration is low and the high buffer capacity indicates that it is very difficult to increase the oxygen concentration. As seen the buffer capacity/ time graph reflects the hysteresis effect very nicely.

## 9.3. Application of Catastrophe Theory on a Lake Ecosystem

Biomanipulation by addition of predatory fish is increasingly used to restore lakes and can lead to dramatic improvement of water quality (Meijer et al., 1989 and Van Donk et al., 1989). The short term results of these and other experiments are encouraging, but it is unclear whether the manipulated system will inevitably return to the initial eutrophic and turbid conditions. Some observations (see Hosper, 1989 and Van Donk et al., 1989), seem to indicate that if low nutrient concentration is combined with a relatively high concentration of predatory fish, a stable steady state will be attained, while high nutrient concentration and high predatory concentration will lead to an unstable clear water state. On the other hand turbid conditions may prevail even at medium nutrient concentrations, provided that the predatory fish concentration is low. By introduction of more predatory fish, the conditions may however improve significantly, even at medium nutrient concentrations.

Willemsen (1980) distinguishes two possible conditions:

1. A "bream state" characterized by turbid water, high eutrophication at least relatively to the nutrient concentration. Submerged vegetation is largely absent from such systems. Large amounts of bream are found, while pike hardly is found.

2. A "pike state" characterized by clear water and low eutrophication relatively to the nutrient level. Pike is abundant, while significantly fewer breams are found compared with the "bream state."

Willemsen's work shows that the pike / bream ratio is strongly correlated with water transparency and that the separation between two states is relatively distinct; see Fig. 9.9.

Scheffer (1990) has used a mathematical model to describe these shifts in structure, which may have catastrophic character. The conceptual dia-

265

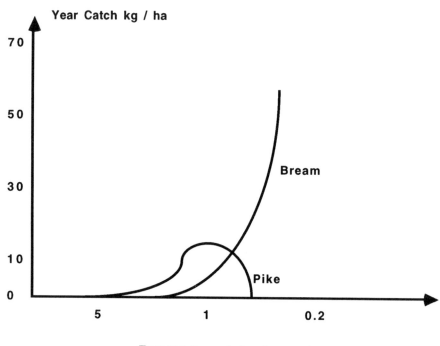

**Fig. 9.9.** Annual catches of pike and bream (kg/ ha) plotted versus transparency (m).

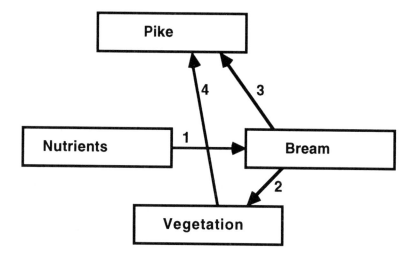

**Fig. 9.10.** Conceptual model applied to describe shifts from "bream state" to "pike state" and vice versa.

gram of the model is presented in Fig. 9.10. The components of the model are

266

gram of the model is presented in Fig. 9.10. The components of the model are connected by four relations, which are incorporated in the model as a simple Monod and Hill function; see Fig. 9.11.

The general features of the model are reflected by the plot of the isoclines. Figure. 9.12 shows the zero isoclines of bream and pike. The low position of the pike isocline at high bream densities is explained by the decrease of vegetation in these situations.

The rise of the bream isocline at low bream density is a result of the functional response used in the model. The isoclines intersect at three points, i. e., the net growth of both pike and bream is equal to zero at these points. The three points therefore represent equilibrium points of the model. While points 1 and 3 are stable equilibria, point 2 represents an unstable equilibrium. The slightest perturbations will cause the system to shift away from this point. The two stable points appear to correspond to the pike (1) and bream state (3).

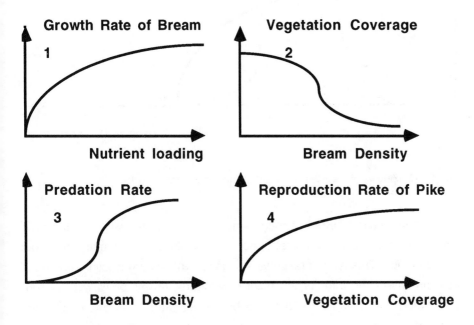

**Fig. 9.11.** Relations incorporated in the model in Fig. 9.10.

The effect of eutrophication on the system may be visualized by plotting isoclines for different values of the nutrient level. The pike isocline is not affected by the nutrient concentration, but the bream isocline changes, as shown in Fig. 9.13, with the nutrient level - the higher the nutrient concentration, the higher the position of the isocline in the diagram; see Fig. 9.13.

The behavior of an oligotrophic situation can easily be derived from Fig. 9.13. The lower bream isocline applies to the oligotrophic state. A low pike equilibrium is the only possible steady state under these conditions.

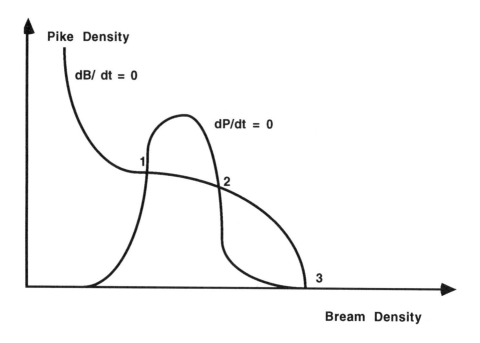

**Fig. 9. 12.** Zero isoclines of the bream (dB/dt = 0) and pike (dP/dt = 0).

At increasing nutrient concentration the equilibrium will shift upwards slowly. Pike density will thereby increase, while bream density does not change much. This type of response continues until bream isocline reaches a position where the intersection point disappears. At this point will the pike population will collapse. The turbid bream equilibrium is attained. If we change the nutrient from high to low concentration, however, the picture will be different. By reduction of the nutrient level the system will stay in the bream type of equilibrium to a very low nutrient concentration, although the bream concentration will decrease slightly. Only at very low nutrient concentration the intersection point representing the bream equilibrium disappears and the

Clearly this behavior is analogous to the example in Section 9.2. and to other examples described by catastrophe theory applied to biological systems.

Figure 9.14 shows the catastrophe fold, where a bream isocline is plotted versus the nutrient concentration, assuming that pike is in steady state. The isocline consists of the stable parts 1 and 3. The unstable part 2 corresponds to the "jump" between the two stable points and it is indicated with the thin line in Fig. 9.14.

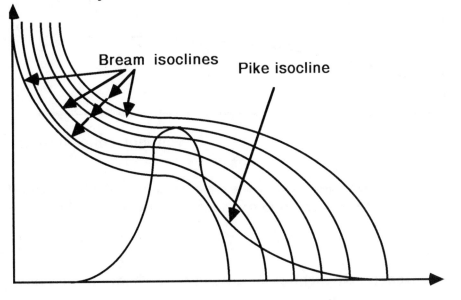

**Fig. 9.13.** The position of isoclines and stable equilibria at different nutrient levels. The highest position of the bream isocline corresponds to the highest nutrient concentration.

The discontinuous response to the increase and decrease of nutrient level implies that decreased nutrient levels will not cause a significant decrease in the eutrophication and a significant increase in water transparency before a rather low level has been attained. However, it may be possible to "push" the equilibrium from point 3 to point 1 by addition of predatory fish, for instance pike.

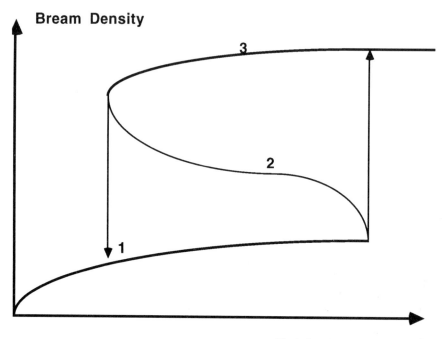

**Nutrient concentration**

**Fig. 9.14.** A catastrophe fold is shown by means of projection of the intersection line of isocline planes of bream and pike on the nutrient-bream plane. The number corresponds to the 3 states in Fig. 9.12.

## 9.4. General Application of Catastrophe Theory in Ecology

The first step in catastrophe modelling should always be a catastrophe analysis which should determine whether a catastrophe is present or not. This can be done from data obtained by sampling the environment or on theoretical grounds alone, although the latter approach should be used very cautiously. Ouimet and Legendre (1988) explain some important principles to be followed when sampling with catastrophe theory in mind. The first step in the catastrophe analysis is an examination of graphs of different system variables as a function of time or space. This type of graphs allows one to find out, if the discontinuities observed in the data are mathematical catastrophes or not.

Figure 9.15 is an example of what might be observed. The state variable d displays a discontinuous behavior. The first discontinuity (1) is linked to a

270

continuous change in variable s, while other variables do not show any variation at that moment.

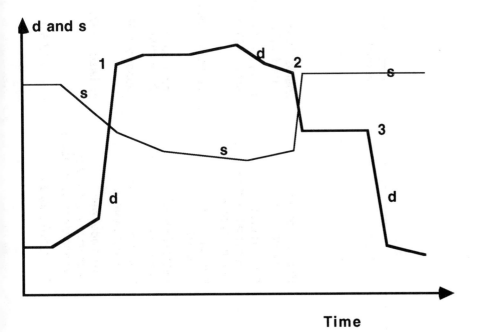

**Fig. 9.15.** The variable d shows discontinuities at 1, 2 and 3 and mathematical catastrophes could therefore be expected here. Further examinations show that 2 can be excluded due to abrupt change in variable s.

Discontinuity (1) can therefore be considered as a mathematical catastrophe, if no other important predictors have been overlooked. The second discontinuity (2) is associated with an abrupt change in the evolution of variable s. Therefore it is not a catastrophe. The last discontinuity (3) is linked to no variation of s and other variables (not shown in the figure). Therefore (3) can be considered a catastrophe. It is obviously important to use small sampling intervals to be able to determine whether the discontinuities are catastrophes or not. For a catastrophe theory approach to be justified, multiple system states should exist. There are two types of evidence of this: there are multiple domains of attraction or multiple stable states and the presence of hysteresis.

**TABLE 9.1**

**Applications of Catastrophe Theory in Ecology**

| Application | Response variable | Control variables | Validity of model | Reference |
|---|---|---|---|---|
| **Predator - Prey Systems** | | | | |
| Grazing | Plant biomass | Stocking level Precipitation | Heuristic, some field data | Loehle (1985), May (1977a) |
| Fishing | Fish stock size | Fleet size Fishing efficiency | Detailed model supported by data for many species | Jones and Walters (1976), May (1977a) |
| | Fish stock size | Exploitation rate Fish fecundity | Detailed model and data | Peterman et al. (1979) |
| Insect-tree | Larval density | Branch density Predation intensity | Detailed model and data | Peterman et al. (1979), Casti (1982) |
| Microbial | Predator biovolume | Predator/prey ratio Time | Time is not a valid control variable | Saunders (1985) |
| Parasite-host | Host population | Transmission efficiency | Fold model well documented, probably extendible to cusp model | Anderson (1979) |
| Timber harvest | Forest biomass | Stocking level Site quality | Qualitative support | Loehle (1989) |

| | Response variable | Control variables | Results | Reference |
|---|---|---|---|---|
| ***Extinction*** | | | | |
| Animals in patchy habitats | Vulnerable species richness | Spatial variance<br>Temporal variance | Hysteresis or multiple stable states not demonstrated | Saxon and Dudzinski (1984) |
| ***Ecosystem properties*** | | | | |
| Structural stability of 3-trophic level aquatic system | Phytoplankton and zooplankton levels | Several combinations of control variables | No catastrophe folds found in simulations but very steep regions found suggested management strategies | Recknagel (1985) |
| Water quality | Oxygen content or chlorophyll a<br>Total algae | Temperature<br>Nutrients<br>Anabaena concentration<br>Soluble phosphate | Detailed model and data<br>Supported by laboratory data | Dubois (1979), Van Nguyen and Wood (1979)<br>Duckstein et al. (1979) |
| | Total algae | Nutrient algae concentration | Supported by observations in Venice Lagoon | Bendoricchio (1988) |
| ***Behavior*** | | | | |
| Herbivore diet switching | % woody vegetation in diet | Season<br>Stocking rate | Supported by data | Rambal (1984) |
| Territory defense | Level of aggression | Distance from nest<br>Reproductive state | Detailed experimental test | Colgan et al. (1981) |
| Nutrient uptake | Internal nutrient concentration threshold | Nutrient uptake rate<br>Total nutrient in system | Some mild data support | Kempf et al. (1984) |
| ***Locomotion*** | | | | |
| Energetics of motion in land animals | Gait (duty factor or shape factor) | Speed<br>Type of animal | Detailed models and data | Alexander (1982) |

Ouimet and Legendre (1988) have presented a procedure for development of a cusp catastrophe model, using graphs and non-linear regressions. If the procedure is followed carefully, it will not be too difficult

1) to state whether the data allow to develop a catastrophe model and

2) To develop the model.

As mentioned in Section 9.1 there are a number of applications of catastrophe theory in ecology which do not violate basic assumptions of the theory. They are listed in Table 9.1, which is mainly based on Loehle (1989), with additions.

The largest number of applications is found in the area of predator-prey models. Often the discontinuity is obvious, as for example in the case of insect pests, that periodically go into outbreak phase (Peterman et al. 1979). Such outbreaks are characterized by a rapid transition from small population size to epidemic, followed by a rapid crash after some years. The spruce budworm case, see Table 9.1, is very consistent with the cusp model. Fishery models may be considered as a prey-predator system with the fleet size and fishing efficiency as control variables.

Examinations of the successful application of cusp models on different predator- prey systems lead to the following conclusions:

1. The predator or the prey may turn out to be the response variable.

2. A number of factors that affect process rates may act as control variables, for instance harvest intensity, food supply and precipitation.

3. Species may have evolved specific attributes to assist in breaking from the endemic to the epidemic phase such as production of toxins.

The range of application of catastrophe theory is beginning to be broader in the ecological field as shown in Table 9.1. It is no longer confined to predator-prey models. Many of the studies included in the table show strong empirical support for the models. The experience from the case studies demonstrates clearly that insights are available with catastrophe theory because it extends our analysis from response as a function of one to a function of two variables, as in the cusp model.

Extension to higher dimensions has so far only been used in a butterfly catastrophe model of a grazing system (Loehle 1989). An unresolved problem in applying catastrophe theory is that of testing the goodness of fit of the model to data. Work is being done, however, in the area of statistical estimators for catastrophe models. The availability of statistical tools will probably speed up application of the techniques.

## 9.5. Ecosystems and Catastrophe Theory

Catastrophe theory has not been widely accepted in ecology, because reductionistic ecology does not believe that it is possible to look through "the mist of complexity". It is, however, clear from the presentation in this chapter that ecosystems show discontinuous stability and that these observations can be modelled and in some cases at least be explained by use of catastrophe theory. The use of catastrophe modelling gives extended insight, which is valuable in our effort to transform our observations to a pattern of ecosystem theory.

It is not surprising that a complex non-linear system such as an ecosystem shows discontinuous stability. Many examples have been observed in physics and chemistry, see for instance Nicolis and Prigogine (1989). It is rather a surprise that it is not met even much more frequently, but this can be explained by the multilevel hierarchy of regulations, see Table 2.1. The flexibility of the system will to a certain extent attempt to prevent the occurrence of catastrophes.

A review of the models in Table 9.1. shows that the catastrophes are probably most frequently met by populations of r-strategists. Their basic strategy is basically opportunistic "boom and burst" and they simply show higher sensitivity to changes in the general conditions particularly those determined by the external factors (Southwood 1973 and 1981). Therefore it is expected that sudden changes of forcing functions (external variables) will first challenge the r-strategists. They will rapidly be on the spot and utilize the recently emerged conditions due to their high potential of growth. On the other hand they will also react violently negatively, i.e., with high mortality, if the conditions would deteriorate.

As discussed in Section 2.2 an ecosystem will be attracted to, but never reach, a steady state. The solar radiation is able to maintain the system far away from thermodynamic equilibrium, and there exists a steady state which can be considered an attractor in a biogeochemical model. It can be found by setting all the derivates to zero. However, the external factors (forcing functions) and even the properties of the species will steadily change. It means that the system at time t will move toward its steady state at time t, but at the time t+1, when the steady state at time t has not been reached yet, the steady state has meanwhile changed and the system moves toward this new steady state and before the new attractor point has been reached, a new steady state = attractor has emerged, etc. The ecosystem is moving toward a moving target and will therefore never reach it. This behavior may also cause the appearance of limit cycles round the attractor point, dependent on the processes involved.

The catastrophe theory has been presented as a theory of equilibria, see Section 9.1, but in an ecological context it should rather be considered a theory, describing a sudden change of the steady state, to which the system is attracted.

The multidimensional concept "buffer capacity" gives the ratio of the change in the external factors to the change in the system (the state variables). It means that if the buffer capacity is high, the steady state or attractor is not far away. It implies that the attractor point is not moving or has lately not been moving very fast. A low buffer capacity corresponds, on the other hand to a fast moving steady state or attractor. Compare with the example presented in Section 9.2, Fig. 9.8, where the buffer capacity has been computed. The low buffer capacity coincides with the jump in steady state or rather the attractor point. Consequently, the occurrence of catastrophes is related to a low value of the very buffer capacity that is based upon the state variable showing drastic changes (jumps) and the external factor, causing these changes. In Section 9.2 it was the buffer capacity based upon the changes in oxygen concentration relatively to the change in temperature. It is even possible to identify the low buffer capacities by examination of a model and thereby the potential catastrophes. The ideas presented above are summarized in Fig. 9.16.

To summarize: An ecosystem will never return to the same situation again and will never again have exactly the same steady state or attractor, because:

**1. The steady state is dependent on the many external factors, which follow some pattern in their changes,** for instance a seasonal and diurnal pattern, but which also show a high extent of randomness. The same combination of external factors will therefore never occur again.

2. **The steady state is dependent on "the history of the system,"** see also Section 8.3. on the indirect effect, which to a certain extent accounts for "the history of the system"- compare the

presentation of the p-direct-t-indirect effect. As an ecosystem will always have a history - all ecosystems in principle have a history of 4 billion years - which in its very sense is a function of time, exactly the same steady state can never be repeated.

**3. The steady state is dependent on the properties of the state variables. As they are changing according to the hierarchy of regulation mechanisms** presented in Section 2.1, the state variables and the steady state will steadily change.

The existence of hysteresis in response of the state variables to changed external factors shows that even the same or in practice "almost the same combination of external factors" may give different steady states. The choice between two or more possible steady states is dependent on the short term history of the system - compare the examples in Sections 9.2 and 9.3. The occurrence of hysteresis phenomena in ecosystems is therefore consistent with point 2 above.

Hysteresis could be explained by the ability of ecosystems to maintain a buffer capacity as high as possible. The jump back to the previous situation is prevented as long as possible. The example in Section 9.3 illustrates how a high eutrophication level (phytoplankton concentration) is maintained; even the nutrient loading is reduced significantly. The reduction to a low phytoplankton concentration may be obtained by patience or by pushing the steady state over the edge of the cusp by increasing the zooplankton concentration (which again may be obtained by increasing the concentration of plantivorous fish). The final steady state situation may be the same in both cases, but the lower level of eutrophication and phytoplankton concentration is obtained faster by the use of an additional push to the system - which is called biomanipulation, see also Chapter 11.

The present application of catastrophe theory in relation to ecosystems is primitive when the complexity of ecosystems is considered. It has been possible in the examples reviewed in Table 9.1. to identify a relationship between one external factor and its possibility to change rapidly the steady state of one state variable, but an ecosystem has many external factors, that are changing simultaneously and influence many state variables.

There are therefore possibilities for many catastrophes in the mathematical sense in an ecosystem. In our effort to identify catastrophes in ecosystems we are therefore facing the same problem of complexity, that was mentioned in Chapter 3 Section 5.

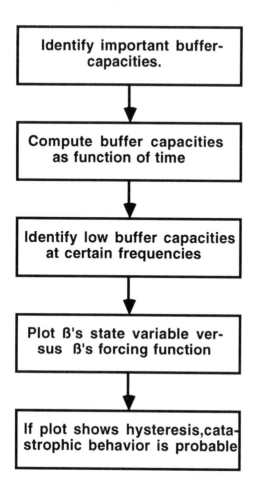

**Fig. 9.16.** Tentative procedure to "trace" a catastrophic behavior of a system.

Having accepted the limitation in our description of the very complex systems, see also Section 2.3, we have to accept that we can only identify catastrophes and the related buffer capacities for the problem in focus, provided it is supported by a good model and good data.

This is, however, the general limitation in modelling and in ecosystem research, that we cannot know all detail with unlimited accuracy - or rather it is the limitation in all sciences. It is a limitation, which the reductionists not have accepted yet. It may be reduced by development of better instruments (tools), but it is impossible to eliminate completely due to the limitations given by the enormous complexity of nature (see Chapter 2) , by the quantum theory (see Section 2.3) and by the chaos theory, which is the topic of the next chapter. All holistic approaches to ecosystem theory and management are, however, based upon a full acceptance of these limitations.

# 10. CHAOS, FRACTALS AND ECOLOGY

## 10.1. Introduction and Definitions

Chaos theory is concerned with unpredictable courses of events. The irregular and unpredictable time evolution of many non-linear systems has been named "chaos". It is a science of global nature of systems and it has brought together scientists from fields that had been widely separated. It makes strong claims about universal behavior of complexity. It occurs in mechanical oscillators such as pendular or vibrating objects, in rotating or heated fluids, in laser cavities, in some chemical reactions and even in biological systems. The most fascinated advocates of this new science go so far as to say that this century science will be remembered for three things: relativity theory, quantum mechanics and chaos theory. Relativity has eliminated the Newtonian illusion of absolute space and time, while quantum theory has eliminated the Newtonian dream of controllable measurements. Chaos theory has eliminated the Laplacian illusion of deterministic predictability and can therefore be conceived as a ticking bomb under reductionistic science.

Chaos theory is best illustrated by Lorentz's (1963 and 1964) famous Butterfly Effect - the notion that a butterfly stirring the air in Hong Kong today can transform storm systems in New York next month. The effect was discovered accidentally by Lorentz in 1961. He was making a weather forecast and wanted to examine one sequence of greater length. He tried to make, what he thought was a shortcut. Instead of starting the whole run over again, he started half way through. To give the computer its initial values, he typed the numbers from the earlier printout. The new run should therefore duplicate the old one, but it did not. Lorentz saw that his new weather forecast was diverging so rapidly from the previous run that within a few months all resemblance has disappeared. There had been no malfunction of the computer or the program. The problem lay in the number he had typed. In the computer six decimal places were stored: 0.506127, but to save time....because he thought it was unessential...he printed a rounded-off number with just three decimals: 0.506.

The explanation is simple: Lorentz's model is very sensitive to initial conditions and so is the weather itself. The effect today is observed in numerous relations and all ecological modellers know this problem. Therefore the initial values of the state variables are most often included in a modeller's sensitivity analysis and he uses much effort to have the seasonal variations of the state variables repeated again and again, when the same forcing functions are imposed on the model; see also Section 3.3. Figure 10.1 gives an ecological example of a model with high sensitivity for the initial value. As seen from the figure a minor difference in the initial value gives two completely different curves after t = 100.

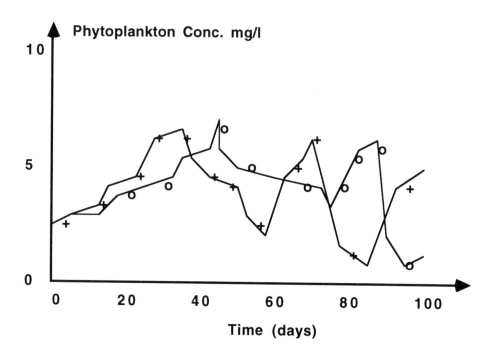

**Fig. 10.1.** A six compartment lake model has been applied to illustrate that the initial value in this case of the zooplankton concentration has great influence on the final results of simulation. The plot shows the phytoplankton simulation according to the model over a period of 100 days, applying zooplankton concentrations on 0.05 (+) and 0.053 (o) as initial values. As seen the phytoplankton concentrations are completely different after 100 days, when using the two initial values of the zooplankton concentration.

The definition of chaos implies that the difference between the two curves with slightly different initial conditions is growing exponentially:

$$d\,(t) \;=\; d(0) * e^{\lambda * t}, \tag{10.1}$$

where d(t) is the distance at time = t, d(0) is the distance at time = 0 and $\lambda$ is a positive number, called the Lyapunov exponent, which is a quantitative indicator for chaos.

After the time $1/\lambda$ the initial conditions are insignificant, i.e. "forgotten".

The Lyapunov exponent for the case study illustrated in Fig. 10.1. can be found by plotting the logarithm to the distance between the two curves neglecting the distance at time 0 (which is 0) versus the time. The plot is approximately a straight line with a positive slope of approximately 0.012 mg / (l * day), indicating chaotic behavior.

The Benard cell presented in Section 5.6 may also expose chaotic behavior. When the temperature difference, $\Delta T$, between the lower and the upper plate exceeds a critical value, convection occurs as described in Section 5.6 as a series of rolls resembling rotating parallel cylinders. The rolls begin to oscillate transversely in complex ways as $\Delta T$ increases beyond a second threshold and chaotic behavior occurs for even higher values of $\Delta T$.

The BZ-reaction, presented in Section 5.6, is a much studied example of a chemical system which exhibits both periodic and chaotic behavior. The following simplified model (Swinney, 1983) illustrates some features of the BZ-reaction:

$$A + B \underset{k'}{\overset{k}{\text{------}}} C \tag{10.2}$$

The reactants A and B are injected into a closed container with flow rate, r, and an exit port relieves the excess material. The rate equations are:

$$dA/dt = -k\,A\,B + k'\,C - r(A - A_0)$$
$$dB/dt = -k\,A\,B + k'\,C - r(B - B_0)$$
$$dC/dt = k\,A\,B - k'\,C - r\,C, \tag{10.3}$$

where $A_0$ and $B_0$ are the reactant concentrations at the input port. $C_0 = 0$. The equations exhibit non-linear coupling between the chemical concentrations. If r is zero the reactions proceed to equilibrium. For larger r the materials are exhausted from the container before they have time to react. For intermediate r the system has periodic states as presented in Section 5.6, but may also show chaotic behavior for certain r-values. r is the control parameter, but the temperature-dependent rate constants and initial conditions also affect the dynamic state.

The existence of chaos in the BZ-reaction suggests that similar behavior might occur for other chemical oscillators such as those found in biological systems. Chaotic behavior in these systems may indicate a pathological condition (Rapp, 1986). This may explain why chaotic behavior does not occur more frequently in ecological systems, despite of the high non-linearity of ecological processes. Processes and components (organisms) with properties (parameters) that will create chaos, are simply outdone. This will be discussed further in Section 10.4.


## 10.2 Bifurcation and Fractal Dimension

Chaos is also known in relation to bifurcation and this form of chaos is nicely illustrated by examination of a simple model in population biology. May (1974,1975 and 1976) has examined the behavior for non-linear differential and difference equations, for instance:

$$N_{t+1} = N_t (1 + r(1-N_t/K)), \tag{10.4}$$

where N is the number of individuals in the population under consideration, r the growth rate per capita, t the time and K the carrying capacity of the environment. Notice that this equation expresses a time delay = 1 in the form the difference equation is given. As long as the non-linearity is not too severe, the time delay built into the structure of the difference equation (10.1) tends to compare to the natural response time of the system and there is simply a stable equilibrium point at N# = K. However for $r \geq 2$ this point becomes unstable. It bifurcates to produce two new and locally stable fixed points of period 2, between which the population oscillates stably in a 2-point cycle. With increasing r, these two points also bifurcate to give four stable fixed points of period 4. In this way through successive bifurcations an infinite hierarchy of stable cycles of the period $2^n$ arises. Figure 10.2 illustrates the formation of bifurcations up to r = 2.75.

Fractal is a word introduced by Mandelbrot and may best be introduced by an example. The example is a typical Mandelbrot question: "How long is the Coast of Britain?". This question does not have an unambiguous answer, because it depends on how many details, the measurement should include. If we use a ruler of one meter, we get another result than if we use a ruler of one cm. This problem inspired Mandelbrot to introduce what he called the fractal dimension.

Suppose you want to measure the length of an irregular curve such as for instance the coastline of Britain. Similar considerations may apply in the measurement of an area of an irregular surface, except that the ruler is replaced by tiles. To probe the system in a manner independent of whether the system is a curve or a surface, you may divide the embedding space into cells (boxes) of side length $\varepsilon$

and count how many are intersected by the curve (or surface).

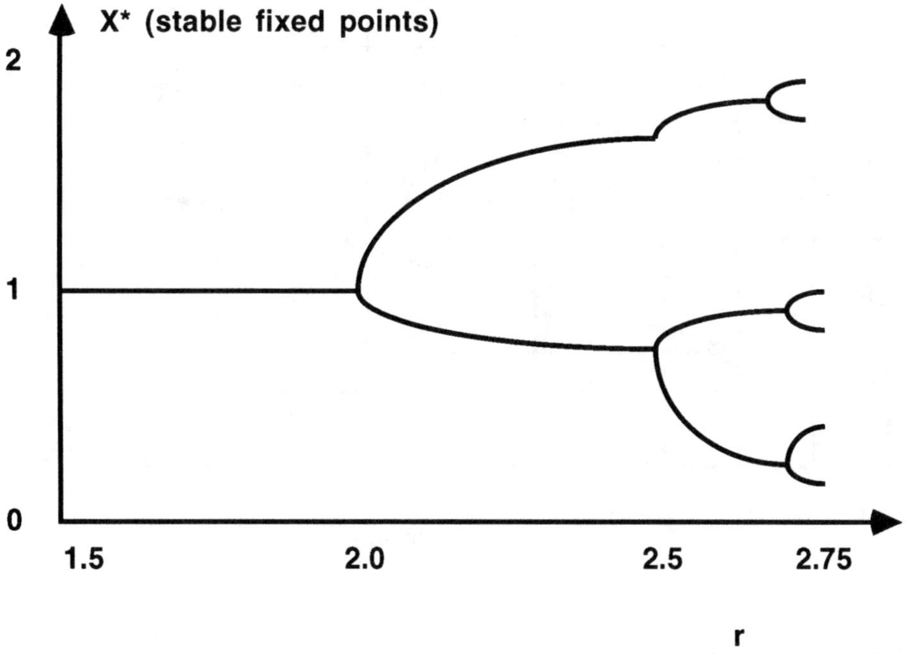

**Fig. 10.2.** The hierarchy of stable fixed points of periods 1, 2, 4, 8... $2^n$, which are produced from equation (10.1) as the parameter r increases. The y-axis indicates relative values.

Figure 10.3 illustrates how you obtain the estimates by counting the number of non-empty cells, N ($\varepsilon$). For the straight line in Fig. 10.4, it is possible to see that the number of boxes is proportional to $\varepsilon^{-1}$, which indicates that the dimension is +1. For a square the number of boxes will correspondingly be proportional to $\varepsilon^{-2}$ and the dimension - not surprising - +2. For a curve; see Fig. 10.4, the irregularity will prevent N ($\varepsilon$) from ever approaching an $\varepsilon^{-1}$ behavior and the dimension will be - dependent on the irregularity - between +1 and +2. In other words fractal dimension becomes a measure of the irregularity.

The fractal dimension D is defined as D in the relationship between N ($\varepsilon$) and $\varepsilon$ :

$$N (\varepsilon) = A * \varepsilon^{-D} \qquad (10.3)$$

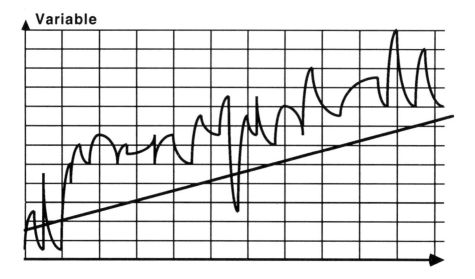

**Variable**

**Time**

**Fig. 10.3.** The straight line has the fractal dimension +1, while the irregular curve will have a dimension between 1 and 2. A magnification will reveal that the curve has continuous irregularity with increasing scale, parallel to the British coastline.

The fractal dimension may be found on the basis of the definition presented above. The number of cells, N, to embed the curve is counted for a decreasing cell length, $\varepsilon$, and log N is plotted versus log ( $\varepsilon$) to provide the dimension D.

Figure 10.4 illustrates this procedure for an irregular relationship between two variables a and y. Table 10.1 gives the data obtained from Fig. 10.4 which were used to determine the fractal dimension. Figure 10.5 gives the log/log plot and as seen a fractal dimension of 1.265 is obtained. In this case the fractal dimension, D, is between 1 and 2, as expected. In this case the analysis stops at $\varepsilon = 0.1$. It is assumed that the irregularity continues with decreasing $\varepsilon$, which is not shown (and can hardly be shown) on Figure 10.4.

Notice that the fractal dimension expresses the irregularity of a curve and may therefore be used as a quantitative measure of the chaotic behavior. This application of the concept fractal dimension will be demonstrated in the last section of the chapter.

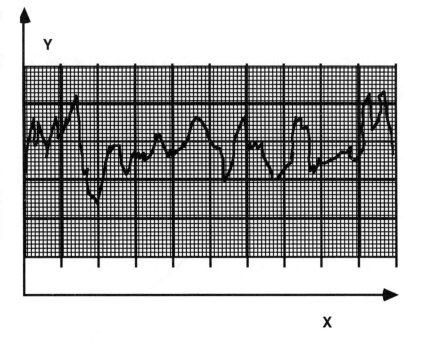

**Fig. 10.4.** Successive subdivisions of overlaying grid to obtain the box counts needed for the application of the procedure to determine the fractal dimension.

**Table 10.1.**

### Determination of the Fractal Dimension by Use of the Data in Fig. 10.5.

| $\varepsilon$ | N ($\varepsilon$) | Log ($\varepsilon$) | Log (N($\varepsilon$)) |
|---|---|---|---|
| 10 | 1 | 1 | 0 |
| 2 | 10 | 0.301 | 1 |
| 1 | 21 | 0 | 1.322 |
| 0.5 | 56 | -0.301 | 1.748 |
| 0.1 | 339 | -1 | 2.53 |

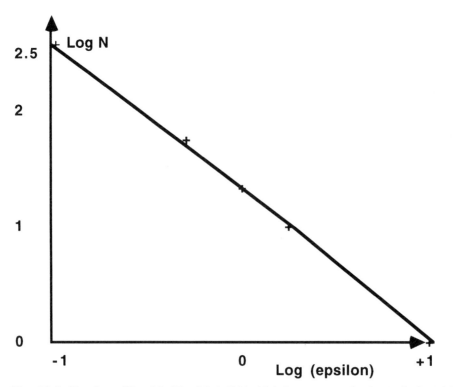

**Fig. 10.5.** The slope of the plot of the data in Table 10.1 gives an approximation to the fractal dimension of the plot in Figure 10.4.

## 10.3. Ecological Implications

When we consider the many non-linear relationships which are valid in ecology, we may wonder why chaos is not observed more frequently in nature or even in our models. An obvious answer could be that nature attempts to avoid chaos and as oppose to the physical system the ecosystem has as discussed in Chapter 2, many possible, hierarchically organized, regulation mechanisms to avoid chaotic situations. This does not imply that chaotic or "almost chaotic" situations are not observed in ecosystems. They are only rarer than would be expected. The classical example is the almost legendary lemming (Shelford 1943). According to this paper $r*T$ is 2.4, $r$ being the growth rate per capita and $T$ the time lag. From Fig. 10.2 it is seen that oscillation between two steady states should be expected as Shelford found; see Fig. 10.6, which is reproduced from Shelford (1943).

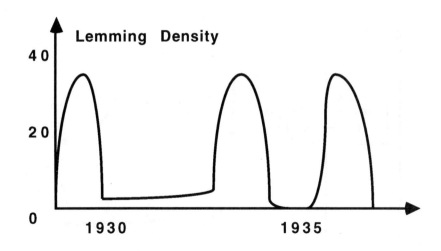

**Fig. 10.6.** Data on the lemming population in the Churchill area in Canada, expressed as numbers per ha. It can be shown that a logistic equation fits nicely with the observations, assuming a relatively large growth rate of the population, (Shelford 1943).

Hassel et al. (1976) have culled data on 28 different populations of seasonal breeding insects. They found that the growth may be described by a difference equation as follows:

$$N_{t+1} = q^* N_t (1 - a^* N_t)^{-\beta} \tag{10.5}$$

q is here related to r as follows: $r = \ln q$. a and ß are constants. Figure 10.7 shows the theoretical domains of stability behavior for equation (10.2) applied on the 28 populations by Hassel et al. By far most of the populations are in the monotonic damping area and only one is in the chaos area (and, as indicated by Hassel et al. it is a laboratory population) and one in the stable limit cycles area.

Notice that there is a tendency for laboratory populations to exhibit cyclic and chaotic behavior, whereas natural populations tend to have a stable equilibrium point. The laboratory populations are maintained in a homogeneous environment and are free from predators and many other natural mortality factors. It means that the indirect effect, which is found in nature (see Section 8.3) ,is omitted and the indirect effect may very well up to a certain level give a stabilizing effect as well.

The most oscillatory natural population is the Colorado potato beetle, *Leptinotarsa*, whose contemporary role in agroecosystems lacks an evolutionary pedigree.

289

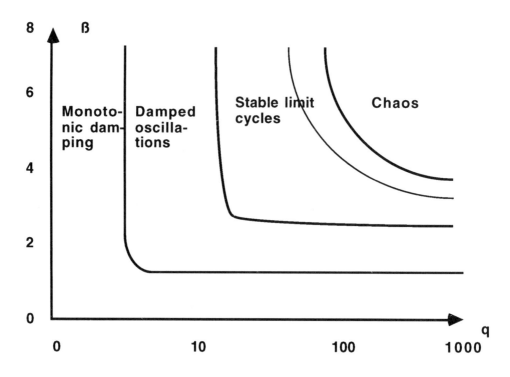

**Fig. 10.7.** The dynamic behavior of equation (10.2). The curves separate the regions of monotonic and oscillatory damping to a stable point, stable limit cycles and chaos. The thin curve indicates where 2-point cycles give way to higher-order cycles. Redrawn after Hassel et al. (1976).

It may be concluded that natural populations are able to avoid chaotic situations to a high extent. The long experience gained during the evolution has learnt the natural population to omit the properties, i.e., the parameters, that may give chaotic situations, because it simply threaten their survival; at least in some situations. Furthermore, the natural populations have the flexibility mentioned in Chapters 2 and 11 - flexibility, which means that the populations have within certain limits the ability to select a combination of parameters that give a better chance for survival.

The relationship between the parameters and the somewhat chaotic behavior is the topic for the following section, which presents an examination of this relationship by the use of models and a concrete case study.

## 10.4. Parameter Estimations and Chaos

Figure 10.8 shows a model with only four state variables: a nutrient., phytoplankton, detritus and bacteria. The reaction of this system is extremely dependent on the parameters given to the state variables, particularly the maximum growth rates of phytoplankton and bacteria. Figure 10.9 shows two situations: one where the maximum growth rates of bacteria and phytoplankton are both 1 day $^{-1}$ and one where the growth rate of the bacteria is maintained on 1 day $^{-1}$, while phytoplankton was given the growth rate of 10 day $^{-1}$. If the growth rate of the bacteria is 10 day $^{-1}$, while the phytoplankton is maintained at 1 day $^{-1}$, almost the same picture is obtained as if the growth rates are inverse. The maximum growth rates are not varied, i.e., there are no fluctuations in temperature or solar radiation.

Exergy is plotted versus the varied growth rate in the figure to capture the biomass of the entire system. From these rather simple modelling experiments it is quite obvious, that if we do have a very simple ecosystem with the components represented in Fig. 10.9, a stable situation is not obtained if the two maximum growth rates are very different (it should be mentioned that almost the same situation is obtained as the one presented in Fig. 10.9., if the maximum growth rates are changed, but the ratio between the two maximum growth rates are varied in a similar way). Stable conditions require that almost the same maximum growth rate is used for phytoplankton and bacteria, while it is not crucial which growth rate is used in the model. Unstable conditions on the other hand appear when significantly different growth rates are allocated to the phytoplankton and the bacteria. The model may represent the situation on the earth about 1.5 billion years ago (we do not know, of course, what the growth rates were then), when only phytoplankton and bacteria were present. Today it can be observed that the bacteria and phytoplankton (still?) have almost the same maximum growth rate. There seems to be some basis, therefore, for the conclusion, that bacteria and phytoplankton have adjusted their maximum growth rate to about 1-2 or maybe 3 day $^{-1}$. The growth rates have been forced to adjust to each-other and when they landed on the level of 1-3 day $^{-1}$, it was simply because that was biochemically feasible, considering the transfer of nutrients through the cell membrane. Any attempt to increase the maximum growth rate would fail unless it were feasible for the bacteria and the phytoplankton simultaneously.

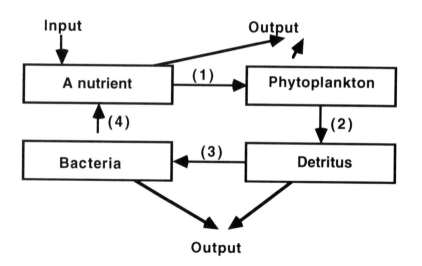

**Fig. 10.8.** The model used for the parameter examination consists of four state variables: a nutrient, phytoplankton, detritus and bacteria. The processes are: growth, expressed by the use of a Michaelis Menten's equation, process number 1; mortality of phytoplankton by use of a first order expression, process 2; growth of bacteria by use of a Michaelis Menten expression, process 3; and mineralization by use of a first-order expression, process number 4.

Figure 10.10 shows another model that has been applied for similar modelling experiments. We have, however, here excluded fish as state variable in the first hand, and we have given the phytoplankton and the bacteria the maximum growth rates experienced from the above-mentioned experiments and ask now what the right maximum growth rate of the two zooplankton state variables to avoid chaotic situations would be. The answer, as seen in Fig. 10.11, is that a maximum growth rate of about 0.35-0.40 day$^{-1}$ seems to give favorable conditions for the entire system, as the exergy is at maximum and stable conditions are obtained. Maximum growth rate of more than about 0.65 -0.70 day$^{-1}$ seems to give chaotic situations for the two zooplankton species.

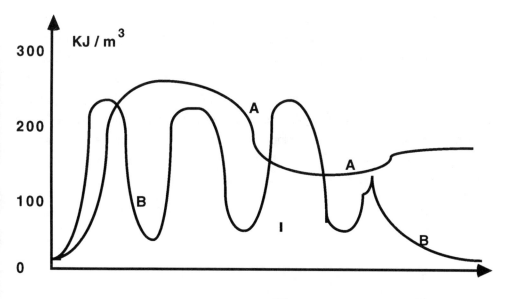

**Fig. 10.9.** Exergy is plotted versus the time for the model shown in Fig. 10.8. A corresponds to an equal maximum growth rate of phytoplankton and bacteria on 1 day[-1], while B corresponds to a growth rate of phytoplankton on 10 day[-1] and of bacteria on 1 day[-1].

Figure 10.10 shows a similar result for fish included as state variable, see Fig. 10.11, and the two zooplankton state variables have been given maximum growth rates of 0.35 and 0.40 day[-1]. A maximum growth rate of about 0.08-0.1 day[-1] seems favorable, but again too high a maximum growth rate (above 0.13-0.15 day[-1]) for the state variable fish will give oscillations and chaotic situations with violent fluctuations.

The parameter estimation is often the weakest point for many of our ecological models. Reasons are:

- an insufficient number of observations to enable the modeller to calibrate the number of more or less unknown parameters
- no or only little literature information can be found.
- ecological parameters are generally not known with sufficient accuracy
- the structure shows dynamical behavior, i.e., the parameters are continuously changing to achieve a better adaptation to the ever changing conditions; see also Jørgensen (1988) and (1992a).
- or a combination of two or more of these points.

The above-mentioned results seem to reduce these difficulties by imposing the ecological facts that all the species in an ecosystem have the properties (described by the parameter set) that are best fitted for survival under the prevailing conditions. The property of survival can currently be tested by use of exergy, since it is survival translated into thermodynamics. Coevolution, i.e., when the species have adjusted their properties to each other, is considered by application of exergy for the entire system. Application of the ecological law of thermodynamics as constraint on our ecological models enable us to reduce the feasible parameter range, which can be utilized to facilitate our parameter estimation significantly.

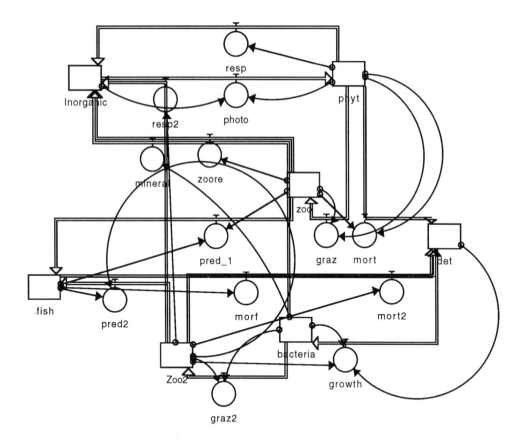

**Fig. 10.10.** Model used to examine the feasible parameters. The model consists of seven state variables. Two zooplankton classes and fish are added in addition to the model in Fig. 10.9.

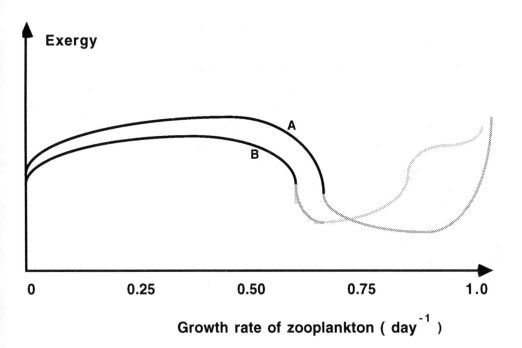

**Growth rate of zooplankton ( day$^{-1}$ )**

**Fig. 10.11.** Exergy is plotted versus maximum growth rate for the two zooplankton classes in Fig. 10.11. A corresponds to the state variable "zoo" and B the state variable "zoo2". The shaded lines correspond to chaotic behavior of the model, i.e., violent fluctuations of the state variables and the exergy. The shown values of the exergy above a maximum growth rate of about 0.65-0.7 day$^{-1}$ are therefore average values.

It is interesting that the ranges of growth rate actually found in nature (see for instance Jørgensen et al. (1991)) are those, which give stable, i.e., non-chaotic conditions. In Chapter 11 we shall apply these plots to further narrow down the ranges using the growth rates giving maximum exergy. All in all it seems possible to conclude that the parameters that we can find in nature today, are in most cases those which assure a high probability of survival and growth in all situations; chaotic situations are thereby avoided. The parameters that could give possibilities for chaotic situations, have simply been excluded by selection processes. They may give high exergy in some periods, but later the exergy becomes very low due to the violent fluctuations and it is under such circumstances that the selection process excludes the parameters (properties) , that cause the chaotic behavior.

Markus et al. (1984, 1987 and 1988) and Markus (1990 and 1991) have examined the occurrence of chaos for populations under periodically and randomly varying growth conditions. An equation similar to (10.2) and (10.4) was applied, but with a varying r-value. It was found that periodically or randomly changing

295

environmental conditions may induce a variety of unexpected dynamic behaviors (see Markus and Hess 1990 and 1990a) which is consistent with the results in Section 4.2. Systems, that are ordered under constant conditions may become chaotic. This effect lowers the threshold for chaos and may explain the fact, that the observed parameters in nature are lower than those leading to chaos in calculations which is according to the results referred to above. The reverse effect is observed, too: a system that is chaotic under constant conditions may become ordered if the conditions change periodically or randomly. Markus et al. (1987) conclude that no generalization on the effect of temporal variation on chaotic behavior can be made, and they assume that the statement that "temporal variations in the environment are a destabilizing influence" is much too simple in view of the diversity of coupling processes.

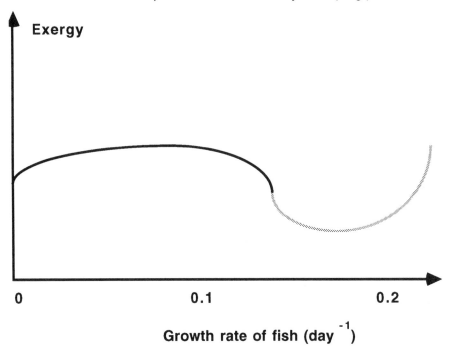

**Fig. 10.12.** The exergy is plotted versus the maximum growth rate of fish . The shaded line corresponds to chaotic behavior of the model, i.e., violent fluctuations of the state variables and the exergy. The shown values of the exergy above a maximum growth rate of about 0.13-0.15 day[-1] are therefore average values.

Kauffman (1991 and 1991a) has studied a Boolean network and finds that network on the boundary between order and chaos may have the flexibility to adapt rapidly and successfully through the accumulation of useful variations. In such poised systems most mutations will have small consequences because of the system's homeostatic nature. Such poised systems will typically adapt to a changing environment gradually, but if necessary, they can occasionally change rapidly - properties that can be found in organisms and ecosystems. It explains, according to Kauffman, why Boolean networks poised between order and chaos can generally adapt most readily and therefore have been the target of natural selection.

The hypothesis is bold and interesting in relation to the results obtained by the use of exergy as indicator in the choice of parameters. The parameters that give maximum exergy are not much below the values that would create chaos, see Figures 10.12 and 10.13. Ecosystems would therefore, according to the ecological law of thermodynamics, select parameters that would guarantee a poised system between order and chaos.

# 11. DYNAMIC OF ECOSYSTEMS

## 11.1. Ecosystem Properties

It has been discussed in Section 2.3 that ecosystems are inconceivably complex and that it will be impossible to produce a description of ecosystem properties that encompasses all the details. Therefore as discussed in Chapter 3, ecological models will always be very simplified pictures of the real ecosystems and can only impinge on a very limited number of problems or aspects related to the focal ecosystem. An ecological model can only be validated in the right context, and only if it is developed according to a sound ecological knowledge of what is essential to include in the model for the focal ecological problem. In addition, it is crucial, that the models possess the basic (holistic) properties of the system that the model is supposed to imitate.

Chapter 2 has attempted to make an inventory of typical ecosystem properties. Table 2.1, for instance, describes the hierarchy of regulation mechanisms and reveals, that ecosystems have a far more ingenious regulation system than you can find to-day even in the most automatized chemical industry. Ecosystems do not only have a regulation of process rates according to feedbacks from both the source and the product, but ecosystems are able to replace ineffective sources, producers and processes with more effective ones to achieve a higher utilization of the resources in their endeavor to move further away from the thermodynamic equilibrium.

The discussion in Section 3.6 on which constraints to impose on ecological models is related to this problem of embedding the properties of the ecosystems into our model. This problem must be solved if we want to improve the predictive capacity of our ecological and environmental models and if we want to understand the system properties of ecosystems. So, the next obvious question is: "would it be possible to account for the entire hierarchy of regulation mechanisms by the introduction of additional constraints on our models?" If we presume that the regulation takes place according to the ecological law of thermodynamics, we may be able use this law as constraints on our model; compare Fig. 3.8. The idea is to use exergy as a goal function and thereby be able to capture the flexibility that characterizes ecosystems in contrast to our present, rigid models, in the hope that we shall be able to improve our models and understanding of ecosystems.

## 11.2 Modelling Structural Dynamics

If we follow the modelling procedure proposed in Fig. 3.2, we will attain a model that describes the processes in the focal ecosystem, but the *parameters* will represent the properties of the state variables as they are in the ecosystem *during* the examination period. They are not necessarily valid for another period of time, because we know that an ecosystem is able to regulate, modify and change them, if needed as response to the change in the prevailing conditions, determined by the forcing functions and the interrelations between the state variables. Our present models have rigid structures and a fixed set of parameters, reflecting that no changes or replacements of the components are possible. We need, however, to introduce parameters (properties) that can change according to changing forcing functions and general conditions for the state variables (components) to be able to optimize continuously the ability of the system to move away from thermodynamic equilibrium. Consequently, we may be able to hypothesize, that the level 5 and 6 in the regulation hierarchy Table 2.1 can be accounted for in our model by a current change of parameters according to the ecological law of thermodynamics. The idea is currently to test if a change of the most crucial parameters is able to produce a higher exergy of the system and, if that is the case, to use that set of parameters. Thereby we obtain a better description of the regulation mechanisms in our model and we obtain simultaneously that our model obeys the Ecological Law of Thermodynamics. If this hypothesis works, we achieve two things: we get more realistic models that are able to describe more accurately our observations, and we get at least a certain support for the hypothetical ecological law of thermodynamics.

The type of models that are able to account for the change in species composition as well as for the ability of the species, i.e., the biological components of our models, to change their properties, i.e., to adapt to the prevailing conditions imposed on the species, are sometimes called structural dynamic models to indicate, that they are able to capture structural changes. They may also be called the next generation of ecological models to underline that they are radically different from previous modelling approaches and can do more, namely describe changes in species composition.

It could be argued that the ability of ecosystems to replace present species with other (level 6 in Table 2.1), better fitted species, can be modelled by construction of models that encompass all actual species for the entire period that the model attempts to cover. This approach has, however, two essential disadvantages. The model becomes first of all very complex, as it will contain many state variables for each trophic level. It implies that the model will contain many more parameters that have to be calibrated and validated and, as presented in Section 3.5, this will introduce a high uncertainty to the model and will render the application of the model very case specific (Nors Nielsen 1992 and 1992a). In addition, the model will still be rigid and not give the model the property of the ecosystems to have continuously changing parameters even without changing the species composition (Fontaine, 1981).

**Table 11.1.**

### Goal functions proposed.

| Proposed for | Objective function | Reference |
|---|---|---|
| Several systems | Maximum useful power or energy flow | Lotka (1922), Odum and Pinkerton (1955); see Chapter 4. |
| Several systems | Minimum entropy | Glansdorff and Prigogine (1971), see Chapter 5. |
| Networks | Maximum ascendency | Ulanowicz (1980) and Chapter 8 |
| Several systems | Maximum exergy | Mejer and Jørgensen (1979) and Chapter 6. |
| Ecological systems | Maximum persistent organic matter | Whittaker and Woodwell (1971) O'Neill et al. (1975) |
| Ecological systems | Maximum biomass | Margalef (1968) |
| Economic systems | Maximum profit | Various authors |

Another related question is the principle of "competitive exclusion", which predicts that two species cannot occupy the same ecological niche at the same time and place (Hardin 1960), while Hutchinson (1953 and 1961) suggests that the vast diversity of phytoplankton observed in many aquatic ecosystems presents an apparent contradiction to this principle. Kemp and Mitsch (1979) have examined this principle and they found, by use of a model with three phytoplankton classes, that the variation of turbulence may explain the coexistence of several phytoplankton species. It may be concluded that ecosystems are more heterogeneous in time and space than presumed and it is therefore difficult to cover this heterogeneity even by use of multi-species models. This does not imply that multi-species models should not be used. The model developed by Kemp and Mitsch illustrates clearly that a multi-species model is able to give reliable results, provided the model contains the essential components and processes for the focal problem.

The following sections in this chapter will present several results of the proposed application of the exergy optimization principle for a continuous change of the parameters. Exergy has been used in some sort of algorithm as a goal function. Other goal functions have been proposed as shown in Table 11.1, but only very few models, that account for change in species composition or for the ability of the species to change their properties within some limits, have been developed.

Bossel (1992) uses what he calls six basic orientors or requirements to develop a system model, that is able to describe the system performance properly. The six orientors are:

1. Existence. The system environment must not exhibit any conditions, which may move the state variables out of its safe range.

2. Efficiency. The exergy gained from the environment should exceed over time the exergy expenditure.

3. Freedom of action. The system is able to react to the inputs (forcing functions) with a certain variability.

4. Security. The system has to cope with the different threats to its security requirement with appropriate but different measures. These measures either aim at internal changes in the system itself or at particular changes in the forcing functions (external environment).

5. Adaptability. If a system cannot escape the threatening influences of its environment, the one remaining possibility consists in changing the system itself in order to cope better with the environmental impacts.

6. Consideration of other systems. A system will have to respond to the behavior of other systems. The fact that these other system may be of importance to a particular system may have to be considered with this requirement.

Bossel (1992) applies maximization of a benefit or satisfaction index based upon balancing weighted surplus orientor satisfactions on a common satisfaction scale. The approach is used to select the model structure of continuous dynamic systems and is able to account for the ecological structural properties as presented in Table 2.1 and Section 11.1. The approach seems very promising, but has unfortunately not been applied to ecological systems except in one case.

The application of the ecological law of thermodynamics as constraint on models corresponds to application of the orientors 2, 4 and 5, while the ecological model, on which this constraint is imposed, should be able to cover orientor 1 and 3. Orientor 6 can only be accounted for by expansion of the model to include at least feed backs to the environment from the focal system.

Straskraba (1979) uses a maximization of biomass as the governing principle. The model computes the biomass and adjusts one or more selected parameters to achieve the maximum biomass at every instance. The model has a routine, which computes the biomass for all possible combinations of parameters within a given realistic range. The combination that gives the maximum biomass is selected for the next time step and so on.

Exergy has been used most widely as a goal function in ecological models, and several case studies will be presented and discussed in the following sections. Exergy has two pronounced advantages as goal function compared with entropy and maximum power: It is defined far from thermodynamic equilibrium and it is related to the state variables, which are easily determined or measured. Equation (6.24) can be used to compute continuously the exergy of the system according to the model. The concentrations of the state variables found by the use of the model at time t, t+1, t+2...t+n are applied in the equation directly to obtain exergy as a function of time.

In the calculation examples given in Section 6.4, $10^{-110}$ mg P/l , was applied as the concentration at thermodynamic equilibrium for phytoplankton which is the thermodynamic equilibrium concentration for E coli according to Morowitz (1968). The exergy is computed for the model rather than for the ecosystem and we can therefore only compute *relative changes* in exergy and not the absolute exergy. It seems of minor importance to discuss this point for a development of a structural dynamic model, where it is the *relative* exergy that is used for selection of values for the parameters.

Zooplankton on the hand side have an even smaller concentration at thermodynamic equilibrium and to account for this, it is proposed to use a concentration for zooplankton that is thousand times smaller, i.e., $10^{-113}$, to account for the lower probability that 100,000 cells are aggregated to form zooplankton. A concentration for fish ($10^{-113}$) a further thousand times smaller at thermodynamic equilibrium should be used; see the discussion in Section 6.3. These proposals for the concentrations of various biological components at thermodynamic equilibrium do, of course, not lead to any exact value of exergy or even of the relative change of exergy, but attempt on top of the exergy coming from the complex biochemical compounds to account an additional contribution - the size of which can be discussed - from the higher level of organization in more developed organisms due to the aggregation of cells. Alternatively, the equations for calculation of the exergy on basis of the chemical composition could be used, as presented in Section 6.3. Some of the short- comings of calculation of exergy in modelling context, including the considerations of the information level, could, however, be accounted for by the development of the applied models for instance by inclusion of information feedbacks.

The inorganic constituents of an ecosystem do not create similar computational difficulties, but the thermodynamic equilibrium concentrations will obviously be the total concentrations of the various elements, corresponding to the fact that all chemical compounds were in inorganic form in the primeval soup, which we often use as reference state for our exergy calculations.

## 11.3 Constraints on Ecological Parameters

The relation between exergy and the most important parameters can also be found and used in the estimations of parameters. It may be best illustrated by use of a simple model of an algae pond, considering only the phosphorus cycle. In this simple case, the model has only two state variables: PA = concentration of phosphorus in algae and PS = soluble inorganic phosphorus. The uptake of phosphorus - the transfer of PS to PA - can be described by use of the Michaelis-Menten expression and the transfer from PA back to PS could be described by the use of a first-order reaction. It means that:

$$dPA/dt = \mu max.^*PS^*PA /(Km + PS) - RE^*PA - Q^*PA/V, \qquad (11.1)$$

where $\mu$max., Km and RE are constants (parameters). Q is the flow of water to and out of the algae pond and V is its volume. The differential equation for PS is:

$$dPS/dt = PIN^*Q/V + RE^*PA - \mu max.^*PS^*PA/(Km + PS) \quad -Q^*PS/V, \quad (11.2)$$

where PIN is the concentration of phosphorus in the inflow to the algae pond. If the steady-state values are found from these equations, it is possible to find the corresponding exergy by use of the exergy equation presented in the first part of this section. We find the following expressions to be used in the equation for computation of exergy:

$$PA_{eq} = [PIN - Km^* (\frac{RE + Q/V}{\mu max. -(RE +Q)})] \tag{11.3a}$$

$$PS_{eq} = [Km^* (\frac{RE + Q/V}{\mu max. -(RE +Q)})] \tag{11.3b}$$

where eq denotes the concentrations of PA and PS at thermodynamic equilibrium.

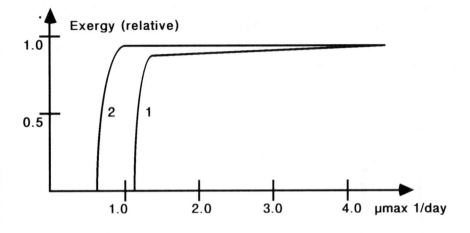

**Fig. 11.1.** Relative exergy is plotted versus μmax. for two Q/V values. 1 corresponds to Q/V = 0.1 and 2 to Q/V = 0.003.

Figure 11.1 shows the relation between Ex and μmax. for two different Q/V values and RE = 0.2, Km = 0.02 and PIN = 1.0. What is interesting about this result, which is *qualitatively* independent of RE, Km and PIN, is that:

1. μmax. has an absolute minimum value, under which no algae can exist. These minimum values agree with observations, as μmax. values below minimum values are not found in nature.

2. The exergy increases very rapidly by increased μmax.- value just above this minimum value and then becomes almost constant. Values slightly above the minimum value could therefore be expected in nature. Such values are in accordance with observations; see for instance Jørgensen et al. (1991). The maximum growth rate of phytoplankton is in the range of about 0.6 to 4

305

day$^{-1}$.

       3) μmax. is dependent on Q/V. The faster the flow rate is, the faster the growth rate must also be to be able to maintain a certain phytoplankton concentration in the lake. This is also according to the observations of Weiderholm (1980).

       It is very difficult to find the analytical solution to the steady state of a non-liear model, if it has more than a few state variables. A relationship between the value of the crucial parameter and the exergy can be found by the use of a computer model. One of the typical results is shown in Fig. 11.2. These results are found by use of a model of the phosphorus cycle in a lake. Four state variables are included: soluble phosphorus, phosphorus in phytoplankton, in zooplankton and detritus-phosphorus. The model is developed by the use of the software STELLA.

       The conceptual diagram is shown in Fig. 2.1. The model was run with fixed values for the forcing functions for 1000 days.

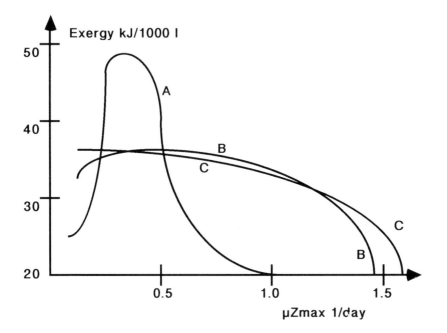

**Fig 11.2.** Exergy is plotted versus value of μZmax. A corresponds to Q/V = 0.1, B to a Q/V = 0.01 and C to Q/V value of 0.003.

As seen from the results in Fig. 11.2, exergy has a maximum at the maximum

306

growth rate for zooplankton of 0.3-0.5 day $^{-1}$, dependent on the flow rate Q/V. It is interesting to observe that the values found are realistic, when they are compared with literature values for this parameter (all the other parameters were given realistic values taken from previous lake modelling studies or the literature), while the highest and lowest values of the maximum growth rate of zooplankton in Fig. 11.2 are unrealistic. The same range of the maximum growth rate for zooplankton is found in many eutrophication modelling studies; see for instance Jørgensen et al. (1986) and Jørgensen et al. (1991) and it is furthermore consistent with the results in Section 10.4. It can be seen from Fig. 11.2 that a high Q/V value gives a high sensitivity to the right maximum growth rate, while a low Q/V value gives almost the same exergy for a wider range of values for the maximum growth rate of zooplankton.

These results may be considered as a certain support for the maximum exergy principle presented in Chapter 6. But they also open the possibilities to use exergy computations to find unknown parameters or to improve the parameter estimation.

It would be interesting to pursue these ideas and investigate whether it would be possible on the basis of such theoretical considerations to give rather narrow ranges for important ecological parameters. It would considerably facilitate the parameter estimation in modelling and would therefore be of a great importance in ecological modelling. It has been shown in Section 10.4 that if parameters are given more extreme values, the model may behave chaotically. It is, of course, not possible to prove that these parameters have been excluded due to the possible chaotic behavior. It seems under all circumstances worthwhile - as it is rather simple - to make an exergy versus parameter value plot for the most crucial parameters to propose some limitations for the parameter estimation.


## 11.4. Application of Exergy as Goal Function in Ecological Modelling

It is obviously of theoretical as well as of environmental management interest to develop models which are able to *predict changes* in the species composition and/or in the ecological structure or at least to indicate the changes of the important properties of the dominant species to account for ecosystem reactions to changes in external factors.

The possibilities of using models with dynamic structure have been tested on two levels:

1) In simple cases where a few species are competing and the result of

the competition is known from observations. The results of such five cases indicated as case A to E are given below.

2) In cases where observations of changes in species composition from entire ecosystems can be used as basis for a modelling test. Two such cases are available and the results are presented in Section 11.5.

**Case A**: It is known that (see for instance Weiderholm, 1980) increased nutrient concentration in a lake often gives larger species of algae with lower growth rate or nutrient uptake rate. Simultaneously the spectrum of algae species becomes more narrow. In oligotrophic waters on the other hand rapid turnover of small phytoplankton should be expected, see for instance Harris (1986) and Margalef (1963 and 1983). The results of this case study are presented in Section 6.4.

**Case B**: Differences in the half-saturation constant for phosphorus and silica may play an important role for the selection of different diatoms, see Tilman and Kilham (1976) If the P/Si ratio is low, the diatoms with a low phosphorus half saturation constant are selected, while a high P/Si ratio is selective for the species with a low silica half-saturation constant. If the Si/P ratio gets very low, diatoms are even replaced by green algae.

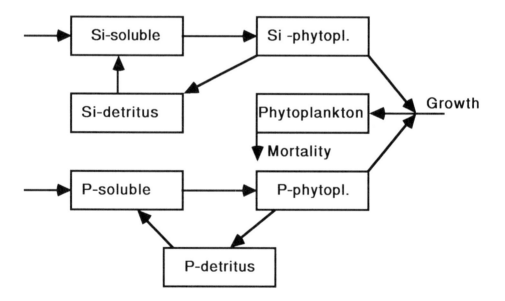

**Fig. 11.3.** One species model applied to show that the results by Tilman and Kilham (1976) are consistent with the maximum exergy principle or the ecological law of thermodynamics. The model has seven state variables. The cycles of phosphorus and silica are independent of each other, while the concentrations of silica and phosphorus in phytoplankton determine the growth of phytoplankton.

An examination with a simple one-species model (see Fig. 11.3) has been carried out to find the relation between the Si/P ratio and the half-saturation constant for silica and phosphorus uptake corresponding to the highest internal exergy value for the system.

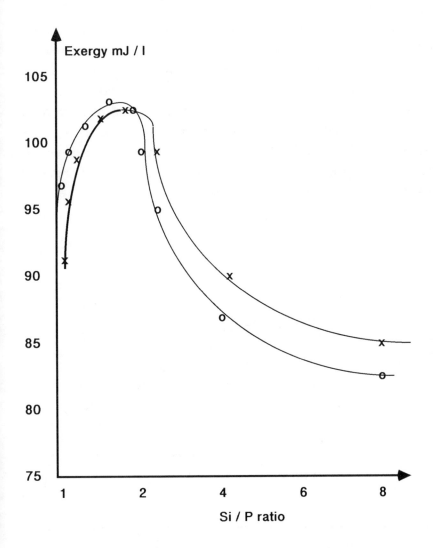

**Fig. 11.4.** Exergy is plotted versus Si/P- ratio for two species of algae: x corresponds to the situation where the half saturation constant for P is 0.003 mg/l and for silica is 0.5 mg/l. o corresponds to the situation where the half saturation constant of P is 0.1 mg/l and for silica is 0.1 mg/l.

The results are shown in Fig 11.4, where the exergy at steady state is plotted versus Si/P-ratio for two species of algae with different half saturation constants. The results are completely according to the chemostate results by Tilman and Kilham (1976). The shift between the two species at the shown Si/P-ratio is completely as found by Tilman and Kilham and the results may therefore be applied as strong support for the maximum exergy principle and for a wider use of this principle in structural dynamic modelling.

Case C: The role of nitrogen-fixing algae species becomes more pronounced, the lower the N/P ratio is and the higher the P-concentration is. A two-species algae model has been used to simulate these observations. The results are shown in Fig. 11.5, where the internal exergy for diatoms and blue- green algae is plotted versus the logarithm of P/N (Si is kept constant at relatively high level). These relations are shown for P= 0.02 mg/l and 1.0 mg/l. The blue-green algae give the highest exergy at a low N/P-ratio and at P= 1.0 mg/l, while the diatoms give the highest exergy in all other situations. It is according to the appearance of blue-green nitrogen-fixing algae in eutrophic lakes with high phosphorus concentrations.

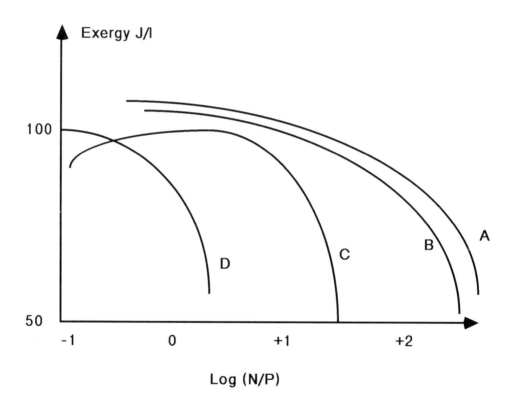

Fig. 11.5. The internal exergy for diatoms and blue-green algae is plotted versus the logarithm of the P/N ratio (Si is kept constant at relatively high level). A corresponds to diatoms and B to blue-green algae at P = 1 mg/l. C corresponds to diatoms and D to blue-green algae at P = 0.02 mg/l.

310

Case D: Diatoms are dominant in many tropical lakes at high rates of precipitation, which usually takes place during the summer. This is surprising, because diatoms usually have a high settling rate and as the retention time under these conditions is often low, diatoms should not be good competitors. However, the very heavy rains stir up the photosynthetic layer and thereby reduce settling and at the same time give diatoms the opportunity to move from time to time to the layer, that offers the most favorable light conditions.

The results of a two-species algae model are shown in Table 11.2. The results: that under the given circumstances (temperature, Si/P ratio and the retention time), the dominance of diatoms gives the highest internal exergy in the rainy season, while a distribution between the two classes of algae in the dry period gives the highest exergy. This is completely according to an actual case reported by T. Tundisi (personal communication 1988).

Table 11.2.

**The ratio of diatoms to green algae at max. exergy by summer and winter situation in a tropical reservoir.**

| Simulation characteristics | Ratio |
|---|---|
| **Summer**    Very low settling rate $Q/V = 0.1$ No light limitations | $\infty$ |
| **Winter**    Normal settling rate $Q/V = 0.02$ Light limitations | 6:4 |

Case E: A model similar to Fig. 11.3, only with the difference that nitrogen and phosphorus were considered instead of silica and phosphorus. All rates were given average values (growth, mortality and mineralization) for the phosphorus and nitrogen cycles. All rates were multiplied by the same factor in each of the two cycles and the inputs of phosphorus and nitrogen were varied. The factors, that give the highest exergy were found, and the ratios, R, between the corresponding nitrogen and phosphorus turnover rates were calculated. The results are summarized in Fig. 11.6., where R is plotted versus N/P ratio and they are completely according to Vollenweider (1975), who considered it a paradox that the higher the N/P ratio, the higher the turnover rate of N to P, as it may be argued that relatively high nitrogen concentrations make it unnecessary to have a rapid turnover of nitrogen.

The five cases discussed above all show that the principle of maximum internal exergy is according to observations of species selections. It would therefore be an obvious step to use the principle to *predict* the selection that will take place under given circumstances, i.e., to develop structural dynamic models.

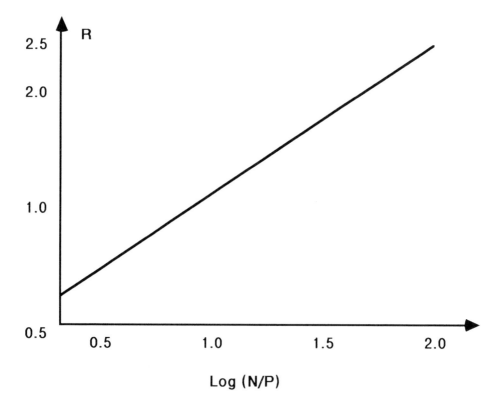

**Fig. 11.6.** The ratio of nitrogen to phosphorus turnover rates, R, at maximum exergy is plotted versus logarithm to the nitrogen phosphorus ratio. Notice that the y-scale is also logarithmic, which makes the relationship almost linear.

## 11.5. Structural dynamic Models of Ecosystems

The idea of the new generation of models presented here is to find continuously a new set of parameters (limited for practical reasons to the most crucial

(=sensitive) parameters) which is better fitted for the prevailing conditions of the ecosystem. "Fitted" is defined in the Darwinian sense by the ability of the species to survive and grow, which may be measured by the use of exergy (see Jørgensen, 1982a, 1986, 1988a and 1990a, Jørgensen and Mejer, 1977 and 1979 and Mejer and Jørgensen, 1979). Figure 11.7 shows the proposed modelling procedure, which has been applied in the cases presented below.

Exergy has previously been tested as a "goal function" for ecosystem development; see for instance Jørgensen (1986), Jørgensen and Mejer (1979) and Herendeen (1989). However in all these cases the model applied did not include the "elasticity" of the system, obtained by use of variable parameters and therefore the models did not reflect real ecosystem properties. A realistic test of the exergy principle would require the application of *variable* parameters.

The use of exergy calculations to vary continuously the parameters has only been used in four cases, of which the two biogeochemical models will be mentioned here. In the first case the growth of algae was used as the only variable parameter (Jørgensen 1986). This gave a significantly improved validation of the model, which encouraged further investigation of the possibilities of developing and applying such new modelling approaches. The maximum growth rate μ-max. and the respiration rate, set equal to 0.15*μ-max., were changed in the model relatively to the previous found value by calibration μ-c:

$$\mu\text{-max.} = F \ast \mu\text{-c.} \qquad\qquad (11.4)$$

The model was run for several F-values and several levels of phosphorus input. The result is plotted in Fig. 11.8. As seen the μ-max. giving maximum exergy decreases when P increases, which is in accordance with ecological observations; see also Section 6.4 When nutrients are scarce, the phytoplankton species compete on the uptake rates of nutrients. Smaller species have a faster uptake due to a greater specific surface and they grow more rapidly. On the other hand, high nutrient concentrations will not favor small species, because the competition rather focuses on avoidance of grazing, where a greater size is more favorable. The results were used to improve the prognosis published in Jørgensen et al (1978) by introducing a continuous change of the parameters according to the procedure in Fig. 11.7. The validation of the prognosis gave the result that the standard deviation between model and measurement was reduced slightly compared with the prognosis applying fixed parameters, although it was also needed to introduce silica as nutrient to account for the appearance of diatoms, see Jørgensen (1986).

The second case where a structural dynamic model was developed by use of exergy as goal function is a lake study, too. The results from Søbygaard Lake (Jeppesen et al 1989) are particularly fitted to test the applicability of the described approach to structural dynamic models. As an illustration to structural dynamics of

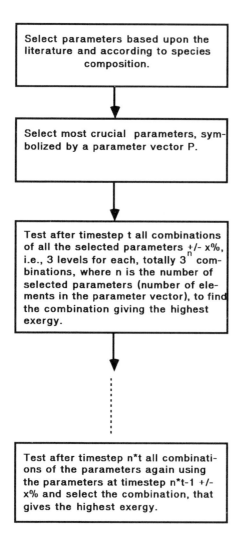

Fig. 11.7. The procedure used for the development of structural dynamic models.

ecosystems and the possibilities to capture the flexibility of ecosystems, the case study of Søbygaard Lake will be presented in detail.

Søbygaard Lake is a shallow lake (depth 1 m) with a short retention time (15-20 days). The nutrient loading was significantly reduced after 1982, namely for phosphorus from 30 gP/ m²y to 5 gP/ m²y. The reduced load did, however, not cause reduced nutrients and chlorophyll concentrations in the period 1982-1985 due to an internal loading caused by the storage of nutrients in the sediment (Søndergaard, 1989 and Jeppesen et al., 1989).

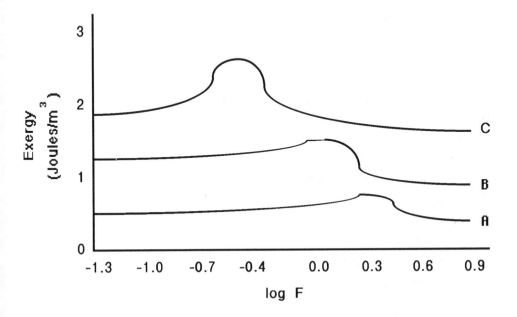

**Fig. 11.8.** Exergy is plotted versus F at different levels of P in a lake. As seen, the maximum exergy occurs at different F-values for different P-loadings. A is an oligotrophic situation that corresponds to a nutrient input of 0.04 mgP/l and 0.3 mgN/l. B corresponds to a nutrient input of 1 mg P/l and 8 mgN/l. C corresponds to a hypereutrophic situation, where the input is 2 mgP/l and 16 mgN/l.

However, radical changes were observed in the period 1985-1988. The recruitment of planctivorous fish was significantly reduced in the period 1984-1988 due to a very high pH caused by the eutrophication. As a result zooplankton increased and phytoplankton decreased in concentration (the summer average of chlorophyll A was reduced from 700 µg/l in 1985 to 150 µg/l in 1988). The phytoplankton population even collapsed in shorter periods due to extremely high zooplankton concentrations. Simultaneously the phytoplankton species increased in size. The growth rate decreased and a higher settling rate was observed (Kristensen and Jensen, 1987). The case study shows, in other words, pronounced structural changes. The primary production was, however, not higher in 1985 than in 1988 due to a pronounced self-shading by the smaller algae in 1985. It was therefore very important to include the self-shading effect in the model, which was not the case in the first mo-

**Table 11.3.**

### Equations of the model for Søbygaard Lake.

---

fish = fish + dt * ( -mort + predation )

INIT(fish) = 6

na = na + dt * ( uptake - graz - outa - mortfa - settl - setnon )

INIT(na) = 2

nd = nd + dt * ( -decom - outd + zoomo + mortfa )

INIT(nd) = 0.30

ns = ns + dt * ( inflow - uptake + decom - outs + diff )

INIT(ns) = 2

nsed = nsed + dt * ( settl - diff )

INIT(nsed) = 55

nz = nz + dt * ( graz - zoomo - predation )

INIT(nz) = 0.07

decom = nd* (0.3)

diff = (0.015)*nsed

exergy = total_n*(Structuralexergy)

graz = (0.55)*na*nz/(0.4+na)

inflow = 6.8*qv

mort = IF fish > 6 THEN 0.08*fish ELSE 0.0001*fish

mortfa =(0.625)*na*nz/(0.4+na)

outa = na*qv

outd = qv*nd

outs = qv*ns

pmax = uptake*7/9

predation = nz*fish*0.08/(1+nz)

qv = 0.05

setnon = na*0.15*(0.12)

settl = (0.15 )*0.88*na

Structuralexergy

= (nd+nsed/total_n)*(LOGN(nd+nsed/total_n)+59)+(ns/total_n)*(LOGN(ns/total_n)-
LOGN(total_n))+(na/total_n)*(LOGN(na/total_n)+60)+(nz/total_n)*(LOGN(nz/total_n)+
62)+(fish/total_n)*(LOGN(fish/total_n)+64)

total_n = nd+ns+na+nz+fish+nsed

uptake = (2.0-2.0*(na/9))*ns*na/(0.4+ns)

zoomo = 0.1 *nz

---

del version, which therefore gave wrong figures for the primary production.

Simultaneously a more sloppy feeding of the zooplankton was observed, as zooplankton was shifted from *Bosmina to Daphnia.*

The model applied has 6 state variables: N in fish, N in zooplankton, N in phytoplankton, N in detritus, N as soluble phosphorus and N in sediment. The equations are given in Table 11.3. As seen, only the nitrogen cycle is included in the model, but as nitrogen is the nutrient controlling the eutrophication, it may be sufficient to include only this nutrient.

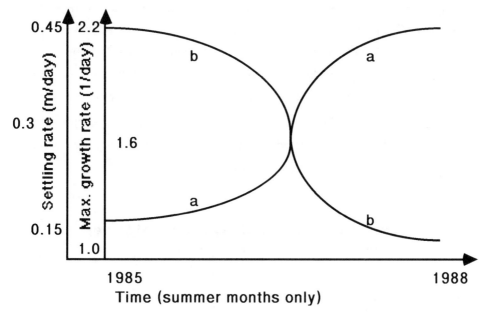

**Fig. 11.9.** The continuously changed parameters obtained from the application of a structural dynamic modelling approach on Søbygaard Lake are shown. a covers the settling rate of phytoplankton and b the maximum growth rate of phytoplankton.

The aim of the study is to be able to describe by use of a structural dynamic model the continuous changes in the most essential parameters using the procedure shown in Fig. 11.7. The data from 1984-1985 were used to calibrate the model and the two parameters that it is intended to change from 1985 to 1988 received the following values by this calibration:

Maximum growth rate of phytoplankton:  2.2 day$^{-1}$

Settling rate of phytoplankton:  0.15 day$^{-1}$

The state variable fish-N was kept constant = 6.0 during the calibration period, but an increased fish mortality was introduced during the period 1985-88 to reflect the increased pH. The fish stock was thereby reduced to 0.6 mgN/l - notice the equation mort = 0.08 if fish > 6 (may be changed to 0.6) else almost 0.

A time step of t = 5 days and x% = 10% was applied; see Fig. 11.7. This means that 9 runs were needed for each time step to select the parameter combination that gives the highest exergy.

The results are shown in Fig. 11.9 and the changes in parameters from 1985 to 1988 (summer situation) are summarized in Table 11.4. The proposed procedure (Fig. 11.7) is able to simulate approximately the observed change in structure. The maximum growth rate of phytoplankton is reduced by 50% from 2.2 day$^{-1}$ to 1.1 day$^{-1}$, which is approximately according to the increase in size. It was observed that the average size was increased from a few 100 $\mu m^3$ to 500 - 1000 $\mu m^3$, which is a factor of 2-3 (Jeppesen et al. 1989). It would correspond to a specific growth reduction by a factor f= $2^{2/3}$ - $3^{2/3}$ (see Jørgensen and Johnsen, 1989).

Table 11.4.

Parameter Combinations giving the highest Exergy.

| | Maximum Growth Rate (day$^{-1}$) | Settling Rate (m*day$^{-1}$) |
|---|---|---|
| 1985 | 2.0 | 0.15 |
| 1988 | 1.2 | 0.45 |

It means that:

$$\text{growth rate in 1988} = \text{growth rate in 1985} / f, \qquad (11.5)$$

where f is between 1.58 and 2.08, while 2.0 is found by use of the structural dynamic modelling approach.

Kristensen and Jensen (1987) observed that the settling was 0.2 m day$^{-1}$ (range 0.02-0.4) in 1985, while it was 0.6 m day$^{-1}$ (range 0.1-1.0) in 1988. By the structural dynamic modelling approach an increase was found from 0.15 day$^{-1}$ to 0.45

day$^{-1}$, the factor being the same - three - but with slightly lower values. The phytoplankton concentration as chlorophyll-A was simultaneously reduced from 600 µg/l to 200 µg/l, which is approximately according to the observed reduction.

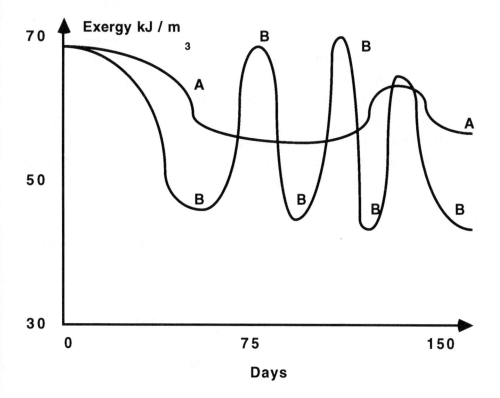

**Fig. 11.10.** Exergy changes by two simulations: A is continuously changed parameters and B is the 1985 parameter set maintained. Start of simulation 1986 summer situation with current changes to the summer situation in 1987.

All in all it may be concluded that the structural dynamic modelling approach gave an acceptable result and that the validation of the model and the procedure in relation to structural changes was positive. It is, however, necessary to expand the model to account for *all* the observed structural changes, including zooplankton, to be able to demonstrate a completely convincing case study. This will therefore be done at a later stage, when all the data from the case study are available. The structural dynamic modelling approach is of course never better than the model applied, and the presented model may be criticized for being too simple and not accounting for the structural dynamic changes of zooplankton.

For further elucidation of the importance to introduce a parameter shift, it has been tried to run the 1985 situation with the parameter combination found to fit the 1988 situation and vice versa. These results are shown in Table 11.5. The results demonstrate that it is of great importance to apply the right parameter set to given conditions. If the parameters from 1985 are used for the 1988 conditions a lower exergy is obtained and the model to a certain extent behaves chaotically while the 1988 parameters used on the 1985 conditions give a significantly lower exergy. This is also demonstrated in Fig. 11.10, where the exergy as a function of time is plotted, when current parameter changes are applied and compared with the 1985 parameters maintained throughout the entire period. For the latter case violent fluctuations of the exergy are observed. Sometimes the exergy is above the level of the simulation based on continuously changed parameters, but the final exergy level is significantly lower. As discussed in Section 10.4. the change in parameters may play a role in avoidance of chaotic conditions of the system.

**Table 11.5**

**Exergy and Stability by different Combinations of Parameters and Conditions**

| Parameter | Conditions | |
| | 1985 | 1988 |
| --- | --- | --- |
| **1985** | 75.0 Stable | 39.8 (average) Violent fluctuations. Chaos. |
| **1988** | 38.7 Stable | 61.4 (average) Only minor fluctuations. |

The results of the two discussed cases show that it is important for ecological and environmental models to contain the property of flexibility, which we know ecosystems possess. If we account for this property in the models, we obtain models that are better able to produce reliable predictions, particularly when the forcing functions on the ecosystems change and thereby provoke changes in the properties of the important biological components of the ecosystem. In some cases we get completely different results, when we apply a continuous change of the parameters from when we use fixed parameters. In the first case we get results that are better in accordance with our observations and as we know that the parameters do actually change in the natural ecosystems, we can only recommend the application of this approach as far as possible in ecological modelling.

The property of dynamic structure and adaptable parameters is crucial in our description of ecosystems and should therefore be included in all descriptions of the system properties of ecosystems. The few examples presented here show that it is feasible to account for the adaptability of the properties in models, although a more general experience is needed before clear recommendations on the application can be given.


## 11.6. Structural Dynamic Models in Population Dynamics

The structural dynamic approach presented in Fig. 11.7 has been applied to two models of population dynamics. The two case studies confirm the applicability of the approach. Both case studies are very simple, but they may be considered theoretically sound.

The first case study deals with a simple two-level predator-prey system, using the following equations:

$$dx/dt = b^*x\,(1 - x/K) - s^*x^*y \quad \text{and}$$
$$dy/dt = s^*y^*x^2/(k + x) - m^*x, \tag{11.6}$$

where x is the prey, y is the predator, b is the growth rate of the prey, K is the carrying capacity, s is the specific predation rate, k is a half-saturation constant, and m is the mortality coefficient for the predator. The procedure described in Fig. 11.7. was used on this model, starting with the following parameters:

b = 2,
K = 100,
s = 0.25,
m = 0.2.

It is known that random mutations will lead to an increase in b and K and a decrease in m, while the evolution of s will have no clear direction; see Allen (1985). All the parameters were set to be changed up to 10% relatively for each ten days. The initial values of x and y were found by running the model to steady state and apply the corresponding x and y values as initial values. The starting exergy was 2400*R*T. The result after 1000 time steps was a new system with exergy as much as ten times higher and the following parameters:

321

b = 5
K = 150
s  = 0.05
m = 0.05

The second population dynamical case study focused on competition and the role of the width of the ecological niche versus the size of the resources available for the competing species. According to Allen (1975 and 1976), it should be expected that a rich system will show an evolution towards specialization, meaning less competition and narrow ecological niches, while a poor system will lead to generalists; it implies more competition and wide ecological niches.

The model presented in Table 11.6 was used to simulate the competition of three species.The procedure in Fig. 11.7. was again applied to allow the model to change the parameters to values giving higher exergy. Up to a 10% change was allowed every ten days for *either* the competition factors *or* the carrying capacities. The change, that gave the highest increase in exergy was realized. The model was run at five different combinations of the other parameters, giving five different utilizations of the carrying capacities at steady state. The results are summarized in Table 11.7, where the change in competition factors starting at 1.0 and the carrying capacities starting at 500 are given after 1000 time steps. It was found that the competition factors (all 0.5 in the version for the model in Table 11.6 for all combinations of competitions) were mainly adjusted, when the carrying capacities were high compared with the numbers of the three species. The carrying capacities were on the other hand adjusted when the number of species was closer to the carrying capacities. These results are completely according to the  evolution of the system which we expected: a rich system should reduce the competition factor and a poor system should increase the carrying capacities.

**Table 11.6.**

**Source code for the equations of the competition model.**

---

```
spec_1 = spec_1 + dt * ( growth - mort )
INIT(spec_1) = 5
spec_2 = spec_2 + dt * ( growth2 - mort_2 )
INIT(spec_2) = 4
spec_3 = spec_3 + dt * ( growth_3 - mort3 )
INIT(spec_3) = 5
carrying_capacity = 500
carry_cap_2 = 500
carry_cap_3 = 500
growth = 0.44*spec_1*(1-((spec_1+0.5*spec_2+0.5*spec_3)
/carrying_capacity))
growth2=0.38*spec_2*(1-(spec_2+0.5*spec_1+0.5*spec_3)/carry_cap_2)
growth_3 = 0.475*spec_3*(1-(spec_3+0.5*spec_2+0.5*spec_1)/carry_cap_3)
mort = 0.4*spec_1
mort3 = 0.45*spec_3
mort_2 = 0.35*spec_2
sum = spec_2+spec_1+spec_3
```

---

**Table 11.7.**

**Results of the use of structural dynamic approach
on the competition model.**

---

| Utilization of carrying capacity | Change in competition factors | Change in carrying capacity |
|:---:|:---:|:---:|
| 60% | 0 | +300 |
| 32% | 0 | +300 |
| 11% | 0.5 | +200 |
| 3% | 0.7 | +50 |
| 0.5% | 0.9 | 0 |

---

# 12. A TENTATIVE PATTERN OF ECOSYSTEM THEORIES

## 12.1. Presentation of a Pattern

The properties of ecosystems can only be revealed by the use of a pluralistic view. It is therefore not surprising that there are many different ecosystem theories presented in this volume. It is on the other hand necessary to try to unite the theories and examine if they are tied up in contradictions or form a pattern that can be used to give a better understanding of the nature of ecosystems and to solve the global environmental problems.

It is probably not surprising for the reader, after reading the 11 preceding chapters, that we *are* able to form a pattern of the presented theories. They are highly consistent .

The pattern is presented in this chapter and should be considered tentative. The goal of the presentation is to give a common framework of reference for further development of a more profound and comprehensive ecosystem theory than the one that we are able to present today. The pattern should serve as a "conceptual diagram," which can be used as basis for further discussion of how ecosystems behave. We are still in an early stage of ecosystem-theoretical developments and it may be argued that this attempt is premature, but I must admit that my experience from modelling has taught me that it is better to conclude one's thoughts in a conceptual diagram at an early stage and then be ready to make changes than to let all modelling efforts wait until all details are known, as this will never be the case due to the immense complexity of nature.

It is too easy in science to fall into the trap of criticizing one's opponent, who is supporting an alternative view to one's own, for blindly pursuing their own view and for failing to see the obvious. Science and particularly ecology is not that simple, as pointed out by the complementarity theory. Therefore we need to be open-minded to other people's approaches to assure progress in ecosystem theory. Only then will our continued effort inexorably lead to the understanding that we are seeking.

The center of the presented pattern is the fourth or ecological law of thermodynamics and the following section is devoted to present this focal law and its direct implications for the complexity of ecosystems. What can we conclude from this law about ecosystem properties? As pointed out in Chapter 6, this law is not only valid for ecosystems - the name "ecological law of thermodynamics" refers solely to its possible application to ecosystems. The law describes the development of systems, that have a through-flow of energy (exergy) and is valid for all systems, i.e., living and non-living systems. The difference between living and non-living systems is not the basic characteristic for this development; rather it is the fact that living systems have better embodied possibilities for utilization of the energy flow.

The relation between the presented pattern and other ecosystem theories is the topic for the following section. The relation to the concepts of entropy, maximum power, emergy and ascendency will be discussed.

The immense complexity of ecosystems has provoked a wider use of non-traditional, scientific tools for a deeper understanding of the ecosystems such as the use of modelling, network theory and hierarchical contemplations. The fourth section of the chapter therefore focuses on these tools.

The two last sections are devoted to ecosystem properties in their widest sense. All the properties mentioned previously in the volume will be related to the pattern and some characteristic additional properties will be included in the pattern as examples. It will not be possible to treat a very wide spectrum of ecosystem properties concerning the developed pattern due to limited space, but the examples will hopefully serve as a source of inspiration for others.


## 12.2. A Central Law of Ecosystem Theories

The previously presented ecological law of thermodynamics seems to be the best candidate for a central law of ecosystem theory, because it is consistent with the holistic approaches of thermodynamics, with the central theory of biology - Darwin's theory - and it is not in contradiction to any of the other theories presented. The formulation that will be given here is based on exergy, but it does not mean that other formulations are not valid. On the contrary, other formulations, using other concepts, are equally valid. In some context they may be more useful and in other contexts the formulation based on exergy gives a better understanding. The other possible formulations will be mentioned in the next section.

Ecosystems are open (or at least non-isolated) systems and can not exist without a through-flow of low-entropy energy. The maintenance of the ecological structure in an ecosystem requires energy, i. e., the life processes, including for instance respiration, require addition of energy or even "first-class energy" (exergy), because addition of heat is not sufficient. The ecosystem receives a through-flow of exergy from the sun, even more than needed (at least in periods). The first-class energy is the radiation energy, which is utilized by the plants to form biomass, i.e., biogeochemical energy or exergy.

The ecological law of thermodynamics gives information on which of the many possible processes, that will be realized as a result of a competition among more possibilities, than the flow of exergy can accomplish. The law asserts, that: **A system, that receives a through-flow of exergy (high quality energy) will utilize the energy to move away from thermodynamic equilibrium and if more combinations of components and processes are offered to utilize the exergy flow, the organization that will obtain the highest (storage of) exergy in the system, will win.**

The support for the validity of the law is strong and may be summarized in the following points (see also Chapter 6):

1. It may be considered a translation of Darwin's theory to thermodynamics and is consistent with the basic, thermodynamic laws.

2. Model studies, that are supported by ecological observations, show that the pathways giving the highest biomass (exergy) will win.

3. The application of the hypothetical law in models gives (many) results, that are consistent with ecological observations (see Chapters 6 and 11, and Section 12.6).

The chemical interpretation of the law is furthermore consistent with an extended version of "Le Chatelier's principle". The focal processes may be described as:

Energy + nutrients  = molecules with more free energy and organization (12.1)

If we pump energy into the system, the equilibrium will according to Le Chatelier's principle shift in a way that tends to relieve the stress (changes), i.e., more molecules with free energy and organization will be formed. If more pathways are offered, the pathways, that give most relief, i.e., that use most energy and thereby form molecules with most free energy (exergy) will win according to the interpretation of the ecological law of thermodynamics (abbreviated ELT). A repetition of the extended "Le Chatelier's principle," is formulated in proposition 15, see Section 12.4.

As already mentioned in Section 6.5, the law is valid for *all* systems, not only ecosystems. The name "The ecological law of thermodynamics" refers to the particular applicability the law has for ecosystems. All systems will - also systems without living matter - utilize a through-flow of exergy to gain more organization, to move away from thermodynamic equilibrium or to attain a higher level of (stored) exergy. The difference between ecosystems and non-living systems is that the latter only have one or very few possibilities to utilize the exergy flow, which means that no, or at the most a very simple *selection* of organization will take place, compare with Benard's cell in Section 5.7.

An ecosystem will on the other hand offer many possible pathways for the utilization of the exergy flow, which is a result of the evolution. It has been rendered possible by a step-wise development of a better and better strategy 1)to maintain pathways, that have already shown to give good solutions, and 2) to create new and better and often more sophisticated pathways to enable the system to move even farther away from the thermodynamic equilibrium.

It seems to be a workable hypothesis to accept ELT, and attempt to form an ecological theory on the basis of ELT. We shall in this section try to explain on the basis of ELT why ecosystems are so complex, as described in Chapter 2, and why the presented law has such a high applicability in ecosystem theory.

The ecosystems on the earth have received an exergy flow in four billion years and have been continuously able to test by trial and error, if occasionally newly formed pathways would be able to do a better job in moving away from the thermodynamic equilibrium. Better and better solutions were found by this method but the big jump forward was made when the selfish gene emerged (Dawkins 1982 and 1989). It implied that information about "good solutions" could be stored and used as basis for moving further away from equilibrium. It was an inconceivable progress in the evolution and as demonstrated in Section 6.5, it meant that the biological evolution actually became possible at all. Of course life as we know it on earth requires additional factors that are based upon biochemical considerations: the presence of the important nutrients, of water as transport medium and of the right temperature range.

Other important progress in the evolutions should also be mentioned: when the cells were formed to protect the storage of information, when multicellular organisms emerged to assure a better division of labor, when nursery and teaching of offspring developed, when communication emerged to transfer information from one organism to another of the same species, when intelligence developed and was used to protect the species, when a language was formed to expand the communication significantly, when the written language was invented, when book printing was invented and when the computer was invented. Notice that in this chain of evolutionary steps that information is becoming more and more important. Mass is the limiting factor in process (12.1) , which implies that to move father away from equilibrium on the basis of the same amount of nutrients will require a better utilization of the nutrients, i.e., formation of more sophisticated organic compounds is required. This possibility, however, also has limits and it is therefore naturally to attempt to put more information "into the organic molecules" to obtain more exergy for the system. The evolution in grams of DNA per cell, number of genes and number of cell types strongly support this hypothesis; see Table 12.1. The evolution may be described by use of a graphic representation as in Fig. 2.5. in Section 2.2. Exergy versus time will show the same curve and the sudden increase in exergy corresponds to the development of new methods (it implies a jump in the level of organization and information) to move away from the thermodynamic equilibrium. This is already achieved for instance by the development of the selfish gene, the cell, and so on.

**Table 12.1.**

**The evolution of g DNA / cell, number of genes and cell types.**

**Approximate figures are given.**

| Organisms | $10^{-12}$g DNA / cell | Number of genes | Number of cell type |
|---|---|---|---|
| Bacteria | 0.005 | 600 | 1-2 |
| Algae | 0.009 | 850 | 6-8 |
| Yeast | 0.02 | 2000 | 5-7 |
| Fungus | 0.03 | 3000 | 6-7 |
| Sponges | 0.1 | 9000 | 12-15 |
| Jellyfish | 0.9 | 50,000 | 23 |
| Annelid worms | 20 | 100,000 | 60 |
| Field mouse | 50 | 140,000 | 100 |
| Human | 90 | 250,000 | 254 |

The above-mentioned milestones in the evolution are all characterized by a better preservation of what is already obtained to assure a higher probability of moving away from thermodynamic equilibrium. Simple model exercises will easily demonstrate that it is of crucial importance to be able to work on "the back" of what is already attained. The dinosaur paradox could for instance be explained in this light. The difference in nursery and protection of the offspring between dinosaur and mammals seems to be sufficient to explain that mammals took over very fast (during maybe one or a couple of millions years). A little advantage is sufficient to give a far better probability of survival, which is easily demonstrated by simple calculations or by the use of simple models. The selection pressure will rapidly favor even the slightest advantage and an advantage in survival of the young ones is incredibly important for preservation of the selfish gene (Dawkins 1989).

It may be claimed on this background that :

1) ELT,

2) the pronounced spatial and

3) temporal heterogeneity and

4) the very long time, that has been available to find new and better solutions to the problem of getting the highest possible storage of exergy,

explain the immense complexity of the ecosphere to day.

The same factors may explain why life has been able to find numerous extremely ingenious solutions to build up biogeochemical energy (biomass, exergy) under all conditions including the most extreme conditions from the deepest sea to the highest mountains (see as examples Figs. 12.1. and 12.2.). The solutions to the problems that life is facing due to extreme external factors, are often surprisingly sophisticated and thousands of pages have been devoted to describe these interesting aspects of life. It may therefore be concluded that life is able to develop a wide spectrum of pathways to be able to meet the challenge of moving further and further away from thermodynamic equilibrium, utilizing all possible combinations of conditions and utilizing all available resources in whatever form they may have. H.T. Odum (1971, 1988 and 1989) uses the expression "self-organization" and " feed back allows the circuit to learn" to cover this description, see also Section 4.2.

These considerations also explain why we are able to find such a wide spectrum of strategies for survival and growth. We distinguish two classes of strategies, K-strategists and r-strategists, but the strategies found in ecosystems may rather be explained as a spectrum of strategies from the clearest K-strategy (high maintenance, little growth and few off-spring) to the clearest r-strategy (little maintenance, high growth and many off-spring).

It is a clear advantage for the ecosystems to have the entire spectrum of strategies available to gain more exergy due to the huge heterogeneity in time and space. Sudden changes in the external factors create suddenly new conditions, that r-strategists can utilize better in the first instance, while the very stable conditions are better utilized by the K-strategists.

Biological growth is dependent on a number of factors:

- some 30 nutrients and micro nutrients,
- a number of climatic factors (temperature, wind, etc.) including the amount of energy flowing through the system,
- the transport processes in the systems, which are, of course, again dependent on a number of other factors including the climatic factors.
- all the other biological and abiological components in the system.

All these factors are functions of time and space. The conditions on formation of life *are* extremely heterogeneous in time and space. The process (12.1) therefore never has the same conditions in time or space.

**Fig. 12.1.** Lichen is able to grow at very high altitude, because it has solved the problem of the low temperature and the high intensity of ultraviolet radiation.

There is therefore a need for many different solutions to utilize the exergy flow and it is therefore not surprising, given the long period available for development of many different and good solutions, that the ecosystems have high complexity and

331

many beautiful solutions. Nor it is surprising that almost *all* possible mechanisms have been tested. It may explain why genes can also be modified by the organisms, i.e., that the organisms attempt to change the environment to modify the selection pressure and why a strong coevolution in general has taken place; see Section 2.2.

Species in the same ecosystem have lived together for a very long time and the influences from the other species have been among the many factors that have determined the selection pressure. The species have "polished each other as an old married couple." As ecosystems are open, the various ecosystems have furthermore influenced each other and have exchanged "knowledge" in the form of genes. Emigration and immigration are common processes in ecosystems.

Fig. 12.2. In Yellowstone National Park algae grow at extreme temperatures even above $80^{\circ}$C.

Symbiosis has again and again been favored, because it gives advantages to two or more species simultaneously and has thereby been considered as a part of the factors mentioned above. A more and more complex interrelationship among the biological components evolves and implies that a more and more complex network develops over time, where the components are more and more dependent on each other. It explains why the indirect effect becomes so dominant (see Section 8.3.), and why the Gaia effect has become more and more pronounced. The presence of a dominant indirect effect can only be interpreted as a *full* cooperation of *all* components in a network, as discussed in Section 8.3. Direct negative effects become positive indirect effects and there seems to be a network mutalism. This, again together with the long period which has been available for evolution, may be able to explain how the Gaia-effect emerged. The indirect effect may be considered as an explanation and as a quantitative measure of the Gaia-effect, see Section 8.3.

The most essential contemplations, presented in this section, are summarized in Fig. 12.3 and we may summarize the presented ecosystem properties in the tentative seven propositions, presented below. The propositions are the result of the discussion in this section and the previous 11 chapters. Some parts of the propositions may be shown by use of ELT in combinations with well examined models - a technique discussed in Sections 3.7. and 12. 4.

**Proposition 1. Ecosystems are open systems and are dependent on a through-flow of first class energy (=exergy). When the energy needs for maintenance (catabolic processes) have been covered, the exergy is stored and the system thereby moves away from thermodynamic equilibrium.**

**Proposition 2. Developments of methods to maintain the biogeochemical energy already stored, i.e., increase in the level of organization and information of the ecosystems, are important milestones in the evolution.**

**Proposition 3. Ecosystems show a very wide spectrum of solutions to survival and growth under all even extreme conditions on the earth. The wide spectrum observed may be considered a result of the combination of 1) ELT, 2) the very long time that has been available for the evolution (4 billion years), 3) the immense heterogeneity in time and 4) in space. The examinations of the development tendencies due to the available spectrum of solutions may be performed by use of ELT and models that must reflect the possibilities that the ecosystem may offer for utilization of the through flow of exergy.**

**Proposition 4. A wide spectrum of strategies from clear K-strategies to clear r-strategies is available to assure survival and growth under all conditions and in spite of the immense heterogeneity in time and space.**

**Proposition 5. Life in the form, that we know from the earth is not possible without the presence of 1) 20-30 essential elements, 2) the temperature range presented on earth (approximately from -40°C to + 90°C) (see Section 5.3) and 3) water.**

**Proposition 6. The long period of selection pressure under the influence of all other biological components throughout the entire**

evolution (about 4 billion years) has developed a high extent of symbiosis or network mutalism, which explains the emergence of the Gaia-effect.

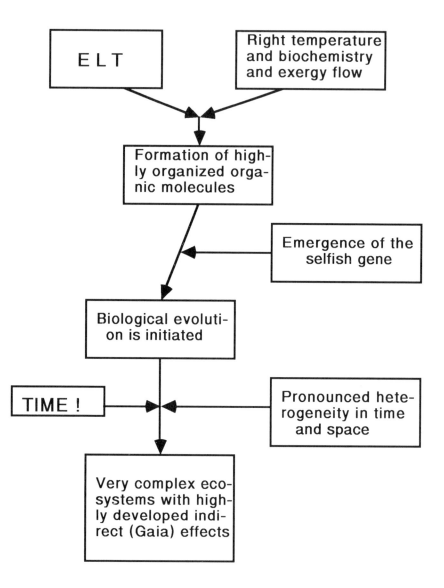

**Fig. 12.3.** The diagram shows the application of ELT (ecological law of thermodynamics) to explain the high complexity and the properties of present ecosystems.

Proposition 7. As a result of the endeavor of ecosystems to find new pathways to move father away from thermodynamic equilibrium, self-organization abilities of ecosystems and feedbacks that allow the circuit to learn from previous experience, have been developed.


## 12.3. The Relation to Other Theories

The relations to other ecological theories have already been mentioned throughout the volume, but we shall here summarize the conclusions to achieve an overview of the relations between the various theories presented. The linkages to the theories related to the perception of ecosystems as integrated networks, i.e., the theories of hierarchical organization, indirect effect, network mutalism and network utility, are mentioned in the next section on the applied tools in ecosystem research.

1. **The theory of maximum entropy production or rather of maximum dissipation of energy** is very closely related to ELT. The difference is whether you focus on the exergy embedded in the construction or on the energy / exergy needed for maintenance of the construction. The two amounts of exergy are of course closely related. Maintenance in general decreases per unit of biomass with size of the organisms and with the size of the system, i.e., the system evolves towards a better utilization of the available exergy (see Figure 5.12., Section 5.7), as the need for energy is related to the surface. It can, however, not change the fact, that the overall biomass (construction) has become bigger and bigger and a better and better energy dissipator (see Fig. 5.13, Section 5.7). Therefore it requires more energy (exergy) for the maintenance. The energy used for maintenance is decreasing relative to the biomass, but as the biomass increases faster, the overall trends are toward dissipation of more energy (exergy). The point of the theory, however, clearly is that there is a direction to the process of self-organization and evolution and this is away from equilibrium in response to the thermodynamic forces, which is completely consistent with ELT.

It is the strength of ELT, that it has more roots in biology by being a thermodynamic translation of Darwin's theory, and as "construction" comes before "maintenance", it is in the first instance at least more obvious to focus on the construction than on maintenance. However, the theories of ELT and maximum energy dissipation *are* , of course, two sides of the same coin. **It may therefore be concluded that ELT involves that more energy is utilized on the earth (or less is reflected to the open space), as we are moving more and more away from thermodynamic equilibrium due to the need for more energy for maintenance.** If we exclude shading effects, energy seems generally not the most important limiting factor, because with the present process rates the nutrients are used up faster than the energy. It is expressed by Kay (1984) as follows: "The supersystem will evolve so as to maximize energy degradation, make efficient use of material resources and be internally stable. Given sufficient time, the supersystem will develop adaptive mechanisms to cope with abiotic environmental changes". Therefore it is not surprising that the evolution has not created very energy-saving organisms, but rather organisms that are able to store more information per unit of mass (and energy, because mass and energy cannot be separated). Information becomes the key to obtain more exergy, when nutrients are limiting. Compare also Table 12.1.

2. **The maximum power principle** focuses on the flow of *useful* energy, (useful to what ? Useful for the system, of course). It may be interpreted as maximization of the energy flow used to increase the free energy (exergy) of the system. The maximum power principle may therefore be interpreted as the derivate of exergy $dEx / dt$. It is, of course, an open question, whether the rate of increase in exergy or the exergy itself is optimized. Most organisms have memory , however,  and take for instance the seasonal variations into consideration and therefore have the possibilities to optimize the exergy on a long term basis. $dEx / dt$ does therefore probably not serve as the right goal function. It seems more correct to use exergy, which leads to the open question, however, on what time horizon to apply for the optimization. In the example in Section 11.4 time-steps of 5 days were used to capture the structural dynamics, but too short a time interval for adjustment of the parameters will only be beneficial. Five days  were, however,  also used as the period to examine which parameters gave the highest exergy. This choice of period length may be acceptable for the selection of algae parameters, but may be too short for the selection of zooplankton  or fish  parameters. Generally , it may be recommended to test the structural dynamic technique presented in Chapter 11 by the use of not too long intervals between two possible adjustments of parameters and not too short intervals for examination of which parameters give the highest exergy.

3. **The Maximum Ascendency Principle** is based upon network considerations. It is a simultaneous measure for growth and development or size and organization. Exergy can also be divided into a size, concentration and structure terms, as presented in Section 6.3. There are therefore clear reasons to anticipate that the two concepts are consistent. It is not possible, or at least very difficult, to show analytically  that exergy and ascendency are parallel measures for the development of ecosystems, but a  few model examinations confirm that they give parallel results.

Ascendency may therefore be considered a convenient concept to apply when ecosystems are viewed as networks and the flows are known. The latter is sometimes difficult to obtain, however, by many ecosystem studies, but the concept is probably more easily conceived than exergy for an ecosystem theorists thinking in terms of networks.

**4. Emergy** may be considered as an attempt to incorporate a quality factor into ecosystem energy. The factor is based upon the energy costs, but when the foodweb gets more complex, as shown in Section 8.2, the energy costs become very complicated to calculate and the simple food chain calculations presumed in Section 4.5. will inevitably give only approximately correct results. The idea behind emergy is to a certain extent adopted in the application of much lower thermodynamic equilibrium concentrations of higher levels in the food web; see Sections 6.3 and 11.2. It is, however, preferable to apply exergy, because it considers that higher life forms have higher exergy due to their higher level of organization, while emergy considers the higher cost of energy in solar equivalents to form higher life forms, which is less relevant for our attempt to express the development of ecosystems.

## 12.4. Tools: Networks and Models

A general discussion of the crucial question on the applicability of models as scientific tools was already presented in Section 3.7. Some additional points will be touched on in this section.

Ecosystems are inconceivably complex and if we want to capture the holistic ecosystem properties, it is necessary to use models as a tool to overview the complexity. Analysis of the individual parts and processes in the ecosystem is necessary and the prerequisite for all deeper understanding. Taken alone, however, analysis is not sufficient. The whole shows properties that are absent from its isolated parts. The problem of ecosystems is that of organization and to capture the properties behind the organization, we need networks and models as tools.

It has been demonstrated in Chapter 11 how it is possible to improve the models, i.e., to build more ecosystem properties into the models - in this case to account for the flexibility of ecosystems - that describe their adaptability and their ability to exchange unsuitable components for better fitted ones. More and more ecosystem properties must be built into our models to improve them; this is the most essential challenge to ecological modellers in the next decade.

Models have been used in this volume to develop important ecosystem theoretical components or to test hypotheses on ecosystem properties. Ecosystems are irreducible systems and therefore the properties cannot be revealed by analytical methods, because they cannot consider the interactions of many components simultaneously. Models therefore seem the only tool, in spite of their shortcomings. As far as possible models have been used to reveal properties of systems with a similar construction as reflected in the models. The general idea is to observe the properties, that are related to a complex network of linkages similar to the ecosystem's. The results will inevitably be only qualitative or semi-quantitative. An illustrative example is the discussion of indirect effect versus the direct one, see Chapter 8. The ratio between the two types of effects cannot be observed without looking into the propagation of effects in the entire system, because the type and number of linkages are determinant. The exact ratio of the direct to the indirect effect found by the use of models is not necessarily valid for the ecosystem. As ecosystems, however, have linkages as the model, the result that the indirect effect is dominant is therefore most probably valid for ecosystems. The results are furthermore supported by ecological observations in the ecosystem; see Chapter 8, which present a natural next step to get the hypothesis tested. So, to conclude: models may be used as tool to reveal ecosystem properties and get inspiration for new hypotheses on ecosystem reactions, provided that:

1. The models are realistic, i.e., they are based upon sound ecological knowledge and good ecological observations. It should be recommended to use models that have proved their capability on several modelling studies - of course with modification from one case study to the next as discussed in Chapter 3.

2. It is important that the models possess the properties that are crucial for the test. If we are testing the consequence of many linkages, as for instance in relation to the indirect effect, it is important that the applied models have these properties, too.

3. The model examinations should be carried out for several different case studies and several different models. Thereby it may be possible to conclude that the results are model independent, see also the Preface.

4. The results should be used to develop hypotheses, that can be tested (observed) in ecosystems.

Networks may be considered as a particular type of models. They focus on the flows from one compartment to another. Chapters 7 and 8, which are devoted to network theories, demonstrate the application of the above mentioned principles for development of ecosystem-theoretical results by the use of models. The two chapters present many properties deducted from energy- and mass flows through a network.

The hierarchical approach presented in Chapter 6 clearly shows the inconceivable complexity of ecosystems and demonstrates that it would be impossible to overview ecosystem components without organizing them in a hierarchy. This organization shows furthermore how the different levels in the hierarchy are influencing each other, so the theory is not only a method to organize our thoughts but also shows that ecosystems *are* organized hierarchically (Müller 1992). It is important to accept this organization to understand ecosystem reactions and properties. Some scientists apply the term "autopoiesis" to refer to the dynamic, self-producing and self-maintaining activities of all living beings. Autopoietic entities are organized hierarchically, the smallest autopoitic entity being a single bacterial cell and the largest probably being Gaia.

The hierarchical organization must, of course, be reflected in modelling, whenever the examination considers more than one level of the hierarchy (Müller 1992) or whenever the considered properties are influenced by more than one level. All in all the hierarchical theory is so important that is should be incorporated into all ecosystem research.

The application of quantum mechanical concepts should also be mentioned in this context. It is important to realize that we simply can not attain the detailed descriptions that are characteristic for many laboratory studies. We are dealing with such complex systems in ecosystem research that the complexity makes it impossible to reveal all details. That is the challenge to ecosystem research: to try to capture the properties of such complex systems as the ecosystems by looking into the entire systems and forgetting the details. The proverb "you cannot see the forest for the trees" is valid here. If we do not study the forest, but only the trees, we will never reach a proper conclusion about the forest. We need to study the ecosystem on the system level. It is hopeless to study the system through an investigation of the details, because they are too many.

## 12.5. Ecosystem Properties

This section is devoted to the ecosystem properties that have been discussed earlier in the volume and can be deduced from ELT or the other ecological theories presented in combination with models. The properties will be presented as tentative theoretical propositions for ecosystems in addition to those already presented in

Section 12.2. References to the discussion / presentation earlier in the volume are given. As presented in Sections 3.7. and 12.4, the idea is to use well tested models, which at least contain the qualities that are crucial for the ecosystem properties under investigations. All the propositions presented in these sections have been tested by this method and the results have at least partially been documented earlier in the volume.

**Proposition 8. Ecosystems have a balanced (medium) connectivity. Too high a connectivity would create instability (chaos) and too low a connectivity would reduce the indirect effects which are beneficial for the ecosystem.**

This ecosystem property is discussed several times; see equation (2.1), Section 2.2 and Sections 7.2 and 10.4.

**Proposition 9.The biological components of ecosystems adjust their properties (parameters) to obtain the highest possible organization and avoid chaos. The boundary between high organization and chaos offers a poised system with high adaptability and probability of survival and growth.**

This property is discussed in Sections 10.3, 10.4 and 11.3.

**Proposition 10. Both matter and energy cycle in ecosystems, as a consequence of the flow of exergy through the system.**

See Sections 4.1 and 8.2.

**Proposition 11. Due to the high complexity of ecological networks, the indirect effect becomes dominant.**

See Section 8.3.

**Proposition 12. The selection process must consider the forcing functions as well as all other components in the ecosystem, which together with the long evolution period may explain why the indirect effects are beneficial for the entire system in contrast to many direct effects and why a network mutalism is formed as a result of the evolution process.**

This property is discussed in Sections 8.3 and 10.4. This property is named network mutalism and the Gaia-effect, because it is able to explain why an ecosystem is a cooperative unit, why symbiotic effects are more pronounced, when the indirect effects are accounted for and why the entire ecosphere is able to work as a cooperative unit of open cooperative ecosystems. The proposition is a variation of the same theme presented in Proposition 6, see Section 12.2.

**Proposition 13. Ecosystems have developed many pathways to**

340

assure survival of the selfish gene, i.e., the selection processes use a wide spectrum of different methods.

This topic is mainly discussed in Section 2.2, point 7, where the applied methods are listed.

**Proposition 14. Ecosystems possess buffer capacities, i.e., an ability to meet changes in external variables by such changes in the internal variables that the direct influence of the changes in the external variables is reduced.**

The issue is presented in Sections 2.2 and 6.4. The proposition may also be formulated as follows: Le Chatelier's Principle is also valid for ecosystems.

**Proposition 15. Ecosystems meet changes in external factors by such changes in internal variables that the buffer capacities, which are related to meet the changes caused by the external factors, are increased.**

This proposition may be called an extended Le Chatelier's Principle (see also Section 12.2), because it asserts not only that ecosystems have buffer capacities, but they are able to develop in such directions that the buffer capacities that are needed for a given change in external factors, are increased. It is not surprising that ecosystems, which are much more flexible than chemical systems, are able to change their composition and structure in such a way, that they increase their resistance to actual changes. This proposition is consistent with the hierarchy of regulation mechanisms presented in Table 2.1, Section 2.1. The validity of the proposition is shown in Section 6.4. and is based upon a statistical analysis of modelling results. The proposition therefore does not have as much support as the other propositions, but it fits nicely into the pattern of ecosystem theories.

**Proposition 16. High diversity does not necessarily give higher stability, buffer capacity or less probability for chaotic behavior, but gives more possibilities to find a better solution by selection processes for the ecosystem as entity, i.e., to find solutions for a higher probability of survival and growth.**

This topic is mainly discussed in Sections 2.2 and 8.3.

**Proposition 17. Ecosystems attempt by use of the entire hierarchy of regulation mechanisms to prevent catastrophic events. This ability is covered by the concept of buffer capacity (see proposition 14). Catastrophic events may, however, occur due to a sudden emergence of particular combinations of external factors, which cause a shift in the focal buffer capacity. The maintenance of certain levels of buffer**

capacities explains  the appearance of hysteresis phenomena in relation to catastrophic behavior.

This proposition is presented in Chapter 9. The sudden change described in the proposition gives the r-strategists occasion to utilize the emerging opportunities by their "boom and burst" strategy.

**Proposition 18. A sudden change in the life conditions of an ecosystem is utilized by r-strategists, as they are characterized by the ability to grow rapidly. It can explain the occurrence of catastrophic behavior (jumps) of ecosystems. K-strategists on the other hand are associated with relatively predictable environment and biologically crowded communities.**

The development of ecosystems from the initial to the mature stage is covered in Section 4.2. Table 4.5 summarizes all the development tendencies; it is adapted from E.P. Odum (1969 and 1971) with some minor modifications. All the development tendencies mentioned here are according to ELT and with propositions 4 and 16, which focus on the development of information. The concept is further discussed in Sections 5.2 and 6.2, where the relations between information, entropy and exergy are presented.

**Proposition 19. As the conservation principles, valid for energy and matter, limit  further development of ecosystems based upon matter and energy, increase of information plays a major role in ecosystem development. It implies that diversity, organism size, organization of patterns, niche specialization, the complexity of life and mineral cycles, internal symbiosis, homeostatis and feedback control  will all increase to make the fullest possible use of the available resources.**

This proposition is concerned with the development toward a better organization and regulation of the system; see the discussion on efficiency of information transfer. The energetic development  is already covered in ELT and in Section 12.3. The better regulation and organization give a higher exergy. In addition they give a higher biomass, and therefore more exergy and higher entropy production. The latter is realized not only by respirations but also by evapotranspiration. The trends in organism size explain that the specific entropy is reduced, see Fig. 5.12, Section 5.7.

An ecosystem will develop along a particular path under normal environmental conditions. The path will attempt to take the ecosystem away from thermodynamic equilibrium according to ELT. It will according to Kay (1984) continue along the path until it reaches an operating point, which represents a balance between the thermodynamic forces, which drives it away from thermodynamic equilibrium and the environmental forces (dissipation of energy including metabolism) which tend to disrupt development and drive the system back toward equilibrium. This point of balance between the two forces may be called the optimum operating point.

**Proposition 20. An ecosystem attempts to find a steady state at the optimum operating point, which may be considered a balance between the thermodynamic and environmental forces.**

If stress is introduced into the system, it will be driven to a new optimum operating point. If the stress is removed, the system will not return exactly to the previous optimum operating point, because the system will have changed its history and the same combination of external and internal factors will with extremely high probability never occur again.

**Proposition 21. An ecosystem will never return exactly to the same operating point again, because the history and the combination of internal and external factors will never be the same again.**

This property of ecosystems and the stability concepts are discussed in details in Section 2.2, where the properties of flexibility are presented. The proposition may be extended from "operating point" to attractor point or steady state.

**Proposition 22. The steady state of ecosystems may be considered as attractor points. An ecosystem will never get the same attractor point (equal to the steady state) again, because the history and the combination of internal and external factors will never be repeated.**

**Proposition 23. The entire ecosystem evolves as all the components of the ecosystem are linked in a network. The evolution of the ecosystem is irreversible, because it is dependent on the history of the system.**

Compare Dollo's Law, presented in Section 6.3, and the computation of the historical indirect effect, which is found to be more important than the direct effects; see Section 8.3.

**Proposition 24. Ecosystems (and the entire ecosphere) are characterized by an intermediate number of components (medium number systems). The components are all different and show a structured interrelationship.**

These characteristics of ecosystems are discussed in Section 2.2. An ecosystem encompasses many *different* components, which explain the complexity of ecosystems. Physical and chemical systems may contain more components, but due to the similarity of the components and the lack of structured interrelationship, they

343

often show less complexity.

Proposition 25. Both "bottom-up" and "top-down" effects may be of importance for ecosystem dynamics.

This proposition is covered in Section 2.2. It does not exclude that there are cases, where only one of the two effects may be sufficient to explain the observed dynamics of the ecosystem.

Proposition 26. The ecosystems have evolved to utilize the oscillations of forcing functions and the spatial heterogeneity to the benefit of the ecosystem, i.e., to gain exergy.

This proposition is touched upon in Sections 2.2 and 4.2, and has been demonstrated by the use of models.

Proposition 27. The development and evolution of ecosystems can be described in many parallel ways: by the use of entropy production, exergy destruction, exergy production and ascendency. The selection of the most appropriate description method is dependent on the case study, the data and the aim of the description.

This proposition is a result of the discussion throughout the entire volume: we need a pluralistic view to capture the ecosystem properties; see for instance Section 8.4.


## 12.6. The Application of ELT in Specific Cases

The ecosystem properties presented in this section have not been treated previously in this volume, because they are less general, as they focus on more specific case studies. They illustrate how it is possible by the use of models and ELT in a similar way as mentioned in Section 12.5, to come to useful conclusions for ecosystem reactions, when the specific conditions are given. The case studies presented have all been mentioned in the literature. References related to observations of the examined ecosystem reactions and properties are given. The step-by-step examinations by use of a the model + ELT are not included, only the results in form of properties or propositions. The applied procedure is however not different from the one used in the similar examinations listed in Sections 2.2, 4.4, 6.4., 6.5, 8.2, 8.3, 8.4, 9.2, 9.3, 10.1, 10.3, 10.4, 11.3, 11.4, and 11.5.

An interesting and very illustrative example of the use of a combination of models + ELT may be based on Sommer's studies of the algae succession in different types of lakes (Sommer, 1987). He has classified algae according to their hydromechanical properties and nutrient requirements and used these classifications to explain the various phytoplankton life forms observed in Lake Constance. Sommer attempts to make predictions for other lakes as well, using the experience gained for Lake Constance. He predicts that in stratified, temperate, oligotrophic lakes with P-limitations the vernal growth pulse will consist mainly of diatoms. Zooplankton will rather be dominated by copepodes, which take larger food particles, are less fertile and have higher longevity. A lake model exercise (Jørgensen, 1976 and 1986) shows very clearly that diatoms and zooplankton with the above-mentioned properties give the highest exergy by low nutrient concentrations and P-limitations.

Sommer et al. (1986) has made a detailed and comprehensive study of the seasonal succession of planktonic events in an idealized standard lake, based upon the well-studied Lake Constance. He has set up 24 different statements that have been confronted with the real situations which exist in 24 different lakes, reservoirs and ponds. Four of these statements have been examined by the use of a eutrophication model and ELT and it was found that these four statements were all consistent with ELT under the conditions given in the "standard lake." The four statements are:
- planktonic herbivores with short generation time increase their population first and are followed by species growing more slowly and with longer generation time.
- Fish predation accelerates the decline of herbivorous planktonic populations and is accompanied by a shift toward a smaller average body size of the surviving crustaceans.
- Competition for phosphorus leads to a replacement of green algae by large diatoms, which are only partly available to zooplankton as food.
- Nitrogen depletion favors a shift to nitrogen-fixing species of filamentous blue-green algae.

Gabriel (1985) has studied the development of cannibalism and found that food limitation may be overcome by cyclopoids by cannibalism. The observed shift in feeding habits by many cyclopoid copepodes is according to ELT, and the model results show that the shift may be considered a stabilizing factor for maintenance of a relatively high exergy level.

Six cases of the application of a model in combination with ELT have been listed above. Several more case studies have been mentioned throughout the volume

345

and the conclusion has been the same: the combination of a good workable model and ELT is often able to explain observed dynamic behavior of ecosystem, which may be considered a strength of ELT. These studies have, however, also shown, that it is absolutely necessary to have a well examined model, that reflects the properties of the ecosystem and the state variables included in the model. It implies that a good (detailed) knowledge of the biological components is crucial. The results of analytical work are therefore important for our possibilities to build appropriate models for ecosystem-dynamical studies.

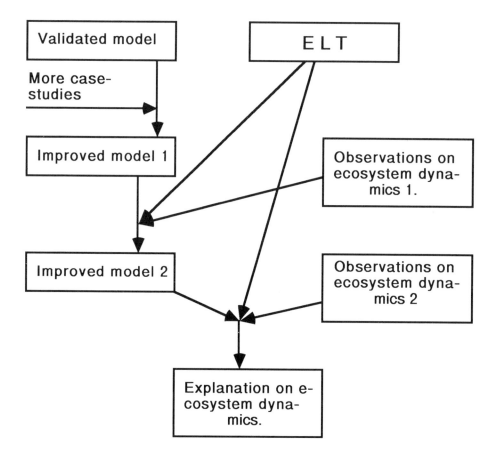

**Fig. 12.4.** The figure shows how ELT and a well examined model may be used to attain explanation of ecosystem dynamics. The procedure should be considered tentative, for instance more observations on ecosystem dynamics may be available and could be used to improve the theoretical basis of the explanations further. Notice that the model, although validated was improved by application to more case studies, before it was used as a basis for explanation of ecosystem dynamics. The procedure has with some modifications been used in six case studies in this section.

The analytical and synthesizing approaches have to work hand in hand to enable us to arrive at major conclusions on ecosystem theory, and particularly when we want to be able to draw conclusions on ecosystem dynamics in specific cases. The ecological scientific literature has an overwhelming number of case studies that could be examined in a similar way to the one demonstrated here by the mentioned six cases. Figure 12.4 shows the idea behind the application of models and ELT in combination to attain a better understanding of ecosystem dynamics.

# 13. EPILOGUE

A close cooperation of analysis and synthesis of ecosystems is necessary, if we want to achieve a profound understanding of our environment. This volume hopefully shows that we cannot do without either approach. Similarly, we cannot do without the many ecosystem theories presented in this volume, because they all contribute to a better understanding of the system properties of ecosystems. They are only in a few points in opposition to each other and form a nice pattern that can hopefully serve as a common framework - or maybe rather as a conceptual diagram - for further development of ecosystem theory.

We urgently need an ecosystem theory - not only to serve as a scientific tool to give a better description and understanding of nature, but also because adequate explanations of long-term global, regional and local changes in the biosphere require an understanding of how ecological systems function and of how they respond to human activities on all levels. The environmental problems on all levels are so pressing that we should already have had a much more comprehensive understanding of ecosystems a decade or two ago. Hopefully, we will achieve a profound understanding of ecosystes in the coming decade and thereby be better able to determine the "health" of the ecosystems and the entire ecosphere. The aim of this volume is to present a tentative pattern of ecosystem theories, that can hopefully contribute to a faster development toward a complete and comprehensive ecosystem theory - or the pattern presented may serve as a first tentative approach to an ecosystem theory.

We are in urgent need of an ecosystem-theoretical pattern, because ecology as a science cannot make major progress without it and because the environmental problems - particularly the global ones - seem impossible to solve without a far better understanding of the system properties of ecosystems and the entire ecosphere. In addition, if we can attain a better general system understanding of nature, we may benefit from such an understanding also in other contexts. We are dependent on good, practical management of other complex systems than ecosystems: our society as a whole, our economical system, our cities and so on. If we gain a better understanding of natural systems, that are so ingeniously designed, we may be able to learn from these systems and adopt some of the stabilizing features to improve the stability of the other systems.

349

General system theory can serve as a tool to distinguish analogies from homologies, to lead to legitimate conceptual models and transfer of laws from one realm to another and to prevent deceptive and inadmissible analogies. With this in mind it may therefore be interesting to ask: Are the properties of quick feedbacks, decentralized control, adaptability and flexibility essential for all complex systems? Should we enhance the development of the man-made systems in this direction?

It was originally my idea to devote a few chapters to these questions, but as the pattern of ecosystem theories evolved, it became clear to me that the issues related to the question: "What can we learn from ecosystems in our design of other complex systems?" is such a comprehensive question that it deserves its own volume. So, later I hope to be able to write a book to cover this interesting topic.

# APPENDIX 1

## 14. DEFINITIONS OF CONCEPTS.

**Buffer capacity:** $\beta = 1/(\partial(\text{State variable}) / \partial(\text{forcing function}))$ or the inverse sensitivity.

**Calibration** is an adjustment of a model to give a better accordance with measured data by change of selected parameters.

**Complexity**. Complexity is a relative concept dependent on the observer. We distinguish between *structural complexity* defined as the number of interconnections between components in the system and *functional complexity*, defined as the number of distinct functions carried out by the system. Many people associate increase in complexity with increase in randomness. This is a misconception. It is the capacity for randomness that increases with complexity.

**Connectance**. The number of food links in the food web as a fraction of the total number of topologically possible links.

**Connectivity** is defined as the number of 1s in the adjacency matrix divided by $n^2$. Connectance and connectivity are therefore almost identical concepts. The differences are: Connectivity implies application of a network and accounts for all connections, while connectance is related to any food web and only accounts for food links.

**Elasticity**. Ability to return to the previous state after the perturbations have been removed. The concept cannot be used quantitatively, because an ecosystem will never return to the same state again due to the immense heterogeneity in time and space.

**Forcing functions = external variables** are functions of time and describe the natural and anthropogenic impacts on the focal system.

**Order** is the antithesis of randomness. The more ordered a system is, the less information is required to describe the system.

**Organized systems** are to be carefully distinguished from ordered systems. Neither kind of systems is random, but whereas ordered systems are generated according to simple algorithms and therefore may lack complexity, organized systems must be assembled element by element according to an external wiring diagram with a high level of information. Organization is functional complexity and carries functional information. It is non-random by design or by selection, rather than by a priori necessity.

**Parameters** are time- and space-dependent coefficients, applied in process equations. They may be constant in a model, but are to be distinguished from constants that always have the same values independent of time, space and model application.

**Persistence**. Ability of an ecosystem or a population not to be disturbed by perturbations.

**Randomness**. The more information is required to describe the system, the more random it is.

**Resilience**. Ability of an ecosystem to return to the same steady state after disturbance. The concept cannot be used quantitatively, because the ecosystem will never return to the same state again due to the immense heterogeneity in time and space.

**Resistance**. A qualitative application of buffer capacity.

**State variables = internal variables** are functions of time and possibly space and describe the state of the focal system.

**System**. A system is defined as a complex of elements subject to interaction.

**Validation**. The expression is mainly used in relation to models. Validation is a test of a model, according to which the model is compared with measurements by some criteria set up by the modeller on the basis of the model goals. Validation is foreseen to be carried out on an already calibrated model.

**Verification**. The test of the internal logic of a model.

# 15. References

Ahern, J.E., 1980. The Exergy Method of Energy Systems Analysis. J. Wiley and Sons, New York.

Ahl, T. and Weiderholm, T., 1977. Svenska vattenkvalitetskriterier: Eurofierande ämnen. SNV PM, Sweden, 918 pp.

Alexander, R.M., 1982. Optima for Animals. Edward Arnold, London.

Allen, P.M., 1975. Evolution in a predator prey ecology. Bull. Math. Biol., 37: 389-405.

Allen, P.M., 1976. Evolution, population dynamics and stability. Proc. Natl. Acad. Sci., 73: 665-668.

Allen, P.M., 1985. Ecology, thermodynamics, and self-organization: Towards a new understanding of complexity. In: R.E. Ulanowicz and T. Platt (Editors), Ecosystem Theory for Biological Oceanography. Can. Bull. Fish. Aquat. Sci., 123: 3-26.

Allen, P.M., 1988. Evolution: Why the whole is greater than the sum of the parts. In: W. Wolff, C.-J. Soeder and F.R. Drepper (Editors), Ecodynamics: Contributions to Theoretical Ecology, Part 1: Evolution. Proc. Int. Workshop, 19-20 October 1987, Jülich, Germany. Springer-Verlag, Berlin, pp. 2-30.

Allen, T.F.H. and Koonce, J.F., 1973. Multivariate approaches to algal stratagems and tactics in systems analysis of phytoplankton. Ecol., 54: 1234-1246.

Allen, T.F.H., O'Neill, R.V. and Hoekstra, T.W., 1984. Interlevel relations in ecological research and management: some working principles from hierarchy theory, General Technical Report RM-110. United States Department of Agriculture, Rocky Mountains Forest and Range Experiment Station, Fort Colins, Colorado.

Allen, T.F.H. and O'Neill, R.V., 1991. Improving predictability in networks: system specification through hierarchy ecology. In: M. Higashi and T.P. Burns (Editors), Theoretical Studies of Ecosystems: The Network Perspective. Cambridge Univ. Press, pp. 101-114.

Allen, T.F.H. and Starr, T.B., 1982. Hierarchy: Perspectives for Ecological Complexity. Univ. of Chicago Press.

Anderson, R.M., 1979. The influence of parasitic infection on the dynamics of host population growth. In: R.M. Anderson, B.D. Turner and L.R. Taylor (Editors), Population Dynamics. Blackwell, London, pp. 245-281.

Anon., 1968. The lead we breathe. Chemistry, 41: 7.

Anon., 1973. Computer Program Documentation for the Stream Quality Model, QUAL-II. Prepared for U.S. Environmental Protection Agency, Systems Analysis Branch. Water Resources Engineers, Inc., Washington, D.C.

Aoki, I., 1987. Entropy balance in Lake Biwa. Ecol. Modelling, 37: 235-248.

Aoki, I., 1988. Entropy laws in ecological networks at steady state. Ecol. Modelling, 42: 289-303.

Aoki. I., 1989. Ecological study of lakes from an entropy viewpoint - Lake Mendota. Ecol. Modelling, 49: 81-87.

Aoki, I., 1992. Inclusive Kullback index - a macroscopic measure in ecological systems. Ecol. Modelling, in press.

Arino, O., Axelrod, D.E. and Kimmel, M., 1991. Mathematical Population Dynamics. Marcel Dekker Inc., New York.

Armstrong, N.E., 1977. Development and Documentation of Mathematical Model for the Paraiba River Basin Study, Vol. 2 - DOSAGM: Simulation of Water Quality in Streams and Estuaries, Technical Report CRWR-145. Center for Research in Water Resources, The University of Texas at Austin, Texas.

Augros, R. and Stanciu, G., 1987. The New Biology: Discovering the Wisdom of Nature. Shambhala, Boston.

Axelrod, R., 1984. The Evolution of Cooperation. Basic Books.

Barlow, C. (Editor), 1991. From Gaia to Selfish Genes: Selected Writings in the Life Sciences. MIT Press, Cambridge, Massachusetts.

Bendoricchio, G., 1988. An application of the theory of catastrophe to the eutrophication of the Venice lagoon. In: A. Marani (Editor), Advances in Environmental Modelling. Elsevier, Amsterdam.

Berry, S., 1972. Bulletin of the Atomic Scientists, 9: 8-20.

Bohm, D., Hilay, B. and Kaloyerou, P.N., 1897. An ontological basis for quantum theory. Phys. Reports, 144(6): 323-329.

Boltzmann, L., 1905. The Second Law of Thermodynamics. Populare Schriften, Essay No. 3 (address to Imperial Academy of Science in 1886). Reprinted in English in Theoretical Physics and Philisophical Probelms, Selected Writings of L. Boltzmann. D. Reidel, Dordrecht.

Bormann, F.H. and Likens, G.E., 1967. Nutrient cycling. Science, 155: 424-429.

Bossel, H., 1992. Real structure process description as the basis of understanding ecosystems. In: Workshop "Ecosystem Theory", 14-17 October 1991, Kiel. Special Issue of Ecol. Modelling, in press.

Bosserman, R.W., 1980. Complexity measures for assessment of environmental impact in ecosystem networks. In: Proc. Pittsburgh Conf. Modelling and Simulation, 20-23 April 1980, Pennsylvania.

Bosserman, R.W., 1982. Structural comparison for four lake ecosystem models. In: L. Troncale (Editor), A General Survey of systems Methodology. Proc. 26th Annu. Meet. Soc. General Systems Res., 5-9 January 1982, Washington, D.C., pp. 559-568.

Brabrand, A, Faajeng, B., Kallqvist, T. and Petter Nilssen, J. et al., 1984. Can iron defecation from fish influence plankton productivity and biomass in eutrophic lakes? Limnol. Oceanogr., 29: 1330-1334.

Brillouin, L., 1949. Life, thermodynamics, and cybernetics. Am. Sci., 37: 554-568.

Brillouin, L., 1956. Science and Information Theory, 1st ed. Academic Press, New York.

Brillouin, L., 1962. Science and Information Theory, 2nd ed. Academic Press, New York.

Brooks, D.R., Collier, J., Maurer, B.A., Smith, J.D.H. and Wiley, E.O., 1989. Entropy and information in evolving biological systems. Biology and Philosophy, 4: 407-432.

Brooks, D.R., Cumming, D.D. and LeBlond, P.H., 1988. Dollo's law and the second law of thermodynamics: Analogy or extension? In: B.H. Weber, D.J. Depew and J.D. Smith (Editors), Entropy, Information, and Evolution: New Perspectives on Physical and Biological Evolution. MIT Press, Cambridge, Massachusetts, pp. 189.

Brooks, D.R. and Wiley, E.O., 1986. Evolution as Entropy. The University Press, Chicago and London.

Brown, W., 1973. Heat-flux transitions at low Rayleigh number. J. Fluid Mech., 69: 539-559.

Brzustowski, T.A. and Golem, P.J., 1980. Second Law Analysis of Energy Processess, Part 1: Exergy - An Introduction. Transactions of the C.S.M.E., 4: 209-218.

Cairns, J., Overbaugh, J. and Miller, S., 1988. The origin of mutants. Nature, 355: 142.

Cairns, J., Jr., 1991. The need for integrated environmental systems management.

In: J. Cairns, Jr. and T.V. Crawford (Editors), Integrated Environmental Management. Lewis Publishers, Inc., Chelsea, Michigan.

Carson, R., 1962. Silent Spring. New American Library, New York.

Casti, J., 1982. Catastrophes, control and the inevitability of spruce budworm outbreaks. Ecol. Modelling, 14: 293-300.

Casti, J.L. and Karlqvist, A. (Editors), 1986. Complexity, Language, and Life: Mathematical Approaches. Springer-Verlag, Berlin.

Chemistry (1968), see Anon., 1968.

Coleman, D.C., 1985. Through a ped darkly: an ecological assessment of root-soil-microbial-faunal interactions. In: A.H. Fitter et al. (Editors), Ecological Interactions in Soil. Blackwell, Oxford, pp. 1-21.

Colgan, P.W., Nowell, W.A. and Stokes, N.W., 1981. Spatial aspects of nest defense by pumpkinseed sunfish (*Lepomis gibbosus*): Stimulus features and an application of catastrophe theory. Anim. Behav., 29: 433-442.

Colinvaux, P.A., 1973. Introduction to Ecology. John Wiley and Sons, New York.

Collier, B.D., Cox, G.W., Johnson, A.W. and Miller, C.P., 1973. Dynamic Ecology. Prentice-Hall, Englewood Cliffs, New Jersey.

Collier, J., 1988. The dynamics of biological order. In: B.H. Weber, D.J. Depew and J.D. Smith (Editors), Entropy, Information, and Evolution: New Perspectives on Physical and Biological Evolution. MIT Press, Cambridge, Massachusetts, pp. 227-242.

Costanza, R. and Sklar, F.H., 1985. Articulation, accuracy and effectiveness of mathematical models: a review of freshwater wetland applications. Ecol. Modelling, 27: 45-69.

Cox, J.L., 1970. Accumulation of DDT residues in *Triphoturus mexicanus* from the Gulf of California. Nature, 227: 192-193.

Cummins, K.W., Coffman, W.P. and Roff, P.A., 1966. Trophic relationships in a small woodland stream. Verh. Int. Ver. Limnol., 16: 627-638.

Currie, D.J. and Paquin, V., 1987. Large scale biogeographical patterns of species richness of trees. Nature, 329: 326-327.

Darwin, C.E., 1859. On the Origin of Species by Means of Natural Selection, or the Preservation of Favoured Races in the Struggle for Life. John Murray, London.

Dawkins, R.D., 1982. The Extended Phenotype. W.H. Freeman, Oxford.

Dawkins, R.D., 1989. The Selfish Gene, 2nd ed. Oxford Univ. Press.

De Angelis, D.L., 1975. Stability and connectance in food web models Ecol., 56: 238-243.

Dubois, D.M., 1975. A model of patchiness for prey-predator plankton populations. Ecol. Modelling, 1: 67-72.

Dubois, D.M., 1979. Catastrophe theory applied to water quality regulation of rivers. In: S.E. Jørgensen (Editor), State-of-the-Art of Ecological Modelling. Environmental Sciences and Applications, 7. Proc. Conf. Ecological Modelling, 28th August-2nd September 1978, Copenhagen. International Society for Ecological Modelling, Copenhagen, pp. 751-758.

Eriksson, B., Eriksson, K.E. and Wall, G., 1976. Basic Thermodynamics of Energy Conversions and Energy Use. Institute of Theoretical Physics, Göteborg, Sweden.

Evans, R.B., 1969. A Proof that Essergy is the Only Consistent Measure of Potential Work, Thesis. Dartmouth College, Hannover, New Hampshire.

Evans, R.B., et al., 1966. Exergy. In: K.S. Spiegler (Editor), Principles of Desalination. New York, pp. 108-118.

Ferracin, A. et al., 1978. Self-organizing ability and living systems. Biosystems, 10: 307-317.

Fidelman, M.L. and Mikulecky, D.C., 1986. Network thermodynamic modelling of hormone regulation of active $Na^+$ transport in cultured renal epithelium. Am J. Physiol., 250: C928-C991.

Fisher, J. and Hinde, R.A., 1949. The opening of milk bottles by birds. Brit. Birds, 42: 347-357.

Fontaine, T.D., 1981. A self-designing model for testing hypotheses of ecosystem development. In: D. Dubois (Editor), Progress in Ecological Engineering and Management by Mathematical Modelling. Proc. 2nd Int. Conf. State-of-the-Art Ecological Modelling, 18-24 April 1980, Liège, Belgium, pp. 281-291.

Frautschi, S., 1988. Entropy in an expanding universe. In: B.H. Weber, D.J. Depew and J.D. Smith (Editors), Entropy, Information, and Evolution: New Perspectives on Physical and Biological Evolution. MIT Press, Cambridge, Massachusetts, pp. 11-22.

Fränzle, O., 1981. Vergleichende Untersuchungen über Struktur, Entwicklung und Standortbedingungen von Biozönosen in den immerfeuchten Tropen und der gemässigten Zone. Aachener Geogr. Arb., 14: 167-191.

Gabriel, W., 1985. Overcoming food limitaion by cannibalism: A model study on cyclopoids. Arch. Hydrobiol. beih. Ergebn. Limnol., 21: 373-381.

Gardner, M.R. and Ashby, W.R., 1970. Connectance of large dynamical (cybernetic) systems: critical values for stability. Nature, 288: 784.

Glansdorff, P. and Prigogine, I., 1971. Thermodynamic Theory of Structure, Stability, and Fluctuations. Wiley-Interscience.

Gliwicz, Z.M. and Pinanowska, J., 1989. The role of predation in zooplankton succession. In: U. Sommer (Editor), Plankton Ecology: Succession in Plankton Communities. Springer-Verlag, Berlin, pp. 253.

Grant, W.E., 1986. Systems Analysis and Simulation in Wildlife and Fisheries Sciences. John Wiley & Sons, New York.

Gödel, K., 1986. Collected Works, Vol. I, (S. Feferman et al. (Editors)). Oxford Univ. Press, New York.

Halfon, E., 1983. Is there a best model structure? II. Comparing the model structures of different fate models. Ecol. Modelling, 20: 153-163.

Halfon, E., 1984. Error analysis and simulation of Mirex behaviour in Lake Ontario. Ecol. Modelling, 22: 213-253.

Halfon, E., Unbehauen, H. and Schmid, C., 1979. Model order estimation and system identification theory to the modelling of 32P kinetics within the trophogenic zone of a small lake. Ecol. Modelling, 6: 1-22.

Hannon, B., 1973. The structure of ecosystems. J. Theor. Biol., 41: 534-546 eller 535-546.

Hannon, B., 1979. Total energy cost in ecosystems. J. Theor. Biol., 80: 271-293.

Hannon, B., 1982. Energy discounting. In: W. Mitsch, R. Ragade, R. Bosserman and J. Dillon, Energetics and Systems. Ann Arbor Science Publishers, pp. 73-100.

Hardin, G., 1960. The competitive exclusion principle. Science, 131: 1292-1297.

Harris, G.P., 1986. Phytoplankton Ecology: Structure, Function and Fluctuation. Chapman and Hall, London.

Hassell, M.P., Lawton, J.H. and May, R.M., 1976. Patterns of dynamical behaviour in single species populations. J. Anim. Ecol., 45: 471-486.

Herendeen, R., 1981. Energy intensity in ecological and economic systems. J. Theor. Biol., 91: 607-620.

Herendeen, R., 1989. Energy intensity, residence time, exergy, and ascendency in dynamic ecosystems. Ecol. Modelling, 48: 19-44.

Herendeen, R., 1990. System-level indicators in dynamic ecosystems: comparison based on energy and nutrient flows. J. Theor. Biol., 143: 523-553.

Higashi, M., Burns, T.P. and Patten, B.C., 1989. Food network unfolding: an extension of trophic dynamics for application to natural ecosystems. J. Theor. Biol., 140: 243-261.

Higashi, M. and Burns, T.P. (Editors), 1991. Theoretical Studies of Ecosystems: The Network Perspective. Cambridge Univ. Press.

Higashi, M. and Patten, B.C., 1986. Further aspects of the analysis of indirect effects in ecosystems. Ecol. Modelling, 31: 69-77.

Higashi, M. and Patten, B.C., 1989. Dominance of indirect causality in ecosystems. Am. Nat., 133: 288-302.

Higashi, M., Patten, B.C. and Burns, T.P., 1991. Network trophic dynamics: an emerging paradigm in ecosystems ecology. In: M. Higashi and T.P. Burns (Editors), Theoretical Studies of Ecosystems: The Network Perspective. Cambridge Univ. Press, pp. 117-154.

Holling, C.S., 1973. Resilience and stability of ecological systems. A. Rev. Ecol. Syst., 4: 1-24.

Hosper, S.H., 1989. Biomanipulation, new perspective for restoring shallow eutrophic lakes in The Netherlands. Hydrobiol. Bull., 23: 5-11.

Huf, E.G. and Mikulecky, D.C., 1986. Role of topology in bioenergetics of sodium transport in complex epithelia. Am. J. Physiol., 250: F1107-F1108.

Hurlbert, S.H., 1975. Secondary effects of pesticides on aquatic ecosystems. Residue Rev., 57: 81-148.

Hutchinson, G.E., 1941. Lecture notes on Limnology. Distributed upon request from the Osborn Zool. Lab., Yale University, New Haven, Connecticut (copyright author).

Hutchinson, G.E., 1948. Circular causal systems in ecology. Ann. N. Y. Acad. Sci., 50: 221-246.

Hutchinson, G.E., 1953. The concept of pattern in ecology. Proc. Natl. Acad. Sci. Philadelphia, 105: 1-12.

Hutchinson, G.E., 1961. The paradox of the plankton. Am. Nat., 107: 405-425.

Hutchinson, G.E., 1978. An Introduction to Population Ecology. Yale Univ. Press, New Haven.

Jeppesen, E., Mortensen, E. Sortkjær, O., Kristensen, P., Bidstrup, J., Timmermann, M., Jensen, J.P., Hansen, A.-M., Søndergård, M., Muller, J.P., Jerl Jensen, H., Riemann, B., Lindegård Petersen, C., Bosselmann, S., Christoffersen, K., Dall, E. and Andersen, J.M., 1989. Restaurering af søer ved indgreb i fiskebestanden. Status for igangværende undersøgelser. Del 2: Undersøgelser i Frederiksborg slotssø, Væng sø og Søbygård sø. Danmarks Miljøundersøgelser, 114 pp.

Jizhong, Z., Shijun, M. and Hinman, G.W., 1992. Ecological exergy analysis: A new method for ecological energetics research. Ecol. Modelling, in press.

Jones, D.D. and Walters, C.J., 1976. Catastrophe theory and fisheries regulation. J. Fish Res. Board Can., 33: 2829-2833.

Jørgensen, S.E., 1976. A eutrophication model for a lake. Ecol. Modelling, 2: 147-165.

Jørgensen, S.E., 1979. Modelling the distribution and effect of heavy metals in an aquatic ecosystem. Ecol. Modelling, 6: 199-222.

Jørgensen, S.E., 1981. Application of exergy in ecological models. In: D. Dubois (Editor), Progress in Ecological Modelling. Cebedoc, Liege, pp. 39-47.

Jørgensen, S.E., 1982. A holistic approach to ecological modelling by application of thermodynamics. In: W. Mitsch et al. (Editors), Systems and Energy. Ann Arbor.

Jørgensen, S.E., 1982a. Modelling the eutrophication of shallow lakes. In: D.O. Logofet and N.K. Luchyanov (Editors), Ecosystem Dybnamics in Freshwater Wetlands and Shallow Water Bodies, Vol. 2. UNEP/SCOPE, Academy of Sciences, Moscow, pp. 125-155.

Jørgensen, S.E., 1984. Parameter estimation in toxic substance models. Ecol. Modelling, 22: 1-13.

Jørgensen, S.E., 1986. Structural dynamic model. Ecol. Modelling, 31: 1-9.

Jørgensen, S.E., 1988. Fundamentals of Ecological Modelling. Elsevier, Amsterdam, 390 pp.

Jørgensen, S.E., 1988a. Use of models as experimental tool to show that structural changes are accompanied by increased exergy. Ecol. Modelling, 41: 117-126.

Jørgensen, S.E., 1990. Application of models in limnological research. Verh. Internat. Verein. Limnol., 24: 61-67.

Jørgensen, S.E., 1990a. Ecosystem theory, ecological buffer capacity, uncertainly and complexity. Ecol. Modelling, 52: 125-133.

Jørgensen, S.E., 1990b. Modelling in Ecotoxicology. Elsevier, Amtserdam, 340 pp.

Jørgensen, S.E., 1991. Modelling in Environmental Chemistry, Developments in Environmental Modelling, 17. Elsevier, Amsterdam, 505 pp.

Jørgensen, S.E., 1992. Development of models able to account for changes in species composition. Ecol. Modelling, 60: in press.

Jørgensen, S.E., 1992a. Parameters, ecological constraints and exergy. Ecol. Modelling, 60: in press.

Jørgensen, S.E., Friis, M.B., Henriksen, J., Jørgensen, L.A. and Mejer, H.F., 1979. In: S.E. Jørgensen (Editor), Handbook of Environmental Data and Ecological Parameters. ISEM, Copenhagen.

Jørgensen, S.E. and Johnsen, I., 1989. Principles of Environmental Science and Technology, Studies in Environmental Science 33. Elesvier, Amsterdam.

Jørgensen, S.E., Jørgensen, L.A., Kamp Nielsen, L. and Mejer, H.F., 1981. Parameter estimation in eutrophication modelling. Ecol. Modelling, 13: 111-129.

Jørgensen, S.E., Kamp-Nielsen, L., Christensen, T., Windolf-Nielsen, J. and Westergaard, B., 1986. Validation of a prognosis based upon a eutrophication model. Ecol. Modelling, 32: 165-182.

Jørgensen, S.E., Kamp-Nielsen, L. and Jørgensen, L.A., 1986. Examination of the generality of eutrophication models. Ecol. Modelling, 32: 251-266.

Jørgensen, S.E., Logofet, D.G. and Svirezhev, Y.M., 1992a. Exergy principles and exergical ecosystems. In: B.C. Patten and S.E. Jørgensen (Editors), Complex Ecology. Prentice-Hall, Englewood Cliffs, New Jersey.

Jørgensen, S.E. and Mejer, H.F., 1977. Ecological buffer capacity. Ecol. Modelling, 3: 39-61.

Jørgensen, S.E., Mejer, H.F. and Friis, M., 1978. Examination of a lake model. Ecol. Modelling, 4: 253-279.

Jørgensen, S.E. and Mejer, H.F., 1979. A holistic approach to ecological modelling. Ecol. Modelling, 7: 169-189.

Jørgensen, S.E., Mejer, H.F. and Nielsen, S.N., 1992. The second law of thermodynamics. Nature, submitted.

Jørgensen, S.E., Nors-Nielsen, S. and Jørgensen, L.A., 1991. Handbook of

Ecological Parameters and Ecotoxicology. Elsevier, Amsterdam, 1270 pp.

Jørgensen, S.E., Patten, B. and Straskraba, M., 1992. Ecosystem emerging. Ecol. Modelling, 60: in press.

Kamp-Nielsen, L., 1983. Sediment-water exchange models. In: S.E. Jørgensen (Editor), Application of Ecological Modelling in Environmental Management, Part A. Elsevier, Amsterdam.

Kamp-Nielsen, L., Jørgensen, L.A. and Jørgensen, S.E., 1983a. Modelling the distribution of heavy metals between sediment and water in the Upper Nile lake system. In: W.K. Lauenroth, G.V. Skogerboe and M. Flug, Analysis of Ecological Systems: State-of-the-Art in Ecological Modelling, Developments in Environmental Modelling, 5. Elsevier, Amsterdam, pp. 623-630.

Kauffman, S.A., 1991. Antichaos and adaptation. Scientific American, 265(2): 64-70.

Kauffman, S.A., 1992. Origins of Order: Self-Organization and Selection in Evolution. Oxford Univ. Press, Oxford.

Kay, J., 1983. Measures of Structural Organization of Ecosystems, Lecture Notes. University of Waterloo, Ontario, Canada.

Kay, J., 1984. Self Organization in Living Systems, Ph.D. Thesis. Systems Design Engineering, University of Waterloo, Ontario, Canada, 458 pp.

Kay, J.J. and Schneider, E.D., 1990. On the applicability of non-equilibrium thermodynamics to living systems. Internal paper, Waterloo University, Ontario, Canada.

Kay, J.J., 1991. A non-equilibrium thermodynamic framework for discussing ecosystem integrity. Environmental Management, 15: 483-495.

Kay, J. and Schneider, E.D., 1992. Thermodynamics and Measures of Ecological Integrity. In: Proc. "Ecological Indicators". Elsevier, Amsterdam.

Keenan, J.H., 1951. Availability and irreversibility in thermodynamics. Br. J. Appl. Phys., 2: 20-27.

Keller, E.F., 1983. A Feeling for the Organism. W.H. Freeman and Co., New York.

Keller, E.F., 1986. One woman and her theory. New Scientist, July 1986.

Kemp, W.M. and Mitsch, W.J., 1979. Turbulence and phytoplankton diversity: a general model of the "paradox of plankton". Ecol. Modelling, 7: 201-212.

Kempf, J., 1980. Multiple steady state and catastrophes in ecological models. ISEM J., 2: 55-79.

Kempf, J., Duckstein, L. and Casti, J., 1984. Relaxation oscillations and othe non-Michaelian behavior in a slow-fast phytoplankton growth model. Ecol. Modelling, 23: 67-90.

Kerfoot, W.C. and DeMott, W.R., 1984. Food web dynamics: dependent chains and vaulting. In: D.G. Meyers and J.R. Strickler (Editors), Trophic Interactions within Aquatic Ecosystems, AAAS Selected Sympos. 85. Westview, Boulder, pp. 347-382.

Koestler, A., 1967. The Ghost in the Machine. Macmillan, New York.

Koestler, A., 1969. Beyond atomism and holism - the concept of the holon. In: A. Koestler and J.R. Smythies, Beyond Reductionism. Hutchinson, London, pp. 192-232.

Kristensen, P. and Jensen, P., 1987. Sedimentation og resuspension i Søbygård sø. Univ. Specialerapport. Miljøstyrelsens Ferskvandslaboratorium & Botanisk Institut, Univ. Århus, 150 pp.

Landauer, R., 1989. Computation, measurement, communication and energy dissipation. In: S. Haykin (Editor), Selected Topics in signal Processing. Prentice-Hall, Englewood, New Jersey, pp. 18.

Landauer, R., 1991. Information is physical. Physics Today, May 1991: 23-29.

Langton, C.G., 1989. Artificial Life: Proceedings of an Interdisciplinary Workshop on the Synthesis and Simulation of Living Systems. Santa Fè Institute Studies in the Sciences of Complexity VI. Addison-Wesley, Redwood City.

Larsen, J.A., 1922. Effect of removal of the virgin white pine stand upon the physical factors of site. Ecol., 3: 302-305.

Layzer, D., 1976. The arrow of time. Scientific American December; Astrophysical J., 206: 559.

Layzer, D., 1988. Growth of order in the universe. In: B.H. Weber, D.J. Depew and J.D. Smith (Editors), Entropy, Information, and Evolution: New Perspectives on Physical and Biological Evolution. MIT Press, Cambridge, Massachusetts, pp. 23-40.

Lehninger, A.L., 1970. Biochemistry. Worth Publishers, New York.

Leontief, W.W., 1966. Input-Output Economics. Oxford Univ. Press.

Levins, R., 1974. The qualitative analysis of partially specified systems. Ann. N. Y. Acad. Sci., 231: 123-138.

Lieth, L., 1976. Biophysikalische Fragestellungen in der Ökologie and Umweltfor-

schung: Teil 1: Versuch eines Vergleiches von Biomasse- und Intelligenzent-
wicklung in der Menschheit. Rad. and Environm. Biophys., 13: 329-335.

Lieth, L., 1976a. Biophysikalische Fragestellungen in der Ökologie and Umweltfor-
schung: Teil 2: Extremalprinzipien in Ökosystemen. Rad. and Environm.
Biophys., 13: 337-351.

Likens, G.E., 1983. A priority for ecological research. Bull. Ecol. Soc. of Amer., 64:
234-243.

Likens, G.E. (Editor), 1985. An Ecosystem Approach to Aquatic Ecology: Mirror
Lake and Its Environment. Springer-Verlag, New York, 516 pp.

Lindeman, R.L., 1941. Seasonal food-cycle dynamics in a senescent lake. Am. Midl.
Nat., 26: 636-673.

Lindeman, R.L., 1942. The trophic dynamic aspect of ecology. Ecology, 23: 399-
418.

Loehle, C., 1985. Optimal stocking for semi-desert range: a catastrophe theory
model. Ecol. Modelling, 27: 285-297.

Loehle, C., 1989. Catastrophe theory in ecology: a critical review and an example of
the butterfly catastrophe. Ecol. Modelling, 49: 125-144.

Lorenz, E., 1964. The problem of deducing the climate from the governing equations. Tellus, 16: 1-11.

Lorenz, E., 1963. Chaos in Meteorological Forecast. J. Atmos. Sci., 20: 130-144.

Lotka, A.J., 1922. Contribution to the energetics of evolution. Proc. Natl. Acad. Sci.,
U.S.A., 8: 147-150.

Lotka, A.J., 1925. Elements of Physical Biology. Williams and Wilkins, Baltimore.

Lovelock, J.E., 1979. Gaia, A New Look at Natural History. Oxford Univ. Press.

Lovelock, J.E., 1988. The Ages of Gaia. Oxford Univ. Press.

Maarel, see Van der Maarel.

MacArthur, R.H., 1955. Fluctuations of animal populations and a measure of
community stability. Ecol., 36: 533-536.

MacArthur, R.H., 1971. Patterns of terrestrial bird communities. In: D.S. Farner and
J.R. King (Editors), Avian Biology. Academic Press, New York, pp. 189-221.

MacArthur, R.H., 1972. Strong or weak interactions? Trans. Conn. Acad. Arts and

Sci., 44: 177-188.

Mann, C., 1991. Lynn Margulis: Science's unruly earth mother. Science 252: 378-381.

Margalef, R., 1963. On certain unifying principles in ecology. Amer. Nat., 97: 357-374.

Margalef, R., 1968. Perspectives in Ecological Theory. Chigaco Univ. Press, 122 pp.

Margalef, R., 1983. Limnologia. Ed. Omega, Barcelona.

Margalef, R., 1991. Networks in ecology. In: M. Higashi and T.P. Burns (Editors), Theoretical Studies of Ecosystems: The Network Perspective. Cambridge Univ. Press, pp. 41-57.

Margalef, R. and Gutierrez, E., 1983. How to introduce connectance in the frame of an expression for diversity. Am. Nat., 121: 601-607.

Markus, M., 1990. Chaos in maps with continous and discontinous maxima: A dramatic variety of dynamic behavior is revealed by graphical display of the Lyapunov exponent. Computers in Physics, 5: 481-485.

Markus, M., 1991. Unvorhersagbarkeit in einer deterministischen Welt: Der Tod der Laplaceschen Dämons. UNI Report 13, Berichte aus der Forschung der Universität Dortmund.

Markus, M. and Hess, B., 1990. Control of metabolic oscillations: Unpredictability, critical slowing down, optimal stability and hysteresis. In: A. Cornish-Bowden and M.L. Cárdenas (Editors), Control of Metabolic Processes. Plenum Press, New York, pp. 303-313.

Markus, M. and Hess, B., 1990a. Isotropic cellular automaton for modelling excit able media. Nature, 347: 56-58.

Markus, M., Hess, B., Roessler, J. and Kiwi, M., 1987. In: H. Degn, A.V. Holden and L.F. Olsen (Editors), Chaos in Biological Systems. Plenum Press, New York, pp. 267-277.

Markus, M., Kuschmitz, D. and Hess, B., 1984. FEBS Lett., 172: 235-238.

Markus, M., Müller, S.C. and Nicolis, G. (Editors), 1988. From Chemical to Bi- ological Organization, Springer Series in Synergetics, Vol. 39, Springer-Verlag, Berlin.

Mauersberger, P., 1979. On the role of entropy in water quality modelling. Ecol. Modelling, 7: 191.

Mauersberger, P., 1982. Logistic growth laws for phyto- and zooplankton. Ecol. Modelling, 17: 57-63.

Mauersberger, P., 1983. General principles in deterministic water quality modeling. In: G.T. Orlob (Editor), Mathematical Modeling of Water Quality: Streams, Lakes and Reservoirs, International Series on Applied Systems Analysis, 12. Wiley, New York, pp. 42-115.

Mauersberger, P., 1985. Optimal control of biological processes in aquatic ecosystems. Gerlands Beitr. Geiophys., 94: 141-147.

Mauersberger, P. and Straskraba, M., 1987. Two approaches to generalized ecosystem modelling: thermodynamic anmd cybernetic. Ecol. Modelling, 39: 161-176.

May, J. and Mikulecky, D.C., 1983. Glucose utilization in rat adipocytes: the interaction of transport and metabolism as affected by insulin. J. Biol. Chem., 258: 4771-4777.

May, R.M., 1972. Will A large complex system be stable? Nature, 238: 413-414.

May, R.M., 1973. Stability and Complexity in Model Ecosystems. Princeton Univ. Press.

May, R.M., 1974. Ecosystem patterns in randomly fluctuating environments. Progr. Theor. Biol., 3: 1-50.

May, R.M., 1975. Biological populations obeying difference equations: stable points, stable cycles and chaos. J. Theor. Biol., 49: 511-524.

May, R.M., 1976. Mathematical aspects of the dynamics of animal populations. In: S.A. Levin (Editor), Studies in Mathematical Biology. American Mathematical Society, Providence, Rhode Island.

May, R.M., 1977. Stability and Complexity in Model Ecosystems, 3rd ed. Princeton Univ. Press.

May, R.M., 1977a. Thresholds and breakpoints in ecosystems with a multiplicity of stable states. Nature, 269: 471-477.

May, R.M., 1979. The structure and dynamics of ecological communities. In: R.M. Anderson, B.D. Turner and L.R. Taylor (Editors), Population Dynamics, Symp. Brit. Ecol. Soc. 20. Blackwell Scientific Publications, Oxford, pp. 385-407.

May, R.M. (Editor), 1981. Theoretical Ecology: Principles and Applications, 2nd ed. Blackwell Scientific Publications, Oxford.

McMurtrie, R.E., 1975. Determinants of stability of large, randomly connected systems. J. Theor. Biol., 50: 1-11.

Meadows, D.H., Meadows, D.L., Randers, J. and Behrens, W.W., III, 1972. The Limits to Growth: A Report for the club of Rome's Project on the Predicament of Mankind. Earth Island Ltd., London.

Meijer, M.L., de Haan, M.W., Breukelaar, A. and Buitenveld, H., 1990. Effects of biomanipulation in shallow lakes: High transparency caused by zooplankton, macrophytes or lack of benthivorous fish? Hydrobiologica

Mejer, H.F. and Jørgensen, S.E., 1979. Energy and ecological buffer capacity. In: S.E. Jørgensen (Editor), State-of-the-Art of Ecological Modelling. Environmental Sciences and Applications, 7. Proc. Conf. Ecological Modelling, 28th August-2nd September 1978, Copenhagen. International Society for Ecological Modelling, Copenhagen, pp. 829-846.

Mesarovic, M.D., Macko, D. and Takahara, Y., 1970. Theory of Hierarchical Multilevel Systems. Academic Press, New York.

Mikulecky, D.C., 1991. Network thermodynamics: a unifying approach to dynamic nonlinear living systems. In: M. Higashi and T.P. Burns (Editors), Theoretical Studies of Ecosystems: The Network Perspective. Cambridge Univ. Press, pp. 71-100.

Monod, J., 1972. Chance and Necessity. Random House, New York, 176 pp.

Montague, C.L., 1980. The Net Influence of the Mud Fiddler Crab, *Uca pugnax*, on Carbon Flow through a Georgia Salt Marsh: The Importance of Work by Macroorganisms to the Metabolism of Ecosystems, Ph.D. Dissertation. University of Georgia, Athens.

Mooney, H.A., Bonnicksen, T.M., Christensen, N.L., Lotan, J.E. and Reiners, W.A. (Editors), 1981. Fire regimes and ecosystem properties, Technical Report wo-26. U.S. Forest Service, Washington, D.C.

Morowitz, H.J., 1968. Energy Flow in Biology. Academic Press, New York.

Murdoch, W.W., 1979. Predation and the dynamics of prey populations. Fortschn. Zool., 25: 295-310.

Müller, F., 1992. Hierarchy theory. Ecol. Modelling, in press.

Nicholis, G., and Prigogine, I., 1977. Self-Organization in Non-Equilibrium Systems: From Dissipative Structures to Order through Fluctuations. Wiley Interscience, New York.

Nicolis, G. and Prigogine, I., 1989. Exploring Complexity: An Introduction. W.H. Freeman & Co., New York.

Nielsen, S.N., 1992. Application of maximum exergy in structural dynamic models, Ph.D. Thesis. National Environmental Research Institute, Denmark, 51 pp.

Nielsen, S.N., 1992. Strategies for structural-dynamical modelling. Ecol. Modelling, in press.

O'Neill, R.V., 1976. Ecosystem persistence and heterotrophic regulation. Ecol., 57: 1244-1253.

O'Neill, R.V., Hanes, W.F., Ausmus, B.S. and Reichle, D.E., 1975. A theoretical basis for ecosystem analysis with particular reference to element cycling. In: F.G. Howell, J.B. Gentry and M.H. Smith (Editors), Mineral Cycling in South-eastern Ecosystems, NTIS pub. CONF-740513.

O'Neill, R.V., DeAngelis, D.L., Waide, J.B. and Allen, T.F.H., 1986. A Hierarchical Concept of Ecosystems. Princeton Univ. Press.

Odling, Smee, and Patten, B.C., 1992. Ecological interscience. In: B.C. Patten and S.E. Jørgensen (Editors), Complex Ecosystems. Prentice-Hall, Englewood, New Jersey, in press.

Odum, E.P., 1953. Fundamentals of Ecology. W.B. Saunders, Philadelphia.

Odum, E.P., 1968. Energy flow in ecosystems: a historical review. Am. Zool., 8: 11-18.

Odum, E.P., 1969. The strategy of ecosystem development. Science, 164: 262-270.

Odum, E.P., 1971. Fundamentals of Ecology, 3rd ed. W.B. Saunders, Philadelphia.

Odum, H.T., 1957. Trophic structure and productivity of Silver Springs, Florida. Ecol. Monogr., 27: 55-112.

Odum, H.T., 1971. Environment, Power, and Society. Wiley Interscience, New York, 331 pp.

Odum, H.T., 1972. An energy circuit language. In: B.C. Patten (Editor), Systems Analysis and Simulation in Ecology, Vol. 2. Academic Press, New Yrok, pp. 139-211.

Odum, H.T., 1983. System Ecology. Wiley Interscience, New York, 644 pp.

Odum, H.T., 1988. Self-organization, transformity, and information. Science, 242: 1132-1139

Odum, H.T., 1989. Ecological engineering and self-organization. In: W.J. Mitsch and S.E. Jørgensen (Editors), Ecological Engineering: An Introduction to Ecotechnology, John Wiley & Sons, New York.

Odum, H.T., Cantlon, J.E. and Kornicker, L.S., 1960. An organizational hierarchy postulate for the interpretation of pecies-individuals distribution: Species entropy and ecosystem evolution and the meaning of a species-variety index. Ecology, 41: 395-399.

Odum, H.T. and Pinkerton, R.C., 1955. Time's speed regulator: The optimum efficiency for maximum power output in physical and biological systems. Amer. Sci., 43: 331-343.

Olmsted, J, III, 1988. Observations on evolution. In: B.H. Weber, D.J. Depew and J.D. Smith (Editors), Entropy, Information, and Evolution: New Perspectives on Physical and Biological Evolution. MIT Press, Cambridge, Massachusetts, pp. 243-262.

Onsager, L., 1931. Reciprocal relations in irreversible processes, I. Phys. Rev., 37: 405-426.

Orians, G.H., 1975. Diversity, stability and maturity in natural ecosystems. In: W.H. van Dobben and R.H. Lowe-McConnell (Editors), Unifying Concepts in Ecology. W. Junk, Hague, pp. 139-150.

Ouimet, C. and Legendre, P., 1988. Practical aspects of modelling ecological phenomena using the cusp catastrophe. Ecol. Modelling, 42: 265-287.

Overton, W.S., 1972. Toward a general model structure for forest ecosystems. In: J.F. Franklin, Proc. Symp. on Research on Coniferous Forest Ecosystems. Northwest Forest Range Station, Portland.

Overton, W.S., 1974. Decomposability: a unifying concept? In: S.A. Levin (Editor), Ecosystem Analysis and Prediction. Society for Industrial and Applied Mathematics, Philadelphia, pp. 297-298.

Pahl-Wosti, C., 1990. Organization of the dynamic network structure in the dimesion of time. Ecol. Modelling, 52: 115-124.

Paine, R.T., 1966. Food web compelxity and species diversity. Am. Nat., 100: 65-75.

Paine, R.T., 1974. Intertidal community structure: experimental studies on the relationship between a dominant competitor and its principal predator. Oecologia, 15: 93-120.

Paine, R.T., 1980. Food webs: linkage, interaction strength, and community infrastructure. J. Anim. Ecol., 49: 667-685.

Pattee, H.H., 1969. Physical conditions for primitive functional hierarchies. In: L.L. Whyte, A.G. Wilson and D. Wilson (Editors), Hierarchical Structures. Elsevier, New York, pp. 161-177.

Pattee, H.H., 1972. The evolution of self-simplifying systems. In: E. Lazlo (Editor), The Relevance of General Systems Theory. Braziller, New York, pp. 31-42.

Patten, B.C., 1978. Systems approach to the concept of the environment. Ohio J. Sci., 78: 206-222.

Patten, B.C., 1982. Environs: relativistic elementary particles for ecology. Amer. Nat., 119: 179-219.

Patten, B.C., 1982a. Indirect causality in ecosystem: its significance for environmental protection. In: W.T. Mason and S. Iker, Research on Fish and Wildlife Habitat, Commemorative monograph honoring the first decade of the US Environmental Protection Agency, EPA-600/8-82-022. Office of Research and Development, US Env. Prot. Agency, Washington, D.C.

Patten, B.C., 1985. Energy cycling in the ecosystem. Ecol. Modelling, 28: 7-71.

Patten, B.C., 1991. Network ecology: indirect determination of the life-environment relationship in ecosystems. In: M. Higashi and T.P. Burns (Editors), Theoretical Studies of Ecosystems: The Network Perspective. Cambridge Univ. Press, pp. 288-351.

Patten, B.C. and Higashi, M., 1984. Modified cycling index for ecological applications. Ecol. Modelling, 25: 69-83.

Patten, B.C., Higashi, M. and Burns, T.P., 1989. Network trophic dynamics: the food web of an Okefenokee Swamp aquatic bed marsh. In: R.R. Sharitz and J.W. Gibbons, Freshwater Wetlands and Wildlife, Proc. Savannah River Ecol. Lab. Conf. on Wetland Ecology, 24-27 March 1986. US Dept. of Energy, Aiken, South Carolina.

Patten, B.C., Higashi, M. and Burns, T.P., 1990. Trophic dynamics in ecosystem networks: significance of cycles and storage. Ecol. Modelling, 51: 1-28.

Peterman, R.M., Clark, W.C. and Holling, C.S., 1979. The dynamics of resilience: shifting stability domains in fish and insect systems. In: R.M. Anderson, B.D. Turner and L.R. Taylor (Editors), Population Dynamics. Blackwell, London, pp. 321-342.

Peters, R.H., 1983. The Ecological Implications of Body Size. Cambridge Univ. Press.

Pimm, S.L., 1980. Food web design and the effects of species deletion. Oikos, 35: 139-149.

Pimm, S.L., 1982. Food Webs. Chapman and Hall, London.

Pimm, S.L. and Lawton, J.H., 1980. Are food webs divided into compartments? J. Anim. Ecol., 49: 879-898.

Pomeroy, L.R., 1974. The ocean's food web: a changing paradigm. BioScience, 24: 499-504.

Pomeroy, L.R., 1985. The microbial food web of the southeastern U.S. continental shelf. In: L.P. Atkinson, D.W. Menzel and K.A. Bush (Editors), Oceanography of the Southeastern U.S. Continental Shelf. Am. Geophys. Union, Washington, D.C., pp. 118-129.

Poston, T. and Stewart, I., 1978. Catastrophe Theory and Its Applications. Pitman, London, 461 pp.

Prigogine, I., 1947. Etude Thermodynamique des Processus Irréversibles. Desoer, Liege.

Prigogine, I., 1980. From Being to Becoming: Time and Complexity in the Physical Sciences. W.H. Freeman & Co., San Francisco, 272 pp.

Prigogine, I., Nicolas, G. and Babloyantz, A., 1972. Thermodynamics of evolution, I. Physics Today, 23(11): 23-28.

Prigogine, I., Nicolas, G. and Babloyantz, A., 1972a. Thermodynamics of evolution, II. Physics Today, 23(12): 38-44

Prigogine, I,. and Stengers, I., 1979. La Nouvelle Alliance. Gallimard, Paris.

Quinlin, A.V., 1975. Design and Analysis of Mass Conservative Models of Ecodynamic Systems, Ph.D. Dissertation. MIT Press, Cambridge, Massachusetts.

Rabinowitch, E.I., 1951. Photosynthesis and Related Processes (3 volumes). Intersciences, New York, 2088 pp.

Rambal, S., 1984. Un modèle de simulation de paturage en Tunisie présaharienne. Acta OEcol. (OEcol. Gen.), 5: 351-364.

Rapp, P.E., 1986. Oscillations and chaos in cellular metabolism and physiological systems. In: A.V. Holden (Editor), Chaos. Princeton Univ. Press, pp. 179-208.

Raup, D.M. and Sepkowski, J.J., 1982. Mass extinctions in the marine fossil record. Science, 215: 1501-1503.

Recknagel, F., 1985. Analysis of structural stability of aquatic ecosystems as an aid for ecosystem control. Ecol. Modelling, 27: 351-364.

Reynolds, C.S., 1989. Physical determinants of phytoplankton succession. In: U. Sommer (Editor), Plankton Ecology: Succession in Plankton Communities.

Springer-Verlag, Berlin, pp. 9.

Richardson, J.R. and Odum, H.T., 1981. Power and a pulsing production model. In: W.J. Mitsch, R.W. Bosserman and J.M. Klopatek (Editors), Energy and Ecological Modelling. Elsevier, Amsterdam, pp. 641-648.

Riley, G.A., 1966. Theory of food-chain relations in the ocean. In: M.N. Hill (Editor), The Sea, Vol. II. Interscience, London, pp. 438-463.

Rosenzweig, M.L., 1971. Paradox of enrichment: destabilization of exploitation ecosystems in ecological time. Science, 171: 385-387.

Rutledge, R.W., 1974. Ecological Stability: A Systems Theory Viewpoint, Ph.D. Thesis. Electrical Engineering, Oklahoma State University.

Salomonsen, J., 1992. Properties of exergy. Power and ascendency along a eutrophication gradient. Ecol. Modelling, in press.

Saunders, P.T. and Ho, M.W., 1981. On the increase in complexity in evolution, II: The relativity of complexity and the principle of minimum increase. J. Theor. Biol., 90: 515-530.

Saunders, P.T., 1985. Catastrophe theory in biology. In: V. Capasso, E. Grosso and S.L. Paveri-Fontana (Editors), Lecture Notes in Biomathematics. 57. Mathematics in Biology and Medicine. Springer, New York, pp. 510-516.

Saxon, E.C. and Dudzinski, M.L., 1984. Biological survey and reserve design by Landsat mapped ecolines - a catastrophe theory approach. Aust. J. Ecol., 9: 117-123.

Scavia, D., 1980. Conceptual model of phosphorus cycling. In: D. Scavia and R. Moll (Editors), Nutrient Cycling in the Great Lakes, Special Report 83. Great Lakes Research Division, University of Michigan, Ann Arbor, pp. 119-140.

Scheffer, M., 1990. Simple Models as Useful Tools for Ecologists. Elsevier, Amsterdam.

Schneider, E.D., 1988. Thermodynamics, ecological succession, and natural selection: A common thread. In: B.H. Weber, D.J. Depew and J.D. Smith (Editors), Entropy, Information, and Evolution: New Perspectives on Physical and Biological Evolution. MIT Press, Cambridge, Massachusetts, pp. 107.

Schneider, E.D. and Kay, J., 1990. Life as a Phenomenological Manifestation of the Second Law of Thermodynamics. Environment and Resource Studies, University of Waterloo, Canada.

Schoffeniels, E., 1976. Anti-Chance. Pergamon Press, New York.

Schrödinger, E., 1944. What is Life? Cambridge Univ. Press.

Sellers, P.J. and Mintz, Y.A., 1986. A simple biosphere model (SiB) for use within general circulation models. J. Atmos. Sci., 43: 505-531.

Shannon, C.E. and Weaver, W., 1963. The Mathematical Theory of Communication. University of Illinois Press (1st ed. 1949).

Shellford, V.E., 1943. The relation of snowy owl migration to the abundance of the collared lemming. Auk, 62: 592-594.

Sherry, D.F. and Galef, B.G., 1984 Cultural transmission without imitation: milk bottle opening by birds. Animal Behav., 32: 937-938.

Shieh, J.H. and Fan, L.T., 1982. Estimation of energy (enthalpy) and energy (availability) contents in structurally complicated materials. Energy Resources, 6: 1-46.

Shugart, H.H. and West, D.C., 1981. Long-term dynamics of forest ecosystems. Amer. Sci., 25: 25-50.

Simon, H.A., 1962. The architecture of complexity. Proc. Amer. Phil. Soc., 106: 467-482.

Simon, H.A., 1969. The Sciences of the Artificial. MIT Press, Cambridge, Massachusetts.

Simon, H.A., 1973. The organization of complex systems. In: H.H. Pattee, Hierarchy Theory. Braziller, New York, pp. 3-27.

Sommer, U., 1987. Factors controlling the seasonal variation in phytoplankton species composition - A case study for a deep, nutrient rich lake. In: Round and Chapman (Editors), Progress in Phycological Research, Vol. 5. Biopress Ltd., pp. 124-148.

Sommer, U., 1989. Toward a Darwinian ecology of plankton. In: U. Sommer (Editor), Plankton Ecology: Succession in Plankton Communities. Springer-Verlag, Berlin, pp. 1.

Sommer, U., Gliwicz, Z.M., Lampert, W. and Duncan, A., 1986. The PEG (Plankton Ecology Group)-model of seasonal succession of planktonic events in fresh waters. Arch. Hydrobiol., 106: 433-471.

Sousa, W.P., 1979. Experimental investigation of disturbance and ecological succession in a rocky intertidal algal community. Ecol. Monogr., 49: 227-254.

Southwood, T.R.E., 1973. The insect/plant relationship - an evolutionary perspective. Symp. Roy. Ent. Soc. Lond., 6: 3-30.

Southwood, T.R.E., 1981. Bionomic strategies and population parameters. In: R.M. May (Editor), Theoretical Ecology: Principles and Applications, 2nd ed. Blackwell Scientific Publications, Oxford, pp. 30-43.

Stenseth, N.C., 1986. Darwinian evolution in ecosystems: a survey of some ideas and difficulties together with some possible solutions. In: J.L. Casti and A. Karlqvist (Editors), Complexity, Language, and Life: Mathematical Approaches. Springer-Verlag, Berlin, pp. 105-129.

Sterner, R.W., 1989. The role of grazers in phytoplankton succession. In: U. Sommer (Editor), Plankton Ecology: Succession in Plankton Communities. Springer-Verlag, Berlin, pp. 107-123.

Stonier, T., 1990. Information and the Internal Structure of the Universe. Springer-Verlag, London.

Straskraba, M., 1979. Natural control mechanisms in models of aquatic ecosystems. Ecol. Modelling, 6: 305-322.

Straskraba, M., 1980. The effects of physical variables on freshwater production: analyses based on models. In: E.D. Le Cren and R.H. McConnell (Editors), The Functioning of Freshwater Ecosystems. International Biological Programme 22. Cambridge Univ. Press, pp. 13-31.

Straskraba, M. and Gnauck, A., 1980. Cybernetic-categories of ecosystem dynamics. ISEM J., 2: 81-96.

Straskraba, M. and Gnauck, A., 1983. Aquatische Ökosysteme - Modellierung und Simulation. VEB Gustav Fischer Verlag, Jena, 279 pp. English Translation: Freshwater Ecosystems - Modelling and Simulation, Developments in Environmental Modelling, 8. Elsevier, Amsterdam.

Straskraba, M. and Gnauck, A.H., 1985. Freshwater Ecosystems: Modeling and Simulation, Developments in Environmental Modelling, 8. Elsevier, Amsterdam.

Streeter, H.W. and Phelps, E.N., 1925. A Study of the Pollution and the Natural Purification of the Ohio River. Public Health Bulletin No. 146. U.S. Public Health Service.

Swartzman, G.L. and Kaluzny, S.P., 1987. Ecological Simulation Primer. Macmillan Publishing Co., New York.

Swinney, H.L., 1983. Obsevations of order and chaos in nonlinear systems. Physica, 7D: 3-15.

Søndergård, M., 1989. Phosphorus release from a hyperthropic lake sediment; experiments with intact sediment cores in a continous flow system. Arch. Hydrobiol., 116: 45-59.

Tansky, M., 1978. Stability of multispecies predator-prey systems. Memoirs Coll. Sci., Univ. Kyoto, Ser. B, 7(2): 87-94.

Tansley, A.G., 1935. The use and abuse of vegetational concepts and terms. Ecol., 16: 284-307.

Tellegen, B.D.H., 1952. A general network theorem, with applications. Philips Res. Rep., 7: 259-269.

Thom, R., 1972. Stabilité Structurelle et Morphogénèse. W.A. Benjamin Inc., Reading, Massachusetts.

Thom, R., 1975. Structural Stability and Morphogensis. W.A. Benjamin Inc., Reading, Massachusetts.

Thoma, J., 1977. Energy, Entropy and Information, Research Memorandum. International Institute for Applied Systems Analysis, Laxenburg, Austria, pp. 77-32.

Thomann, R.V., 1984. Physico-chemical and ecological modelling the fate of toxic substances in natural water systems. Ecol. Modelling, 22: 145-171.

Tilman, D. and Kilham, S.S., 1976. Phosphate and silicate growth and uptake kinetics of the diatoms *Asterionella formosa* and *Cyclotella meninghiniana* in batch and semi-continuous culture. J. Phycol., 12: 375-383.

Tribus, M. and McIrvine, E.C., 1971. Scientific American, 224: 179-186.

Ulanowicz, R.E., 1979. Prediction chaos and ecological perspective. In: E.A. Halfon (Editor), Theoretical Systems Ecology. Academic Press, New York, pp. 107-117.

Ulanowicz, R.E., 1980. An hypothesis on the development of natural communities. Ecol. Modelling, 85: 223-245.

Ulanowicz, R.E., 1983. Identifying the structure of cycling in ecosystems. Math. Biosci., 65: 219-237.

Ulanowicz, R.E., 1986. Growth and Development, Ecosystems Phenomenology. Springer-Verlag, New York.

Ulanowicz, R.E., 1989. A phenomenology of evolving networks. Systems Research, 6: 209-217.

Ulanowicz, R.E., 1990. Ecosystem trophic foundations: Lindeman exonerata. In: B.C. Patten and S.E. Jørgensen (Editors), Complex Ecology: The Part-Whole Relation in Ecosystems. SPB Academic Publishing, The Hague.

Ulanowicz, R.E., 1991. Formal agency in ecosystem development. In: M. Higashi and T.P. Burns (Editors), Theoretical Studies of Ecosystems: The Network

Perspective. Cambridge Univ. Press, pp. 58.

Ulanowicz, R.E. and Kemp, W.M., 1979. Toward canonical trophic aggregations. Am. Nat., 114: 871-883.

Ulanowicz, R.E. and Norden, J.S., 1990. Symmetrical overhead in flow networks. Int. J. Systems Sci., 21: 429-437.

Ulanowicz, C.J. and Puccia, C.J., 1990. Mixed trophic impacts in ecosystems. COENOSES, 5: 7-16.

Van der Maarel, E., 1976. On the establishment of plant community boundaries. Ber. Deutsch. Bot. Ges., 35: 36-55.

Van Donk, E., 1989. The role of fungal parasites in phytoplankton succession. In: U. Sommer (Editor), Plankton Ecology: Succession in Plankton Communities. Springer-Verlag, Berlin, pp. 171.

Van Donk, E., Gulati, R.D. and Grimm, M.P., 1989. Food-web manipulation in Lake Zwemlust: positive and negative effects during the first two years. Hydrobiol. Bull., 23: 19-35.

Van Nguyen, V. and Wood, E.F., 1979. On the morphology of summer algae dynamics in non-stratified lakes. Ecol. Modelling, 6: 117-131.

Vollenweider, R.A., 1975. Input-output modles with special reference to the phosphorus loading concept in limnology. Schweiz. Z. Hydrol., 37: 53-84.

Vollenweider, R.A., 1990. Eutrophication: Conventional and non-conventional considerations and comments on selected topics. In: R. de Bernardi, G. Giussani and L. Barbanti (Editors), Scientific Perspectives in Theoretical and Applied Limnology. Mem. Ist. Ital. Idrobiol., 47: 77-134.

von Bertalanyffy, L., 1952. Problems of Life. Wiley.

Webster, J.R., 1979. Hierarchical organization of ecosystems. In: E. Halfon (Editor), Theoretical Systems Ecology. Academic Press, New York, pp. 119-131.

Weiderholm, T., 1980. Use of benthos in lake monitoring. J. Water Pollut. Control Fed., 52: 537-557.

Weinberg, G.M., 1975. An Introduction to General Systems Thinking. John Wiley and Sons, New York.

Whittaker, R.H. and Woodwell, G.M., 1971. Evolution of natural communities. In: J.A. Weins (Editor), Ecosystem Structure and Function. Oregon State Univ. Press, Corvallis, pp. 137-159.

Wicken, J.S., 1976. The chemical organizing effects of entropy maximization. J. Chem. Ed., 53: 623-625.

Wicken, J.S., 1978. The entropy gradient: A heuristic approach to chemical equilibrium. J. Chem. Ed., 55: 701-703.

Wicken, J.S., 1978a. Information transformations in molecular evolution. J. Theor. Biol., 72: 191-204.

Wicken, J.S., 1979. The generation of complexity in evolution: A thermodynamic and information-theoretical discussion. J. Theor. Biol., 77: 349-365.

Wicken, J.S., 1980. Thermodynamic theory of evolution. J. Theor. Biol., 87: 9-23.

Wicken, J.S., 1988. Thermodynamics, evolution, and emergence: Ingredients for a new synthesis. In: B.H. Weber, D.J. Depew and J.D. Smith (Editors), Entropy, Information, and Evolution: New Perspectives on Physical and Biological Evolution. MIT Press, Cambridge, Massachusetts, pp. 139.

Wiley, E.O., 1988. Entropy and evolution. In: B.H. Weber, D.J. Depew and J.D. Smith (Editors), Entropy, Information, and Evolution: New Perspectives on Physical and Biological Evolution. MIT Press, Cambridge, Massachusetts, pp. 173.

Willemsen, J., 1980. Fishery aspects of eutrophication. Hydrobiol. Bull., 14: 12-21.

Wilson, D.S., 1978. Prudent predation: a field test involving three species of tiger beetles. Oikos, 31: 128-136.

Wilson, D.S., 1980. The Natural Selection of Populations and Communities. The Benjamin/Cummings Publishing Company, Inc.

Wolfram, S., 1984. Cellular automata as models of complexity. Nature, 311: 419-424.

Wolfram, S., 1984a. Computer software in science and mathematics. Sci. Am., 251: 140-151.

Woodwell, G.M. et al., 1967. DDT residues in an East Coast esturay: A case of biological concentration of a persistent insecticide. Scinece, 156: 821-824.

Zeeman, E.C., 1978. Catastrophe Theory: Selected Papers 1972-1977. Addison-Wesley, London.

Zeigler, B.P., 1976. Theory of Modelling and Simulation. Wiley, New York, 435 pp.

Zotin, A.I., 1978. The second law, negentropy, thermodynamics of linear irreversible processess. In: I. Lamprecht and A.I. Zotin (Editors).

Zotin, A.I. and Lamprecht, I. (Editors), 1978. Thermodynamics of Biological Processes. Walter de Gruyter, Berlin.

Zotin, A.I., 1984. Bioenergetic trends of evolutionary progress of organisms. In: I. Lamprecht and A.I. Zotin (Editors), Thermodynamics and Regulations of Biological Processes. Walter de Gruyter, Berlin, pp. 451-458.

# INDEX